plant
solutions

plant
solutions

Nigel Colborn

Collins

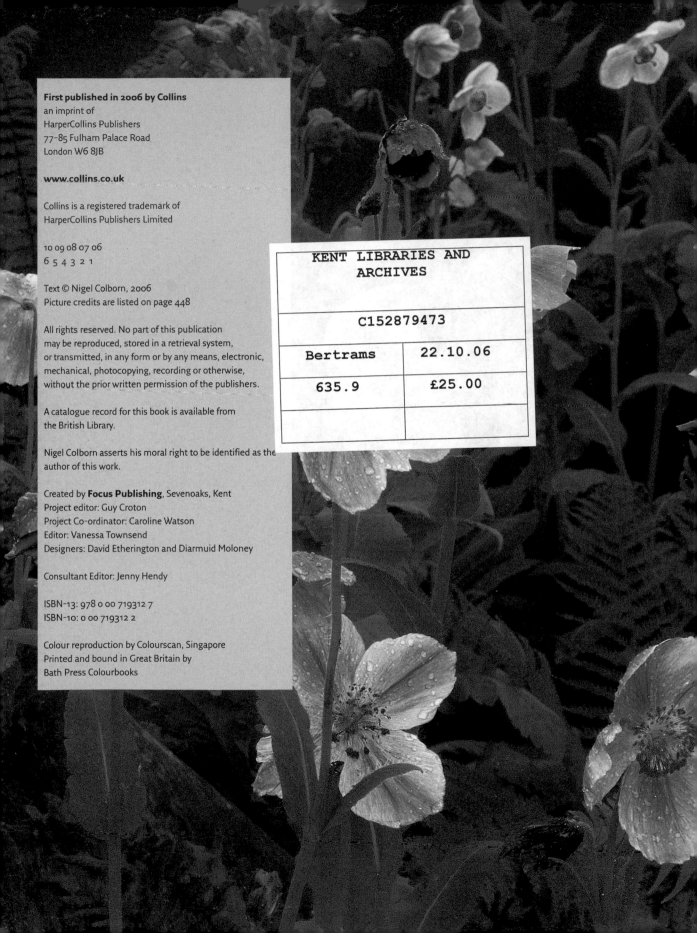

First published in 2006 by Collins
an imprint of
HarperCollins Publishers
77–85 Fulham Palace Road
London W6 8JB

www.collins.co.uk

Collins is a registered trademark of
HarperCollins Publishers Limited

10 09 08 07 06
6 5 4 3 2 1

Text © Nigel Colborn, 2006
Picture credits are listed on page 448

Created by **Focus Publishing**, Sevenoaks, Kent
Project editor: Guy Croton
Project Co-ordinator: Caroline Watson
Editor: Vanessa Townsend
Designers: David Etherington and Diarmuid Moloney

Consultant Editor: Jenny Hendy

ISBN-13: 978 0 00 719312 7
ISBN-10: 0 00 719312 2

Colour reproduction by Colourscan, Singapore
Printed and bound in Great Britain by
Bath Press Colourbooks

Contents

How to Use This Book

The aim of this book is to stimulate planting ideas, rather than give prescriptive formulae. Feel free, therefore, to flick through the pages at random and alight on any plants that catch your eye. The main section of the book consists of the plant directory pages, categorised as shown in the contents table, with each group – shrubs, annuals etc. – further subdivided to offer selections for specific sites. Thus, if you are searching for a medium sized shrub that prefers partial sun, you will find a choice on pages 300–3. Each plant entry gives essential details and a brief description, and lists suggestions for companion plants. Alternative varieties are also frequently mentioned.

Interspersed among the directory pages, you will find occasional spreads devoted to a specific plant group. Limited space allows these to represent but a tiny sample from such extensive genera as roses (pages 314 and 316) or clematis (pages 250 and 252). They are intended for use as a starting point, perhaps for a more detailed search elsewhere.

Examples of plant associations are also included, for example, on pages 32–3, where a scheme with annuals is described and illustrated. Like the special spreads, these are intended as prompters for further ideas, rather than as specific recipes to which one must adhere.

Although the information given is as accurate as possible, it is important to bear in mind that plants can cope with a surprisingly wide range of conditions outside their recognized 'comfort zones'. Species which are deemed tender, can often survive low night temperatures, certain wetland plants can be surprisingly drought tolerant and plants adapted to sunny conditions may thrive in shade. Heights and dimensions can vary, too, depending on growing conditions, so be experimental, when you plant, and prepare for some surprises!

Plant type Brief description of the plant's characteristics

Planting solution Growing conditions or garden use for which plants are particularly well suited

Description Detailed description of the plant's qualities and specific needs, including habitat

Plant name Latin name first, followed by the plant's common name

Planting information At a glance round-up of the plant's preferences

Companions Outline of other plants that complement or are similar to the one being described

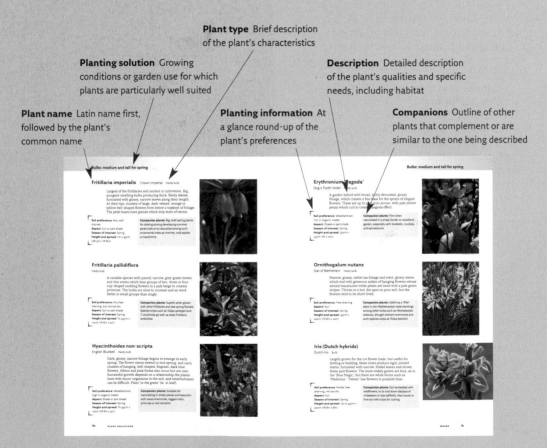

Introduction

Choosing plants can be one of the greatest pleasures of gardening, but it can also give rise to the most agonising dilemmas. The number of species and varieties in cultivation is so vast and so varied that deciding which ones to select, for a particular planting scheme, is almost impossible. And as garden sizes reduce, in an increasingly urban world, that choice becomes ever more crucial.

Every part of every garden, regardless of design or style, presents its own special planting opportunities. Whether on a grand scale, such as in a big mixed border, or in a space so confined that only tiny plants will fit, there are decisions to be made, combinations to be composed and solutions to be found. Which perennial group will blend well in this partly shaded bed? What climbers would thrive on that sheltered wall? Is there a plant that can grow in that baking hot corner or that waterlogged bog? Didn't I even see a plant grown on nothing more than a house brick once? Every garden situation, regardless of prevailing conditions, presents a planting challenge and, for every challenge, there is a planting solution.

The purpose of this book is to serve as a launching pad for your own creative planting ideas. As many typical situations as possible have been included, with specific plant suggestions offered for each. Ample cross referencing and special sections on selected plant combinations help to develop design ideas further so that among the hundreds of individual plants mentioned in the following pages, you are bound to find inspiration to come up with the very best plant solutions for your own garden.

We assess the plants, not merely on their own merit, but as core elements of good garden design. Detailed planting recipes are not included, since these could influence or even cramp individual creativity, and cultural advice is kept to a minimum. However, once a number of potential plants has been identified for a specific site, your next step will be to develop that initial choice into a growing composition in which plants will not only thrive, but will also look beautiful together. And if such a composition works well, that beauty and interest becomes a dynamic art form which changes almost daily but sustains its constant allure, through each of the seasons.

The choice of plants, for any garden situation, will be rich and varied, even if growing conditions are less than ideal.

Some Thoughts on Planting and Design

Garden design has recently experienced a stimulating revolution. In an age of growing prosperity since the mid 1990s, interest in private outdoor spaces increased sharply and by the turn of the century, gardens and gardening had entered a new era. Growth in hard landscaping burgeoned, with ever-expanding areas of paving, decking, gravel, terracing, walls and fancy fencing. Such colourful new materials as tumbled glass gravel, raw sheet copper or dyed sands were deployed, often in dramatic and mould-breaking styles. This brave new gardening world continues to develop and to evolve in all aspects of design bar one: creative planting.

Plants are a crucial element to almost all popular garden designs but their importance is often overlooked. Plant choice, even by able and experienced designers, is sometimes inappropriate, resulting in ill-composed schemes which go badly wrong, or worse, in plants that simply languish or die. Plant associations can be unsympathetic, either to the hard landscaping that surrounds them, or within the mix of chosen species. There are plant-minded designers, of course, many of whom develop original and creative planting schemes, but these are exceptions, and in the great bulk of new gardens, from major public spaces, to tiny urban oases, plants have tended to become misunderstood components.

Creative planting schemes, with varied colours, textures and sizes, help to soften the harsh effect of hard landscaping.

Creative planting is a dynamic, ongoing art form. The mixed border, below, has been boosted with temporary colour from a mid-season introduction of tender, summer-flowering perennials. These could, in turn, be underplanted with spring bulbs.

Texturing Plants

Given a sound structure, usually provided from a combination of hard materials and woody plants, the bulk of any planting scheme is likely to be concerned with filling the spaces in between. The term 'in-fill' or 'space filling' suggests that these plants are less important than the structure but the opposite is true. The soft planting, in all its guises and styles, plays the most important role of all. These are the plants that create the desired mood. They will often be the most rapidly changing, and so will deliver the essential dynamic of a well-tempered garden. Since, by volume, texturing plants usually make up the largest area, they will have the most influence on colour schemes, on texture, on planting styles and on ensuring sustained interest.

By policing in-fill plants, one can develop changes of mood and style from one part of the garden to another, or from one season to another. Bursts of special interest can be engineered to take place in specific garden spots, by concentrating in-fill plants that will synchronise their performance with their neighbours. A woodland garden, for example, may be a cool, shady, green retreat from the heat of summer where little is in

Plants for bedding can be used in exactly the same way as a decorator might deploy paint or carpet – to cover a surface with a chosen colour. These African marigolds, planted after the last frost, in spring, paint a bright golden surface for the whole of the summer. While they flourish, the effect is spectacular, but when the bed is stripped away, only bare soil will remain.

flower and berries have yet to ripen, but in winter and spring, the same area could host a mass of highly coloured bulbs and perennials from snowdrops, hellebores and yellow winter aconites in mid-winter to wild narcissus, epimediums, primulas, and fritillaries in mid-spring. A dry garden, developed for minimal water use, will benefit from being well furnished with evergreens – especially those with distinctive foliage – so that the seasons are linked by a constant background, and so that there is something beautiful to look at during extreme summer heat or in the depths of winter.

Planting for the Senses

Although it seems pretty obvious, it may be worth remembering that good planting will stimulate more than just the eyes and nose. In a richly planted garden, there will be plants to listen to and to touch, as well as those that look pretty. This dimension becomes doubly important if a planting scheme is designed for people who lack one or more of the five senses.

Sight The most obvious of the senses, for gardeners, but there are subtleties frequently overlooked. Pale pastel colours and whites, for example, are best for planting schemes which may be viewed mainly in poor light or at night. Very dark colours tend to vanish into shadow, when viewed from a distance, whereas pale ones stand out. In bright light, pale colours appear washed out, whereas strong hues become more arresting. Large flowers, in strong colours, have far more influence in the overview of a border or plant group than do lots of small flowers in even much brighter colours.

Fragrance The second most important of the senses, in a garden, is the sense of smell. Plants with a desirable fragrance are best placed where they are readily accessible to the nose; those which have an unpleasant odour should never be placed where they can spoil the garden experience, but may still be worth growing for other reasons. When blending fragrances, some go better together than others. The richness of summer jasmine, for example is expanded to Wagnerian sensuality if teamed with the perfume of honeysuckle and *Nicotiana affinis*. The smell of lavender adds a firmer dimension to the sweeter perfume of old roses.

Touch So many plants are pleasant to stroke, or to feel. Many of the artemisias, for instance, have silky textured filigree leaves and are

When plants are teamed, colours in one variety can pick up sympathetic tones in the hues of its neighbours. Here, the bell flowers of the tall Campanula echo the mauve and pink hues of the annual candytuft.

aromatic as well. The shining, bright tan trunk of the Chinese cherry species *Prunus serrula* makes it worth growing, just to look at, but extra pleasure comes from being able to caress that smooth, polished bark.

Taste Taste is less critical, but if you want to grow a hazel nut for its beautiful foliage, or edge a border with wild strawberries for their decorative value, being able to eat the produce provides an added bonus.

Sound Sound can help to create special moods. A breeze blowing through aspen leaves makes a noise identical to falling rain; wind in a pine tree sighs and sobs whereas winter gales make the tall dead stems of Miscanthus grass hiss in a disturbing manner. Classical Chinese gardeners were said to have had the tradition of planting large, broad leaved specimens just below the eaves of a building, and close to a window, so that during rain, the sound of water drops striking them would be audible from within. The effect, apparently, was to enhance the melancholy mood of a wet day.

The best plants make multiple contributions (above). The pink, variegated petals are the obvious asset of this old gallica rose, 'Rosa Mundi', but it also provides sweet fragrance and makes a sumptuous texture contrast with the yellow-green lady's mantle growing nearby.

The long, curving leaves of Bowles golden sedge, *Carex elata* 'Aurea' (left), harmonise with the yellow-leaved form of meadowsweet, *Filipendua ulmaria* 'Aurea', while their textures make a dramatic contrast.

Planting for the Emotions

Less obvious than planting for the physical senses, carefully devised planting will also stimulate an emotive response. A feeling of calm, for example, is enhanced when gentle colours and subtly blended foliage textures are deployed. But when colours are strident and there are strong colour contrasts, the viewer tends to feel more agitated, particularly when plants with spiky outlines are used, or where trees have irregular limbs. Examples abound, of how specific planting schemes stimulate particular emotions. Here is a small selection, presented in opposing pairs:

Hot/cool; calm/agitated As a general rule, cool colours – blue, white, green – are calming, whereas hot oranges, reds and golds can be agitating. But blues are cold and can lack passion whereas bold, burning reds stir the blood and hot oranges actually make one feel warmer.

Low-key/high key In some parts of a garden, planting is best if low-key. Uniform ground cover – or a lawn for that matter – makes a gentle foil, allowing neighbouring features, whether plants or objects, to stand out. A frequent mistake made by people who remove their lawns is to install a gravel surface, but then to plant it so busily that it becomes a strong feature in its own right, perhaps overshadowing surrounding borders or planting schemes. Where a strong, bold statement is needed, however, planting must rise to the need, drawing one's eye and dominating the scene. A single main architectural plant, or a small group, may suffice, but a canny plant designer will keep an eye on such a group and keep finding ways to make its impact even stronger.

Inviting/forbidding Careful placing of plants, particularly near entrances or where different sections of a garden are divided, are able either to make a welcoming pitch, or to discourage entry. Both techniques are valuable. Where the entrance is narrow – through a gateway, perhaps, or under an arch, a carefully placed plant with interesting foliage colour or conspicuous blossoms will help to draw people in. If the arches or gateways are themselves well furnished with handsome climbing plants, perhaps with special treasures also grown at their feet, a visitor might pause there, to enjoy the moment, before passing through.

A sea of spring daffodils induces a feeling of calm and well-being thanks to the delicate contrast between the soft, pastel colour of the flowers and the subtle greens of the stems and foliage.

Where there needs to be private access, whose use is to be limited, the opposite of these measures can be taken. Shrubs can be allowed to expand and disguise the thoroughfare, or planting in front can be staggered so that only those 'in the know' are inclined to slip through. And in places where security is a concern, ostentatiously thorny, dense vegetation can do a lot to back up the threat of any spiked railings or fencing which stands between it and the outside world.

Intellectual versus emotional This is a more difficult concept to believe in, but with planting, just as in an instrumental concerto, there is often a tension between two forms. With the musical analogy, the solo instrument converses with the orchestra, sometimes in unison, but mostly in a melodious dialogue. In a garden, formal landscaping – whether with plants or structures – can have a similar dialogue with more naturalistic planting. Formal geometric shapes are the result of an intellectual exercise, Man imposing himself on Nature. Line and form have been carefully considered and structures – be they plants or man-made objects – are laid out in strictly disciplined patterns. Eighteenth century parterres, Victorian bedding schemes and some modern day public plantings are examples of these. Wild, natural landscapes are the antithesis of this cerebral approach. Topography and vegetation are seen as nature intended and the rules of symmetry appear to be broken. Naturalistic designs in gardens take the main elements of beauty from truly wild landscapes and compose them to create romanticised scenes. Streams or ponds appear like natural water courses and planting is in layers – trees, shrubs, understorey – more or less as you would find in rural regions.

In most gardens, however, both concepts are adopted and there is a stimulating tension between the two. An artificial flower meadow, for example, might be skirted – as in the author's garden – by fine-mown lawn, and a clipped shrub screen. In many modern versions of Elizabethan knot gardens, summer perennials are allowed to progress and flower fairly freely, whereas the originals would have been much more formally planted.

A gateway that is well furnished with interesting plants and flowers (above) will be more inviting than bare pillars and a gate. If this many plants decorate the entrance, how much more will there be to enjoy inside?

Floral fireworks (right)! The seed heads of *Allium schubertii* bring a touch of drama to this dense, mixed Mediterranean planting scheme.

Planting in Specific Styles

Planting styles will depend very much on overall design, and on personal preference, but it is worth considering some of the most popular and distinctive of these:

Classic mixed borders

Mixed borders must be large enough to accommodate shrubs – perhaps even trees – along with herbaceous perennials of all sizes, probably interspersed with annuals or biennials for gap-filling and even a succession of bulbs. These are the most malleable and, over time, will run through gentle but profound changes. Colour can be carefully controlled, with main themes, such as red, white, hot or cool hues, or may roll through a series of intriguing changes with the season.

It is important to view such borders at all levels, and to bear in mind how they are likely to look in all seasons. Whenever any major changes are made to the planting, this is likely to have a 'knock on' effect on other times of year, so that one big change necessitates

Cottage-style planting works well beneath the walls of a 300 year-old building. The climbing Bourbon rose, 'Kathleen Harrop' furnishes the limestone, without hiding too much of it, and teams with the colour of the pink valerian which is allowed to seed around freely.

further changes down the line. These are ongoing, long-term planting schemes which can be adjusted and tinkered with over decades, and which will keep most keen gardeners both occupied and pre-occupied for a very long period. It is said that the Edwardian garden guru, Gertrude Jekyll, spent over forty years adjusting the borders at her garden, Munstead Wood.

Mediterranean

With water becoming a scarce commodity and, in some areas, an expensive one, much attention is being turned to low-water planting schemes. Typical natural landscapes, whose arid beauty is well worth imitating, occur in such places as the rocky Mediterranean coastal regions, the southern tip of Africa, the American Chaparral and in many parts of Australasia. Such areas have amazingly rich floras and many of their native plants have become garden staples. Gladiolus, Lavandula and Eschscholzia are examples of the thousands of widespread plants which enjoy similar conditions.

Trees, in such habitats, tend to be small and slow growing and many of the shrubs are evergreen, often thorny, either with waxy cuticles to their foliage, or with silvery or grey leaf surfaces. The secret, with Mediterranean gardens, is to include a rich number of short, medium and long term feature plants. Winter and spring bulbs, which grow during the cool, wet periods, give short spells of drama, but disappear for much of the year. Speedy annuals, such as Cerinthe or Papaver will splash summer colour among the shrubs which will become increasingly gnarled and characterful as they age, providing a longer term outline. Mediterranean-style herbs come in and out of colour all year, linking seasons and extending colour, from such spring bloomers as Erysimum to the autumn flowering, vivid orange Zauschnerias.

Cottage

The romanticised concept of a cottage garden conjures up images of roses or honeysuckle round doorways and window frames, mossed apple trees, flower borders with plants all hugger-mugger, a vegetable patch and possibly even a chicken coop. To be well planted, however, a cottage garden must retain elements of order and pleasing form. Colours should be blended with care, especially where cultivated varieties of plants with large flowers are used.

Plants look best when arranged to complement one another, with consideration given to height, spread, denseness or looseness and so on. They must also be chosen for succession so that an autumn cottage border is as attractive as an early summer one.

Naturalistic

The aim is to mimic plant distributions as they might occur in nature. Apparently random groups of plants are arranged in drifts or small groups of irregular sizes and shapes. Where shrubs or walls obstruct light, shade plants are placed just as they might grow naturally, in a wild setting. Plants can be allowed to seed around, even if this means that they spill over onto pathways, softening lines and edges and extending their colonies.

Closest to a truly wild, flowery meadow, this is a style which contrasts sharply with contemporary landscaping where hard materials and objects such as gabions or sheet metal are used. Grasses blend sweetly with other perennials whose gentle outlines are full of movement and dreamy romantic colours. Woodland plantings are also best when kept as naturalistic as possible, and where woodland species can be allowed to propagate themselves, and perhaps blend with native species in the same habitat.

Formal

Bedding, a traditional planting style, is still popular and, despite going through minor fashion changes, remains one of the great Victorian legacies. The importance is to understand that plants are used as colouring materials to paint surfaces and make patterns or shapes which, for the most part, last but a season. Overwintered bedding which reaches its climax in mid-spring – perhaps six months after planting – is a dying culture but has immense value.

Meadow and cornfield

Growing plants naturalised in grass is a technique that still has some way to go before all its secrets have been revealed. As a growing medium for spring bulbs and early flowers, grass has long been proven, but as a feature for a summer garden, particularly on a small scale, there is still some way to go. The decision has to be made, each season, when to cut the meadow back and how to manage the aftermath in late summer and autumn.

A stimulating composition in which colours and textures work well together. The velvet leaves of the verbascum find some sympathy with the fluffiness of the Ageratum flowers, but when their tall yellow flower spikes emerge, later in the year, the effect might be a little too startling!

Annuals such as poppies and cornflowers are frequently, mistakenly, planted in grass meadows where they are bound to be short-lived. However, a new concept in gardening is the notion of a small fragment of cornfield, even sown with barley or wheat, and where such annuals could be made to thrive. Management is simple: 'harvest' in late summer, removing straw and plant material after it has shed its seed; disturb the ground and wait for next year's self sown crop to grow!

Paving and gravel

Even the most unsympathetic hard landscaping can often be persuaded to yield up a planting opportunity or two. Where space is limited and plants few, immense care is needed to select exactly the right ones, since each specimen will be making a large statement. This is like comparing a string trio, where a missed note on the violin jars the whole performance, with a huge orchestra and choir where, if a bass sings temporarily out of tune, only the sharpest ear will pick up the drone. Not only must the most suitable plants be selected, for such key roles, they must also stay in near perfect condition.

Problem Site

Every planting site comes with its own special advantages and its own problems. It is important to assess both, in terms of plant choice. Disadvantages should not be viewed in negative terms, but should be recognised so that plant choice is limited to those species which will thrive in the prevailing conditions.

The main challenges to plants are caused by the following typical situations, either in isolation or – more usually – in combination:

Exposure to wind Plant robust trees and shrubs to windward, to create shelter. Hedges and shrub screens are more effective at wind protection than walls or solid fences which cause damaging eddy currents. Be prepared to plant for more extreme conditions, as your sheltering plants develop, and, as shelter becomes more available in the garden, adjust your planting plans to take advantage of the new conditions.

Excess shade Thinning out the overhead branches of mature trees often lets in more daylight. It may also help to paint any surfaces with white or a light colour. In moist shade, select plants from damp woodland habitats. Where trees are intended, as part of a planting scheme, select varieties such as Robinia, whose leaves are late emerging. The delay will enable spring plants under the branches to flower and begin to seed before light levels are reduced.

Excessively dry shade Moisture-retaining mulches will help, as will establishing a dense vegetative ground cover. Under trees, focus on plants that flower during winter and spring, when overhead branches are bare. Be content with a narrow choice of plants, but try any that you think might survive. All conditions differ, and plants that languish in one person's dry shade, may perform well in another. Once you know the plants that will live, focus hard on these, selecting them in as many different forms as you can.

Excessively hot, sunny and dry Hardly a problem site! The number of plants that love such hot conditions is vast and varied, from desert succulents to winter and spring flowering bulbs. Count your blessings and get to love small bulbs, sedums, helianthemums, dwarf irises and so on.

Excessive wet – especially when caused by poor drainage Good drainage is essential for most plants to thrive. However, some wetland species are better at coping with poor drainage than others. Try to minimise the problems associated with bad drainage by installing raised beds, or following the advice given for excessively heavy soil below. Select wetland plants such as hostas, water iris, ligularias and *Lobelia cardinalis*.

Heavy or light soil Surprisingly, the same improving measures apply to both: dig in as much compost or leafmould as possible, building up the levels of organic matter. Heavy clays can be improved by digging in coarse grit, leaf mould or rotted compost. Light sand also benefits from a boost to its organic content and also needs a heavy mulch each summer, to assist with moisture retention.

Excessively alkaline (limy) or acid soil Limy soil can be made less alkaline by applying sulphur, but the effect is limited. Acid soil can be limed to bring the up the pH, but that effect is difficult to reverse. Of all problem sites, these two are the easiest to solve, simply by wise plant selection. If your soil is limy, learn to live without rhododendrons, but to revel in pinks, clematis and the thousands of species which love alkaline conditions. If your soil is acid, your azaleas, camellias, summer heathers and ravishing blue Himalayan poppies will be the envy of your friends.

Having an Open Mind

With so much at stake, it is far too easy to forget that we garden largely for pleasure – or if we don't, we should! You can therefore be pretty relaxed about how you try out various planting combinations, and can afford to make mistakes. Plants and planting schemes are plastic, that is, they can be moulded or changed as you go. Only the boldest artist who dares to try something outrageous or at least, unprecedented, is likely to end up with a creation that is special.

New gardeners sometimes become so anxious about getting everything right that they forget to take pleasure in what they are doing. Experienced gardeners, however, are constantly learning. They make frequent mistakes and will enjoy a lifetime of adjusting, re-planting, devising new projects, trying out new plants and just generally messing about in their gardens. In fact the only serious, damaging and lasting mistake you can ever make, with your garden, is to think that you have finished.

Flowers come in a rush, through spring and summer, and mid-winter plants are always sought-after. Too few of us, however, remember to plan for the 'forgotten season' – the autumn. This border of asters, chrysanthemums and other short-day flowers shows what superb colour autumn can bring.

annuals

Agrostemma githago

Corn Cockle   Annual

Cornfield annual with long, thin, somewhat lax stems, narrow, slightly hairy leaves and a long summer succession of large, rosy purple flowers, each with dotted lines leading to the centre. Support is necessary, either from other plants or with stakes or sticks. Selections include 'Ocean Pearl' – white with silver lines – and the pale 'Pink Pearl'.

Soil preference: Any
Aspect: Full sun
Season of interest: Summer
Height and spread: 1m plus (3ft plus)

Companion plants: Excellent annual for the border back, especially if it can lean against shrubs or come up among perennials with better standing qualities. Also fine in a naturalistic annual border with other cornfield annuals such as cornflower and larkspur.

Adonis annua   Pheasant's Eye   Annual

A cornfield annual with emerald green, feathery or filigree foliage on narrowly branched stems. From early summer, a succession of small, intensely blood red buttercup-like flowers nestle among the soft foliage, creating a strong contrast. Autumn sown plants grow larger and flower more profusely and for longer than those which germinate in spring.

Soil preference: Any, not too dry
Aspect: Sun, part shade
Season of interest: Summer
Height and spread: 45cm x 15cm (18in x 6in)

Companion plants: A wild species with modest beauty, but effective when dotted among perennials in a mixed border or growing in gravel where it will take over from such late spring bulbs as fritillaries or late tulips.

Malcolmia maritima

Virginian Stock   Annual

Almost every child's first plant from seed, since it will flower a few weeks after sowing. Narrow foliage and slender stems produce a short but intense succession of brightly coloured, four-petalled flowers. Good seed series include flowers in shades of pink, white, cream, purple or near red, but these plants need to grow in bold drifts to create a strong effect.

Soil preference: Sandy, free-draining but not too dry
Aspect: Sun or part shade
Season of interest: Summer
Height and spread: 20cm x 10cm (8in x 4in)

Companion plants: Best sown in patches at a border front, with taller perennials behind, or among cottage garden flowers in an informal planting. These are often blended with night scented stock, *Matthiola bicornis*, for evening fragrance.

Papaver rhoeas 'Shirley Series'

Shirley Poppy   Annual

Developed in the 19th Century by the rector of Shirley, Rev. Wilkes, from the showiest of cornfield weeds, this series has flowers ranging from lemon through pink to red, some with picotee edges in pale pink or white. The pollen is always golden, in contrast with wild field poppies, whose pollen is dark grey. More annual poppies on pages 42 and 43.

Soil preference: Any
Aspect: Sun
Season of interest: Summer
Height and spread: 30–60cm (1–2ft) x 20–40cm (10in–1ft 4in)

Companion plants: Other annual poppies work beautifully with Shirley seedlings, especially if allowed to naturalize in a gravel garden or sown at random in an annual border with such annuals as marigolds, clarkias, larkspurs and cornflowers.

Nigella damascena

Love-in-a-mist   Annual

Lacy, filamentous foliage makes a soft and alluring background for the flowers, whose distinctive blue petals nestle among the feathery leaves. Garden series such as 'Persian Jewels' have purple and white flowers, as well as those in various shades of blue. The large, inflated, lantern-like seed capsules are almost as decorative as the flowers and last until autumn.

Soil preference: Any
Aspect: Sun or part shade
Season of interest: Summer, autumn
Height and spread: 30–45cm (1ft–1ft 6in) tall

Companion plants: A lovely annual to naturalize among roses, especially the older varieties. Also effective for gap-filling, in a mixed border or for lining a lavender hedge.

Lagurus ovatus

Hare's Tail Grass   Annual grass

Mediterranean species with grassy foliage and silvery grey flowers which are broadly oval and furry to the touch, resembling the tail of a hare or rabbit. This grass grows taller on rich soil but thrives as a smaller plant in harsh conditions. A dwarf form, 'Nanus', may be more suitable for gardens with rich soil.

Soil preference: Any free-draining
Aspect: Sun
Season of interest: Summer, autumn
Height and spread: 15–50cm (6in–1ft 8in) x 30cm (12in)

Companion plants: A worthy addition to a grass border, especially if planted with other annual grasses such as *Briza maxima*, but also lovely among flowering annuals. Scatter seed among pot marigolds, cornflowers or tagetes.

Anagallis monellii

Shrubby Pimpernel   Perennial grown as a tender annual

A low, straggly plant with semi-trailing stems and small, triangular leaves grouped in threes along the stem. At each leaf joint, buds form which open as conspicuous, five-petalled flowers in the deepest, most intense blue. Similar, but larger in all its parts, to the wild blue pimpernel, *Anagallis foemina*.

Soil preference: Fertile, well-drained
Aspect: Sun
Season of interest: Summer
Height and spread: 20cm x 30cm (8in x 12in)

Companion plants: An excellent hanging basket or container plant which is especially effective when contrasted with bright yellow *Bidens ferulifolia* or harmonized with variegated trailing Plectranthus or with red pelargoniums.

Cerinthe major 'Purpurascens'   Honeywort   Annual

Cornfield annual from the Mediterranean with curious, glaucous foliage and, in early summer, metallic purple bracts which are remarkably luminous and which half conceal the strange brownish purple and yellow tubular flowers. The seeds are large and stone-hard. Although when established it will self-sow, the species is not hardy in sustained frost.

Soil preference: Any well-drained
Aspect: Sun
Season of interest: Summer
Height and spread: 50cm x 30cm (1ft 8in x 12in)

Companion plants: A distinctive plant for a Mediterranean garden among grey and silver-leaved herbs such as lavenders, Teucrium and sages. Excellent in gravel, too, among brown sedges such as *Carex buchananii* and also with Californian poppies.

Brachyscome hybrids

Swan River Daisy   Annuals

The narrow, fresh, often lacy green leaves on these Australian native plants are almost hidden behind a generous covering of bright daisy flowers, in mauve, pink or white. A neat, but semi-trailing habit, coupled with summer-long flowering makes them ideal for container use. Good varieties include 'Blue Haze', the lilac coloured 'City Lights' and the purple-blue 'Toucan Tango'. Tender.

Soil preference: Any, reasonably fertile
Aspect: Best in full sun
Season of interest: Summer
Height and spread: 45cm x 45cm (18in x 18in)

Companion plants: Yellow-flowered *Bidens ferulifolia* makes a good contrast, but the silver filigree leaves of *Artemisia* 'Lambrook Silver' or 'Powis Castle' also blend pleasingly.

Convolvulus tricolor   Annual

A non-climbing, but somewhat lax plant with small, oval leaves and saucer shaped flowers, similar to those of morning glories, but 5cm (2in) wide. The typical species has dark, royal blue petals, fading white or creamy yellow at the throat. Selected varieties include 'Ensign Mixed', with pink, maroon, blue and white shades, and the pale 'Light Blue Flash'.

Soil preference: Any
Aspect: Sun
Season of interest: Summer
Height and spread: 50cm x 30cm (1ft 8in x 1ft)

Companion plants: Great for a mixed annual border or to dot in among such perennials as Mexican salvias, osteospermums or grasses.

Lavatera trimestris   Annual

Tall, bold, with thick, rigid stems and large, slightly hoary leaves, this native of the Mediterranean regions has large, saucer shaped flowers whose stamens and stigma fuse to form a central spike. Colours range from rich pink, in 'Silver Cup' and 'Ruby Regis', to a startling white in 'Mont Blanc'. Each petal is veined with darker lines.

Soil preference: Well-drained, fertile
Aspect: Sun
Season of interest: Summer
Height and spread: 60–90cm x 45cm (2–3ft x 18in)

Companion plants: Careful siting is necessary, with so conspicuous a plant. Excellent in bold groups on its own or among such large perennials as Galega, leucanthemums and *Phlox paniculata*, with perennial asters to follow.

Galactites tomentosa   Annual

A thistle with spiky, divided white and green foliage, which emerges in autumn or early spring, forming an attractive rosette. In summer, the stem lengthens and branches, eventually bearing lilac-mauve, tufted thistle flowers. Seed is borne on thistledown. This native of the Canary islands and Mediterranean self-seeds freely, but young seedlings will not survive prolonged frost.

Soil preference: Any free-draining
Aspect: Sun
Season of interest: Spring, summer
Height and spread: 1m x 75cm (3ft 4in x 2ft 6in)

Companion plants: Attractive when allowed to colonize areas between shrubs – especially such Mediterranean species as rosemary, lavender, Santolina or *Phlomis fruticosa*, or to pop up at random in a mixed border.

Briza maxima

Greater Quaking Grass   Annual

A free-seeding annual grass which performs best in hot, dry conditions, where the plants are less likely to become invasive. Mid-green, soft grass foliage emerges in autumn or spring. The flower stems are wiry and much branched, bearing cone-shaped flowers which shimmer and tremble in the slightest breeze. Superb for cutting and drying.

Soil preference: Dry, not too fertile
Aspect: Sun or part shade
Season of interest: Summer
Height and spread: 60cm x 45cm (2ft x 18in)

Companion plants: A beautiful foil for showy herbaceous plants such as scabious, cornflowers, Linum or Oenothera.

Eschscholzia californica

Californian Poppy   Annual or short-lived perennial

A beautiful combination of blue-green, lacy foliage and bright, silky-textured flowers makes this American native a valuable plant, especially for a dry garden. The wild species has bright orange flowers, but seed selections come in a range of sunset hues from cream or primrose yellow, through peachy tones to burnt orange. Best in free-draining soil.

Soil preference: Dry, not too fertile
Aspect: Sun
Season of interest: Summer
Height and spread: 30cm x 30cm (1ft x 1ft)

Companion plants: The orange form makes a stirring companion to such bronze-tinted grasses as *Stipa tenuissima* or the sedge *Carex buchananii*. Also good in a gravel garden, where its misty foliage and silky petals will soften hard textures.

Geranium robertianum

Herb Robert   Annual

An invasive annual with spreading habit, pungent-smelling, ferny foliage and a long run of tiny, pink, five-petalled flowers. The albino form, 'Album', is more distinctive. A thug in the wrong place, but charming when allowed to self-sow in drifts in gravel or along the edges of a path.

Soil preference: Any free-draining
Aspect: Sun or part shade
Season of interest: Spring, summer, autumn
Height and spread: 20cm x 40cm (8in x 1ft 4in)

Companion plants: Naturalize this one with other gravel or paving crack plants such as *Viola riviniana* or Alchemilla.

Consolida ajacis   Larkspur   Annual

Classic cornfield annual which has been bred to improve height, standing power, and colour range. The leaves are finely divided and the tall, straight stems are furnished with spurred flowers in shades of pink or blue or white. Easy to raise from seed sown in autumn or spring, directly where they are expected to flower.

Soil preference: Fertile, well-drained
Aspect: Sun
Season of interest: Summer
Height and spread: Up to 1m x 30cm (3ft 4in x 1 ft)

Companion plants: Good as a cut flower and therefore effective grown among vegetables in a kitchen garden or in a mixed border. Attractive with roses, where the straight spikes make a strong contrast and where the blues and pinks of the flowers harmonize.

Helianthus annuus   Sunflower – large varieties   Annual

Biggest of the hardy annuals and raised as food crops in Central America since prehistoric times. The stout stems are strong enough to carry the massive flowers and seed heads without support. Some ornamental varieties are sterile and bear no pollen. Field crop sunflowers are golden yellow, but cultivated forms include such colourful series as 'Ring of Fire', whose flowers have concentric ring patterns in hues of dusky red and yellow, or 'Moonshadow', whose flowers are cream.

Soil preference: Rich, fertile
Aspect: Sun
Season of interest: Summer
Height and spread: Up to 3m x 1m (10ft by 3ft)

Companion plants: Useful plant to create a temporary screen, or to use as accent plants in a bedding scheme, cottage border or kitchen garden.

Linum grandiflorum

Flowering Flax   Annual

Slender, almost wiry stems with narrow, pointed leaves bear a long succession of disc-shape flowers up to 4cm (1¾in) across. In the wild, these are rosy purple, but seed selections include 'Bright Eyes', whose flowers are white with conspicuous wine red centres, and 'Rubrum', whose petals are a deeper rose with dark crimson centres.

Soil preference: Any, free-draining
Aspect: Sun
Season of interest: Summer
Height and spread: 45cm x 30cm (1ft 6in x 1ft)

Companion plants: The waving stems and frail flowers look delightful among coloured grasses or sedges such as *Carex comans* or *Molinia caerulea*. Also lovely when naturalized among low-growing shrubs in a Mediterranean-style planting scheme.

Cynoglossum amabile

Chinese Forget-me-not   Annual

Narrow, pointed leaves on branched stems are joined in early and mid-summer by clusters of small forget-me-not flowers in an intense blue. Pink and white flowered varieties are also available. The seeds are large and exceptionally hard.

Soil preference: Fertile, free-draining
Aspect: Sun or part shade
Season of interest: Summer
Height and spread: 50cm x 30cm (20in x 12in)

Companion plants: Blue forms contrast sharply with the yellows of verbascums or, from later sowings, goldenrods and yellow daisies such as rudbeckias and heleniums. The intense blue would also relieve the monotony of a cool, silvery or white theme.

Datura inoxia

Downy Thorn Apple   Annual

A large, much branched, characterful annual with big, oval leaves which are downy and slightly tacky to the touch. The huge trumpet flowers – 15cm (6in) or more long – are purple tinged when in bud, but open to a soft white. In the evening and at night they are heavily scented.

Soil preference: Any fertile soil
Aspect: Sun
Season of interest: Summer, autumn
Height and spread: Up to 1m x 1m (3ft 3in x 3ft 3in)

Companion plants: One to grow on its own, but for a heady cocktail of night fragrance, plant with fragrant tobacco *Nicotiana affinis* and the vanilla scented heliotrope.

Malope trifida   Annual Mallow   Annual

Similar to annual *Lavetera trimestris*, but slightly smaller with more downy, heart-shaped leaves that hang down as the plant matures. Big saucer shaped flowers appear in succession throughout summer and colours in the various seed selections range from dusky and rose pink to bright magenta, deep plum and white.

Soil preference: Fertile but well-drained
Aspect: Sun
Season of interest: Summer
Height and spread: 50-75cm x 45cm (1ft 8in-2ft 6in by 1ft 6in)

Companion plants: Better than lavatera for mixing with other such hardy annuals as cornflowers, clarkia, larkspurs, *Convolvulus tricolor* and corn cockle.

Zinnia elegans   Annual

The species has been used to develop a colourful range of tender annuals, with simple leaves, slightly rough to the touch, and flowers with attractive layered florets, often with dark ochre or yellowish fertile centres. Flower colours include white, yellow, pink, mauve, orange, red, maroon and even pale green with a variety of flower forms from single to pompon.

Soil preference: Fertile, free-draining but not too dry
Aspect: Sun, shelter
Season of interest: Summer
Height and spread: From 20cm x 30cm to 1m x 50cm (from 8in x 3ft to 3ft 3in x 1ft 8in)

Companion plants: As desirable for cutting as for garden use, Zinnias will benefit from softer, more diffuse shapes nearby. Goldenrods add extra summer yellow, with a contrasting texture. Pale mauve or blue varieties of perennial aster will tone down the zinnias' jazz.

Borago officinalis

Borage   Annual

Large, heart-shaped to oval puckered, hairy leaves and thick, fleshy, branched stems carry myriads of small, star shaped flowers which are intense sky blue, with pale centres and dark, spiky stamens. A rapid annual which self-seeds copiously.

Soil preference: Any
Aspect: Any
Season of interest: Summer, autumn
Height and spread: Up to 1m x 75cm (3ft 3in x 2ft 6in), usually smaller

Companion plants: Beautiful anywhere but easily pulled out if not welcome. Herbs such as lavenders, herbaceous perennials, shrubs, large grasses, roses and bedding plants all make great companions.

Phacelia tanacetifolia

Fiddleneck   Annual

Handsome American species, often used as a 'green manure' crop. The compound leaves, reminiscent of Jacob's Ladders, create a ferny effect as the branched stems develop and lengthen. Buds are carried on tightly curled scapes, like violin heads, which uncurl and straighten as the violet blue flowers open. A free seeder.

Soil preference: Any, not too wet
Aspect: Sun or part shade
Season of interest: Summer
Height and spread: Up to 1m x 60cm (up to 3ft 3in x 2ft)

Companion plants: Another charming annual to sow in drifts among grasses or naturalistically planted perennials. The soft lavender-blue haze they create is also pretty with creamy or sunset-hued achilleas or among blue cranesbills.

Antirrhinum pulverulentum

Trailing Snapdragon   Half hardy perennial, grown as an annual

A compact, but trailing plant with oval, dull-green leaves and a long succession of 'snapdragon' flowers whose lips gape when gently pinched. Hybrids include the series 'Pendula Lampion' with pale pink, white or purplish flowers and pale yellow markings. *Antirrhinum hispanicum* subsp. *hispanicum* has silvery grey leaves and purplish pink blooms.

Soil preference: Any free-draining
Aspect: Sun
Season of interest: Summer and autumn
Height and spread: 15cm trailing 30cm (6in trailing 1ft)

Companion plants: Equally effective in hanging baskets, window boxes or alpine troughs. Their pastel hues blend gently with the grey-green foliage of *Helichrysum petiolare* or with white-variegated *Glechoma hederacea* 'Variegata'.

Celosia argentea

Cockscomb or Wool Flower   Tender annual or shortlived perennial

Vigorous, soft-textured plants with pointed leaves and successions of bold, highly coloured plume-like flowers in vivid shades including red, orange, yellow and purple. 'Fresh Look Red' has scarlet flowers. The mixed 'Look Eternal Flames' has either bright yellow or burning red flowers, accompanied by foliage which is green or deep purple-bronze.

Soil preference: Free-draining but moist and fertile
Aspect: Sun
Season of interest: Summer
Height and spread: from 30cm x 30cm (from 1ft x 1ft)

Companion plants: Their sub-tropical looks and strong flower colour make these plants good companions for Solenostemon (Coleus). Also try cooling with deep blue bedding lobelias.

Nemesia strumosa

Nemesia   Tender annual

A South African member of the foxglove family, whose main features are the massed flowers in bright sunny colours which include orange, red, white, pink and yellow. 'Nebula Mixed' has hot, single colours whereas 'KLM' is a blue and white bicolour. The series 'Sundrops' has a remarkably long flowering period.

Soil preference: Any moisture retentive and fertile
Aspect: Sun
Season of interest: Summer
Height and spread: Variable to 30cm x 15cm (1ft by 6in)

Companion plants: The hot colours benefit from the cooling effect of blue-flowered bedding lobelia or a blue variety of Laurentia.

Phlox drummondii   Annual Phlox   Tender annual

Delicate plants, with rather weedy growth and nondescript simple leaves produce large heads of brightly coloured, disc-shaped flowers, often with contrasting centres. Superb when in full bloom but the flowering season can be brief. 'Phlox of Sheep' is an excellent series, with flowers in sunset hues; 'Silver Blossom' has mauve, dusky pink and even beige suffusions; and the petals of 'Twinkle Stars' are white-edged picotee types.

Soil preference: Free-draining but fertile
Aspect: Sun
Season of interest: Summer
Height and spread: Variable to 30cm x 30cm (1ft x 1ft)

Companion plants: Best when backed up by the strong characterful foliage of Plectranthus or when planted with such annual grasses as *Briza maxima* and *Lagurus ovatus.*

Sanvitalia procumbens

Creeping Zinnia   Tender annual

Trailing stems with simple, deep-green leaves and a summer-long succession of abundant small daisy flowers with broad, orange or yellow sterile ray florets and deep green or dark centres. The variety 'Irish Eyes' is golden yellow with glowing green flower centres. 'Orange Sprite' is dwarfer, with bright orange semi-double flowers whose centres are dark.

Soil preference: Any fertile and free-draining
Aspect: Sun
Season of interest: Summer
Height and spread: 15cm (6in), spreading 30cm (1ft)

Companion plants: Good in a bold colour scheme with perhaps compact varieties of nasturtiums and purple-leaved basil. Excellent contrast with dark blue trailing lobelia.

Dorotheanthus bellidiformis

Livingstone Daisy   Tender annual

A South African member of the ice plant family with small, fleshy leaves, mealy in texture, and a long succession of bright, daisy-like flowers in day-glow colours. 'Apricot Tutu' has pinkish sunset-hued flowers, but 'Sparkles' has a wider range including pale cream, purplish pink and orange, many flowers being bicoloured. The flowers will only open in full, direct sunlight.

Soil preference: Free-draining, not rich
Aspect: Full sun
Season of interest: Summer
Height and spread: To 15cm x 25cm (6in x 10in)

Companion plants: Good on their own in a hot, dry container in the sun or to add colour to such succulents as echeverias, sedums or sempervivums.

Rudbeckia hirta   Half hardy perennials grown as annuals

Dwarf, intermediate and tall hybrids of this North American genus have dark stems and simple leaves, lightly covered with short hairs. The daisy flowers, with their conspicuous ray florets and dark central cones, come in warm tones from yellow through to mahogany. Good cutting varieties include the double-flowered 'Cherokee Sunset', spidery-bloomed 'Chim-chimenee', and the green and golden 'Irish Eyes'.

Soil preference: Fertile, moisture-retentive and heavy but drained
Aspect: Sun or part shade
Season of interest: Summer, autumn
Height and spread: 15–60cm x 30cm (6in–2ft x 1ft)

Companion plants: Use these plants to extend summer displays and blend with late flowering blue and purple salvias and perennial asters. They are also bewitching with soft, flowing grasses or sedges such as bronze leaved Carex and *Stipa arundinacea*.

Antirrhinum majus **tall varieties**

Half hardy to hardy perennial, usually grown as an annual

Familiar snapdragons such as 'Axiom Series' which have been bred to grow as tall plants, each with a straight, single stem ending in a long spike bearing the flowers in a broad colour range, including red, pink, yellow and bicolours. Plant in a sheltered spot or raise under glass.

Soil preference: Fertile, well-drained
Aspect: Sun, often raised under glass
Season of interest: Constant, depending when planted
Height and spread: To 75cm (30in)

Companion plants: Pretty plants for a summer kitchen garden, along with such cutting flowers as marigolds, larkspurs, dahlias and Gladiolus.

Helianthus annuus

Sunflower – pollen-free varieties   Hardy annual

Single or branched stems may grow from a single seed, furnished with broad, slightly hoary, simple leaves and massive flowerheads with bright yellow, orange or maroon ray florets. Selections for cutting include pollen-free 'Bees Knees', whose flower colours include orange, lemon yellow, rich gold and deep reddish brown and orange, as well as the powderpuff-like 'Double Shine'.

Soil preference: Fertile, free-draining
Aspect: Sun
Season of interest: Summer
Height and spread: Variable to 2m x 30cm (6ft x 1ft)

Companion plants: Too dominant to harmonize with other annuals, but very effective when planted as short-term screens or along walls or hedges. Pollen-free varieties are NOT GOOD for wildlife.

Dianthus barbatus 'Summer Sundae'

Annual Sweet William   Hardy annual or biennial

An annual form of the familiar sweet William described on page 54. Although spring-sown seed will produce flowers the same season, autumn-sown plants will grow a little larger and flower for longer. A valuable variety, though, for speedy cut flowers. The multi-headed flowers are sweetly fragrant and last well in water.

Soil preference: Any free-draining
Aspect: Sun
Season of interest: Summer
Height and spread: 45–60cm x 20cm (18in–2ft x 8in)

Companion plants: All sweet Williams make excellent border plants, as they are at home with most perennials. Particularly effective with such flowery summer annuals as cornflowers, larkspurs, marigolds and poppies.

Callistephus hybrids

Bedding Asters   Half hardy annual

Popular both as bedding or for cut flowers, these daisy relatives have showy ray florets in pink, purple, white, cream and wine red. Many different forms are widely available. Good cutting kinds, with long lasting qualities, include 'Truffaunt's Peony Mixed', whose petals are incurved, and 'Super Chinensis', which has single flowers with bold, yellow centres.

Soil preference: Fertile, free-draining
Aspect: Sun or part shade
Season of interest: Summer
Height and spread: 30cm x 20cm (1ft x 8in)

Companion plants: If varieties are chosen with gentle colours, asters make great companion plants for red, pink or white bedded roses. Also fine in rows in a kitchen garden.

Molucella laevis

Bells of Ireland   Half hardy annual

A member of the deadnettle family whose main features are the large, pale green, bell-shaped bracts which surround the tiny, off-white flowers, and which persist for the whole growing season. The foliage is unremarkable. Stems with the bracts are as effective when used dried as when they are fresh.

Soil preference: Fertile, free-draining
Aspect: Sun
Season of interest: Summer
Height and spread: 60cm x 25cm (2ft x 10in)

Companion plants: Normally grown for cutting though Molucella can look attractive among white flowers or with silvery foliage plants such as *Artemisia ludoviciana* or *Salvia farinacea* 'Victoria'.

Planting Schemes Using Annuals

The main point about annuals – and therein lies their charm – is that they are shortlived. Even the most stalwart, enduring individuals are done after a few months; few last for more than half a summer and many flower and die within a few weeks. Effective planting, therefore, depends on rotation, careful timing, large numbers and bold placing.

Many annuals are also somewhat unpredictable, growing larger and brighter than expected in favourable years, but failing to achieve their potential in difficult seasons. Since they seed copiously and since many adopt the role of biennials and will survive a winter, having germinated in the autumn, their short lives are often compensated for by rapid reproduction and a sustained succession. With the hardiest, such as Nigella, Calendula or Papaver, flowering can sometimes come in waves, with early and copious summer flushes from seed sown the previous autumn, a further wave from spring-germinated seed and a finale from summer-sown seed. Flowering times can also be brought forward by artificial sowing, pre-season, in trays or cells and planting out the young plants. Tender annuals will not sustain their colonies outdoors, where winter frost is expected, but hardy species can be left to their own devices and should ensure colour through much of the growing season.

Annuals as blenders

Although they work very well in their own company, the most common use of annuals is as gap fillers, or to accompany other, more permanent plants in mixed schemes. The main picture shows an informal grouping of *Campanula lactiflora* (bellflower) with red-flowered opium poppies. The foliage of both plants contrast well, the pale, glaucous leaves of the poppy having a markedly different colour, texture and shape from the smaller, rougher leaves of the bellflower. As they bloom, the large poppies are backed up by the starry, curled petals of the bells in their pastel lavender tones.

The photograph represents a tiny moment, probably no more than a 60th of a second! The plant association needs to last for several weeks at least and preferably for months, and yet each poppy blooms for no more than a day. The display, however, is far less ephemeral than it looks. After flowering, the campanula would be cut hard back to promote a second flush of flowers. As the opium poppy loses the last of its petals, the shapely seed capsules, held on stiffening stems, will continue to provide an architectural outline. By the time the bellflower has re-grown and is blooming again, the spent poppy will shift in colour from glaucous green to beige, and hence will continue to provide a contrast.

Caution is needed with the poppy, as with many annuals, to prevent unnecessary spread of seed by destroying seedlings while still young. Poppies, among all annuals, are probably the most fecund, and their seeds have a staggeringly long period of viability, countable in decades rather than years!

An informal grouping of *Campanula lactiflora* with a red flowered opium poppy.

This group is spectacular for the present, but less successful as a lasting association. The candytuft (Iberis) makes a strong companion to the Korean perennial *Campanula takesimana*, picking up some of its tones but with cleaner, brighter colours and making a bright carpet. However, although it is slightly longer in flower than the poppy, it lacks an attractive aftermath and has undistinguished foliage.

Clarkia pulchella   Hardy annual

A pretty annual from the Rocky Mountains with thin stems furnished with attractively ruched, funnel-shaped flowers in soft hues of pink, mauve or rosy purple. Gardenworthy seed series include 'Choice Double Mixed' and 'Apple Blossom', whose flowers, being apricot with white touches, could hardly look less like apple blossom!

Soil preference: Any free-draining, reasonably fertile
Aspect: Sun
Season of interest: Summer
Height and spread: 45cm x 30cm (18in x 12in)

Companion plants: Plants with an understated beauty, best placed with other pastel, crimson or purple annuals. Or use as gap fillers in a mixed or perennial border.

Euphorbia lathyrus

Caper Spurge   Hardy annual

A member of the spurge family which produces an erect, single stem with leaves held opposite one another in pairs, forming an unusual cross pattern. The green flowers, despite resembling capers, are highly poisonous and attract many species of fly which, in turn, attract predators. If wounded, all parts of the plant exude a milky, irritant sap.

Soil preference: Any
Aspect: Any
Season of interest: Spring, summer
Height and spread: Up to 1.5m x 25cm (5ft x 10in)

Companion plants: Not a great beauty but effective as a foil for more colourful plants. Its erect stance makes a pleasing contrast with more pendulous shapes including arching grasses and phormiums.

Linaria maroccana   Morocco Toadflax   Hardy annual

A pretty annual whose branching stems are furnished with simple, narrow leaves, which terminate with long-lasting spikes of small, spurred 'snapdragon' flowers. Colours are very variable in the wild species, with pink, yellow, dusky red, white or purple, each bloom usually having a deep yellow pollen guide. Garden varieties include 'Fairy Bouquet' in mixed colours, 'Fantasy blue' and 'Northern Lights', which has fragrant blooms.

Soil preference: Any free-draining
Aspect: Sun
Season of Interest: Summer
Height and spread: 20cm x 30cm (8in x 1ft)

Companion plants: A pretty annual to seed in a gravel garden, among low-growing grasses or to follow on from helianthemums and dwarf bearded irises.

Iberis umbellata

Candytuft   Hardy annual

Often a child gardener's first success, candytuft is an easily grown, quick-acting plant with simple leaves and branched stems which bear umbels of four-petalled, lilac, pink or white flowers. The outer petals on each umbel are larger than the inner, creating a lace-cap effect. Self sows freely in friable soil. Attractive to bees and butterflies.

Soil preference: Any
Aspect: Sun or part shade
Season of interest: Spring, summer
Height and spread: Up to 30cm x 15cm (12in x 6in)

Companion plants: Useful gap filler among the leaves of perennials which will flower later or naturalized in cottage style plantings with pinks, sweet Williams or other annuals.

Limnanthes douglasii   Poached Egg Plant   Hardy annual

A remarkably versatile, wildlife-friendly, low energy plant. Produces a moisture-retaining dense carpet of vivid green vegetation and when the bright yellow and white flowers open, in late spring and early summer, they are irresistible to bees. Though annual, self-seeding will usually allow these plants to develop self-sustaining colonies.

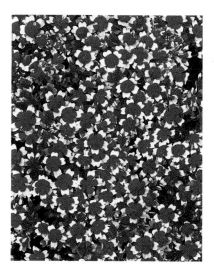

Soil preference: Any, not too dry
Aspect: Sun or part shade
Season of interest: Spring, summer
Height and spread: 15cm x 20cm (6in x 8in)

Companion plants: Useful to plant in front of shrubs, where they will make a bright carpet, or to scatter along the front of an annual border. Limnanthes also looks handsome grown among tuft-forming grasses such as *Festuca glauca*.

Calendula officinalis

Marigold, Pot Marigold   Hardy annual

Familiar, aromatic annual with big daisy flowers, single or double, in the yellow and orange colour range. Modern series include the dwarf 'Citrus Cocktail' and taller 'Touch of Red', whose petals have dark edges. 'Art Shades' are tall, traditional marigolds with orange to yellow, fully double flowers. Prone to mildew in damp years.

Soil preference: Any free-draining and fertile
Aspect: Sun, partial shade
Season of interest: Summer, autumn
Height and spread: From 15–60cm x 45cm (6–24in x 18in)

Companion plants: The hot colours are excellent to contrast with blue larkspur and annual Convolvulus or to pep up a cottage border. Also good for creating a wild meadow effect with other hardy annuals and cornfield blooms.

Reseda odorata

Mignonette, Bastard Rocket   Hardy annual

An unassuming little plant from Southern Europe, with simple leaves and spikes of tiny greenish flowers, each with a tuft of orange stamens. The plant's main distinguishing feature is its sweet fragrance, making it perfect to plant near an outdoor seating area. Attractive to moths and other nectar-seeking insects.

Soil preference: Any, fertile, free-draining
Aspect: Sun, part shade
Season of interest: Summer
Height and spread: 45cm x 20cm (1ft 6in x 8in)

Companion plants: Pretty among such annuals as calendulas and Nigella or perhaps in a fragrant border with roses, pinks and nicotianas.

Nemesia cheiranthus 'Masquerade'

Half hardy annual

An odd-looking relative of the more familiar bedding plant whose branching stems bear bicoloured flowers with elongated, narrow upper petals in white, contrasting with broad, two lobed lower petals which are yellowish orange. The plant has a the rich fragrance of roasted or candied coconut.

Soil preference: Fertile but free-draining
Aspect: Sun
Season of interest: Summer
Height and spread: 30cm x 20cm (12in x 8in)

Companion plants: An interesting plant for a hanging basket, perhaps planted with golden flowered *Bidens ferulifolia* or with *Lamium* 'Golden Anniversary'.

Tagetes lucida

Mexican Mint or Spanish Tarragon   Perennial, usually grown as an annual

Differing from better known members of the genus by having simple, rather than filigree, leaves, this plant has culinary value as well as beauty. The leaves and branched stems are highly aromatic - reminiscent of aniseed. It has bright golden flowers whose outer ray florets are broad, surrounding a raised central tuft of fertile florets.

Soil preference: Free-draining but fertile
Aspect: Sun
Season of interest: Summer
Height and spread: 60cm x 40cm (2ft x 1ft 8in)

Companion plants: One for the herb garden, perhaps planted with marjoram, basil and summer savory.

Scabiosa atropurpurea 'Dwarf Double'

Hardy annual

A shorter, more compact form of the familiar Southern European plant described on page 133. The blooms are as large as those on taller varieties and come in a rich colour range, which includes blue, mauve, cream, pink and white. The flowers, which are excellent for cutting, have a gentle fragrance.

Soil preference: Rich, fertile but free-draining
Aspect: Sun or part shade
Season of interest: Summer
Height and spread: 45cm x 30cm (1ft 6in x 1ft)

Companion plants: A fine selection for mixed flower borders or simply to line out for cutting. Also effective with annual grasses, hardy geraniums and other meadow flowers.

Matthiola longipetala subsp. bicornis

Night Scented Stock   Hardy annual

An intensely fragrant annual from Southern Europe which looks far more spectacular when illustrated in seedsmen's catalogues than when seen growing in a garden. The thin, frail stems bear small, irregularly shaped, pinkish-mauve four-petalled flowers. Improved series such as 'Scentsation' have white, deeper purple and pale pink among their colours.

Soil preference: Any
Aspect: Sun or part shade
Season of interest: Spring, summer
Height and spread: 30cm x 16cm (12in x 6in)

Companion plants: Frequently mixed with Virginian stocks before sowing or grown in a bed under a window or by a door so that the fragrance can be enjoyed at twilight. A positive cocktail of fragrances can be mixed with mignonette and dwarf sweet peas.

Laurentia axilliaris *syn.* Isotoma axilliaris *or* Solenopsis axilliaris   Tender annual

Narrow leaves and trailing stems form a shapely dome on which the star-shaped flowers appear over many weeks and exude a gentle but telling fragrance. Interesting varieties include 'Stargazer Mixed', whose colours may be white, blue or pink, and the compact 'Blue Stars'.

Soil preference: Fertile, free-draining
Aspect: Sun
Season of interest: Summer
Height and spread: 20cm (8in), trailing

Companion plants: Ideal for hanging baskets, especially if planted with Callibrachoa, Scaevola, ivy leaved pelargoniums or trailing petunias.

Impatiens glandulifera

Himalayan Balsam, Policeman's Helmet   Hardy annual

Tall, fast growing annual with fleshy stems and hairless leaves. From early summer onwards, a succession of large, helmet-shaped flowers precedes the pressure-packed seed capsules which explode, when touched, scattering their seed. An invasive plant that can be damaging in the wild, but an unusual garden annual.

Soil preference: Moist
Aspect: Part shade
Season of interest: Summer
Height and spread: To 1.5m x 45cm (5ft x 1ft 6in)

Companion plants: Best grown as a marginal or bog plant, with such other large species as *Ligularia clivorum* or Rodgersias.

Nigella papillosa   Hardy annual

A curious annual with single, five-petalled, dusky blue flowers and very finely divided foliage. The spidery seed heads are as interesting as the flowers, and can also be cut and used dry. *Nigella sativa* is a similar species, with aromatic seeds which are sometimes used as spices, hence the colloquial name Nutmeg Flower or Roman Coriander.

Soil preference: Any, free-draining
Aspect: Sun
Season of interest: Summer, autumn
Height and spread: 75cm x 30cm (2ft 6in x 1ft)

Companion plants: Useful as a border gap filler, where the seedheads can be left to accompany late summer daisies such as rudbeckias and heleniums or goldenrods.

Scabiosa prolifera

Carmel Daisy   Hardy annual

A sun-loving scabious which produces a mass of pale yellow flowers followed by dramatic, rounded seedheads whose sepals form cells rather like those of a honeycomb. Excellent for indoor decoration - fresh or dried.

Soil preference: Any free-draining, reasonably fertile
Aspect: Sun
Season of interest: Summer
Height and spread: 60cm x 20cm (2ft x 8in)

Companion plants: Pretty in an annual border, perhaps with nigellas, which also have pleasing seedheads and with such annual grasses as Lagurus or *Briza maxima*, whose drying heads are also handsome.

Papaver somniferum   Opium Poppy   Hardy annual

The leaves of opium poppies are bold, ruffled, blue-green and hairless. Many-branched stems produce large conspicuous flowers that are single or double and vary in hue from mauve, purple and pink to crimson or white. Shapely pepperpot seed capsules follow the flowers and persist into autumn. See also pages 42 and 43 for more poppies.

Soil preference: Free-draining, well worked
Aspect: Sun
Season of interest: Summer, autumn
Height and spread: Variable to 1.5m x 45cm (5ft x 1ft 6in)

Companion plants: Surprisingly pretty among shrub roses, particularly when the leaves contrast, but also popular in cottage schemes with early perennials such as lupins, campanulas or cranesbills.

Lobelia erinus

Lobelia   Half hardy perennial usually grown as an annual

A low allergen bedder with predominantly cool blue or white flowers – although some series come in mauve hues. 'Cambridge Blue' is an excellent, compact and long-flowering variety in pale blue. 'Crystal Palace' has bronze-tinted foliage and deep blue flowers. The old variety, 'Mrs Clibran Improved', is extremely neat with white-eyed blue flowers. (For other lobelias, see pages 67 and 155.)

Soil preference: Fertile, not too dry
Aspect: Sun or part shade
Season of interest: Summer
Height and spread: Variable to 20cm x 20cm (8in x 8in)

Companion plants: Traditionally used in pots or as border edging but also handsome when used informally amongst low growing border plants such as *Euphorbia myrsinites* or with purple-leaved heucheras.

Begonia semperflorens

Begonia   Tender perennial grown as an annual

Ubiquitous but invaluable bedding plant, tolerating drought and shade, which produces fleshy stems and leaves and a constant run of small pink, white or red blooms on low, bushy plants. The 'Alfa' series have bronze-suffused foliage; the 'Inferno' series are remarkably vigorous; 'Prelude' series begin flowering very early.

Soil preference: Fertile, not too dry but free-draining
Aspect: Sun or part shade
Season of interest: Summer
Height and spread: Variable to 30cm x 20cm (12in x 8in)

Companion plants: Often used in large floral bedding schemes because of their uniformity, they are useful edgers for the patio or lawn and single colours work well in pots or to fill in spaces in box parterres.

Omphalodes linifolia

Venus' Navelwort   Hardy annual

A rather fetching European member of the forget-me-not family with pale, grey-green, simple, narrow leaves and a long display of opalescent white flowers with navel-like centres. Though short-lived as an annual, this is a free-seeding species which, if happy, will form self-sustaining colonies.

Soil preference: Any free-draining, but not too dry
Aspect: Sun, part shade
Season of interest: Summer
Height and spread: 30cm x 20cm (1ft x 8in)

Companion plants: Best if allowed to spread in drifts among low-growing summer flowers such as violas and Mimulus, or to front low-growing shrubs. The foliage also harmonizes well with garden pinks, whereas the flowers make a pretty contrast in both colour and shape.

Orlaya grandiflora   Tender annual

A Mediterranean member of the carrot family whose finely divided foliage is crowned, from late spring to mid-summer, by a succession of shallow, dome shaped umbels. The outer, sterile flowers on each umbel carry large, creamy white asymmetrical petals, creating a beautiful lace-cap effect. Can be directly sown in warm regions, where it will also self-sow.

Soil preference: Any free-draining
Aspect: Sun
Season of interest: Summer
Height and spread: 30cm x 15cm (12in x 6in)

Companion plants: An exquisite, lacy companion to annuals with more solid-looking flowers, such as godetias, red poppies or Calendula. With deep blue larkspurs, the cream white lace caps make a cool contrast.

Cleome hassleriana

Spider Flower   Near hardy annual

A tall, rangy annual with decorative, seven-lobed palmate leaves held on short stalks along the tall, erect spike which terminates in a series of fragrant, distinctive white or pink flowers whose narrow petals and elongated stamens and stigma give the impression of colourful, long-legged spiders. Native of South America.

Soil preference: Any fertile, free-draining, not too dry
Aspect: Sun, part shade
Season of interest: Summer
Height and spread: 1.2m x 30cm (4ft x 1ft)

Companion plants: Ideal for the border back or to grow among tall perennials such as perennial asters since it brings earlier colour. The exotic appearance makes it a good companion to broad-leaved plants such as banana, canna or hedychiums (ginger lilies.)

Atriplex hortensis   Red Orache   Hardy annual

An easy annual, distinguished – especially when young – by its conspicuous slightly downy-textured, rich purple leaves which are oval, pointed and borne on flexible stems. Some of the early colour intensity is lost as the plant matures to produce, in summer, foxtail flowers which are brownish green. Self-seeds freely but is easy to control.

Soil preference: Any
Aspect: Sun, part shade, shade
Season of interest: Spring, summer
Height and spread: 1m x 30cm (3ft x 1ft)

Companion plants: Prettiest when allowed to dot itself among other plants in mixed borders or among shrubs. The foliage contrasts dramatically with the silver grey of young artemisias or with the gentle gold of *Milium effusum* 'Aureum'.

Silene coeli-rosa (Viscaria oculata)

Hardy annual

A hairless, reasonably erect annual with slender stems and narrow, oblong leaves. The small but showy, pale pink or two-tone pink and white flowers are produced in profusion on longish stems for much of the summer. Tolerant of hot, dry conditions and usually trouble-free.

Soil preference: Any free-draining
Aspect: Sun
Season of interest: Summer
Height and spread: 30cm x 15cm (1ft x 6in)

Companion plants: Prettiest with other annuals such as nigellas, poppies or Anagallis, but also handy to blend with other low growing perennials such as pinks and carnations, sedums, *Origanum rotundifolium* and *Euphorbia myrsinites*.

Rhinanthus minor

Hay Rattle, Yellow Rattle   Hardy, semi-parasitic annual

An interesting member of the foxglove family which can only germinate in the presence of host plants – grasses – from which it derives much of its sustenance during the early part of its life. The narrow, toothed leaves, bright yellow, lipped flowers and semi-translucent, pale green calyces make this a distinctive grassland species.

Soil preference: Moist, grass sward
Aspect: Sun
Season of interest: Summer
Height and spread: 30cm x 15cm (1ft x 15cm)

Companion plants: The 'impoverishing' effect Rhinanthus has on grass growth is of great benefit because it enables other broad-leaved flowering plants to colonize more easily. Wonderful with *Cardamine pratensis*, cowslips, cranesbill and knapweeds.

Planting Naturalistic Schemes

Many annuals which occur in the wild are opportunist plants which grow wherever the ground is disturbed. As fieldcrop weeds, many of them occur worldwide and among the most beautiful are those which colonize the ground among growing cereal crops. This cornfield scene, with its red poppies, blue cornflowers, yellow corn marigold and daisy-like corn chamomile would be simple to reproduce as part of a naturalistic planting scheme in an informal garden. Some wild annuals, however, may be too invasive to risk introducing into a garden – especially a small one.

To avoid creating problems with over-exuberant self-seeding, beds of annuals or 'arable patches' imitating cornfields should be contained. Solid pathways around their edges or other non-cultivable ground surfaces can help to prevent seed spread but may compromise the natural appearance. Annuals that are allowed to spill over their boundaries by self-seeding can be far more beautiful than those regimented in strict beds.

Blue *Centaurea cyanus* produces an attractive picture when combined with red poppies, corn chamomile and corn marigold.

biennials

Myosotis sylvatica

Forget-me-not   Hardy biennial

Narrow, bright green leaves that form neat clumps over winter are joined from early spring by expanding spikes of tiny, pale centred, blue flowers. The first flowers nestle among the leaves, but as spring advances, the stems extend, creating a soft blue haze. A ready self-seeder. 'Blue Ball' is the most widely grown variety, but other seed series include 'Victoria' which has blue, white or pink flowers.

Soil preference: Any well-drained
Aspect: Sun or part shade
Season of interest: Spring, early summer
Height and spread: Up to 30cm x 40cm (1ft x 1ft 4in)

Companion plants: One of the finest companions for tulips, since it creates a soft, blue base. Charming when dotted among spring perennials such as *Lathyrus vernus*, yellow doronicums or polyanthus.

Erysimum cheiri

Bedding Wallflowers   Hardy biennial

Shrubby biennial or short-lived perennial with narrow, evergreen leaves and from mid-spring spikes with bold-coloured, four-petalled flowers, which are sweetly fragrant. Dwarf bedding varieties include the mixed 'Persian Carpet'. 'Fire King' is a taller orange red variety and 'Blood Red' an old breed with deep blood red flowers.

Soil preference: Any, preferably alkaline
Aspect: Sun
Season of interest: Spring
Height and spread: Up to 60cm x 40cm (2ft x 1ft 4in)

Companion plants: Pretty when bedded with tulips, but also handy for gap filling in a mixed or herbaceous border. Wallflowers work well with emerging lupin foliage, with tulips or with the hazy blue flowers of *Brunnera macrophylla*.

Erysimum   Perennial Wallflowers   Short-lived

perennials, can be grown as biennials

Shrubby wallflower varieties with narrow, sometimes blue-grey leaves and a steady succession of stiff flower spikes held well clear of the leaves, and bearing four-petalled blooms in mauve, bronze, cream, yellow or red. *Erysimum* 'Bowles Mauve' is the best known but 'Sunlight' has yellow flowers and 'Harpur Crewe' small, double yellow, richly fragrant blooms.

Soil preference: Free-draining
Aspect: Sun
Season of interest: Spring, summer
Height and spread: Variable to 75cm x 60cm (2ft 6in x 2ft)

Companion plants: Good in a dry gravel or Mediterranean garden, with yellow-flowered *Genista lydia* and silver-leaved shrubs and herbs.

Digitalis purpurea   Foxglove   Hardy biennial

Large, downy basal leaves in the first year are followed by tall, slender spikes furnished with many tubular downward-hanging flowers. The typical species has purplish pink flowers whose throats are thickly spotted with rusty marks, but garden forms come in a range of colours from white, through pale pink and apricot to deep purple.

Soil preference: Well-drained, but not too dry
Aspect: Shade or part shade
Season of interest: Late spring, early summer
Height and spread: Up to 2m x 60cm (6ft 6in x 2ft)

Companion plants: Excellent for woodland planting or to fill spaces between shrubs. Foxgloves are also lovely in cottage-style gardens, alongside cranesbills, old fashioned roses or with columbines.

Smyrnium perfoliatum   Biennial

A biennial with branched, winged stems and from mid-spring, showy, bract-like leaves which surround the flower umbels and are a vivid golden green. Lovely with the light coming through them, but this is an invasive plant which seeds a little too freely.

Soil preference: Any, not too damp
Aspect: Sun or shade
Season of interest: Spring
Height and spread. 1m x 45cm (3ft 3in x 1ft 6in)

Companion plants: Good for filling up spaces below trees, or allowing to spread with such other umbelliferous plants as sweet cicely or cow parsley. Also handsome when planted with red tulips, or with purple honesty *Lunaria annua*.

Hesperis matronalis

Dames Violet, Sweet Rocket   Biennial or short-lived perennial

Cabbage family member with narrow leaves held on stout flower spikes that are topped with generous clusters of four-petalled fragrant blooms, the perfume being especially strong at twilight. Colours range from white, through pale mauve to soft purple. Replace flowered plants with self-sown seedlings.

Soil preference: Any, moist
Aspect: Sun or part shade
Season of interest: Spring, early summer
Height and spread: 1m x 30cm (3ft x 1ft)

Companion plants: A lovely species whose pale colours which show up well in poor light, and which go well with such bolder-hued early perennials as lupins, campanulas or even oriental poppies.

Campanula medium   Canterbury Bells   Hardy biennial

The showiest of all bell flowers, with rough-textured, simple leaves and thick, ribbed stems. The stems develop into generously endowed spikes whose huge, tubular bell flowers may be shades of blue, pink or white. 'Cup and saucer' varieties have a bell flower resting on a petal-like, coloured calyx. Double-flowered varieties are available from seed catalogues.

Soil preference: Well-drained
Aspect: Sun
Season of interest: Summer
Height and spread: 1m x 50cm
(3ft x 1ft 8in)

Companion plants: A perfect cottage plant, showy but in gentle colours and along with sweet Williams, ideal for bridging the gap between spring and mid-summer, following on from wallflowers. Beautiful with roses!

Salvia farinacea

Mealy Sage   Tender biennial

Technically a perennial, but grown as a tender biennial or annual, the leaves are glossy but the flower stems are coated with a white mealy substance. The lipped flowers, produced throughout summer, are purple, blue or white. *Salvia farinacea* 'Victoria' is a popular bedding plant.

Soil preference: Any, fertile but free-draining
Aspect: Sun
Season of interest: Summer
Height and spread: 1m x 60cm
(3ft x 3 ft)

Companion plants: Attractive when included in a tropical mix, perhaps with cannas, bold grasses such as *Chasmanthium* or ornamental sorghums.

Ratibida columnifera

Mexican Hat   Biennial or short-lived perennial

A member of the daisy family from Mexico, with divided leaves and erect stems bearing flowers whose broad, yellow, or red and yellow sterile ray florets surround an extended central cone. Viewed from the side, these Rudbeckia relatives resemble the sombreros worn by Mexican bandits in cowboy films.

Soil preference: Any well-drained, but not too dry
Aspect: Sun
Season of interest: Summer
Height and spread: 60cm x 45cm (2ft x 1ft 6in)

Companion plants: A delightful cottage garden plant whose shape contrasts well with campanulas, delphiniums or with perennial asters.

Lysimachia atropurpurea

Hardy biennial or short-lived perennial

A striking, if somewhat sparse growing species with pewter-suffused foliage when young and, during mid-summer, narrow spikes of deep purple-red flowers which contrast with the grey-green tones of the leaves. From the distance, the flowers look black and disappear, but close-to, especially if used as cut flowers, they are superb.

Soil preference: Fertile, free-draining
Aspect: Sun
Season of interest: Summer
Height and spread: 45cm x 30cm (1ft 6in x 1 ft)

Companion plants: Best planted with light-coloured foliage plants such as *Artemisia ludoviciana* or *Convolvulus cneorum* so that the sombre blooms can make a strong contrast.

Oenothera biennis   Evening Primrose   Biennial

Broad, pointed leaves form loose rosettes producing, in their second year, tall, somewhat lax stems with large pale yellow blooms that open at twilight and are spent by the following midday. May be a nuisance self-seeder, but a late summer delight.

Soil preference: Any
Aspect: Sun or part shade
Season of interest: Summer
Height and spread: 1.2m x 45cm (4ft x 1ft 6in)

Companion plants: One to dot about or allow to come up where it will in an informal planting scheme. Especially good among the soft mauves, purples and blues of perennial asters or in a late season annual border.

Scabiosa atropurpurea

Mournful Widow, Egyptian Rose   Biennial

Lobed or divided leaves and thin, branched stems carry, in summer and early autumn, a long succession of pincushion-like flowers in dusky maroon or near black. The form 'Chile Black' is dark crimson, 'Chile Sauce' is rose red and 'Salmon Queen' a deep salmon pink.

Soil preference: Any fertile soil
Aspect: Sun
Season of interest: Summer
Height and spread: 90cm x 45cm (3ft x 1ft 6in)

Companion plants: Beautiful grown with summer annuals such as corn cockle or field poppies, and with taller ornamental grasses like Deschampsia.

Eryngium giganteum 'Miss Willmott's Ghost'

Short-lived perennial

A very large perennial with prickly leaves and stems. The leaves are suffused with silvery white and each dome-shaped, thistle-like flower carries a spiky ruff at its base. The common name arises from the habit of Edwardian garden guru Ellen Willmott who, presumptuously, scattered seeds of it in other people's gardens.

Soil preference: Any fertile
Aspect: Sun or part shade
Season of interest: Summer, autumn
Height and spread: 1.5m x 80cm (5ft x 2ft 8in)

Companion plants: Plants of great character, making strong focal points in mixed borders. Useful for lightening up dark evergreen shrubs at the back of borders, or to dot among tall perennials such as *Verbena bonariensis* and with big grasses.

Geranium maderense

Madeiran Cranesbill   Tender biennial

Palmate leaves grow from a stumpy base, forming a large, impressive rosette. When the necessary size has been reached, a big branched flowerhead forms and erupts into a spectacular display of rich cerise to rosy purple flowers, each with a more intense eye. Once seed has formed, the plant dies. Must have winter protection.

Soil preference: Any not too dry, but well-drained
Aspect: Part shade
Season of interest: Summer
Height and spread: Up to 1.3m x 1m (4ft x 3ft 3in)

Companion plants: Best in a container in cold regions. Perfect in the company of ferns or of broad-leaved, shade-loving plants such as the larger hostas.

Meconopsis napaulensis

Technically a perennial but seldom survives flowering

As valued for the beautiful rosettes of felty lobed leaves, each one covered in rust-coloured hairs, as for the huge flower spikes which will grow well over 2m (6ft) before producing a generous supply of poppy flowers in pinkish red, purple or dusky blue.

Soil preference: Preferably lime-free, not too dry
Aspect: Shade or part shade
Season of interest: Summer.
Height and spread: 2m x 75cm (6ft 6in x 2ft 6in)

Companion plants: A plant for the woodland garden, or at least for dappled shade and therefore wonderful with foxgloves or perhaps teamed up with other Himalayan poppies such as *Meconopsis grandis*.

Digitalis   Foxglove   Hardy biennial or short-lived perennial

The common foxglove (*Digitalis purpurea*) has several equally dramatic and unusual cousins. One of the finest is *D. grandiflora* (pictured), which has bold, dark green tooth-edged leaves and early summer flower spikes of large butter yellow blooms. *D.* 'Carillon' is similar but shorter and *D.* x *mertonensis*, a cross between *D. grandiflora* and *D. purpurea*, has crushed strawberry blooms.

Soil preference: Any free-draining
Aspect: Sun or part shade
Season of interest: Summer
Height and spread: Up to 1m x 50cm (3ft 3in x 1ft 8in)

Companion plants: Foxgloves are excellent for adding height and flower power to shady borders. *Digitalis grandiflora* works particularly well in a cool-colour planting scheme with blue, white and clear yellow flowers.

Echium russicum

Red Bugloss   Marginally tender to hardy biennial

Tidy rosettes of narrow, dark grey-green leaves develop during autumn and winter. During the following spring and early summer, rigid spikes appear, carrying narrow leaves along their lengths and, later, clusters of small, rose-red flowers which are irresistible to bees. The plants must be in a free-draining, sheltered spot to survive winter.

Soil preference: Any well-drained
Aspect: Sun
Season of interest: Summer
Height and spread: 45cm x 30cm (1ft 6in x 12in)

Companion plants: Best in bold groups where the spikes can make a contrast with lower growing early summer plants such as helianthemums, *Verbascum* 'Letitia' or Alchemilla.

Petroselinum crispum

Parsley, Curled Parsley   Hardy biennial or short-lived perennial

Familiar kitchen herb which also makes a first rate ornamental foliage plant. The leaves are vivid, emerald green, tightly curled and crisped, or flat, ferny and much divided. Sprays of greenish umbels appear in late summer but are not particularly decorative. Will self-seed.

Soil preference: Any
Aspect: Sun or part shade
Season of interest: Year round
Height and spread: Foliage 25cm (10in), flower to 60cm (2ft)

Companion plants: Cooling foil for bright, hot coloured flowers such as tulips in spring, annual poppies, pansies or marigolds in summer.

Lunaria biennis

Honesty   Hardy biennial or annual

Toothed, heart-shaped green or variegated foliage with soft, fast growing stems, in spring, which produce sprays of four-petalled flowers in magenta, white or dark purple. The flat, rounded, transparent seedheads are pretty in late summer, but are easily damaged by wind. Attracts bees and butterflies; food for the Orange Tip butterfly.

Soil preference: Any
Aspect: Any
Season of interest: Spring, summer
Height and spread: 90cm x 45cm (3ft x 1ft 6in)

Companion plants: A pretty woodlander to naturalize in dapple shade among bluebells, red campion and species tulips.

Primula elatior hybrids

Polyanthus   Hardy perennials grown as biennials

Very close relative of primroses and cowslips, these are the colourful hybrids whose oblong, wrinkled leaves form winter rosettes from which spring stems or 'scapes' topped with clusters of fragrant, five-petalled flowers in shades of yellow, blue, pink, red or white. Valuable to early bees, especially bumble bees. 'Crescendo' series are large-flowered; 'Guinevere' has dark leaves and pale flowers.

Soil preference: Moist but well-drained. Fertile
Aspect: Part shade
Season of interest: Spring
Height and spread: To 25cm x 25cm (10in x 10in)

Companion plants: Usually bedded when grown as biennials and excellent with tulips or with wall flowers. Yellow or red series look fine with blue forget-me-nots.

Verbascum bombyciferum

Giant Mullein   Hardy biennial

Huge rosettes of downy, pale grey leaves develop in the first year, followed in the second summer by towering, white felted flower spikes which are furnished for months with chrome yellow flowers. Food plant of the Mullein moth caterpillar; flowers attractive to bees.

Soil preference: Any free-draining
Aspect: Sun
Season of interest: Year round
Height and spread: 2.5m x 1.5m (7ft 6in x 4ft 6in)

Companion plants: One for bringing drama to a dry border. Try with airy grasses, or with other large, drought tolerant perennials such as *Crambe cordifolia* or *Colquhounia coccinea*.

Echium pininana   Tower of Jewels, Pride of Tenerife, Tree Echium   Tender biennial

A bizarre giant bugloss from the Canary islands. Bristling, thick stems with narrow leaves extend during summer and carry thousands of small, violet blue or pinkish-tinged flowers. May take more than a year to reach flowering size, but always dies after flowering. Loved by bees.

Soil preference: Any free-draining
Aspect: Sun
Season of interest: Summer
Height and spread: 3m x 1m (10ft 9in x 3ft 3in)

Companion plants: Grown as a curio, but handsome when the flower stem begins to rear up amongst plants in a Mediterranean style border.

Salvia argentea   Hardy biennial or short-lived perennial

Large, oval, densely felted foliage forms large, flat rosettes from early summer. The small, greenish white, lipped flowers are held on branched stems which are square in section. A free self-seeder but young plants are susceptible to water logging, especially in winter. Loved by bees, butterflies and adult hoverflies.

Soil preference: Any free-draining
Aspect: Sun
Season of interest: Summer
Height and spread: 45cm x 45cm (1ft 6in x 1ft 6in)

Companion plants: The broad leaves contrast sharply with the small, spiky stems and foliage of rosemary, lavender and Russian sage (Perovskia)

Rudbeckia hirta   Half hardy biennial or short-lived perennial

Oval, pointed leaves and somewhat hairy, branched stems bear, during late summer and autumn, big daisy flowers whose prominent central cones are usually dark and whose outer ray florets are broad, long and richly coloured in yellow, orange, mahogany or combinations of these hues.

Soil preference: Fertile, well-drained but moisture retentive
Aspect: Sun or part shade
Season of interest: Late summer and autumn
Height and spread: Variable to 1m x 45cm (3ft 3in x 1ft 6in)

Companion plants: Bright companions for red salvias or among cooler blues and mauves of autumn-flowering asters. Also useful for late bedding schemes.

Dianthus barbatus

Sweet William   Hardy annual or short-lived perennial

Member of the pink family, its branching stems furnished with broad or narrow dark green or purple-bronze leaves, are topped with clusters of flowers. The sepals are narrow and extended like little green beards. The fragrant blooms are maroon, red, pink, white or bicoloured and last for several weeks.

Soil preference: Any free-draining
Aspect: Sun
Season of interest: Early to mid-summer
Height and spread: To 60cm x 45cm (2ft x 1ft 6in)

Companion plants: Great favourite for cottage planting and good company for annuals such as larkspurs and cornflowers, or to grow at the feet of climbing or bush roses. Also prized as a cut flower.

Viola x williamsii 'Bedding Supreme'

Miniature pansy   Hardy biennials or short-lived perennials

Seed-raised selections of small-flowered pansies or violas with honey-scented, five-petalled flowers produced above lobed leaves. Short-lived as perennials, but can be kept in flower for months by regular deadheading. Good series: 'Bedding Supreme' comes in a broad colour mix, 'Singing in the Blues' in shades of purple, violet and blue.

Soil preference: Any free-draining but not too dry
Aspect: Sun, part shade
Season of interest: Winter, spring, summer
Height and spread: 20cm x 30cm (8in x 12in)

Companion plants: Like all pansies and violas, these plants fit anywhere with anything. Lovely in a cottage border, seeding among pinks, antirrhinums or in semi-shade with small dicentras or between polyanthus.

Matthiola incana

Stock, Brompton Stock   Biennial

Glaucous, slightly downy, grey-green foliage which produces multiple short stems, or long single stems bearing highly fragrant single or double blooms in white or shades of violet, mauve or pink. Cutting varieties include Ten Week stocks, but the wild species is attractive for cottage garden use. Excellent bee plant.

Soil preference: Any free-draining
Aspect: Sun
Season of interest: Summer.
Height and spread: Variable to 1m x 20cm (Variable to 3ft 3in x 10in)

Companion plants: Once popular for over-wintered bedding, Brompton Stocks are more frequently used to dot among early summer mixed borders, preludes to pinks or border carnations, or to grow among bush roses.

Onopordon nervosum

Scottish Thistle   Hardy biennial

Metallic, silvery-grey leaves form dramatic rosettes in autumn and thick, winged, branched stems rear up during spring and summer, creating tree-like structures decorated in summer with purplish red thistle flowers. Viciously armed in all its parts. A prolific self-seeder.

Soil preference: Any free-draining
Aspect: Full sun
Season of interest: All year, mainly summer
Height and spread: Up to 3m x 1.5m (10ft 9in x 4ft 6in)

Companion plants: Their architectural shape make these ideal plants for providing dramatic summer statements, particularly among soft outline perennials such as cranesbills. Also excellent in sparse gravel planting.

Lychnis coronaria

Rose Campion   Hardy biennial

Loose rosettes of oval, felty, grey leaves develop in the first year. Branched, erect stems develop during the second spring and in summer carry a long succession of bright cerise, disc-shaped flowers. The form 'Alba' has white flowers which age to pale pink, whereas the petals of 'Atrosanguinea' are blood red.

Soil preference: Well-drained
Aspect: Sun
Season of interest: Summer
Height and spread: 1m x 50cm (3ft 3in x 1ft 8in)

Companion plants: A free self-seeder, which is lovely dotted about among the more rigid spikes of lupins or to harmonize with lavenders and Perovskia.

Silybum marianum

Our Lady's Milk Thistle, Blessed Thistle   Hardy biennial

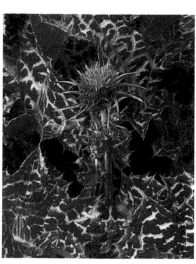

Dark green, undulating, prickly leaves, each marbled with white streaks, form a loose-knit groundcover during spring. Flower spikes develop in summer producing deep purple thistle flowers, but the value is in the foliage. The name arises from the legend that the Blessed Virgin Mary dripped milk onto the leaves. Watch for slugs and snails.

Soil preference: Any well-drained
Aspect: Sun or part shade
Season of interest: Summer
Height and spread: 50cm x 1m (1ft 8in by 3ft 3in)

Companion plants: Valuable for linking spring with summer and lovely among early flowering perennials such as lupins, early poppies and perennial wallflowers.

Trifolium rubens   Hardy biennial

A compact, bushy clover with typical three-lobed leaves and, during summer, elongated, slightly furry buds which open to produce tight groups of crimson flowers. An excellent cut flower and extremely bee-friendly. Like all legumes, the plant fixes its own nitrogen from the atmosphere.

Soil preference: Any free-draining
Aspect: Sun or part shade
Season of interest: Summer
Height and spread: 45cm x 20cm (18in x 8in)

Companion plants: A plant to blend harmoniously with the annual hare's foot grass, *Lagurus ovatus*, whose flowers are similar in shape, but contrast in colour. Also good in a mixed border, to fill gaps between later flowering perennials.

Trifolium incarnatum

Italian Clover, Crimson Clover   Annual or biennial plant

A vigorous annual or biennial whose young foliage is vivid emerald green. The three-lobed leaves form a neat mound during autumn followed, in late spring, by a succession of waving stems topped with oblong clover flowers in bright claret red. Not suitable for autumn sowing where winters are hard.

Soil preference: Any free-draining
Aspect: Sun
Season of interest: Summer
Height and spread: 60cm x 30cm (2ft x 1ft)

Companion plants: Valuable as a green manure, to be dug in before seeds are set, but also highly decorative among annuals or dotted among sun-loving Mediterranean shrubs such as Cistus, Artemisia and Helichrysum.

Dianthus chinensis   Hardy biennial

Fast-maturing species which has given rise to many garden series. The simple, narrow green leaves are all but hidden by the crop of brightly coloured flowers with pinked or serrated petals. Fine forms include the maroon and white 'Black and White Minstrels', brilliant red or white 'Magic Charms' and the pink or red 'Victoriana' series.

Soil preference: Any free-draining
Aspect: Sun
Season of interest: Summer
Height and spread: 30cm (1ft), variable by 20cm (8in)

Companion plants: Superb container plants, to blend with other summer flowers such as *Lobelia erinus* or with the foliage of Plectranthus and *Glechoma hederacea* 'Variegata.'

Angelica gigas   Giant Angelica   Hardy biennial or short-lived perennial

A big, clump-forming plant which may take two or three years to flower. The three-part leaves are large and green but carried on purplish stems. The flower buds form in dark, bulging sheaths and open to form attractive, purplish umbels. An East Asian plant of great character which, if happy, will self-seed.

Soil preference: Fertile, not too dry
Aspect: Sun or part shade
Season of interest: Spring, summer, autumn
Height and spread: 2m x 1m (6ft x 3ft)

Companion plants: A big monster to grow with lilies, perhaps, in semi-shade among shrubs, or to bring later interest in a woodland garden, perhaps among Fothergilla, magnolias, Enkianthus or to grow under wide-spaced trees in a large scale planting.

Brassica oleracea   Kale 'Redbor'   Hardy biennial

Purple curly kale. A decorative and edible member of the cabbage family with thick, erect stems and deeply creased and ruched leaves. The stem colour is bright rose purple, darkening to deep red-purple in the puckered leaves. In its second spring, pale yellow flowers are produced. Excellent for flavour, as well as ornament.

Soil preference: Any fertile, free-draining
Aspect: Sun
Season of interest: Summer, winter
Height and spread: 75cm x 45cm (2ft 6in x 1ft 6in)

Companion plants: Superb with the strong colours of late summer perennials such as chrysanthemums, rudbeckias, Mexican salvia spieces and with Swiss or Rhubarb chard.

Beta vulgaris   Chard   Hardy biennial

Usually grown as a vegetable, but a highly decorative plant. Huge, puckered leaves with thick midribs which may be coloured. When the plants bolt, coarse seedheads form and the ornamental and culinary value diminishes. Pretty varieties include 'Bright Lights' (red, white and yellow stems), 'Lucullus' (white stems) and 'Charlotte' (bright red stems with dark leaves).

Soil preference: Any
Aspect: Sun
Season of interest: Spring, summer
Height and spread: To 75cm x 30cm (2ft 6in x 1ft)

Companion plants: Lovely for an ornamental kitchen garden, or simply to mix in with a summer flower border to add substance and colour.

Planting Biennials for Spectacular Schemes

Biennials can be useful among more permanent flowering plants such as shrubs or perennials. Their temporary nature can be advantageous, enabling them to provide a spectacular show in their season, and then disappearing to leave an uncluttered space for the permanent plants to take over. Alternatively, they can be timed to complement their companion shrubs or perennials.

Spring-flowering biennials such as wall flowers or forget-me-nots are useful, not only for early colour, but also to relieve the monotony of deciduous shrubs or emerging perennials whose period of beauty is yet to come. They can be deployed as fillers, giving background colour to more brilliant performers such as tulips, or can be used to provide drifts of colour in their own right.

Pastel-coloured Brompton stocks (*Matthiola incana*) not only create attractive displays in any garden, but also attract bees with their powerful scent.

Stark contrast

The rose 'Climbing Iceberg' is teamed (below, left) by a white seedling foxglove, *Digitalis purpurea*. The colours harmonize, but the shapes and character of the plants are in stark contrast with each other. When the flowers of the foxglove are over, the whole plant can be pulled out or can be allowed to set seed for next year's repeat show.

Informal air

A very loose, informal planting of climbing roses along an old limestone wall is enhanced by a drift of sweet Williams – *Dianthus barbatus* (below, right). The contrasting rose colours – 'Scharlachglut' ('Scarlet Fire') and 'Gloire de Dijon' – make a cheerful splash above the biennials, which help to draw the eye downwards and along the border. This is an early summer display but later, when the Dianthus are over, the scarlet rose will carry a conspicuous crop of orange hips, accompanied in the border by lilac-coloured colchicums.

Dual-purpose biennials

Some biennials are valuable as dual-purpose plants, creating attractive displays in beds or borders, or as cut flowers. In the main picture, opposite, these Brompton stocks have rich pastel colours and an intense fragrance, making them ideal for both purposes.

Although the same colour, the shape of *Digitalis purpurea* (foxglove) contrasts with that of the rose, 'Climbing Iceberg'.

Sweet Williams, loosely planted in drifts, go well with roses up against a garden wall.

bedding

Bedding: spring flowering, full and dappled shade

Bedding: summer flowering, full sun

Bedding: summer flowering, dappled shade

Bedding for attracting wildlife

Bellis perennis   Double Daisy, Lawn Daisy   Perennial

Rounded or spoon-shaped leaves create mats of foliage above which blooms are held on thin stems. The wild species has a golden flower centre, surrounded by white sterile florets whose edges are flushed pink. Garden varieties include the double 'Pomponette' series, pale pink 'Dresden China' and the reddish 'Rob Roy'.

Soil preference: Any
Aspect: Sun or partial shade
Season of interest: Spring
Height and spread: Up to 15cm x 20cm (6in x 8in)

Companion plants: Beautiful when bedded with forget-me-nots and with such bulbs as hyacinths or tulips.

Hyacinthus orientalis   Hyacinth   Bulb

Fleshy, dark green leaves emerge in early spring. Later, chunky flower buds appear and extend to form thick flower spikes in shades of pink, blue, purple, white, pale yellow and orange. Intensely fragrant. 'L'innocence' is a fine bedding white, 'Delft Blue' is mid-blue, 'Queen of the Blues' darker and 'Anna Marie' pale pink.

Soil preference: Any free-draining
Aspect: Sun or shade
Season of interest: Spring
Height and spread: Up to 25cm x 15cm (10in x 6in)

Companion plants: Effective when bedded with winter pansies or polyanthus, but also superb when massed on their own. Fewer colours works better than a mix.

Viola   Winter Pansies   Biennials or short-lived perennials

Low, mound-forming plants with diamond-shaped, slightly lobed leaves. The flowers, large in proportion to the plants, are flattened, disc-shaped, sweetly fragrant and almost perpetually in flower. Colours run through blue, orange, maroon, purple, yellow, pink and white. 'Universal' and 'Ultima' series are among the most popular winter flowering varieties. Deadhead to extend flowering.

Soil preference: Any well-drained, not too dry
Aspect: Part shade
Season of interest: Mainly winter but also year round
Height and spread: Approx 15cm x 20cm (6in x 8in)

Companion plants: Superb for long-lasting bedding, as well as for gap filling or providing winter interest in containers. Pretty with small bulbs such as Muscari, or with such spring plants as wallflowers or Aubrieta.

Primula vulgaris   Hybrid Primroses   Perennial

Rosette-forming with broad, deeply veined, oval leaves and from winter through spring, a succession of five-petalled flowers. The wild species has pale yellow or flush mauve blooms but garden hybrids vary in flower size and colour. Red, blue, yellow, orange, pink and white hues are common. Sweetly fragrant. Should be divided and replanted regularly.

Soil preference: Medium to heavy, moisture retentive
Aspect: Shade or part shade
Season of interest: Spring
Height and spread: To 15cm x 20cm (6in x 8in)

Companion plants: Attractive bedded on their own, or with such spring bulbs as Muscari, Tulipa or smaller Narcissus such as N. 'Hawera' for companions. Also excellent as container plants.

Primula elatior hybrids

Polyanthus   Short-lived perennials

Leaves as primroses but the primula flowers appear in loose umbels of several blooms atop stems which may extend to 30cm. Developed from the wild oxlip, whose flowers are butter yellow, but cultivars come in all shades making them useful for colour scheming. Deadhead and remove yellowing leaves regularly. Divide annually and watch for vine weevil.

Soil preference: Moisture retentive
Aspect: Shade or partial shade, excellent under deciduous trees
Season of interest: Spring
Height and spread: Up to 30cm x 20cm (1ft x 8in)

Companion plants: Excellent for partially shaded bedding schemes but perfectly happy in full sun when they are bedded out in autumn and lifted in late spring after flowering.

Doronicum 'Leopard's Bane'

Perennial

Bright green, heart-shaped, slightly toothed leaves which form a basal clump as well as furnishing the flower stems. These lengthen in mid-spring, and bear big, golden daisy flowers which last into early summer. The foliage tends to burn away in hot weather.

Soil preference: Moist but free-draining
Aspect: Part-shade or shade. Excellent under deciduous trees
Season of interest: Spring
Height and spread: 30cm x 60cm (1ft x 2ft)

Companion plants: Beautiful planted with contrasting tulips such as the scarlet 'Apeldoorn' or deep purple 'Negrita'. Also interesting when teamed with aquilegias, which will extend the flowering season further into summer.

Petunia

Petunias   Perennial (frost tender)

The most widely grown bedding plant, worldwide. A mat-forming herbaceous plant with oval leaves and a constant succession of vivid, saucer-shaped, fragrant flowers. Flowers can be ruined by damp weather, but blooming is copious. Wide colour range available, some with stripes, edging or darker veins. Series include 'Mirage', 'Wave', 'Celebrity' and trailing 'Surfinia'.

Soil preference: Any, not wet
Aspect: Full sun
Season of interest: Summer
Height and spread: Various, to 30cm x 60cm (1ft x 2ft)

Companion plants: Traditionally bedded on their own or with contrasting colours of bedding salvias or tagetes, petunias are also useful for gap filling in mixed planting schemes and for containers.

Tagetes patula, T. tenuifolia

French/African/Afro-French Marigold, Tagetes   Annual

Annuals with divided, sometimes filigree foliage and a succession of flowers in hot hues from yellow, through gold to orange, red or pale cream. African Marigolds such as 'Antigua Gold' grow tallest; French Marigolds such as 'Little Hero' (orange) or 'Safari' series are mid-height; and Tagetes such as 'Starfire' form sprays of yellow or orange flowers.

Soil preference: Free-draining, fertile
Aspect: Sun
Season of interest: Summer
Height and spread: Variable up to 60cm x 45cm (up to 2ft x 1ft 6in)

Companion plants: These hot colours are difficult to team in more naturalistic bedding schemes but their power and distinctive aroma make them great value for bulking up summer colour. Tagetes are superb with blue daisies such as *Felicia amelloides*.

Pelargonium hybrids   Geraniums   Tender perennials

A huge group of highly popular perennials, originating almost exclusively from Africa but hybridized and grown all over the world. Sizes vary from miniature hybrids and dwarf species to the largest kinds such as *P. papilionaceum* which can exceed 2m (6ft) in height and width. The single or double blooms occur in sprays or small clusters. Colours include most shades excluding blue and yellow. Zonal types have darker or lighter banding on leaves.

Soil preference: Any free-draining
Aspect: Full sun
Season of interest: Summer
Height and spread: Variable

Companion plants: Traditionally bedded on their own with contrasting 'dot plants'. Red zonals look good with pale blue Plumbago or purple Cordyline; pink or violet can be set off with standard fuchsias or Abutilon.

Verbena hybrid cultivars Tender perennials

Plants have lobed leaves and flattened flower umbels which attract butterflies. Those with a spreading habit include the vigorous 'Homestead Purple' which may overwinter, the old cultivar 'Sissinghurst' with abundant pink blooms and the popular 'Tapien' and 'Temari' series which offer a wide colour range. 'Quartz' is an excellent upright bedder from seed.

Soil preference: Well-drained
Aspect: Sun
Season of interest: Summer
Height and spread: Up to 30cm (1ft), spreading

Companion plants: Spreading or trailing types work well as temporary summer groundcover spilling onto the patio or in containers. Try dotting with taller plants such as *Lobelia* 'Compliment Series'. Upright bedding verbenas contrast nicely with petunias.

Dahlia hybrid bedding varieties Perennial

Variable range of tender perennials developed from Central American species. These hybrids vary in height from dwarf, compact and bushy forms with smaller blooms suitable for containers and low bedding to tall upright types, often with spectacular flowers, that add colour and drama to the late summer border. Bedding dahlias are usually raised from seed and discarded at the end of the season. Lift dahlia tubers after first frosts.

Soil preference: Fertile, well-drained but not too dry
Aspect: Sun
Season of interest: Summer, autumn
Height and spread: From 30cm to 1.75m (1ft to 5ft)

Companion plants: Taller, large-flowered dahlias are excellent in a mixed border with late flowering perennials such as asters and crocosmias. Compact, tuberous or seed raised dahlias combine well with red bedding salvias and Solenostemon (Coleus).

Antirrhinum majus Snapdragons Short-lived perennial

Herbaceous plants with simple leaves and spikes bearing lipped flowers which, when squeezed, open like jaws. Colours range from white and pale yellow through pinks and crimson to scarlet red or orange. Prone to rust disease. More resistant seed strains are available but to reduce rust problems remove surviving plants at the end of the season. Series include the dwarf 'Chimes' and taller 'Liberty'.

Soil preference: Fertile, well-drained
Aspect: Sun or part shade
Season of interest: Summer, autumn
Height and spread: To 45cm–1m (1ft 6in–3ft 3in) for cutting varieties

Companion plants: Excellent as link plants between spring and summer bedding, since they can be planted out in very early spring before the frost risk has passed. Try them after tulips or polyanthus.

Salvia splendens

Scarlet Sage, Bedding Salvia   Tender perennial

Shrubby perennial with angular stems and toothed, nettle-like leaves. The flowers are sheathed in colourful bracts and, in the wild species, are vivid red. Garden forms, which come in red, pink or purplish hues, include 'Scarlet King', 'Empire Purple' and 'Vista Salmon'. The 'Sizzler' series are smaller, more compact plants in a similar colour range.

Soil preference: Rich, not too dry, but well-drained
Aspect: Part-shade or sun
Season of interest: Summer, early autumn
Height and spread: Up to 1.2m (4ft), but usually grown shorter

Companion plants: A good choice for part-shaded bedding schemes or for high rainfall areas. The strong colours work well with sombre heliotropes or with the rich foliage patterns of Plectranthus or with Solenostemon (Coleus).

Impatiens walleriana hybrids

Busy Lizzie, Balsam   Tender perennial

Shrubby perennials with thick but brittle stems and smooth, glossy, slightly toothed leaves. The flowers are flattened, asymmetrical and come in a broad range of hues from red, through mauve, pink or salmon to white. F1 hybrid seed strains offer single colours. Some types are picotee edged, striped or have 'eyed' flowers, for example 'Dazzler Merlot'.

Soil preference: Fertile, not too dry
Aspect: Part shade or sun but not too hot
Season of interest: Summer
Height and spread: 20–30cm x 20–50cm (8–12in x 8in–1ft 10in)

Companion plants: Best when encouraged to form dense mats of colour by planting in groups, but softened by foliage plants such as *Senecio* 'Silver Dust' or with taller dot plants such as *Eucalyptus gunnii* or Plumbago.

Limnanthes douglasii   Poached Egg Plant   Hardy annual

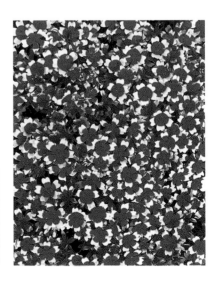

Vivid emerald green, feathery leaves create a dense ground cover persisting through winter, where seed has germinated in autumn. In late spring, the bright foliage is all but blotted out by even brighter, disc-shaped or shallow cupped flowers, each about 3cm (1in) across, with brilliant yellow centres and white petal margins. An excellent plant for attracting wildlife, especially beneficial hoverflies. Self-sows copiously.

Soil preference: Any, not too dry
Aspect: Sun or part shade
Season of interest: Spring, summer
Height and spread: 15cm x 20cm (6in x 8in)

Companion plants: Perfect for creating green or coloured ground cover between shrubs, particularly along border edges. Best when allowed to spread naturally, by self-sowing.

Mimulus   Monkey Flower, Musk

Short-lived perennials and half hardy annuals

Mat forming perennials with slightly toothed leaves and a summer-long run of trumpet-shaped flowers in bright colours, often with stippling at the throat. Cultivars include 'Highland Park' (tomato red), 'Puck' (yellow) and 'Wisley Red' (scarlet). Seed series offer speckled and dramatically blotched blooms in shades of pink and cream though orange, red, maroon and yellow. 'Monkey Magic' is white with red markings.

Soil preference: Moist, but well-drained and fertile
Aspect: Sun or shade
Season of interest: Summer
Height and spread: From dwarf to 30cm x 45cm (1ft x 1ft 6in)

Companion plants: Ideal plants for a moist, part-shaded bedding scheme where they can accompany some of the taller primulas, such as *Primula viallii*. Seed series are useful for shaded containers with dark blue lobelia.

Lobelia erinus

Bedding Lobelia   Tender perennial, invariably grown as annuals

Compact or trailing herbs with thin stems, sometimes bronze-hued foliage and a constant succession of small flowers, with broad lower petals and a contrasting white eye. Colours include dark, mid- or pale blue, mauve, purple and white. Popular compact varieties include non-trailing 'Palace Series' and 'Mrs Clibran'. Trailing kinds include the 'Cascade Series' and light blue 'Periwinkle Blue'.

Soil preference: Moisture-retentive
Aspect: Sun or part shade
Season of interest: Summer
Height and spread: Variable to 20cm (8in), but trailing kinds have longer stems

Companion plants: The classic plant for edging borders, or for trailing from baskets. The blue is valuable for cooling colour schemes or for making strong contrasts with, for example, golden-flowered *Bidens ferulifolia*; looks attractive almost anywhere.

Tanacetum parthenium   Feverfew   Perennial

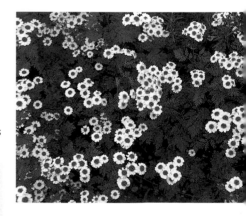

Bright green or gold, lobed leaves which are acridly aromatic when bruised. The yellow-centred, white flowers begin to emerge in late spring and are produced all summer. Cultivars include 'Snowball' (button blooms) and 'Santana'. Will flower naturally but also responds well to frequent trimming. A prolific self-seeder, sometimes becoming a nuisance, but also a handy gap filler. The leaves are reputed to cure headaches.

Soil preference: Any
Aspect: Sun, partial shade or shade
Season of interest: Spring, summer, autumn
Height and spread: Variable to 45cm (1ft 6in), usually smaller

Companion plants: Useful as part of a carpet bedding scheme, or when the gold-leaf form 'Aureum' is planted among such plants as Impatiens or petunias, to tone down the intensity of the flowers.

Viola   Violas   Perennials

Mat-forming perennials with compact foliage and a constant succession of flowers, many of which are marked with face-like features. Garden violas are almost constantly in bloom with colours similar in range to pansies with many being bi-coloured, plain or picotee. Varieties include 'Ardross Gem', 'Irish Molly' and 'Martin'. Seed series include 'Baby Face', 'Gemini Twins' and 'Sorbet'.

Soil preference: Any, well-drained, not too dry
Aspect: Sun or part shade
Season of interest: Year round
Height and spread: Up to 20cm x 30cm (8in x 1ft)

Companion plants: Universally loved and useful almost anywhere. New seed series of small flowered violas are superseding bigger flowered pansies because they can bloom throughout the year. Violas and pansies look good with almost any other garden plant.

Geranium pratense

Meadow Cranesbill   Perennial

Raise from seed sown in autumn to provide flowers the following summer. Decorative foliage is divided with first flower stems developing in early summer producing bright blue flowers. Cut hard back to provide a second flush in late summer. There is a pure white form, and 'Mrs Kendall Clark' has pale slate-blue flowers.

Soil preference: Any
Aspect: Sun
Season of interest: Summer and autumn
Height and spread: 1m x 60cm (3ft 3in x 2ft)

Companion plants: Wild bedding is an unusual but exciting concept. Try this cranesbill with ox eye daisies (*Leucanthemum vulgare*) and with annual grasses such as *Briza maxima* or *Lagurus ovata* for a soft, meadow effect.

Aquilegia   Granny's Bonnets, Columbine   Perennials

Sustainable bedding. Seed series of big, showy columbines are popular as bedding plants. Sown in spring, they will produce plenty of flower the following year and can be planted in situ in autumn. The 'Songbird series' have big, long-spurred blooms in red, blue, yellow and creamy white, which also make good container plants and can even be used for early conservatory displays.

Soil preference: Any, preferably fertile
Aspect: Sun, part-shade
Season of interest: Spring, early summer
Height and spread: Variable from dwarf to 1m (3ft 3in)

Companion plants: Best on their own in a bedding scheme, but beautiful if dotted among perennials or shrubs in a mixed border, or grown in containers.

Verbena bonariensis

Purple Top, Tall Verbena   Short-lived, marginally hardy perennial

Tall stems, sparsely furnished with narrow, dark green leaves are topped, through summer, by dense bunches of tiny bright purple blooms. The stems are so thin and the leaves so few that the flowers seem suspended by invisible supports. Attractive to butterflies and a wide range of insects. A prolific self-seeder.

Soil preference: Any, even very dry
Aspect: Full sun
Season of interest: Summer, autumn.
Height and spread: 2m x 30cm (6ft 6in x 1ft)

Companion plants: Most effective when used to create an extra, ephemeral layer of bedding above more moderately sized plants such as bedding dahlias, pelargoniums or petunias.

Gaillardia hybrids

Blanket Flower; Fire Wheel   Hardy perennials

Brilliantly coloured, daisy flowers with hot coloured outer rays and raised, furry central 'cones' are produced throughout summer. Typical flower colours are red and yellow, as in the old variety 'Kobold'; 'Burgunder' is red and 'Dazzler', a shorter-stemmed variety. Divide or propagate from root cuttings frequently, since these perennials are short-lived. Loved by butterflies and bees.

Soil preference: Any free-draining
Aspect: Sun
Season of interest: Summer, autumn
Height and spread: Variable from dwarf to 60cm x 75cm (2ft x 2ft 6in)

Companion plants: For a hot effect, gaillardias mix well with annual varieties of Rudbeckia, such as 'Marmalade' or 'Rustic Dwarfs', whose flowers will continue long into autumn. Besides bedding, they also work well in mixed or herbaceous borders.

Nicotiana x sanderae   Tobacco Plant   Half hardy annual

Bold perennial with large, oval, sticky leaves and branched stems bearing narrow-necked, trumpet-shaped flowers. Blooms on scented varieties wilt by day, but perk up at dusk and produce a rich fragrance. Best scented varieties are 'Fragrant Cloud' or 'Evening Fragrance Mixed'. Decorative, non-scented kinds include 'Domino' and 'Nikki' series in pastel pink hues, and red, pink, cream or white. Particularly attractive to bees and moths.

Soil preference: Any
Aspect: Sun or part shade
Season of interest: Summer
Height and spread: Variable to 1m x 75cm (3ft 3in x 2ft 6in)

Companion plants: Coloured varieties call for strong foliage contrasts from silvery plants such as *Centaurea cineraria* or a filigree-leaved Artemisia. Scented kinds are good with the huge *Nicotiana sylvestris*.

Torenia

Wishbone Flower   Tender perennial

Bushy or slowly spreading perennials with toothed leaves and a long succession of lipped, trumpet flowers with dark petal edges and contrastingly pale throats. Good varieties for containers include 'Amethyst', 'Blue Panda' (royal blue and pale violet blue) and 'Duchess Series', which comes in two-tone blue, white and pink or white and blue.

Soil preference: Any, not too dry
Aspect: Sun or part shade
Season of interest: Summer
Height and spread: 25cm x 30cm (10in x 12in)

Companion plants: Best co-ordinated with attractive foliage plants, particularly with silvery or grey leaves. Trailing plants such as Sutera, *Dichondra argentea* 'Silver Falls' and the very silvery *Lotus berthelotii* would make fine companions.

Calibrachoa 'Million Bells'

Tender perennial

Close relative of the petunia, producing masses of long, trailing stems, richly furnished with flattened, flared, trumpet flowers up to about 3cm (1in) across. One of the best trailing plants for hanging baskets or large containers. 'Million Bells' series has flowers in pink, mauve, dusky yellow, white and terracotta.

Soil preference: Any well-drained
Aspect: Sun
Season of interest: Summer
Height and spread: 15cm (6in) high, trailing 1m (3ft 3in) stems

Companion plants: Teams will with such trailing foliage plants as *Lotus berthelotii* or *Helichrysum petiolare* 'Variegatum' but also excellent when grown alone.

Felicia amelloides

Blue Daisy, African Blue Daisy   Tender perennial

Bushy or slowly trailing perennial with rounded, deep green, slightly pubescent leaves and masses of yellow-centred, bright blue daily flowers held on thin, erect stems. The form 'Santa Anita' is the toughest, sometimes surviving a touch of frost, and flowers throughout summer.

Soil preference: Any free-draining
Aspect: Sun
Season of interest: Summer, early autumn
Height and spread: 40cm x 60cm (1ft 4in x 2ft)

Companion plants: Magnificent if contrasted with bright yellow or orange flowers. Tagetes, especially clear yellow varieties, blend sweetly as does *Bidens ferulifolia*.

Nemesia denticulata and allies   Tender perennial

Mound-forming perennial with thin, easily snapped stems, which are quick to regenerate, and generous, long-lasting sprays of sometimes fragrant flowers shaped like small, open snapdragons. Colours range from white to pastel lilac, purple and pink tones.

Soil preference: Any, not too dry
Aspect: Sun or part shade
Season of interest: Summer
Height and spread: 30cm x 40cm (1ft x 1ft 4in)

Companion plants: Best grown on its own, especially in a large pot or hanging basket.

Bidens ferulifolia

Bidens, Beggarticks   Tender perennial

Lax perennial, whose much branched stems trail elegantly among other vegetation. The deeply divided foliage makes a pretty foil for the big, golden, honey-scented blooms which are produced constantly through summer. A classic and drought-tolerant basket plant, but also fine in a border, where it can sprawl among other perennials.

Soil preference: Any
Aspect: Sun
Season of interest: Summer
Height and spread: Up to 45cm (1ft 6in) trailing

Companion plants: Lovely with silver foliage of trailing Helichrysum or trailing Plectranthus. Superb when making a startling contrast with the vigorous *Verbena* 'Homestead Purple'.

Sutera (syn. Bacopa)   Tender annuals or perennials

South African plants with bushy but trailing or sprawling habit and slightly toothed triangular or rounded leaves. The flowers are tiny – forget-me-not sized – but are produced in profusion through much of summer. Pastel shaded cultivars include 'Blue Showers', 'Lilac Showers' and 'Pink Domino'. White forms include 'Snowstorm', 'Snowflake' and *Sutera cordata* 'Blizzard'.

Soil preference: Any
Aspect: Sun
Season of interest: Summer
Height and spread: 10cm x 45cm (4in x 1ft 6in)

Companion plants: Suteras have become standard basket and window box plants and will mix with practically anything. They are ideal for softening edges and disguising pot sides, making excellent companions for erect varieties of pelargonium and fuchsias.

Lathyrus odoratus Dwarf varieties

Sweet Pea   Hardy annual

Most have the attributes of climbing sweet peas – fragrance, colourful blossoms, good cutting value – but dwarf plants need minimal support. Varieties include 'Snoopea', which lacks tendrils and has a prostrate but bushy habit, 'Bijou Mixed' and the dwarf 'Cupid Mixed'. Colours run through pink, purples and white. Excellent for containers.

Soil preference: Any fertile, free-draining but moisture-retentive
Aspect: Sun
Season of interest: Summer
Height and spread: Variable to 30cm (1ft)

Companion plants: Effective in small bedding schemes alongside leafy plants such as *Senecio cineraria* or as part of a mixed container, with Nemesia or Torenia.

Heliotropium arborescens

Heliotrope, Cherry Pie   Tender shrub, grown as bedding

A rounded shrub, in the forget-me-not family with handsome oval and deeply veined leaves that are often purple-tinged. Large heads of tiny, rich purple flowers which smell sweetly of vanilla. When used in bedding, heliotropes can be trained as standards or pruned and pinched back to sustain bushiness. Fine varieties include 'Princess Marina', whose flowers are deep purple-blue, 'Chatsworth', slightly paler purple and also very fragrant, and 'White Lady'.

Soil preference: Any
Aspect: Sun
Season of interest: Summer
Height and spread: To 90cm x 60cm (3ft x 2ft)

Companion plants: The classic 'dot' plant of Victorian bedding, useful for giving height to beds of impatiens, petunias or to contrast strongly with French marigolds.

Nicotiana mutabilis 'Marshmallow'

Tobacco Plant   Tender perennial

This plant has large, floppy leaves which are sticky to the touch above which grows a mass of branched, slender stems bearing trumpet-shaped flowers which open white and gradually flush to a pale and then a deep cherry pink. Each flower has a dark eye and in the evening, exudes a delicious fragrance.

Soil preference: Any, fertile and free-draining
Aspect: Sun
Season of interest: Summer
Height and spread: 1.2m x 75cm (4ft x 2ft 6in)

Companion plants: Big, bold bedding plants, ideal to soften the harshness of large dahlias or to intersperse among *Verbena bonariensis* for a light, airy effect.

Viola x wittrockiana

Small-flowered Violas   Hardy perennial or biennial

Neat, mat-forming perennials or biennials with slightly lobed, heart-shaped leaves and stems which are square in section. A constant run of small, pansy flowers is produced in a vast range of colours and patterns, ranging through blues, mauves, yellow, orange, purples and to almost black or tan red. Many have bi-coloured blooms or monkey faces; all have a sweet-sharp, honey fragrance.

Soil preference: Any reasonably fertile, not too dry
Aspect: Sun or part shade
Season of interest: Year round
Height and spread: Variable to 20cm x 30cm (8in x 1ft)

Companion plants: Adaptable to any situation – in containers, beds, rock gardens or even lining vegetables in a kitchen garden. Especially effective with spring bulbs or over-wintered plants such as polyanthus, primroses or wall flowers.

Verbena 'Blue Lagoon'

Verbena   Tender perennial

Oval, toothed leaves and semi-trailing stems which produce a summer-long succession of umbels bearing true blue flowers. Said to be resistant to mildew – a bugbear disease for bedding verbena – and to have sweet fragrance. A seed-raised series, but can be propagated from cuttings or divisions.

Soil preference: Fertile and free-draining
Aspect: Sun
Season of interest: Summer, autumn
Height and spread: 25cm x 30cm (10in x 12in)

Companion plants: An excellent container plant to trail with such gold-leaf companions as *Lamium* 'Golden Anniversary' or with *Lysimachia nummularia* 'Aurea'.

Zaluzianskya capensis

Night Phlox   Tender annual

A member of the foxglove family which looks more like a pink or a campion! Sticky foliage on bushy plants is joined, in summer, by starry flowers with twin-lobed petals, which are crimson on the reverse, but white on their upper surfaces. The flowers open more fully at night when they become sweetly fragrant.

Soil preference: Any free-draining
Aspect: Sun
Season of interest: Summer
Height and spread: To 60cm x 45cm (2ft x 1ft 6in)

Companion plants: Try fusion planting, growing these South African beauties along with the equally sweetly scented and nocturnal Marvel of Peru or *Mirabilis jalapa*, and with tobaccos.

Begonia semperflorens Tender perennial

Universally popular bedding plant with thick, fibrous roots, succulent stems and glossy, fleshy leaves which are rounded and may be bright green, or bronze or purple tinted. A constant run of flowers in colours ranging from scarlet, through reds and pinks to white. Good seed series are legion, for example, 'Doublonia' series and 'Stara Mixed'.

Soil preference: Any
Aspect: Sun or part shade
Season of interest: Summer
Height and spread: To 30cm x 30cm (1ft x 1ft)

Companion plants: Best for bedding schemes, on account of their ability to make long-lasting carpets of colour. Also effective as texturing plants with grasses, perhaps, or for use in mixed containers with *Helichrysum petiolare*, Brachyscome or *Senecio* 'Silver Dust'.

Brassica oleracea

Ornamental Cabbage, Ornamental Kale Hardy biennial

Valuable for their winter displays, ornamental cabbages and kales provide strong colours from their colourful foliage. The cabbages form loose but symmetrical rosettes with purple, rose-mauve, pink or creamy suffusions mixed with green. The kales have a more open, lax habit. The flowers, which follow in late spring, are yellow and usually clash with the coloured leaves.

Soil preference: Any
Aspect: Sun
Season of interest: Autumn, winter, spring
Height and spread: To 45cm x 30cm (1ft 6in x 1ft)

Companion plants: Useful for a strong colour display for winter but difficult to team with smaller flowers. Certain tulips, particularly in white, purple or pink shades, go surprisingly well.

Salpiglossis sinuata Tender annual

A South American member of the potato family with slender habit, sparsely branched stems and slightly sticky foliage. During much of the summer, these plants produce a long succession of trumpet-shaped flowers. These are deeply veined and come in attractive, dusky colours ranging through yellows, brick red and orange to violet and purple-blue.

Soil preference: Any free-draining
Aspect: Sun
Season of interest: Summer
Height and spread: 60cm x 30cm (2ft x 1ft)

Companion plants: Striking, characterful plants which need backing up with other, foliage-rich companions such as heliotropes, *Centaurea cineraria* or scented leaf pelargoniums.

Canna indica, C. iridiflora   Tender perennials

Large, coarse perennials with broad, oar-shaped, glossy surfaced leaves which unfurl like rolled banners; in some varieties these are dark-tinted or striated. The flowers, which resemble untidy irises, are produced in bunched panicles and come in shades of pink red, yellow, orange or white. The species *C. iridiflora* (pictured) grows taller and has gracefully hanging pink flowers.

Soil preference: Moist, fertile
Aspect: Sun
Season of interest: Summer
Height and spread: To 2.5m x 1m (8ft x 3ft)

Companion plants: Traditionally used as dot plants, in bedding schemes and effective when presiding over drifts of French marigolds, pelargoniums, Impatiens or nicotianas. Also fine in containers with Mexican salvias and *Solanum rantonetii*.

Cosmos bipinnatus, C. sulphureus

Hardy or near hardy annuals

Two variable species, with divided, often lacy foliage and an open, branching habit. The flowers are composite with yellow central florets and broad, showy outer ray florets which may be flat or, in some varieties such as 'Seashells', tubular. Flowers of *C. bipinnatus* range from deep rose or crimson through pinks to white. *C. sulphureus* comes in hotter colours ranging from yellow to coppery orange or near red.

Soil preference: Fertile but free-draining
Aspect: Sun
Season of interest: Summer
Height and spread: Variable to 2m x 45cm (6ft x 1ft 6in)

Companion plants: Fast-growing plants whose soft, lacy foliage provides a gentle tracery, striking when accompanied by bedding such as annual Lavetera, petunias or dense masses of fuchsias. Also pretty dotted in a flower border, perhaps with cleomes.

Dahlia   Half hardy perennials

A variable genus with huge plants, bearing vast blooms the size of a hat down to more modest, dwarf varieties. Many-branched stems rise from fleshy tubers in late spring and are furnished with divided, glossy, sometimes dark foliage. The late summer flowers are variable, usually brightly coloured with every hue except pure blue. Seed series such as 'Duo' or the dark-leaved 'Bishop's Children' are good for bedding.

Soil preference: Any fertile, free-draining but not too dry
Aspect: Sun
Season of interest: Summer, autumn
Height and spread: Variable to 2m x 75cm (6ft x 2ft 6in)

Companion plants: Medium and small flowered varieties, especially those with dark foliage, are popular, blending with lilies among shrubs or in a late summer border with heleniums, late daisies or chrysanthemums.

Bedding Schemes Used Formally and Informally

Bedding schemes can be tailored to suit a diverse range of tastes and preferences. Plants, in formal bedding, are used en masse to create a colourful surface and their use can appear to be more akin to painting than to planting! Bold brush-strokes of colour, sometimes creating formal patterns or shapes, often in the commemoration of an event, are popular in public planting schemes and are intended to provide sudden drama and spectacle, rather than to sustain a gentle, changing scene.

However, bedding can also be used in an informal way, simply arranging for drifts of similar plants to make small statements, perhaps as part of a border, or for giving temporary lift to an otherwise dull spot.

Vibrant colours

The main picture opposite shows a harmonious spring bedding display using botanical tulips, *Tulipa kaufmanniana* 'Stresa', with *Hyacinthus orientalis* 'Blue Jacket'. The three strong colours, red, yellow and blue, work superbly together and bring bright spring cheer. The display will not be long-lived, however, and will leave a sizeable gap by the end of spring.

Painting with flowers

In this scheme (see the bottom picture on the opposite page), bold swirls of Tagetes (French and African marigolds) create a dazzling surface which is so intense in colour that it can almost cause physical discomfort to view, particularly in low light conditions.
However, where the sun is strong, hard colours like these can be surprisingly effective. The effect is one of drama, rather than to entice long, lingering looks!

Using dot plants to lift the scheme

Common bedding plants such as these Ageratum (above) can be augmented with less usual choices to add interest to an otherwise rather pedestrian planting scheme. The Verbascums are used here for the silver foliage but later they will produce handsome flower spikes and make strong accent plants.

bulbs

Fritillaria imperialis   Crown Imperial   Hardy bulb

Largest of the fritillaries and ancient in cultivation. Big, pungent-smelling bulbs producing thick, fleshy stems, furnished with glossy, narrow leaves along their length. At their tips, clusters of large, dark-veined, orange or yellow bell-shaped flowers form below a topknot of foliage. The petal bases have glands which drip tears of nectar.

Soil preference: Any, well-drained
Aspect: Sun or part shade
Season of interest: Spring
Height and spread: 1m x 45cm (3ft 3in x 1ft 6in)

Companion plants: Big, bold spring plants for dotting among developing summer perennials or to naturalize among such ornamental trees as cherries, crab apples or hawthorns.

Fritillaria pallidiflora

Hardy bulb

A variable species with paired, narrow, grey-green leaves and thin stems which bear groups of two, three or four cup-shaped nodding flowers in a pale beige to creamy primrose. The bulbs are slow to increase and so work better in small groups than singly.

Soil preference: Any free-draining, but not too dry
Aspect: Sun or part shade
Season of interest: Spring
Height and spread: To 45cm x 10cm (1ft 6in x 4in)

Companion plants: Superb when grown with other fritillaries and late spring flowers. Species tulips such as *Tulipa sprengeri* and *T. acuminata* go well, as does *Fritillaria verticillata*.

Hyacinthoides non-scripta

English Bluebell   Hardy bulb

Dark, glossy, narrow foliage begins to emerge in early spring. The flower stems extend in mid spring, and carry clusters of hanging, bell-shaped, fragrant, dark blue flowers. Albino and pink forms also occur but are rare. Successful growth depends on a relationship the plants have with micro-organisms in the soil, and establishment can be difficult. Plant 'in the green' (ie. in leaf).

Soil preference: Woodland soil, high in organic matter
Aspect: Shade or part shade
Season of interest: Spring
Height and spread: To 45cm x 10cm (1ft 6in x 4in)

Companion plants: Suitable for naturalizing in shady places and beautiful with wood anemones, ragged robin, primulas or red campion.

Erythronium 'Pagoda'

Dog's Tooth Violet   Hardy bulb

A garden hybrid with broad, richly decorated, glossy foliage, which creates a fine base for the sprays of elegant flowers. These are up to 5cm (2in) across, with pale yellow petals which curl to create a pagoda effect.

Soil preference: Woodland soil, rich in organic matter
Aspect: Shade or part shade
Season of interest: Spring
Height and spread: 30cm x 25cm (1ft x 10in)

Companion plants: Fine when naturalised in a shady border or woodland garden, especially with bluebells, Uvularia and epimediums.

Ornithogalum nutans

Star of Bethlehem   Hardy bulb

Narrow, grassy, rather lax foliage and erect, glossy stems which end with generous spikes of hanging flowers whose almost translucent white petals are lined with a pale green stripes. Thrives in a hot, dry spot on poor soil, but the flowers tend to be short-lived.

Soil preference: Free-draining
Aspect: Sun
Season of interest: Spring
Height and spread: 45cm x 20cm (1ft 6in x 10in)

Companion plants: Useful as a 'filler' plant in dry Mediterranean style plantings among other bulbs such as *Hermodactyla tuberosa*, drought tolerant anemones and such species tulips as *Tulipa batalinii*.

Iris (Dutch hybrids)

Dutch Iris   Bulb

Largely grown for the cut flower trade, but useful for dotting or bedding, these irises produce rigid, jointed stems, furnished with narrow, folded leaves and showy three-part flowers. The most widely grown are blue, as in the 'Blue Magic', but there are white forms such as 'Madonna'. 'Telstar' has flowers in purplish blue.

Soil preference: Fertile, free-draining, not too dry
Aspect: Sun
Season of interest: Spring
Height and spread: Up to 45cm x 20cm (1ft 6in x 8in)

Companion plants: Can be bedded with wallflowers, or to cool down displays of midseason or late daffodils. Also handy to line out with tulips for cutting.

Galanthus nivalis, G. elwesii

Snowdrops   Hardy bulbs

Favourite indicator of winter's end. Small, grassy leaves emerge in midwinter, soon joined by dazzling white blooms whose outer tepals cloak the greenish tipped inner parts. Noteworthy are *G. nivalis* in single or double form – easily the best for naturalizing – and *G. elwesii*, whose glaucous leaves are broader and whose flowers may appear earlier.

Soil preference: Any, not too dry
Aspect: Shade or part shade
Season of interest: Winter
Height and spread: Up to 20cm x 10cm (8in x 4in)

Companion plants: Beautiful and welcome everywhere, but best in drifts, with hellebores and winter aconites, perhaps under winter blooming shrubs such as *Cornus mas* or *Salix caprea*.

Eranthis hyemalis

Winter Aconite   Hardy tuber-bearing perennial

Short stems bearing small, buttercup yellow, muskily fragrant blooms appear a day or two after the winter solstice. Each flower is cradled in a pretty ruff of green foliage. The leaves die down by late spring. A much loved plant whose appearance is brief and stature tiny, but whose timing is perfect.

Soil preference: Any
Aspect: Sun or shade
Season of interest: Winter
Height and spread: 10cm x 10cm (4in x 4in)

Companion plants: Beautiful in drifts with snowdrops, under trees or between shrubs. Plant potted specimens in growth.

Cyclamen coum

Hardy tuberous perennial

Kidney-shaped leaves, green or marbled in grey and green, begin to emerge in early winter. By midwinter, flowers shaped like squat ship's propellers begin to open and are held just clear of the leaves by near-prostrate stems. Typical flower colour is rich carmine or cerise, but there are also pale pink and white forms.

Soil preference: Any, free-draining
Aspect: Sun or part shade
Season of interest: Winter
Height and spread: 10cm x 20cm (4in x 8in)

Companion plants: The foliage makes a pretty foil for snowdrops or aconites and the gem-like flowers sparkle among sombre blue winter irises. Also lovely in short grass.

Crocus imperati
Hardy, corm-bearing perennial

Narrow, grassy leaves appear in winter, soon accompanied by the frail crocus blossoms, which are biscuit beige on the outside, decorated with dark blackish purple veining. When the flowers open in sun, their insides are bright violet mauve. See also Crocuses, page 96.

Soil preference: Very free-draining
Aspect: Sun
Season of interest: Late winter, early spring
Height and spread: 10cm x 10cm (4in x 4in)

Companion plants: Precious to include in a crocus collection because of the early blooms. Also pretty with winter irises and *Cyclamen coum*.

Iris danfordiae, Iris 'Katharine Hodgkin'
Hardy bulb

Leafless stems emerge in winter, carrying buds which open to bright golden yellow iris blooms. The narrow leaves extend as the flowers fade. *Iris* 'Katharine Hodgkin' (pictured) is a hybrid with extraordinary colouring: veined dusky blue, yellow and white, with dark spots.

Soil preference: Any free-draining
Aspect: Sun
Season of interest: Late winter, early spring
Height and spread: 15cm x 10cm (6in x 4in)

Companion plants: Best in small specimen groups among other late winter flowers, or to bring interest to an Alpine collection to precede the main spring show, perhaps of saxifrages and dwarf narcissus.

Leucojum vernum
Spring snowflake   Hardy bulb

Clump-forming bulb with dark green, lustrous strap-like leaves which emerge in late winter, just after the flower stems. These carry one, two or three flowers shaped like pleated bells or lanterns; pure white but with a faint green tinge along the tips. Stems and leaves extend after flowering.

Soil preference: Fertile, not too dry
Aspect: Part shade
Season of interest: Late winter, early spring
Height and spread: 20cm x 10cm (8in x 4in), spreading

Companion plants: Beautiful among tufts of lime green *Hacquetia epipactis* or below arching Solomon's Seal (*Polygonatum multiflorum*) stems, both of which flower a little later.

Narcissus

Daffodils are among the most popular of hardy bulbs. Variable in habit, they range from miniature species and hybrids to tall cultivars with large flowers. Leaves may be strap-shaped or, in miniature species, somewhat grassy. The flowers consist of a trumpet- or cup-shaped corona surrounded by flat or reflexed petals known as perianth segments.

1. Narcissus 'Jenny'
A pale-flowered cyclamineus hybrid with white, strongly reflexed petals and pale lemon trumpet which fades to cream as the flower ages.

2. Narcissus 'Ice Follies'
A very large-flowered, commercial variety excellent for cutting but unnatural-looking for small scale wild planting. The pleated lemon cup and white petals, with strong and upright stem give this variety good standing power and, by Narcissus standards, a long life, whether cut or left to bloom outdoors.

3. Narcissus 'Tête à Tête'
Universally popular, *Narcissus* 'Tête à Tête' is early, compact, easy to grow and dependable. The buttercup yellow blooms, which may come singly or in pairs on the stem, have neat petals and small cups contrasting well with the deep green foliage.

4. Narcissus 'Topolino'
One of the earliest varieties to flower. The petals are creamy white, making a lovely contrast with the neatly shaped, flared trumpet. Reasonably quick to multiply, and reliable in good, rich soil, this is a valuable miniature daffodil.

5. Narcissus 'Jetfire'
A vigorous and dependable cyclamineus hybrid with buttercup yellow petals, slightly swept back, and a trumpet which matures to rich orange red. Bulks up more quickly than many hybrids.

6. Narcissus 'Rip van Winkle'
An oddity whose cultivation dates back several centuries. The petals are split or shredded, giving a dandelion-like impression. Short stems, vigorous and, if not beautiful, at least jolly in colour and appearance.

7. Narcissus bulbocodium
The elegant little 'hoop petticoat' narcissus grow wild on the Iberian peninsula. They prefer moist but free-draining soils and, where happy, will self-seed and naturalise readily. For Alpine style meadows, they are superb but will also flourish in gravel, or in a rock garden.

8. Narcissus obvallaris
The Tenby Daffodil, an early species with upright stems and golden flower which are remarkably weather resistant. Ultimate height is 25cm (10in), but the flowers open while the stems are still short.

9. Narcissus pseudonarcissus
The true wild daffodil, short in stature, but big in charm. The pale petals lie along the darker gold trumpet until the flower is fully mature. Best in moist grassland, and easier to establish in high rainfall.

1	2	3
4	5	6
7	8	9

Eremurus robustus

Desert Candle, Giant Foxtail Lily   Bulbous perennial

A beautiful monster with broad, fleshy roots arranged in a
star or spider shape. Coarse, strap-like leaves grow almost
1m (3ft 3in) high before the thick, rigid flower spikes rear
up. These are densely packed with fluffy pink flowers,
whose tepals show greenish brown veining.

Soil preference: Free-draining,
never wet
Aspect: Sun
Season of interest: Summer
Height and spread: Up to 3m x
90cm (9ft 9in x 3ft)

Companion plants: An individualist but
dramatic when included singly or in small
groups among such dry-loving shrubs as
Jerusalem sage (*Phlomis fruticosa*), *Teucrium
fruticans* or against the white clouds of
Crambe cordifolia.

Allium 'Purple Giant'

Drumstick Allium   Hardy bulb

Member of the onion family with green, glossy leaves
which begin to wither before the bold flower spikes
mature. These are topped with massed, deep purple
blooms arranged in a drumstick formation. A free
self-seeder, best sited where other foliage will help to
disguise the withering leaves.

Soil preference: Fertile, but free-
draining
Aspect: Sun or part shade
Season of interest: Early
summer
Height and spread: 1m x 20cm
(3ft x 8in)

Companion plants: Frequently used to
furnish the base of a laburnum tunnel,
where the purple and yellow flowers can
contrast, but also beautiful naturalized with
other drumstick alliums among tall grasses.

Dierama pulcherrimum

Angel's Fishing Rod, Wand Flower   Corm-bearing perennial

A South African native and strikingly beautiful in outline.
Narrow, evergreen, sword-shaped leaves form a dense
clump from among which graceful, arching wands develop.
These divide into branches of wiry, nodding stems whose
almost transparent, papery buds open to reveal bold
reddish-purple flowers which hang like lanterns.

Soil preference: Free-draining
Aspect: Sun
Season of interest: Summer
Height and spread: 1.5m x 30cm
(5ft x 1ft)

Companion plants: Best when sited to
create a focal point, perhaps in gravel,
where it can set off sedges and grasses.
Smaller species such as *Dierama
dracomontanum* also make interesting
companions.

Galtonia candicans

Summer Hyacinth   Marginally hardy bulb

Bold, strap-like leaves surround a big, rigid stem whose top third, in summer, is furnished with bell-shaped waxy white flowers. These are held well away from the stem and hang downwards gracefully. Gently fragrant and a relatively free self-seeder.

Soil preference: Any free-draining
Aspect: Sun
Season of interest: Summer
Height and spread: 1m x 30cm (3ft 3in x 1ft)

Companion plants: A good plant to distribute among old fashioned roses or to include with a cool colour scheme of anchusas, campanulas and Anaphalis.

Gladiolus hybrids   Tender, corm-bearing perennials

Large group of frost tender, corm-bearing plants derived mainly from South African species, with flat, ribbed, sword-shaped leaves and tall spikes bearing showy, open-throated blooms with flared tepals in mainly vivid colours through purples, pinks, reds, oranges, and yellows to lime green and white. Many are bicolours. 'Grandiflorus' kinds have the largest blooms; 'Primulinus' have narrower leaves and hooded flowers and 'Nanus' types are dwarf.

Soil preference: Free-draining
Aspect: Sun
Season of interest: Summer
Height and spread: Variable to 1m x 30cm (3ft 3in x 1ft)

Companion plants: Developed largely as competition blooms or cut flowers. Larger varieties are hard to place in mixed plantings; newer smaller kinds make attractive groups in a late summer border, among hybrid dahlias, perennial asters or taller phloxes.

Agapanthus (deciduous hybrids)

African Lily, Nile Lily   Tender or marginally hardy bulb-bearing perennials

Deep green, shiny, strap-shaped leaves form dense clumps among which, in late summer, tall stems emerge, bearing at their tips short-stalked umbels of many six-petalled flowers in shades of blue or white. Varieties, whose leaves die right down in winter. Free-flowering kinds include the deep blue 'Midnight Star', 'Jack's Blue', and 'Loch Hope' and 'Bressingham White'.

Soil preference: Any well-drained
Aspect: Sun
Season of interest: Summer
Height and spread: Up to 1.2m x 75cm (4ft x 2ft 6in)

Companion plants: Good in containers, or in mixed herbaceous plantings among such late summer flowers as phloxes and asters, or to contrast with hot-coloured daisies such as rudbeckias, heleniums or coreopsis.

Colchicum speciosum

Autumn Crocus, Naked Ladies, Naked Boys   Hardy bulb

Crocus-shaped flowers emerge directly from the ground at the end of summer, disappearing completely after blooming. In spring, glossy foliage appears and forms a bold clump, with seed heads carried at the base of the leaf. Flower colours are typically lilac or mauve, with pale petal bases, but *C. speciosum* 'Album' has soft white flowers.

Soil preference: Any free-draining
Aspect: Sun or part shade
Season of interest: Late summer, early autumn
Height and spread: Flowers to 20cm (8in), foliage 45cm (1ft 6in)

Companion plants: One to site where the coarse spring leaves will not be troublesome. Lovely naturalized in grass or in a border with softly coloured late perennials including aster and *Sedum spectabile* and dainty flowered hardy fuchsias.

Amaryllis belladonna

Belladonna Lily, Jersey Lily   Near hardy bulb

Thick stems emerge naked from the ground in early autumn rapidly extending until the plump buds at their ends have opened to reveal a cluster of large pink flowers with white centres. The strap-like leaves follow in spring and summer. Bulbs flower best when congested and when baked in summer sun.

Soil preference: Free-draining
Aspect: Sun, very hot and dry
Season of interest: Autumn
Height and spread: 60cm x 15cm (2ft x 6in)

Companion plants: The flowers come as a delightful surprise, in autumn and are beautiful among Mediterranean shrubs such as French lavenders and silver, feathery artemisias.

Crocus speciosus

True Autumn Crocus   Hardy corm-bearing perennial

Slender, wineglass-shaped flowers emerge, without foliage, in autumn, followed, in late winter, by the grassy leaves. The violet blue flowers are marked with darker pencil veining and have showy, orange stigmas. Slow to establish but superb in large numbers.

Soil preference: Any free-draining
Aspect: Sun
Season of interest: Autumn
Height and spread: 12.5cm x 10cm (5in x 4in)

Companion plants: Not a showy plant, except when grown in bold drifts, preferably in short grass, or among autumn flowering cyclamen such as *C. hederifolium* or *C. cilicium*. See also Crocuses on page 96.

Cyclamen hederifolium

Sowbread   Hardy tuberous perennial

Loaf-like tubers lie just beneath the surface of the ground. From them come masses of pink or white flowers, each with five petals swept right back to give the typical cyclamen shape. Some races are sweetly scented. From late autumn the flowers are joined by decoratively marbled leaves which persist through winter until the end of spring.

Soil preference: Any, but not wet
Aspect: Any
Season of interest: Autumn, winter, spring
Height and spread: 15cm x 30cm (6in x 1ft)

Companion plants: An essential part of any wild or woodland garden, going well both with autumn colchicums and with spring primroses and other bulbs. The leaves are lovely with *Anemone blanda* popping up among them.

Leucojum autumnale

Autumn Snowflake   Hardy bulb

Thin, dusky green foliage emerges in winter, looking like dusty grass. In early autumn, the tiny, fragrant, pink-tinged-white, nodding flowers are hard to see as individuals but are beautiful when grown in drifts. A native of Spain and North West Africa.

Soil preference: Dry
Aspect: Sun
Season of interest: Autumn
Height and spread: 15cm x 10cm (6in x 4in)

Companion plants: Not spectacular, but charming if colonies are allowed to bulk up among such rock garden plants as alpine pinks, auriculas and Lithodora.

Nerine bowdenii

Guernsey Lily, Spider Lily   Hardy bulb

A South African native which produces stems carrying umbels of brilliant pink flowers, whose petals are curled outwards and crisped or crinkled at their edges. The leaves follow in late winter and spring. Bulbs flower best when congested and when warmed by hot summer sun.

Soil preference: Any well-drained
Aspect: Sun
Season of interest: Autumn
Height and spread: 60cm x 15cm (2ft x 6in), spreading

Companion plants: An outstanding cut bloom. The candy pink contrasts sweetly with the soft violet blues of perennial asters or with the reds and rusts of spray chrysanthemums and autumn foliage.

Lilies

A group of hardy bulbs of diverse habit, lilies are superb for producing elegant, showy flowers throughout summer and and sometimes into early autumn. Many also have fragrant blooms for added appeal.

1. Lilium lancifolium
The tiger lily, whose tiger-orange petals are strongly spotted, rather than striped. The stems produce axilliary buds which develop into bulbils, tiny bulbs from which the plant is easily propagated. Lime tolerant.

2. Lilium regale 'Album'
A pure white form of the regal lily, whose richly fragrant, elongated flowers are more usually flushed pink on the outsides of their petals, but with creamy white interiors.

3. Lilium henryi
Probably the most lime-tolerant of all the lilies, with tall, flexible stems, dark in hue, and narrow, glossy leaves. The flowers, which open late in summer, are bright orange, with raised, dark spots on the petal surfaces. The petals curl back as the flowers mature.

4. Lilium martagon
The Turk's Cap lily, a European native with tall stems whose leaves are attached in whorls on a tall, self-supporting stem which carries generous numbers of purplish pink or white flowers. The petals turn back on themselves to resemble turbans. Lime tolerant.

5. Lilium longiflorum
A vigorous, fast growing lily with the stem-rooting habit. The flower stems carry up to six intensely fragrant, pure white flowers. This variety, 'American White', has green tips to its petals and there is a blush pink variety, 'Casa Rosa'.

6. Lilium 'Golden Splendor Group'
A vigorous strain of lilies suitable for outdoors with sprays of large, elongated, bright yellow blooms, whose petal backs are pinkish, in mid to late summer. Lime tolerant.

7. Lilium 'African Queen'
A very tall, trumpet-flowered hybrid lily whose large, showy blooms are brownish purple in bud, opening to a rich egg-yolk hue, between orange and yellow. Protection from severe frost is necessary.

Narcissus (dwarf hybrids) Bulb

Familiar narcissus and daffodil shapes, but on smaller scale plants. Good varieties include buttercup yellow, small flowered 'Tête à Tête', the lemon and white 'Jack Snipe', whose outer petals are swept back, and the intriguing 'Queen Anne's Double', whose flowers are almost like small yellow roses. Later varieties include the highly scented jonquil 'Trevithian' and 'Hawera', whose tiny cups are accentuated by fully reflexed petals.

Soil preference: Any, not too dry
Aspect: Sun or part shade
Season of interest: Spring
Height and spread: Up to 25cm x 10cm (10in x 4in)

Companion plants: Naturals with almost any small, spring-flowering planting scheme, these narcissi will spice up forget-me-nots, primroses, winter heathers or such big foliage plants as Bergenia.

Eucomis bicolor

Pineapple Lily   Marginally hardy bulb

Undulating dark green leaves surmount a single, thick, cylindrical stem carrying masses of tightly packed flowers in a broad spike. A topknot of foliage, above the greenish, dark-edged flowers, gives the impression of a pineapple. A handsome display of ripening seed capsules follows.

Soil preference: Moist, humus-rich
Aspect: Sun or part shade
Season of interest: Summer, autumn
Height and spread: 6ocm x 45cm (2ft x 1ft 6in)

Companion plants: A streamside plant in its native South Africa, but excellent in containers for summer gardens. Mix with potted cannas and bananas to enhance the tropical feel and create a striking patio display.

Leucocoryne purpurea

Glory of the Sun   Tender bulb

A species from South America with grassy foliage and spikes bearing six-petalled flowers, which are mottled purple with paler centres. Under-used in northern gardens, this plant is, however, a genus of great beauty. *Leucocoryne ixioides* has brilliant blue flowers with white petal bases.

Soil preference: Free-draining
Aspect: Sun
Season of interest: Spring, early summer
Height and spread: 45cm x 15cm (1ft 6in x 6in)

Companion plants: Though tender, these will over-winter with minimal protection and are beautiful near the silvery foliage of, say, *Convolvulus cneorum* or *Artemisia* 'Powis Castle' in a large container.

Lilium hybrids   Hardy bulbs

Highly variable group, always with narrow leaves along the stems which bear sprays of large, often highly scented flowers. These may be funnel shaped or may open to form big, six-pointed star shapes, or can curl back on themselves to resemble turbans. Examples include 'Casablanca', tiger lily (*L. lancifolium*) hybrids and 'Trumpet' lilies.

Soil preference: Fertile but free-draining. Some dislike lime
Aspect: Sun or part shade
Season of interest: Summer, autumn
Height and spread: To 1.5m x 75cm (5ft x 2ft 6in)

Companion plants: Virtually all lilies are excellent container plants and are best grown alone, but with their pots arranged with other, large plants. A pot of lilies placed close to a containerized dwarf maple such as *Acer palmatum* 'Dissectum', for example, will create an Oriental effect.

Gladiolus callianthus

Acidanthera   Near hardy, corm-bearing perennial

Sword-like leaves arranged in a fan shape are joined in late summer by tall flower spikes bearing fragrant white blooms, whose centres are boldly marked with dark crimson or purple. Each flower hangs on a short, but elegantly curved stalk. Previously known as Acidanthera.

Soil preference: Any free-draining
Aspect: Sun
Season of interest: Late summer, early autumn
Height and spread: 120cm x 30cm (4ft x 1ft)

Companion plants: A great mixer, beautiful in pots among Eucomis, lilies or with containerized bedding such as tuberous begonias, hot-coloured dahlias or fuchsias.

Agapanthus africanus   Tender bulb

These evergreen agapanthus – superb for containers – are more tender than deciduous kinds and need winter protection. Bold, strap-shaped leaves and massive stems bear generous umbels of blue, or in 'Alba', white flowers. 'Sapphire' is dark blue; 'Glen Avon', lilac blue and the impressive 'Purple Cloud', deep purple-blue.

Soil preference: Free-draining
Aspect: Sun
Season of interest: Summer
Height and spread: Up to 1.5m x 1m (5ft x 3ft 3in)

Companion plants: Beautiful as solo performers, but also effective with mixed containers of architectural foliage plants. A cool effect is achieved with the silver foliage of artemisias, *Helichrysum petiolare* or *Felicia amelloides*.

Crocus tommasinianus

Hardy corm-bearing perennial

Tiny crocuses which appear at winter's end. The outer petals are soft greyish lilac but when the flowers open to the sun, their interiors are bright mauve. Though free seeding, they also spread by underground stolons. Improved forms include 'Whitewell Purple' whose flowers are dark purple.

Soil preference: Any, not too wet
Aspect: Sun or part shade
Season of interest: Late winter, spring
Height and spread: 10cm x 5cm (4in x 2in)

Companion plants: Best for naturalizing in grass with daffodils or narcissus to follow, or perhaps among emerging snake's head fritillaries.

Crocus large Dutch hybrids

Hardy corm-bearing perennial

Grassy leaves, with central white stripe, and bold, goblet-shaped flowers, which are held well clear of the leaves. Colours can be purple, mauve or white – often with bold, contrasting stripes or veins on outer petals – as well as yellow. Out of scale with other species of crocus and being very showy best kept apart.

Soil preference: Any, not wet
Aspect: Sun or part shade
Season of interest: Early spring
Height and spread: 15cm x 10cm (6in x 4in)

Companion plants: Fine in grass, with daffodils, or in border fronts among primulas or winter and spring pansies.

Scilla bifolia

Alpine Squill   Hardy bulb

Twin leaves, grooved and suffused with bronze when young, appear from each bulb on either side of the short stems, which carry a small spray of azure flowers. A free self-seeder, quick to naturalize in a part-shaded or sunny wild garden. Modest, but beautiful.

Soil preference: Fertile but free-draining
Aspect: Sun or shade
Season of interest: Spring
Height and spread: 10cm x 5cm (4in x 2in)

Companion plants: Often found in the wild, growing with *Crocus sieberi* and wild fritillaries – a worthy combination to imitate at home.

Narcissus pseudonarcissus

Wild Daffodil, Lenten Lily   Hardy bulb

The species that inspired the poet Wordsworth. Strap-shaped leaves in glaucous green among which short stems bear blooms with forward-sweeping lemon petals and a darker, flared, yellow trumpet. This species naturalizes best in high rainfall areas where summers are cool, but is not difficult to establish in moisture-retentive, humus-rich soil elsewhere.

Soil preference: Rich, leafy and not too dry
Aspect: Part shade, shade
Season of interest: Spring
Height and spread: 20cm x 10cm (8in x 4in)

Companion plants: A plant of hedgerows, stream sides and woodland borders, beautiful beneath large trees, between shrubs such as camellias or early rhododendrons and lovely in the grass of an established fruit orchard.

Cyclamen repandum

Hardy tuber-bearing perennial

Broad, bluntly pointed leaves, sometimes faintly marbled, unfurl in spring accompanied by small cyclamen blooms whose petals are swept right back. Typical colour is vivid carmine pink, but the subspecies from the island of Rhodes, *C. repandum* var. *rhodense*, has pink-flushed white blooms with darker centres. More difficult to establish than most hardy cyclamen.

Soil preference: Humus-rich, well-drained
Aspect: Part shade or shade
Season of interest: Spring
Height and spread: 15cm x 20cm (6in x 8in)

Companion plants: A woodland species, best among humus-loving plants such as *Anemone nemorosa*, oxlips and violets, perhaps in shaded, sparse grass along the edge of a shrubbery.

Tulipa kaufmanniana 'Guiseppi Verdi'

Hardy bulb

Broad, faintly striped foliage arranged along the stems which bear a single, elongated tulip flower. The outer petals are fiercely flushed with carmine, edged with yellow; the flower interior is bright yellow with a dark centre. A 'botanical' tulip, robust enough to survive in grass.

Soil preference: Fertile but free-draining
Aspect: Sun or part shade
Season of interest: Spring
Height and spread: 25cm x 15cm (10in x 6in)

Companion plants: A good companion, in grassland, to shorter daffodil varieties such as 'Jack Snipe', 'Rip van Winkle' or to *Narcissus pseudonarcissus*. Also striking with cowslips and fritillaries in the grass.

Crocus

Crocuses offer far more than their small stature would suggest. Many of them bloom when colour is most needed, at winter's end; their flower shapes are charming and their nectar is of great value to early stirring bees. When their season is done, they leave minimal aftermath, dying down quickly and gracefully, to rest underground and build up strength for next year's show.

1. Crocus tommasinianus 'Whitewell Purple'
One of the easiest winter-flowering species whose pale blue-grey outer petals belie the brighter mauve interior. The form 'Whitewell Purple' develops a deeper colour than seen in the wild species, but retains its simple charm.

2. Crocus speciosus
A strong-growing species whose naked violet-mauve blooms appear soon after the Autumn Equinox. The petals are feathered with darker purple, making a handsome contrast with the orange stigmata. Leaves follow the flowers, in late winter.

3. Crocus sieberi 'Tricolor'
Wild forms of Crocus sieberi vary considerably, even when found in the same location, but the vivid mauve and ochre flowers of this garden selection make a startling display.

4. Crocus imperati
A striking crocus for late winter whose outer petals are biscuit-beige with bold pencilled feathering in deep purple-black. When the flowers open, to reveal bright lilac-mauve interiors, their appearance is transformed.

5. Crocus hybrid 'Jeanne d'Arc'
Dutch hybrid crocus are much larger and coarser than their wild forebears, but still retain that essential early spring charm. Colours range through purple and mauve shades, often with striped petals, but one of the most outstanding varieties, 'Jeanne d'Arc' is pure white.

6. Crocus sieberi 'Bowles White'
A more delicate, dainty plant altogether, than the hybrid Dutch crocus, this selected white form of the wild Crocus sieberi has been popular in cultivation for almost a century.

7. Crocus chrysanthus 'Cream Beauty'
Another variable wild species has given rise to a broad range of subtly coloured, gem-like beauties. Their flowers are more goblet-shaped than larger, cultivated crocuses.

8. Crocus ancyrensis
The 'golden bunch' crocus, one of the earliest of the yellows to bloom. The small flowers are produced in tight clusters from each corm, and are a vivid egg yolk hue.

1	2	3
4	5	6
7		8

Galanthus reginae-olgae

Hardy bulb

A remarkable snowdrop species, from Greece, which, instead of flowering in midwinter, produces autumnal blooms without leaves. The flowers are similar to those of the common snowdrop, with three outer tepals and green-tipped inner parts. Leaves develop in late winter.

Soil preference: Any free-draining
Aspect: Sun
Season of interest: Autumn
Height and spread: 15cm x 5cm (6in x 2in)

Companion plants: A conversation piece rather than a garden essential, but fun to grow with the yellow, crocus-like *Sternbergia lutea* to create an out-of-season spring effect.

Muscari neglectum

Common Grape Hyacinth   Hardy bulb

The commonest species, with grassy foliage and short stems crowded with small, dusky blue flowers shaped like tiny, rounded jars with restricted openings. Multiplies invasively from small offshoots, as well as seeds, so not a plant to let loose where it could become troublesome.

Soil preference: Any
Aspect: Any except deep shade
Season of interest: Spring
Height and spread: 15cm x 5cm (6in x 2in), spreading

Companion plants: Natural-looking among pebbles, especially when blended with the white *Muscari botryoides* 'Alba' or with crocuses.

Muscari comosum

Hardy bulb

A curious species, tall for a grape hyacinth. The lower spike carries fertile flowers, which are brownish and jar-shaped, but above these are bright mauve plumes or tufts of sterile florets. The garden form *M. c.* 'Plumosum' bears only dense masses of the beautiful mauve sterile florets.

Soil preference: Any free-draining
Aspect: Sun or partial shade
Season of interest: Spring
Height and spread: 30cm x 10cm (1ft x 4in)

Companion plants: Interesting addition to a mix of drought-tolerant bulbs which might also include *Tulipa batalinii*, *Bellevalia dubia* and *Scilla peruviana*.

Ornithogalum thyrsoides

Chincherinchee   Marginally hardy bulb

A South African native with narrow, pointed leaves which tend to wither before the erect, naked flower stems appear. These bear spikes of closely packed, white, cup-shaped flowers. An excellent cut flower, but not very long lived in the garden.

Soil preference: Free-draining
Aspect: Sun
Season of interest: Summer
Height and spread: 60cm x 15cm (2ft x 6in)

Companion plants: The cool, white flowers are refreshing among gravel scree plants, particularly, dark leaved Carex species such as *C. buchananii* and with grasses such as *Stipa tenuissima*.

Anthericum liliago

Hardy bulb

Grassy foliage and in early summer, tall stems bearing widely spaced, lily-like flowers in startling white. The selection *A. l. major* has larger flowers with wider petals. A graceful meadow plant from southern Europe, which seeds freely in gravel when happily established.

Soil preference: Any free-draining
Aspect: Sun
Season of interest: Early summer
Height and spread: 60cm x 15cm (2ft x 6in), spreading

Companion plants: At home with sun-loving shrubs such as rosemary and lavender, and with such annuals as *Cerinthe major* or wild poppies.

Dierama dracomontanum

Marginally hardy, corm-bearing perennial

Clumps of tough, narrow, branched, arching, sword-like stems; flowers appear in summer, bearing papery calyces which enwrap the deep madder pink buds. These open to form clusters of small flowers shaped like lampshades, which dance and sway in the slightest breeze.

Soil preference: Free-draining, but not too dry
Aspect: Sun
Season of interest: Summer
Height and spread: 45cm x 30cm (1ft 6in x 1ft)

Companion plants: At home among rocks or in gravel, either with grassy companions, or *Verbena bonariensis*, or in mild areas alongside South African restios.

Allium karataviense

Turkestan Onion   Hardy bulb

Broad, bold, curved leaves with attractive pleating and in purple-suffused blue green tints develop in pairs, curving outwards as the drumstick flowerheads swell. The flowers themselves are densely packed on short stems and are greyish white.

Soil preference: Any
Aspect: Sun
Season of interest: Spring, early summer
Height and spread: To 30cm x 20cm (1ft x 6in)

Companion plants: A striking spring foliage plant, perfect to set off against colourful bulbs such as *Narcissus* 'Hawera', *N.* 'Jack Snipe' or to distribute among low growing tulips.

Tulipa praestans

Tulip   Hardy bulb

Pale green, broad, pointed leaves are arranged along the stems. These are divided at their ends and bear several vivid scarlet blooms, which are goblet-shaped when closed, but open wide to form six-pointed stars. The variety 'Fusilier' has slightly larger flowers than the wild species which comes from western Asia.

Soil preference: Any free-draining
Aspect: Sun
Season of interest: Spring
Height and spread: 25cm x 20cm (10in x 8in)

Companion plants: Small enough to include among alpines such as aubrieta and arabis, or to distribute among smaller spring perennials such as *Primula auricula*. Startling with the yellow-flowered *Aurina saxatilis*, forget-me-nots or *Allium karataviense*.

Muscari latifolium

Grape Hyacinth   Hardy bulb

Characterful grape hyacinth with single or paired broad, strap-like leaves and thin flower stems, which carry small, tightly clustered, rounded flowers with pinched ends in midnight blue. Above these, in a contrasting paler blue, small sterile flowers also form. Too dark in colour to make a vivid splash, but gently attractive in big drifts.

Soil preference: Any, free-draining
Aspect: Sun
Season of interest: Spring
Height and spread: 20cm x 10cm (8in x 4in)

Companion plants: Muscari work best in large numbers, drifting among brighter flowers such as primroses or small wallflowers. Also beautiful when blended with Bowles' Golden Grass – *Milium effusum* 'Aureum'.

Ranunculus asiaticus

Persian Ranunculus   Perennial with a bulb-like root

Variable wild species from the eastern Mediterranean with tuberous roots. Short-lived stems with divided or lobed leaves bear large, showy blooms, usually with five petals, or double, showing dark, almost black flower centres. Colours in the wild may be white, scarlet or yellow. In addition to these colours, cultivars may be pink, cream, orange. Double series include 'Tecolote' and 'Bloomingdale'.

Soil preference: Fertile, free-draining
Aspect: Sun
Season of interest: Spring
Height and spread: To 45cm x 30cm (1ft 6in x 1ft)

Companion plants: Most cultivars are too startling to blend comfortably with soft planting schemes, but these are excellent for bedding with such bulbs as hyacinths or dwarf tulips, or with forget-me-nots.

Narcissus tazetta and hybrids

Bunch-flowered Narcissus   Hardy bulb

Small cupped, fragrant, multi-headed narcissus types bred from the species, which seldom exceed a height of 20cm (8in). Typically, the cup is darker in hue than the outer petals and may be orange against creamy white, as in 'Geranium' (pictured), deep yellow against pale yellow, as in 'Golden Dawn' or white against pale lemon yellow, as in 'Ziva'.

Soil preference: Fertile, free-draining but not too dry
Aspect: Sun or part shade
Season of interest: Spring
Height and spread: Up to 45cm x 20cm (1ft 6in x 8in)

Companion plants: Most naturalize happily in grass, or are dainty enough to mix with developing perennials or to bed among wallflowers or tulips.

Anemone coronaria (garden forms)

Florist's Anemone   Tuberous rooted perennial

Derived from *A. coronaria*, these plants have divided, ferny leaves and stiff, but hollow stems topped with a solitary bold flower in scarlet, crimson, blue, purple, white or pink, each nestling on a lacy ruff of foliage. Excellent as a cut flower. Favourite varieties include 'De Caen', which have single flowers, and 'Saint Brigid' whose flowers are double.

Soil preference: Free-draining but fertile
Aspect: Sun
Season of interest: Spring, early summer, autumn
Height and spread: To 30cm x 20cm (1ft x 8in)

Companion plants: Frustratingly short-lived, in many soils, but useful to have at the border front or lined out to provide cut flowers. Beautiful among short narcissus or botanical tulips in a spring border.

Tulips

Tulips are universal favourites worldwide, not only for gardeners but also as cut flowers. The name is derived from a Persian word meaning 'Turban' and relates to the shape of the bulbs, rather than the flowers. With roughly a hundred species and more than three millennia of breeding, the choice is understandably vast.

1. Tulipa fosteriana group 'Candela'
A yellow form of the very early *T. fosteriana* group. Large, soft yellow flowers on tall stems.

2. Tulipa fosteriana group 'Purissima'
Best of the early, large flowered tulips, opening cream turning warm white.

3. Tulipa 'Apricot Beauty'
A single early tulip with big, softly peachy flowers which fade prettily as they mature.

4. Tulipa 'Apeldoorn'
The classic red Darwin hybrid tulip and parent of several valuable sports including 'Apeldoorn Elite' and 'Golden Apeldoorn.'

5. Tulipa 'Ballerina'
A lily-flowered tulip pointed, yellow petals.

6. Tulipa 'Prinses Irene'
A single early tulip with dark, bronze suffused leaves and curious tan-orange flowers whose petals bear darker markings.

7. Tulipa 'China Pink'
Lily flowered tulip with clear pink petals.

8. Tulipa turkestanica
A late flowering wild species with multi-headed stems whose greenish buds open to display white interiors with yellow petal bases.

9. Tulipa greigii 'Toronto'
A 'botanical' tulip with marked foliage and multi-headed stems bearing cherry red flowers, opening paler with yellowish petal bases.

10. Tulipa tarda
Wild species with multiple stems bearing narrow buds which open to form brilliant, star-shaped flowers which are white and bright yellow.

11. Tulipa 'Olympic Flame'
A Darwin hybrid tulip whose yellow flowers are streaked with bold orange-red.

12. Tulipa kaufmanniana 'Stresa'
Botanical tulip with elongated flowers on short stems, vivid red and yellow. Supposed to resemble a water lily when open.

Chionodoxa luciliae

Hardy bulb

Paired leaves in spring, accompanied by short stems bearing sprays of star-shaped flowers with pale blue petals fading white at their bases. Among selected garden forms, the 'Gigantea Group' are larger than the typical species and 'Rosea' has pink and white, rather than blue and white, flowers. A less vigorous variety is the white 'Alba'.

Soil preference: Any free-draining
Aspect: Sun
Season of interest: Spring
Height and spread: 15cm x 7cm (6in x 3in)

Companion plants: Best when allowed to multiply either in poor quality grassland or in gravel, perhaps in the company of crocuses, fritillaries and other small bulbs.

Crocus sieberi

Hardy corm-bearing perennial

Mediterranean species with pale violet, mauve or white cup-like flowers which open in sun to form a six-point star shape. Best garden forms include 'Tricolor' – an arresting mix of vivid rose purple, yellow and white, in distinct zones down the petals – and 'Hubert Edelsten', which is purple and white. See also pages 96–7 for Crocuses.

Soil preference: Any free-draining
Aspect: Sun
Season of interest: Late winter, spring
Height and spread: 10cm x 5cm (4in x 2in)

Companion plants: The flowers show well in small groups, among other crocuses or dwarf bulbs in a gravely or rocky scree garden, or in pans in an alpine house. Lovely to follow on from *Iris reticulata*.

Crocus chrysanthus

Hardy corm-bearing perennial

Dainty crocuses with fine, short, grassy foliage and elongated goblet-shaped flowers, sometimes darker striped or marked on the outside, but always opening wide in sun to reveal bright colours. Outstanding varieties include 'Ladykiller', whose outer petals are stained purple, 'Zwanenburg Bronze', which is yellow with dark exteriors and 'Goldilocks', whose egg yolk petals have dark bases.

Soil preference: Free-draining
Aspect: Sun
Season of interest: Late winter, spring
Height and spread: 10cm x 5cm (4in x 2in)

Companion plants: Just big enough to naturalize in grass, but more effective among other dwarf bulbs such as Chionodoxa or Muscari in gravel or a raised bed.

Ipheion uniflorum   Star Flower, Spring Star   Hardy bulb

Pungent, mat-forming perennial with lax, grassy foliage and large, six-petalled, pale blue flowers. 'Wisley Blue' has flowers in a more intense sky blue, each with a darker central vein; 'Froyle Mill' has purple flowers; and 'Alberto Castillo' is white. A rapid spreader, but easy to control.

Soil preference: Very free-draining
Aspect: Sun
Season of interest: Spring, early summer
Height and spread: To 15cm (6in), spreading

Companion plants: One for a sunny bank or the base of a wall, perhaps with *Erigeron karvinskianus* for later colour or with red *Anemone fulgens* or *Anemone blanda* 'White Splendour' for company.

Iris reticulata

Bulb

Erect, thin, spiky leaves emerge soon after the flower buds, which open to form sparse but shapely tripartite, blue, purple or violet iris blooms, often marked with bold, black spotted yellow pollen guides. A variable species with such excellent cultivars as the maroon to purple 'J. S. Dijt' or the light and dark blue 'Harmony'.

Soil preference: Free-draining
Aspect: Sun
Season of interest: Winter, early spring
Height and spread: Up to 20cm x 10cm (8in x 4in)

Companion plants: Fine for pot culture or for blending with crocuses or winter aconites in a rock garden or scree.

Nectaroscordium siculum ssp. bulgaricum

Bulb

Pleated, grass-like leaves and smooth, rigid stems, topped with umbels of bell-like, hanging blooms in a bewitching mix of green, pink and greyish white. As the seeds mature, the flower stems begin to rear up until they are all held erect. The bulbs are short-lived, but the plant is a very free seeder.

Soil preference: Free-draining but not too dry
Aspect: Sun or part shade
Season of interest: Summer
Height and spread: 1m x 15cm (3ft x 6in)

Companion plants: Excellent in a mixed border among shrubs and perennials, especially backing up purples and pinks of *Cistus purpurea* or the soft hues of old shrub roses.

Narcissus obvallaris

The Tenby Daffodil   Hardy bulb

Close relative of the wild daffodil, *Narcissus pseudonarcissus*, but much earlier to flower, sometimes showing colour in mid-winter. The butter-yellow outer petals and golden trumpet make a bold splash, before other spring blooms have emerged and will attract early bumble bees.

Soil preference: Fertile and free-draining, but not too dry
Aspect: Sun, part shade
Season of interest: Late winter
Height and spread: 25cm x 15cm (10in x 6in)

Companion plants: Lovely naturalized, but also beautiful when grouped in a sunny spot with winter crocuses, or under a winter shrub such as *Chimonanthus praecox* or witch hazel.

Hermodactylus tuberosus

Widow Iris, Snake's Head Iris   Hardy corm-bearing perennial

Narrow, sharply creased leaves begin to develop in late winter and by early spring, strangely kinked stems develop, bearing typical three-part iris flowers. The petals are predominantly green with conspicuous, satiny brownish black marks on the falls. Plants must be in sun to develop abundant flowers.

Soil preference: Any free-draining
Aspect: Sun
Season of interest: Early spring
Height and spread: 25cm x 15cm (10in x 6in)

Companion plants: The green and black theme goes well with scarlet anemones such as *Anemone* x *fulgens* or with the brilliant red *Tulipa praestans*.

Tulipa turkestanica

Hardy bulb

An early-emerging bulb with narrow, dark green or bronze suffused foliage and narrow, dark stem which carries between three and ten, slender, green-backed buds which open to show bold, six-pointed star-shaped flowers, which are white with yellow centres. In favourable conditions, this species will self-seed freely.

Soil preference: Any free-draining
Aspect: Full sun
Season of interest: Early spring
Height and spread: 30cm x 10cm (1ft x 4in)

Companion plants: A natural for a rocky or gritty terrain, interspersed with rock roses or such other early flowering bulbs as *Crocus chrysanthus*, *C. sieberi* or *Cyclamen coum*. Pretty when planted densely in a container.

Tecophilaea cyanocrocus Marginally tender bulb

A treasure best suited to Alpine pan growth with grass-like foliage and, during spring, crocus-like blooms whose petals are possibly the most intense blue to be found in the plant world. Each petal bears a thin white margin which amplifies the power of that blue.

Soil preference: Free-draining, sandy
Aspect: Sun
Season of interest: Spring
Height and spread: 10cm x 5 cm (4in x 2in)

Companion plants: Unrivalled in its hue, and best matched with such other pan-cultured treasures as *Cyclamen libanoticum*, delicate saxifrages, challenging fritillaries, and similar plants.

Tritelia ixioides Marginally hardy, corm-bearing

Grass-like basal foliage emerges in spring to form a sparse rosette from which a flower stem emerges, carrying an umbel of a score or so of pretty, star-shaped flowers whose beige-yellow colour is set off by darker but subtle purplish central line. Reasonably hardy in sharp drained soil, but will succumb to sustained frost.

Soil preference: Any free-draining
Aspect: Sun
Season of interest: Spring, early summer
Height and spread: 30cm x 15cm (1ft x 6in)

Companion plants: Useful plant for growing in gravel, or for dotting through a Mediterranean style garden among such other bulbs as *Anemone pavonina*, dry-loving fritillaries, Bellevalia, or perhaps following on from Muscari or Chionodoxa.

Arum creticum Near hardy tuberous perennial

Striking wild plant from Crete with big, bold, deep green arrow-head leaves and in spring, large flowers consisting of a white or yellow spathe surrounding a deeper golden spadix. Unlike many of the arum family, which stink, this one has sweetly fragrant flowers. Needs protection from severe frost.

Soil preference: Free-draining
Aspect: Sun
Season of interest: Spring, summer
Height and spread: 30cm x 15cm (1ft x 6in)

Companion plants: Most effective with such other sun-loving spring plants as *Iris unguicularis*, *Arum italicum*, crocuses and dwarf irises, in rocky conditions.

Geranium malviflorum   Hardy tuberous perennial

A cranesbill which produces easily stored tubers. In autumn, attractively divided leaves form a loose carpet over the ground followed, in spring, by sprays of disc- or saucer-shaped, five petalled flowers whose pinkish-blue colours are enhanced by thin, red veining. The leaves tend to disappear in summer.

Soil preference: Poor, dry
Aspect: Sun, part shade
Season of interest: Spring
Height and spread: 30cm x 45cms (1ft x 1ft 6in)

Companion plants: Pretty among shrubs, or to create drifts in a sunny, free-draining corner, perhaps with *Fritillaria verticillata* or *F. pallidiflora* as companions.

Camassia cusickii, C. leichtlinii

Hardy bulb

Vigorous bulbs with broad, strap-shaped leaves among which, in late spring, bold flower stems develop, carrying well-packed spikes of six-petalled flowers in pale blue, deep blue or creamy white. *C. cusickii* 'Zwanenburg' has vivid blue flowers; *C. leichtlinii* subsp. *suksdorfii* has violet blue flowers.

Soil preference: Any, humus-rich, not too dry
Aspect: Sun, part shade.
Season of interest: Early summer
Height and spread: 60 cm x 30cm (2ft x 1ft)

Companion plants: Best naturalised in grass among shrubs or at the edge of a woodland garden and lovely to follow from cowslips and *Fritillaria meleagris*. Also beautiful with cranesbills, particularly *G. pratense*, whose flowers continue as the camassias fade.

Cardiocrinum giganteum   Hardy bulb

A beautiful giant lily with heart-shaped leaves and, from mature bulbs, thick, fleshy flower stems which carry up to a dozen, large, funnel-shaped, scented lily flowers which are white with crimson markings at their throats. The ripening seedheads follow with a quieter beauty.

Soil preference: Deep, humus-rich, reasonably fertile, not too dry but well-drained
Aspect: Part shade
Season of interest: Summer
Height and spread: 2.5m x 45cm (10ft x 1ft 6in)

Companion plants: The ultimate plant for a woodland garden. Bulbs may take several years to bloom, but the foliage is lovely among such woodland shrubs as hydrangeas, Enkianthus, Fothergilla and *Magnolia sieboldii*.

Crocosmia garden forms

Hardy or near hardy corm-bearing perennials

Rapidly multiplying corms quickly form dense clumps of sword-like foliage and, in summer, sprays of funnel-shaped flowers in hot colours. The tallest, *C.* 'Lucifer' has flame red flowers contrasting with emerald green foliage. There are smaller, more sedate varieties available.

Soil preference: Free-draining, not too dry
Aspect: Sun, part shade
Season of interest: Summer, autumn
Height and spread: Variable to 1.5m x 45cm (to 5ft x 1ft 6in)

Companion plants: Valuable constituents of a late summer border, where their hot colours can contrast with mauves and blues of perennial asters, or can harmonise with such yellow daisies as *Bidens heterophylla*, Helianthus, Rudbeckia and Helenium.

Corydalis solida Hardy, tuber-bearing perennial

Divided, ferny foliage emerges in early spring and is soon accompanied by short spikes of curious, narrow, spurred, two-lipped flowers whose colour is pinkish purple. The variety 'George Baker' has brighter, brick red blooms and there are other varieties whose colours range through mauve-pink to creamy white.

Soil preference: Humus rich, free-draining
Aspect: Sun or part shade
Season of interest: Spring
Height and spread: 20cm x 15cm (8in x 6in)

Companion plants: Short-lived, in its season, but a charming species to blend with other spring bulbs such as crocuses, primroses, *Anemone blanda* and the earlier fritillaries.

Freesia corymbsa, Freesia garden forms

Marginally tender corm

Beloved cut flower and member of the iris family with sword-like leaves and elegant, branched sprays of sweetly fragrant, funnel shaped flowers. Colours may be creamy white, yellow, mauve-blue, or darker mahogany. Barely hardy enough for general outdoor use, but in mild areas, freesias will naturalise freely.

Soil preference: Free-draining, sandy
Aspect: Sun
Season of interest: Winter, spring
Height and spread: 45cm x 15cm (1ft 6in x 6in)

Companion plants: With climate change, the safe range in which freesias can be naturalised is expanding. In sharp-draining soils, against a sunny wall, or on a sheltered terrace, try this plant with winter violas, Ipheion or *Arum creticum*.

Blue bulbs

Blue seems to be the predominant colour, among the smaller spring flowering bulbs. From the earliest, *Scilla bifolia*, whose tough buds pierce the melting snow on springtime mountainsides, to the vast drifts of bluebells which carpet the northern woodlands, the choice of good garden varieties is bountiful. Most small blue bulbs are easy to grow and will naturalise speedily.

1. Scilla sibirica
One of the best known, and most adaptable blue bulbs. Rich peacock blue, especially in the form 'Spring Beauty'.

2. Scilla peruviana
A big, bold species from the western Mediterranean. Seeds freely where it is happy.

3. Scilla bifolia
Twin leaves cradle the clusters of intense blue flowers. Not long in bloom, but an excellent naturalising plant.

4. Muscari azureum
A pale blue grape hyacinth whose tiny flowers have serrated tips. There is a gardenworthy white form.

5. Hyacinthoides italica
The Italian bluebell, whose flowers are starry.

6. Hyacinthoides non-scripta
English Bluebells, a rare plant, threatened by habitat loss. The bells hang more gracefully than other species, usually to one side of the stem.

7. Chionodoxa sardensis
An easy species for naturalising in free-draining soils or gravels. Spreads well by self-sowing.

8. Muscari armenaicum
The commonest grape hyacinth. A variable species which, in some gardens, can become invasive.

9. Muscari latifolium
The broad leaves and two-tone flowers make this a pretty plant to feature in drifts among shrubs, in part shade or sun.

10. Puschkinia scilloides
Very pale blue petals, each with its darker blue pencil line, make this species useful for naturalising to create a contrast among other blue bulbs.

11. Hyacinthoides reverchonii
A Spanish bluebell with delicately coloured, starry petals and a vigorous, spreading habit.

alpines

Alpines for year-round and vertical wall shade

Alpines for full light in winter and spring

Alpines for full light in summer and autumn

Alpines for dry conditions

Viola riviniana

Dog Violet, Wood Violet   Alpine

Heart-shaped, evergreen leaves on slender stems among which small, purple-blue, white, pink or violet blooms appear in mid-spring. A prolific seeder, but ideal for encouraging to naturalize in paving cracks or in gloomy corners. Though not scented, the flowers last well when cut. 'Rosea' has pink blooms and 'Alba' is white.

Soil preference: Any
Aspect: Shade, semi shade
Season of interest: Spring
Height and spread: 15cm x 20cm (6in x 8in)

Companion plants: *Viola riviniana* 'Purpurea group' (syn. *V. labradorica*) has deep purple leaves. Sweet violets, *V. odorata*, enjoy similar conditions. Also good with epimediums, *Corydalis solida*, primroses and small spring bulbs.

Ranunculus ficaria

Lesser Celandine, Pilewort   Tuberous perennial

Shiny, spade-shaped leaves emerge in late winter accompanied in early spring by small, buttercup-like flowers whose green-backed petals open wide to the sun. Flowers of the wild species are vivid yellow. Good garden forms are *R. f.* var. *aurantiacus* (orange flowers), the double flowered 'Double Mud' and 'Brazen Hussy'. As happy in a bog as in drained soil.

Soil preference: Not too dry
Aspect: Shade or semi shade; also happy in sun when moist
Season of interest: Early spring
Height and spread: 15cm x 30cm (6in x 12in), spreading

Companion plants: Perfect in a moist woodland garden with ragged robin (*Lychnis flos cuculi*) or among meadow grasses. Spring snowflake, *Leucojum vernum*, and the purple-flowered *Primula* 'Wanda' also go well with this vigorous wildling.

Corydalis solida   Fumewort   Tuberous perennial

Glaucous, finely divided, ferny foliage emerges from an underground tuber-like root in early spring, soon joined by spikes of intricate flowers, each one elongated, lipped in front, with a curved spur behind. Typical flowers are a rather liverish, purple to pink, but *Corydalis solida* 'George Baker' has brick red blooms.

Soil preference: Any, not too dry
Aspect: Shade or part shade
Season of interest: Spring
Height and spread: Compact 20cm x 20cm (8in x 8in)

Companion plants: Beautiful woodlander, happy with primroses, celandines, scillas and miniature daffodils.

Aubrieta x cultorum   Aubretia   Trailing evergreen perennial

Form-hugging, trailing perennial which loves growing in rock crevices or on stony screes. The tiny leaves are slightly lobed and mid-green, covering thin, flexible stems. In spring, the entire plant is smothered by showy four-petalled flowers whose colours range from violet blue, through mauve to magenta. Variegated leaf forms such as 'Argenteovariegata' bring an extra decorative dimension.

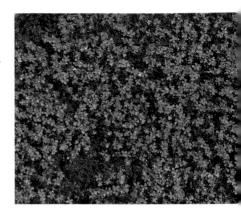

Soil preference: Dry, limy, well-drained
Aspect: Sun
Season of interest: Spring
Height and spread: 15cm (6in), spreading

Companion plants: Traditional companion of yellow alyssum, Arabis, sedums, thrift and houseleeks. Allow to trail down a steep bank or dry stone wall with *Erinus* 'Dr Hähnle', *Dianthus deltoides* and *Saponaria ocymoides*, all of which continue to flower later.

Onosma alborosea

Honey Drops   Alpine

Narrow, hoary grey-green leaves on short, trailing stems produce semi-erect flower spikes from which hang elongated, tubular, cream-coloured flowers with a touch of pink on their outsides when in bud. When plucked, each petal tube yields a drop of sweet nectar. A plant of Mediterranean walls and dry places, loved by bees.

Soil preference: Dry, well-drained, poor
Aspect: Sun
Season of interest: Evergreen, best in spring and summer
Height and spread: 20cm x 30cm (8in x 12in), slowly spreading

Companion plants: Happiest in a wall or a gravel garden with *Corydalis lutea*, wallflowers, Aubrieta and succulent plants. Also useful in the front of a dry, sunny border, perhaps among drought tolerant grasses.

Arabis ferdinandi-coburgi   Alpine

Ground covering plant which creates mats with masses of neat rosettes, many of which overlap. In spring, wiry stems bear small, four-petalled white flowers. The form 'Aureovariegata' has cream edges to the leaves and 'Old Gold' has yellow foliage. Modest in stature and unspectacular in bloom, but a cooling, pleasing plant for a patio corner or dingy part of a terrace.

Soil preference: Any, not too wet
Aspect: Sun, shade or part shade
Season of interest: Year round, flowers in spring
Height and spread: 5-7cm (2-3in), spreading

Companion plants: Best with spring bulbs planted to thrust through the rosettes. Grape hyacinths, species crocuses and *Iris reticulata* are useful for this, perhaps with autumn snowflake, *Leucojum autumnale*, for later.

Aquilegia flabellate 'Nana' Hardy alpine

Lobed, ferny leaves, which emerge in autumn and persist through winter, are joined in spring by extending, branching flower stems. The flowers are large in proportion to the plants, with pale blue and white petals and short spurs. Not long lived, but a free-seeder and ready hybridizer with other columbines!

Soil preference: Humus-rich, free-draining
Aspect: Sun or part shade. Not too hot
Season of interest: Spring, early summer
Height and spread: 20cm x 20cm (8in x 8in)

Companion plants: Interesting in a container with late bulbs such as fritillaries, or in a border front or rock garden with low-growing alpines such as *Geranium farreri* or alpine campanulas.

Saxifraga 'Tumbling Waters' Alpine

Typically found growing in a rock crevice, with clusters of rough-textured, neat, decorative rosettes of leaves. In spring, one or two rosettes will produce long trails of white blossoms which hang downwards. Spectacular when arranged to cascade down the sides of a large rock or when planted in a big hunk of tufa (soft, porous limestone).

Soil preference: Well-drained, poor
Aspect: Sun, but not too hot or part shade
Season of interest: Spring, but leaf rosettes are evergreen
Height and spread: Leaves 10cm x 25cm (4in x 10in); flowers, up to 40cm (16in)

Companion plants: The year-round rosettes team well with equally evergreen *Primula marginata*, with almost any of the cushion saxifrages and with small, non-invasive succulents.

Arabis alpina subsp. caucasica 'Flore Pleno'
Rock Cress   Alpine

Evergreen perennial that grows into thick, leafy mats from which grow spikes bearing clusters of fragrant white flowers in early to mid-spring. As more flowers open, the stems lengthen. Once flowering is done and the stems removed, a pleasing green mat of foliage is left for the rest of the year.

Soil preference: Any well-drained
Aspect: Sun or part shade
Season of interest: Spring
Height and spread: 15cm (6in), slowly spreading

Companion plants: Lovely when grown with its closest relatives, *Arabis* x *arendsii*, varieties which bear flowers in shades of lilac, mauve and pink, as well as white. Good in a rock garden or scree, among alpines such as Aubrieta, Aurinia and Chiastophyllum.

Gentiana verna   Spring or Star Gentian   Alpine

Slow-growing, rosette-forming perennial with simple, oblong leaves and in spring, short stems bearing five-petalled, tubular flowers whose intense blue colour is amplified by contrasting white throat. Though perennial, the plants are short-lived and need regular propagating. A demanding plant, but happy if given gritty, free-draining soil, especially if loaded with leafmould.

Soil preference: Any, but not too dry
Aspect: Sun
Season of interest: Spring
Height and spread: 7cm x 15cm (3in x 6in)

Companion plants: Beautiful with other gentians, such as *G. acaulis* and with the more modest-growing winter and spring flowering heathers. Also good with saxifrages, Androsace and other early spring alpines.

Primula marginata   Alpine

Loose rosettes of leathery, pale grey-green, toothed leaves grow from thick, part-submerged rhizomes. In spring, stems bearing up to a dozen pale, lilac-mauve, five-petalled flowers appear between the leaves. Good garden forms include rich purple-blue 'Kesselring's' variety, 'Linda Pope', which is pale lavender and the white flowered *P. m. alba*.

Soil preference: Any well-drained. A lime lover
Aspect: Full sun in spring; appreciates summer shade
Season of interest: Spring
Height and spread 15cm x 15cm (6in x 6in)

Companion plants: All alpine primulas are highly collectable and go well together. The related *P.* x *pubescens* brings a wider colour range, including maroon 'Boothman's Variety' and the creamy 'Harlow Carr'.

Euphorbia myrsinites

Alpine, small perennial

A superb evergreen from the hottest, most rugged parts of the Mediterranean. Its spiralling, prostrate stems are furnished with triangular, blue-green, hairless foliage. In spring, the stem ends rear up to produce clusters of bright gold-green flowers. Ideal for a hot, dry bank. Reluctant to transplant, but self-seeds generously.

Soil preference: Very dry
Aspect: Hot sun
Season of interest: Year round, flowers in spring
Height and spread: 15cm x 75cm (6in x 2ft 6in), slowly spreading

Companion plants: Teams well with Californian poppies and other drought-tolerant annuals. Effective when drought-loving bulbs such as species crocus, *Leucojum autumnale* or *Tulipa turkestanica* are allowed to grow through the prostrate stems.

Dianthus **Dwarf Hybrid Pinks**   Alpine

Tidy, evergreen mats of silvery blue-green, needle-like foliage create attractive, low mounds from which, in early summer, richly fragrant flowers, often with clove scent, are borne on short stems. The petals of most are 'pinked' or fringed at their ends, hence the name 'pink'. These are dwarf perennials, perfect for border fronts, rock gardens, containers or even to plant between paving cracks. Good varieties include 'Little Jock', 'Pike's Pink' and some of the slightly taller varieties, such as 'Haytor Rock' (pictured).

Soil preference: Lime-rich, dry
Aspect: Sun
Season of interest: Summer
Height and spread: 12cm x 25cm
(5in x 10in)

Companion plants: Little hybrid pinks team well with such Dianthus species as *D. gratianopolitanus*, the Cheddar pink, *D. plumarius* and the Maiden pink, *D. deltoides*.

Dryas octopetala   Mountain Avens   Alpine

Dense, ground-hugging, mat-forming perennial with lobed leaves having glossy, dark green upper sides and pale grey-green undersides. From late spring, short flower stems emerge and are held well clear of the foliage mats, creating a drift of soft cream as the petals emerge. Whiskery seedheads provide a bonus display, lasting long into summer.

Soil preference: Any free-draining
Aspect: Sun or part shade
Season of interest: Summer
Height and spread: 10cm x 75cm
(4in x 2ft 6in)

Companion plants: Mature plants form large mats, which merge pleasingly with other low-spreading species. Creeping thymes, sun roses, low-growing sedums and spreading campanulas such as *C. cochlearifolia* work particularly well together.

Helianthemum **'Wisley Primrose'**

Sun Rose, Rock Rose   Alpine shrub or sub-shrub

Prostrate, evergreen shrubby perennial with small, grey-green leaves and clusters of short-lived flowers whose frail, crinkled petals are pale yellow. One of many superb rock plants coming in a range of colours including red, pink, cream, orange and bright yellow. Hard pruning, straight after flowering, will stimulate a vigorous flush of fresh, evergreen leaves giving beauty through autumn. Other good varieties include 'Raspberry Ripple', 'Mrs C. W. Earle' and 'Ben Nevis'.

Soil preference: Dry and hot
Aspect: Full sun
Season of interest: Summer
Height and spread: 25cm x
45cm (10in x 18in)

Companion plants: Best in their own company, but lovely backed up with Mediterranean oregano – *O. rotundifolium* and *O. laevigatum*.

Penstemon newberryi Alpine sub-shrub

Dark green, glossy, oval, leathery leaves make a beautiful contrast in early summer with the showy, cherry red, tubular flowers which are presented on short stems held clear of the leaves. The woody main stems are brittle, so the plant needs protection from the worst of the wind. One of several excellent rock garden penstemons.

Soil preference: Free-draining but not too dry
Aspect: Sun
Season of interest: Summer
Height and spread: 15cm x 30cm (6in x 12in)

Companion plants: Lovely to blend with the related *Penstemon pinifolius* and *P. fruticosus* var. *scouleri*. The dark leaves also contrast well with the silver foliage of *Convolvulus cneorum*.

Rhodanthemum hosmariense

Alpine or small perennial

Silvery, divided foliage makes a beautiful companion to the continually produced classic daisy flowers, which are up to 5cm (2in) across, with white outer rays and bold, yellow centres. A mountain plant from Morocco, which will tolerate most conditions apart from sustained frost. Plants in very well-drained conditions over-winter better than those in waterlogged soil.

Soil preference: Free-draining, but not too dry
Aspect: Sun
Season of interest: Year round
Height and spread: Up to 25cm x 30cm (10in x 12in)

Companion plants: One of the most dependable rock plants, ready to produce its first flowers alongside spring bulbs such as botanical tulips or fritillaries and still able to accompany autumn gentians or such late perennials as Zauschneria.

Lithodora oleifolia (formerly Lithospermum)

Alpine

Low-growing alpine shrub with twiggy, semi-upright habit bearing dark, evergreen but non-glossy foliage. In early summer, small sprigs of pinkish buds are produced in profusion and open to small, cup-shaped, mid-blue flowers. A useful lime-tolerant alternative to the more widely grown *L. diffusa* 'Heavenly Blue', although the much paler flowers make a less intense statement.

Soil preference: Limy or neutral, free-draining
Aspect: Sun or part shade
Season of interest: Summer
Height and spread: 15cm x 30cm (6in x 1ft), spreading

Companion plants: A good wall plant, attractive with campanulas or alpine cranesbills. The evergreen foliage works well with such spring bulbs as Muscari or Scilla.

Chiastophyllym oppositifolium Alpine

Dark, succulent, evergreen leaves which are oval, slightly toothed and undulate at their margins and which take on bronze tints in the autumn. These make a superb contrasting foil for the catkin-like clusters of rounded, golden yellow flowers, which hang gracefully between spring and summer. A superb plant from the Caucasus and very easy to grow.

Soil preference: Any free-draining
Aspect: Sun
Season of interest: Year round; summer
Height and spread: 20cm x 15cm (8in x 6in)

Companion plants: Bold enough to grow in a border front or in a container, as well as on a rock garden. Fine among feathery or filigree foliage of artemisias or with *Rhodanthemum hosmariense*.

Erinus alpinus Fairy Foxglove Alpine

Diminutive member of the foxglove family, which is short-lived but self-seeds very freely. The foliage is nondescript, slightly lobed and sticky to the touch, but the profusion of bright rosy purple, two-lipped flowers makes this a conspicuous alpine. Other forms include 'Dr Hähnle', which is a deeper rose pink and a white form, *E.a.* var. *albus*.

Soil preference: Any free-draining
Aspect: Sun or part shade
Season of interest: Summer
Height and spread: 10cm x 10cm (4in x 4in)

Companion plants: One of the best plants for naturalizing in cracks in paving or to allow to scatter in a shingly scree. It makes a cheerful accent for greener crevice plants such as *Alchemilla alpina* or Pratia.

Jovibarba heuffelii Alpine

A succulent from the Balkans. Neat, flower-like rosettes up to about 2.5cm (1in) across are formed, with fleshy, pointed leaves which are green suffused with bronze or purple. The whole plant is covered with fine, white hairs, though some forms do without (pictured). When flower spikes are formed, these carry yellowish, bell-shaped blooms, but the plant is primarily grown for its foliage.

Soil preference: Any, dry
Aspect: Sun
Season of interest: Year-round
Height and spread: Rosettes, 7cm (3in); flower spike, 20cm (8in)

Companion plants: Great in a container that need not be watered, or among rocks or in a gravelly scree along with other succulents such as sedums, sempervivums or Rhodiola.

Rhodiola rosea   Rose Root   Alpine

A curious succulent which, as it matures, develops a cluster of knobbly storage stems held above ground. From these, rose-like leaf buds emerge in spring and eventually lengthen to stems, furnished with grey-green, toothed leaves and topped with clusters of greenish yellow flowers. *Rhodiola heterodonta* is taller, with rusty blooms.

Soil preference: Dry
Aspect: Sun
Season of interest: Spring and summer
Height and spread: Up to 30cm x 25cm (12in x 10in)

Companion plants: Good in a border front, where it makes a neat colourful dome among less disciplined perennials. Also contrasts well with helianthemums.

Sempervivum tectorum   Common Houseleek   Alpine

Familiar succulent found growing on old roofs and walls, especially in cottage gardens. The fleshy, pointed leaves are arranged in a perfect rose formation. They are often suffused with purplish or bronze tones and are sometimes dark tipped. Mature rosettes produce spikes of pinkish purple flowers which should be pulled away after flowering to allow more rosettes to form.

Soil preference: Dry
Aspect: Sun or part shade
Season of interest: Year round
Height and spread: 7.5cm (3in); flower spike 25cm (10in)

Companion plants: A charming plant to fit into cracks or crevices to allow to spread around old walls and structures in the company of *Sedum acre*, Jovibarba and any other species able to cling to life in the most inhospitable habitats.

Silene uniflora

Sea Catchfly   Alpine or low perennial

Clump forming perennial with thin, lax stems and narrow, hairless, silvery blue-grey leaves in pairs along them. In early summer, bladder-like buds form and open to stark white blooms with bifurcated petals. The effect is of a silvery white cascade, giving this common European wildflower exceptional garden value.

Soil preference: Sandy and dry
Aspect: Sun
Season of interest: Summer
Height and spread: 25cm (10in)

Companion plants: Beautiful when grown with other maritime plants such as *Armeria maritima* or thrift and *Lotus hirsutum*. Also lovely with pinks, to which it is related, and with *Dryas octopetala*.

Androsace lanuginosa   Rock Jasmine   Hardy alpine

A member of the primrose family with a prostrate, semi-trailing habit. Small grey-green leaves are joined in late summer by small, well packed heads of very pale pink flowers, each with a darker pink eye. The wild-occurring variety, *A. l.* var. *leichtlinii*, has deeper pink flowers.

Soil preference: Free-draining, not too wet
Aspect: Sun, part shade
Season of interest: Summer, autumn
Height and spread: 10cm x 20cm (4in x 8in), spreading

Companion plants: Useful to bridge the gap between summer and autumn and not out of place if grown with gentians, or to follow on from small cranesbills, such as *Geranium dalmaticum*.

Gentiana sino-ornata

Autumn Gentian   Hardy alpine

Prostrate stems, furnished with narrow, deep green leaves produce large, trumpet-shaped flowers at their tips from early autumn onwards. Flower colour is an intense blue, accentuated by dark stripes down the outsides of the flowers. These Himalayan plants enjoy a moist atmosphere and may be difficult to establish.

Soil preference: Lime-free, humus-rich, free-draining
Aspect: Sun or part shade
Season of interest: Autumn
Height and spread: 20cm x 30cm (8in x 12in)

Companion plants: A spectacular container plant to accompany good autumn leaf colour. In a container, *Sorbus reducta* would make a lovely companion.

Geranium dalmaticum

Dalmatian Cranesbill   Hardy alpine

Charming and easy wilding with rounded, lobed foliage that turns reddish in cold autumn weather. Clusters of small but showy, shell-pink flowers are produced in late spring and held above the leaves on short, erect stems. White flowered forms are also available.

Soil preference: Any, free-draining. A lime lover
Aspect: Sun
Season of interest: Late spring, early summer
Height and spread: 15cm (6in), spreading

Companion plants: A vigorous spreader, so best grouped with robust companions such as *Campanula cochlearifolia* and extremely pretty if crocuses are planted to flower through the young, emerging leaves.

Campanula cochlearifolia

Fairy Thimbles   Hardy alpine

One of the prettiest bellflower species with a dense, mat-forming habit and small, diamond-shaped, emerald green leaves. The sprays of light blue flowers, each a compact, thimble shape, are held on thin stems, above the leaf mats. Regular deadheading will ensure a constant run of bloom. Other varieties include white flowered *C. c.* var. *alba* and the double flowered 'Elizabeth Oliver'.

Soil preference: Any, free-draining
Aspect: Sun or part shade
Season of interest: Summer
Height and spread: 15cm x 20cm (6in x 8in) and spreading

Companion plants: A good companion for other mat forming plants such as *Androsace lanuginosa* or to precede *Gentiana sino-ornata*. Also excellent for an alpine trough or sink, perhaps with dwarf conifers or low-growing heathers.

Aquilegia viridiflora Columbine Alpine

Divided, lobed, ferny foliage, hairless and blue-green in colour, surrounds elegant branched stems which bear characteristic columbine flowers whose petals are arranged to resemble a circle of perching doves. Their colour is extraordinary: chocolate brown to black flower centres contrast with sage green outer parts. A short-lived perennial, but easy to raise from seed.

Soil preference: Any, well-drained
Aspect: Sun or part shade
Season of interest: Spring
Height and spread: 30cm x 20cm (12in x 8in)

Companion plants: Excellent in the company of miniature daffodil or botanical tulip bulbs. Creates a subtle display when interspersed with Bowles' Golden Grass, whose young foliage is at is best when the columbine is blooming.

Lewisia cotyledon Alpine perennial

An evergreen perennial which forms clumps of rosettes of simple, fleshy, dark green leaves. Branched flower stems emerge from these in late spring bearing flattened funnel-shaped flowers in rich hues of pink, orange, purple or yellow. Plants can be shortlived unless grown lime-free in humus-rich soil.

Soil preference: Neutral or acidic, free-draining
Aspect: Part shade
Season of interest: Early summer
Height and spread: Variable to 30cm x 45cm (1ft x 1ft 6in)

Companion plants: Beautiful in a raised alpine sink or trough, where the flowers can be enjoyed at close quarters or in the face of a stone wall. Especially fetching with vivid blue *Lithodora diffusa* 'Heavenly Blue'.

Sedum acre

Biting Stonecrop   Hardy alpine

A common European succulent which forms mats of dense, sometimes tangled stems, furnished with tiny, triangular, fleshy leaves which have adapted as water storage organs. In spring, the plant is covered with small, starry, bright yellow flowers. Tiny star-shaped spent seed capsules follow in summer.

Soil preference: Poor, free-draining
Aspect: Sun
Season of interest: Year round
Height and spread: 8cm x 30cm (4in x 1ft)

Companion plants: Fun to grow in a wall, in paving cracks or even on a brick! Good companion to sempervivums, jovibarbas and the tougher of the cushion saxifrages.

Asarum pulchellum

Wild Ginger   Hardy, low-growing perennial

Hardly an 'alpine', but useful for a shaded rock garden, where it will form mats of foliage. The rounded leaves, carried on hairy or downy stems, are deep green, each with a bold silvery grey central stripe. Unexciting flowers, produced in spring, are dirty white with reflexed petals.

Soil preference: Humus-rich, not too dry
Aspect: Shade, part shade
Season of interest: Year round
Height and spread: 5cm (2in)

Companion plants: A pretty woodlander to mix with gentians and perhaps with small bulbs.

Anthyllis vulneraria

Kidney Vetch   Hardy, short-lived perennial

A north European wild flower common on cliff tops and rocky places. The pubescent, nearly prostrate stems carry lobed foliage which has a grey-green hue and, in summer, tightly bunched heads of pea flowers appear. The commonest flower colour is butter yellow but forms appear with orange, carmine, cream or pink flowers.

Soil preference: Free-draining
Aspect: Sun
Season of interest: Summer
Height and spread: 15cm x 15cm (6in x 6in)

Companion plants: A useful rock plant to grow with *Armeria maritima* and *Silene vulgaris* subsp. *maritima* to develop a coastal feel.

Serratula shawii   Saw Wort   Hardy perennial

A neat, compact perennial with stiff, twiggy, branched stems furnished with deeply divided, serrated leaves and, in summer, clusters of hard, bottle shaped buds which open with purple-pink flowers. The spent seed heads persist through autumn and winter, creating an attractive bonus show.

Soil preference: Any free-draining
Aspect: Sun
Season of interest: Summer, autumn
Height and spread: 30cm x 15cm (12in x 6in)

Companion plants: Equally suitable in a rock garden or at the border front where it blends well with garden pinks, low-growing artemisias or among low grasses, especially blue fescue.

Primula auricula   Alpine Auriculas   Hardy perennial

Tough plants forming clumps of leathery, evergreen leaves. In spring, umbels of disc-shaped, sweetly fragrant flowers are carried just clear of the leaves on self-supporting stems. Colours can be muddy – or bewitchingly dusky! – and range through purple, blue, maroon, yellow and cream hues, usually with or contrasting centres.

Soil preference: Free-draining
Aspect: Sun or part shade
Season of interest: Spring
Height and spread: 20cm x 20cm (8in x 8in)

Companion plants: Pretty enough to include almost anywhere, garden auriculas traditionally lined cottage garden pathways. They mix sweetly with botanical tulips, forget-me-nots, fritillaries or anemones and are also superb as spring container plants.

Salix reticulata

Net Leaved Willow   Hardy, dwarf shrub

One of several prostrate willow species suitable for rock gardens or containers. The leaves are broadly oval, strong green with a prominent network of veining which makes their surfaces beautiful. Erect, greenish cream catkins are produced with the leaves. Other fine little willows include *Salix* 'Boydii' and the tiny *S. simulatrix*.

Soil preference: Any, free-draining but not too dry
Aspect: Sun, part shade, shade
Season of interest: Year-round
Height and spread: 10cm x 30cm (4in x 30in)

Companion plants: Dwarf prostrate willows are ideal as solo plants for an alpine pan or pot, but make good companions to ferns.

Planting Schemes Using Alpines

Alpine plants should be more popular and more widely grown than they are. Although some species are demanding and require expert culture, the great majority are no more difficult to look after than most perennials or annuals. Since they originate from widely different habitats, it is difficult to lay down hard and fast culture rules that would apply to all. However, the majority of easy alpines simply require extremely efficient drainage, soil that is not too nutrient-rich and plenty of sunshine.

Gentians

Gentians are among the most prized of alpine plants and, though they have specific needs, are not difficult to grow. This display (below) of the autumn-flowering Himalayan species *Gentiana sino-ornata* has been planted in moist but free-draining soil which has been enriched with leaf mould. Varieties like these, and species from which they have been developed, prefer the humid, cool atmosphere which prevails in their natural mountain habitat. The rich choice of different autumn gentians includes *G. farreri*, *G.* x *macauleyi* and *G. ternifolia* as well as such cultivars as *G.* 'Inverleith' and *G.* 'Kingfisher'.

Alpines are excellent for roaming freely over stony or rocky surfaces, adding interest to an otherwise dull area of the garden.

Wild thyme

The alpines growing in the main picture opposite are suitable for absolute beginners and are, by and large, indestructible. The downside of such qualities is that some of them may prove to be a little too vigorous, overtaking more sedate or delicate neighbours and smothering all in their path. The most colourful plant, at the time the picture was shot, is wild thyme, *Thymus serpyllum*, a species which rapidly forms a network of running stems, each furnished with tiny leaves. The broadening mats of foliage thus formed are mossy in appearance and are decorative through the year. In early summer, however, the bright purple blossoms cover the plants, making vivid patches of colour.

The soft texture of the thyme flowers makes an exciting contrast with the neat rosettes of the sempervivums growing in the side of the wall, a contrast which still holds off-season, when the thyme is only in leaf. Above, larger plants including *Geranium macrorrhizum* and a mound-forming saxifrage will have guaranteed earlier flower colour, and will also give pleasing autumn foliage.

Scale is particularly important. The gem-like quality of alpine plants is easily overpowered if there are outsize specimens growing nearby and, in this case, alpine forms of both Geranium and Iberis would have been a more desirable choice. A very close relative of *G. macrorrhizum* is *G. dalmaticum*, whose growth habits and flowering are very similar, but which is very much smaller in all its parts. There are several alpine species of candytuft which stay small and compact, and which have the added advantage of being evergreen. *Iberis sempervirens* 'Weisser Zwerg' ('Little Gem') would have been a shrewder choice.

The autumn-flowering Gentian, *Gentiana sino-ornata*, is an ideal choice to inject stunning colour into an alpine scheme at the time of year when colour may be disappearing in the garden.

perennials

Doronicum orientale

Leopard's Bane   Hardy perennial

Bold, toothed, heart-shaped basal foliage develops in early spring, from among which sparsely branched or single, erect flower stems rapidly extend. Buds open in early spring sunshine, to form bold, golden daisies whose large, narrow-rayed flowers attract early butterflies and bees. Susceptible to mollusc damage, but otherwise, easy to grow.

Soil preference: Any, not too dry
Aspect: Sun or part shade
Season of interest: Spring
Height and spread: 45cm x 30cm (1ft 6in x 1ft)

Companion plants: Striking flowers which contrast boldly with tulips, especially red-flowered varieties, but also beautiful to harmonise with spring and late winter-flowering euphorbias such as *Euphorbia* x *martini* or *E. characias*.

Gentiana acaulis

Gentian   Low-growing perennial or alpine

A low-growing, mat-forming perennial which, in spring, produces a succession of elongated, tubular, trumpet-shaped flowers held on short stems just clear of the foliage. The petals are an intense deep blue, often with streaks of green, white or dark purple-black in their throats or along the outsides of the tube.

Soil preference: Any not too dry, but free-draining
Aspect: Sun
Season of interest: Spring
Height and spread: 10cm x 30cm (4in x 1ft)

Companion plants: Increasingly useful plant for modern, ground level planting schemes in shingle or among paving where it teams well with such other ground huggers as Pratia, Acaena and with small cranesbills such as *Geranium dalmaticum*.

Iris unguicularis

Algerian Iris   Hardy evergreen perennial

Tough, grassy, somewhat untidy evergreen foliage develops, over several seasons, into a loose tussock. Large but fragile flowers emerge, in winter, among the foliage, in colours ranging through gentle mid-blues, to mauve or white. Varieties to seek include 'Mary Barnard' (violet blue flowers) and 'Alba' (white flowers). Happiest on a dry, sunny bank or tucked into the base of a warm wall.

Soil preference: Free-draining
Aspect: Sun
Season of interest: Winter
Height and spread: 30cm x 45cm (1ft x 1ft 6in)

Companion plants: The flowers are best if picked, but plants are attractive dotted among dwarf bearded iris hybrids, *Euphorbia characias*, with verbascums, perhaps, and Schizostylis for summer and autumn blooms.

Primula veris   Cowslip   Hardy perennial

A rosette-forming, grassland species which stays compact when grown in turf but grows taller and larger in tilled soil. Oblong, spoon-shaped wrinkled leaves and downy stems are topped, in spring, with hanging clusters of pale green calyces and small, mustard yellow flowers which have a faint, but sweet fragrance. Many garden forms are available, but the true cowslip is the most peerless wild beauty.

Soil preference: Any
Aspect: Sun or part shade
Season of interest: Spring
Height and spread: 20cm x 15cm (8in x 6in)

Companion plants: Prettiest in turf among cuckoo flowers, daisies and snakeshead fritillaries, following on from wild daffodils. In a spring border, team it with forget-me-nots, pansies or hybrid daisies.

Lathyrus vernus

Spring Vetch, Spring Pea   Hardy perennial

A clump-forming, early developing perennial with short stems bearing oval, pointed leaves in pairs or groups of up to four. Among these, clusters of vivid magenta pea flowers appear and last through much of spring. Selected forms include 'Cyaneus', whose flowers are steely blue, and the pale pink flowered 'Alboroseus' (pictured).

Soil preference: Any, not too dry but free-draining
Aspect: Sun or part shade
Season of interest: Spring
Height and spread: 30cm x 45cm (1ft x 1ft 6in)

Companion plants: The bright magenta makes a superb contrast with the sharp yellow blooms of *Doronicum orientale* or with daffodils and narcissus. Harmonizes well with honesty, *Lunaria annua*, and with such mauve or purple tulip varieties as 'Queen of the Night' or 'Negrita'.

Pulsatilla vulgaris   Pasque Flower   Hardy perennial

A European limestone species (of a widespread genera) with finely divided foliage and downy, erect stems bearing nodding flowers whose petals have inner surfaces of brilliant purple-mauve, contrasting with intensely golden stamens. Attractively fluffy seedheads follow. Garden selections include *P.* var. *rubra*, whose blooms are dull red, and 'Alba,' but none is so fine as the typical wild form.

Soil preference: Free-draining, preferably limy
Aspect: Sun
Season of interest: Spring
Height and spread: 25cm x 20cm (10in x 8in)

Companion plants: Interesting with the closely related Anemone tribe, especially *A. fulgens* or the Greek anemone, *A. pavonina*, and attractive with small perennial wallflowers such as *Erysimum* 'Moonlight' and other rock garden plants.

Phlox paniculata Border Phlox Hardy perennial

Big, bold, clump-forming perennials with simple leaves, erect stems and generous panicles of fragrant, disc-shaped flowers, ranging through a full spectrum of pastel hues, often with bi-colours. Superb for cutting. Outstanding varieties include 'Mount Fuji' (white), 'Prospero' (mauve, pale centres) and 'Le Mahdi' (purple to blue). 'Windsor' has reddish pink flowers and 'Prince of Orange' is bright salmon orange.

Soil preference: Any fertile, well-drained
Aspect: Sun, or part shade
Season of interest: Summer
Height and spread: Up to 1.3m x 75cm (4ft x 3ft)

Companion plants: Classic border plants to team with hybrid Achillea such as 'Coronation Gold' or 'Terracotta' or to contrast with the big white daisy flowers of *Leucanthemum* x *superbum*, warm-coloured heleniums or rudbeckias.

Armeria juniperifolia Thrift, Sea Pink Hardy perennial

A bushy, compact form of 'thrift' or sea pink from Spain, whose short, grassy leaves form a low, soft mound above which the thin flower stems rise. These are generously clustered with flowerheads tightly packed with bright pink. 'Bevans Variety' has dark foliage and short stems, very well furnished with flowers.

Soil preference: Very free-draining
Aspect: Sun
Season of interest: Summer
Height and spread: 15cm x 20cm (6in x 8in)

Companion plants: A fine candidate for a Mediterranean planting scheme, perhaps set among annual Cerinthe, low-growing varieties of lavender, marjorams (Origanum) and decorative thymes.

Dianthus Border Pinks Hardy perennials

Familiar garden plants with very narrow blue-green or silvery leaves produced in pairs along jointed stems. The flowers are usually intensely fragrant, often of cloves, with single or double petals, usually pinked or fringed along their tips – hence the name 'pink' (the colour derives its name from the flower, not the other way round). Of the wide choice of garden forms, favourite varieties include 'Doris', 'Gran's Favourite', 'Mrs Sinkins' and 'Fenbow Nutmeg Clove'.

Soil preference: Any free-draining
Aspect: Sun
Season of interest: Summer, autumn
Height and spread: Variable to 30cm x 30cm (1ft x 1ft)

Companion plants: Pinks are perfect at the feet of roses, especially *Rosa gallica* 'Versicolor' or 'Maiden's Blush'. Also contrasts well with the compact *Lavandula* 'Hidcote' and artemisia forms or *Salvia argentea*.

Catananche caerulea

Cupid's Dart   Hardy perennial

From clumps of soft, narrow, slightly lobed leaves spring large numbers of thin, waving stems which carry single flowers with papery sepals and soft petals arranged in ray formation. Typical flower colour is azure, but 'Alba' (pictured) has white petals with darker flower centres and 'Major' has deep blue flowers.

Soil preference: Any free-draining
Aspect: Sun
Season of interest: Summer
Height and spread: 6ocm x 30cm (2ft x 1ft)

Companion plants: Excellent in a mixed border of cool colours with low growing phloxes, perhaps, or with Platycodon or low growing campanulas such as *C. carpatica*.

Kniphofia hybrids

Torch Lily, Red Hot Pokers   Hardy or near hardy perennials

Big tussocks or clumps of coarse, grass-like leaves from which spring fleshy, erect stems carrying tightly packed flower buds at their tips. These lengthen as they mature to form tubular flowers in warm hues, often changing colour as they age. Hybrids include 'Little Maid' (creamy white), 'Green Jade', 'Toffee Nosed' (caramel tip, cream lower down the spike) and 'Bees Sunset' (yellowy orange). Natives of southern Africa.

Soil preference: Any free-draining, but not too dry
Aspect: Sun
Season of interest: Summer, autumn
Height and spread: Up to 1.5m x 1m (5ft x 3ft)

Companion plants: Spikes contrast well with round flowers such as marigolds or rudbeckias, but their colours go well with the blues and purples of, say, *Verbena* 'Homestead Purple', the lilac *Penstemon* 'Alice Hindley' or dark plum coloured *P.* 'Blackbird'.

Scabiosa columbaria   Small Scabious   Hardy perennial

Sparsely branched stems, furnished with grey-green, divided foliage, carry conspicuous flowers in a flattened convex shape with larger petals surrounding more tightly bunched central florets. Gardenworthy varieties include *S. c.* subsp. *ochroleuca*, whose flowers are pale primrose yellow, pastel hued 'Butterfly Blue' and 'Pink Mist'. Loved by bees and butterflies.

Soil preference: Any free-draining
Aspect: Sun or part shade
Season of interest: Summer, autumn
Height and spread: 6ocm x 45cm (2ft x 1ft 6in)

Companion plants: Popular in large bedding schemes, but also valuable as border plants to impart a 'cottage garden' feel. Pretty with pale yellow Achillea or with border pinks.

Achillea millefolium

Yarrow, Milfoil   Hardy perennial

A common wild herb with deeply divided foliage and large, flattened umbels of bloom. Selected varieties of this easiest of perennials include 'Terracotta' – tan to apricot orange, 'Lachsschönheit' (translates 'Salmon Beauty'), pale yellow 'Moonshine', 'Cerise Queen', 'Paprika' and Apfelblüte (translates 'Appleblossom'), which is dappled white and blush. Divide frequently to keep them young.

Soil preference: Any free-draining
Aspect: Sun
Season of interest: Summer, autumn
Height and spread: To 75cm x 60cm (2ft 6in x 2ft)

Companion plants: Wonderful border companions for scabious, lupins, bell flowers or the handsome grey foliage of *Anaphalis margaritacea* or *Artemisia ludoviciana*.

Agapanthus

African Lily, Blue Lily of the Nile   Near hardy, bulbous perennials

Glossy, strap-like leaves and tall, straight stems which carry umbels of blue, funnel-shaped or tube shaped flowers. Hardiest varieties are raised from *A. campanulatus* or its forms. *A. c.* var. 'Albidus' is a hardy white form and characterful cultivars include 'Lilliput', a dwarf; 'Midnight Star', dark blue; 'Jack's Blue', vigorous mid-blue; and the variegated leaf form, 'Silver Moon'.

Soil preference: Fertile, free-draining
Aspect: Sun, partial shade
Season of interest: Summer
Height and spread: Up to 1m x 45cm (3ft x 1ft 6in)

Companion plants: Superb container plants, but also beautiful in a mixed border where they can contrast with yellow flowers such as Lysimachia, Oenothera or Coreopsis, or to harmonize with lilac to blue asters or blue and white campanulas.

Anchusa azurea   Alkanet   Hardy perennial

A coarse stemmed, broad leaved perennial whose rugose surfaces are covered with fine bristles. Flowering stems are tall and multi-branched, carrying a long run of intense blue blossoms. 'Loddon Royalist' is the finest deep blue variety; 'Opal' has silvery leaves and pale blue flowers; and 'Little John' is a dwarf.

Soil preference: Any free-draining
Aspect: Sun
Season of interest: Summer.
Height and spread: Up to 1.5m x 75cm (5ft x 2ft 6in)

Companion plants: Large varieties make strong focal points, especially with equally dramatic companions. With the yellow flowered *Verbascum bombyciferum* or with the earlier flowering *Crambe cordifolia*, they are superb.

Anemone x hybrida

Japanese Anemones, Summer Anemones   Hardy perennials

Large, slightly downy three-lobed compound leaves develop from the running rootstock during early summer. The flower stems are well branched and bear large flowers in pink, white or rose-purple, each having a bold central tuft of stamens. Fine varieties include the white 'Honorine Jobert', pale pink 'September Charm' and deeper pink *A. hupehensis* var. *japonica* 'Prinz Heinrich'.

Soil preference: Any free-draining
Aspect: Sun, part shade, shade
Season of interest: Late summer, autumn
Height and spread: To 2m (6ft), spreading

Companion plants: Excellent for naturalizing among trees or shrubs, especially on poor or dry soil. Team them with late-blooming *Aconitum carmichaelii* or with autumn lilies such as *Lilium auratum*.

Campanula lactiflora

Milky Bellflower   Hardy perennial

Tuberous, non-spreading root system produces sturdy, many-branched stems which are richly arrayed with loose clusters of open bell-shaped flowers. Typically, flower colour is pale blue, but white forms are common and a lavender pink selection is 'Loddon Anna'. The blue flowered 'Prichard's Variety' is smaller and more compact.

Soil preference: Any fertile, free-draining
Aspect: Sun, part shade
Season of interest: Summer
Height and spread: To 1.5m x 60cm (5ft x 2ft)

Companion plants: Useful companions for big, sprawling shrubs such as buddlejas or shrub roses – especially old fashioned varieties.

Lupinus polyphyllus   Lupin   Hardy perennial

Distinctive bright green, palmate leaves which are especially beautiful when bejewelled by raindrops. The columnar flower spikes carry closely packed, spicy-scented pea flowers in strong, clean colours across the spectrum. 'Russel' lupins, developed between the two World Wars, are progenitors to modern varieties such as 'Troop the Colour' (red), 'Rosalind Woodfield' (yellow) and, ahem, 'Nigel Colborn' creamy white.

Soil preference: Fertile, well-drained but not too dry
Aspect: Sun or part shade
Season of interest: Spring, summer
Height and spread: To 1.2m x 45cm (4ft x 1ft 6in)

Companion plants: Classic components of an early summer border, especially with big oriental poppies, but also striking among tall grasses or simply lined up with larkspurs, cornflowers and marigolds for cutting.

Aquilegia vulgaris

Granny's Bonnet, Columbine   Hardy perennial

Glaucous green, prettily lobed, almost ferny foliage borne on thin stems, give this perennial much of its charm. Branched, erect flower stems carry complex blooms which resemble groups of perching doves – hence the name, 'Columbine'. The wild form may be blue, pink or white, but selected seed series are available, including the pink double 'Nora Barlow' and its derivatives.

Soil preference: Any
Aspect: Part shade or sun
Season of interest: Late spring, early summer
Height and spread: To 1m x 45cm (3ft 3in x 1ft 6in)

Companion plants: Essentially woodland plants, columbines are handy for following on from winter and spring displays of hellebores, primulas, epimediums and bulbs.

Aconitum napellus

Monkshood, Wolfsbane   Hardy perennial

A poisonous plant with divided, rounded leaves and tall erect, non-branched stems which carry evenly spaced flowers whose upper petals are developed into hoods or cowl-like shapes. Typical colour is a deep, dusky blue, but garden forms and monkshood hybrids come in a wider range, including *A.* 'Ivorine' (cream), 'Bressingham Spire', which is purple blue and 'Bicolor' – blue and white.

Soil preference: Any not too dry
Aspect: Shade, part shade or sun
Season of interest: Summer
Height and spread: 1.5m x 75cm (5ft x 3ft 6in)

Companion plants: The low key blues benefit from leavening companions such as brightly variegated or golden sedges – try *Carex elata* 'Aurea' – and also look beautiful with rich pink blooms of penstemons, say, or sidalceas.

Astilbe

False Spiraea   Hardy perennial

Pleated, toothed compound leaves, often with dark stems, develop into attractive basal mounds in spring and early summer. The plume-like flowers are held well clear of the foliage, and range in colour through white, mauve and pale pink to deep, burning red. Outstanding varieties include 'Deutschland' (white), 'Fanal' (bright red), 'Venus' (soft pink) and 'Perkeo', a dwarf hybrid with pink blooms.

Soil preference: Moist, fertile
Aspect: Shade or part shade
Season of interest: Summer
Height and spread: Variable to 2m (6ft), usually less

Companion plants: The finest plants for a rich, moist border or even a bog garden, where they thrive with *Siberian iris*, Ligularia and Rodgersia. Astilbes are also wonderful unaccompanied except by their own kind.

Astrantia major

Masterwort, Melancholy Gentleman   Hardy perennial

Deeply lobed, rounded leaves and sparsely branched stems which carry the curious flowers. These consist of coloured bracts, in the shape of a multi-rayed star, on which sit the small flowers held in tufts like microscopic bouquets. Colourful varieties include 'Hadspen Blood' (dark red) and 'Sunningdale Variegated'.

Soil preference: Any, not too dry
Aspect: Sun, part shade or shade
Season of interest: Summer, autumn
Height and spread: 60cm x 30cm (2ft x 1ft)

Companion plants: Fine cottage perennials, as attractive among naturalistic plantings of grasses and wild herbs as in a more formal border with dahlias, say, or Anthemis or campanulas.

Cephalaria gigantea

Giant Scabious   Hardy perennial

A gigantic perennial with handsome, compound foliage and very tall, arching, but largely self-supporting, branched stems which carry a scattering of large, typical scabious flowers (see page 133) that are primrose yellow. The pale flower colour shows up well against the dark sepals and stems.

Soil preference: Any, not too dry
Aspect: Part shade
Season of interest: Summer
Height and spread: To 2.5m x 1.5m (8ft x 5ft)

Companion plants: A distinctive focal point plant, but to scale up, try growing it with larger forms of *Miscanthus sinensis*, or perhaps with *Rudbeckia* 'Herbstsonne' for later colour.

Ligularia dentata   Golden Groundsel   Hardy perennial

A massive, fleshy perennial with thick stems and large, rounded, often toothed leaves borne on erect stems. The flower spikes, which develop during midsummer, are well-branched and carry showy orange or yellow daisy flowers. The best garden hybrids include the orange flowered 'Desdemona', whose leaf-backs and stems are dark mahogany, and the later 'Gregynog Gold', with green leaves and rich yellow flowers. *Ligularia przewalskii* (pictured) has narrow, tall flower spikes and oval, toothed leaves.

Soil preference: Fertile, moist
Aspect: Shade, part shade or sun
Season of interest: Summer
Height and spread: 1.25m x 1m (4ft x 3ft)

Companion plants: A fine plant for a big border or bog garden, excellent to plant among willows, or with large wetland species such as Lysichiton or Darmera.

Geum rivale

Water Avens, Wild Geum   Hardy perennial

Downy leaves form basal rosettes from which spring sparsely branched stems that carry the nodding, rose-like flowers. Flower colour, in nature, is variable from creamy or pink to greenish white. Cultivars include 'Lionel Cox' (cream), 'Coppertone' (orange) and 'Leonard's Variety' (bright coppery pink).

Soil preference: Any, not too dry
Aspect: Shade, part shade
Season of interest: Spring, summer
Height and spread: To 30cm x 30cm (1ft x 1ft)

Companion plants: Useful woodlanders to blend with such low, shade tolerant perennials as *Hacquetia epipactis*, *Brunnera macrophylla* or *Omphalodes verna*.

Hypericum olympicum   Hardy, shrubby perennial

From a shrubby base, slender herbaceous stems develop and are furnished with small, oval, simple leaves. Flowers are produced over a long period in summer and are bright yellow with attractive golden stamens. The form *H. olympicum* f. *uniflorum* 'Citrinum' has large, lemon yellow flowers.

Soil preference: Any well-drained
Aspect: Part shade, sun
Season of interest: Spring
Height and spread: 20cm x 20cm (8in x 8in)

Companion plants: Useful for a dry spot, especially when associated with low-growing perennials or alpines such as *Origanum laevigatum* or *Alchemilla conjuncta*.

Dicentra formosa   Wild Bleeding Heart   Hardy perennial

Delicate, lacy foliage whose green is subtly suffused with purple in some varieties. In spring, fleshy, almost glassy stems hold the nodding clusters of narrow, tubular, lipped flowers well above the foliage. 'Stuart Boothman' has dark foliage and dusky pink flowers; 'Langtrees' has white flowers; and 'Luxuriant' has almost crimson blooms. Spreading, but non-invasive.

Soil preference: Any not too dry, but well-drained
Aspect: Part shade
Season of interest: Spring
Height and spread: 30cm (1ft), spreading

Companion plants: A fine ground cover plant between low growing shrubs, such as daphnes. Also lovely for a spring border, among bulbs such as hyacinths or narcissus and polyanthus or oxlips.

Geranium wallichianum 'Buxton's Variety'

Hardy, creeping perennial

Creeping, but by no means invasive stems form a loose network from which, from late summer, produces a succession of pale blue flowers, each five petalled and with white centres. As autumn advances, the foliage often colours up to rusty gold.

Soil preference: Any, not too dry
Aspect: Part shade or sun
Season of interest: Late summer, autumn
Height and spread: 15cm (6in), spreading

Companion plants: Charming companion to shrubs or trees which colour well in autumn. All Japanese maples, *Berberis thunbergii*, *Prunus incisa* 'Kojo-no-mai' and deciduous rhododendron (azaleas) would all make excellent companions.

Heuchera garden hybrids   Coral Bells   Hardy perennials

Rhizome-forming perennials whose basal foliage has been selected to produce a number of richly coloured cultivars, usually with purple leaves, often with pewter or silvery suffusions. Flower stems, thin and numerous, carry misty sprays of small white, greenish or pinkish blooms. Cultivars include 'Plum Pudding', 'Pewter Moon', 'Chocolate Ruffles' and 'Mint Frost' (silvery white on a green background). Prone to vine weevil attack.

Soil preference: Free-draining, not too dry
Aspect: Part shade or sun
Season of interest: Year round
Height and spread: To 60cm x 45cm (2ft x 1ft 6in)

Companion plants: In demand among trendy gardeners for planting in gravel with grasses or for producing rich colour schemes with crimson and scarlet blooms. Some varieties are lovely in woodland plantings with Polygonatum, Convallaria and perhaps wood anemones.

Mimulus naiandinus (syn. 'Andean Nymph')

Monkey Flower, Musk   Near hardy perennial

A mat forming perennial with paired, glossy leaves and an almost constant run of asymmetrical trumpet-shaped flowers whose cream yellow background colour is overlaid with pink and whose throats are stippled with bold purplish pink. Easy to propagate from cuttings or division, but inclined to disappear in all but the gentlest winters.

Soil preference: Fertile, not too dry
Aspect: Sun or part shade
Season of interest: Summer
Height and spread: 20cm x 30cm (8in x 1ft)

Companion plants: Attractive in an informal planting of low perennials, especially in a moist corner with Tricyrtis, such ferns as *Polystichum setiferum* or *Athyrium filix-femina*, or in a sunnier spot along with low-growing penstemons and the grassy *Uncinia rubra*.

Violas and pansies

Pansies and violas are among the most easily cultivated plants in the temperate world and yet few groups offer so much reward for so little input. Flowering can be practically round the calendar, with special selections which bloom in winter and others which are never out of flower. Colours are variable enough to suit every taste and every scheme and many varieties are long-lived perennials. Propagation is easy too, both from cuttings and from seed, but this is a promiscuous genus and it can be difficult to keep colour series pure!

1. **'Tiger Eyes'**
2. **Sorbet 'Ice Blue'**
3. **'Ruby Gold'**
4. **'Blue Blotch'**
5. **'Baby Face Primrose'**
6. **'Rose Blotch'**
7. **'Rose Surprise'**
8. **Viola cornuta**
9. **V. cornuta 'Alba'**

1	2	3
4	5	6
7	8	9

Actaea matsumurae (syn. Cimicifuga)

Bugbane   Hardy perennial

Large, decorative leaf stems which carry many-lobed, irregularly divided leaves, sometimes suffused with purple-black. At summer's end, tall, single stems carry rat-tail flowers, often dusky pink in bud, opening white. 'Elstead Variety' has bronze coloured leaves and dark tinged buds and 'White Pearl' is green-leaved. The *A. simplex* cultivar 'Brunette' has brownish purple foliage.

Soil preference: Any, not too dry
Aspect: Shade, part shade
Season of interest: Summer, autumn
Height and spread: 1.2m x 60cm (4ft x 2ft)

Companion plants: As valuable for the foliage as the flower, but useful as a late follow-on to schemes with Polygonatum, euphorbias or candelabra primulas.

Aruncus dioicus   Goat's Beard   Hardy perennial

A large species from Europe which forms clumps of pleated, divided leaves with red-tinged stems. Male and female plants occur, the former having tall, much-branched stems of creamy white, catkin-like blooms. The less conspicuous female flowers are greenish cream, pendulous and produce attractive arching panicles of seed heads.

Soil preference: Any, not too dry
Aspect: Shade, part shade
Season of interest: Summer
Height and spread: 1.75m x 1m (6ft by 3ft 3in)

Companion plants: A striking woodlander, best among such large plants as *Carex pendula* or with ligularias, Siberian irises or perhaps the closely related filipendulas. Also useful to associate with spring-flowering shrubs for a late summer lift.

Macleaya cordata

Plume Poppy, Tree Celandine   Hardy, creeping perennial

An invasive perennial whose distinctive, rounded, deeply lobed leaves are grey-green, with paler undersides. The flowers are massed but tiny, appearing as plumes atop the very tall stems. A striking and beautiful species, but should be planted only where it can be controlled or where its relentless spread will be welcomed.

Soil preference: Humus-rich, not too dry
Aspect: Shade, part shade or sun
Season of interest: Summer
Height and spread: 2.4m (8ft), spreading

Companion plants: Ideal for filling spaces between large shrubs and ornamental trees, especially spring blooming varieties that turn dull in summer. In herbaceous plantings, try it with Cortaderia, *Gunnera manicata*, *Miscanthus sinensis* and other big thugs.

Chaerophyllum hirsutum 'Roseum'

Pink Cow Parsley, Hairy Chervil   Hardy perennial

Looking like pink cow parsley but blooming earlier than its hedgerow lookalike, this has deeply divided ferny foliage which is gently aromatic - redolent of apples - and makes an enchanting foil for the large umbels of bright purplish pink flowers which are in full colour by mid-spring. Must be divided frequently to keep the roots young.

Soil preference: Humus-rich, not too dry
Aspect: Shade, part shade, sun
Season of interest: Spring
Height and spread: 60cm x 30cm (2ft x 1ft)

Companion plants: A valuable spring perennial to plant with *Lathyrus vernus* or to blend with sweet cicely, *Myrrhis odoratus*, whose larger, white umbels emerge later.

Euphorbia amygdaloides

Wood Spurge   Hardy perennial

Evergreen woodland perennial with thick stems which exude toxic, milky latex if wounded. The dark green leaves are attractively arranged in whorls and contrast with the lime-green bracts which surround the spring flowers. Best forms include the dark 'Purpurea' and reddish, mildew-resistant 'Craigieburn'.

Soil preference: Any, humus-rich
Aspect: Shade or part shade
Season of interest: Spring, summer
Height and spread: Variable to 75cm x 45cm (2ft 6in x 1ft 6in)

Companion plants: Ideal for naturalizing in a woodland with bluebells, campions, violets, primroses, Trillium and oxlips. *E. a.* var. *robbiae* is a rapid colonizer even in dry shade.

Helleborus foetidus

Stinking Hellebore   Hardy perennial

Evergreen plant with distinctive palmate leaves whose leaflets are toothed and pointed. In winter, panicles of bright green flowers develop, sometimes with reddish or purplish edges to their sepals, and persist into early summer. Wester Flisk Group has foliage suffused with pewter grey and reddish stems. A free seeder.

Soil preference: Any, but happiest in calcareous soils
Aspect: Shade, part shade, sun
Season of interest: Winter, spring, summer
Height and spread: 60cm x 45cm (3ft x 1ft 6in)

Companion plants: A 'stand-alone' species often most attractive where it seeds itself along pathways or in gravelly landscapes. The flowers harmonize well with early daffodils or can contrast their green with red or yellow tulips, or with peonies.

Helleborus orientalis hybrids   Hardy perennials

Leathery, palmate leaves which emerge in spring persist through summer, but are best removed each autumn to prevent disease carry-over. The large, five-sepalled flowers appear from late winter. Garden varieties, although known as 'Orientalis Hybrids', are derived from a number of European species and come in a wide range of colours, shapes and sizes. Hues may be white, shades of pink and purple, yellow or bright green.

Soil preference: Humus-rich, fertile, not too dry, yet well-drained
Aspect: Shade, part shade
Season of interest: Winter, spring, early summer
Height and spread: Variable to 40cm x 45cm (1ft 4in x 1ft 6in)

Companion plants: Mainstay of a winter herbaceous display and perfect companions to bulbs such as snowdrops, crocuses, winter irises and *Leucojum vernum*. Also effective among Prunus, Forsythia and Salix.

Anthriscus sylvestris

Cow Parsley, Queen Anne's Lace   Hardy perennial

Deeply divided, ferny foliage develops rapidly during spring before the much-branched, hollow stems extend and produce parachute-shaped umbels of pure white flowers. The foliage is aromatic. Selected garden forms include the dark-leaved 'Ravenswing'. Wild forms are invasive through copious self-seeding.

Soil preference: Any
Aspect: Part shade, shade
Season of interest: Spring, summer
Height and spread: To 1.5m x 75cm (5ft x 2ft 6in)

Companion plants: A fitting climax to a woodland spring display, lovely among pink campion or ragged robin (*Lychnis flos-cuculi*) or to follow from bluebells. Good for creating foamy drifts between large shrubs such as flowering currants, shrub roses or Cytisus.

Myrrhis odorata

Sweet Cicely   Hardy perennial

A large, sweetly aromatic umbellifer with divided, fern-like leaves and stems bearing flattened umbels of small, pure white flowers in early summer. The black seeds that follow are large, ribbed and elongated. Invasive, but beautiful for filling an otherwise dull corner. The leaves can be used in place of sugar for sweetening rhubarb or other tart fruits.

Soil preference: Any
Aspect: Shade or part shade
Season of interest: Spring, summer
Height and spread: 1.5m x 1m (5ft by 3ft 3in)

Companion plants: Too invasive to plant alongside delicate perennials but excellent as a base ground cover in a shrubbery or beneath trees.

Smilacina racemosa

False Spikenard, False Solomon's Seal   Hardy perennial

Arching stems emerge from plump rhizomes and carry paired leaves along their length. The flowers, which develop in mid-spring, consist of creamy tufts which form at the ends of the stems. In late summer and autumn, small, reddish berries develop in clusters and persist while the foliage turns from green to soft gold before withering.

Soil preference: Humus-rich, well-drained but not too dry
Aspect: Part shade, shade
Season of interest: Spring, summer, autumn
Height and spread: 90cm x 75cm (3ft x 2ft 6in)

Companion plants: Pretty with the related Solomon's Seals and with such colourful spring perennials as Pulmonaria or Mertensia. Natural dwellers of the woodland floor, with epimediums, trilliums and wild columbines.

Symphytum caucasicum   Comfrey   Hardy perennial

A relatively compact comfrey with large, oval, pointed dark grey-green leaves and branched flower stems which carry a long succession of tubular flowers, pinkish in bud but opening to an intense blue. Cutting back spent flower stems will stimulate new growth. Adored by bees.

Soil preference: Any, preferably moist
Aspect: Part shade, shade or sun
Season of interest: Spring, summer
Height and spread: 80cm x 80cm (2ft 6in x 2ft 6in)

Companion plants: The lush foliage and relatively sparse number of flowers associate well with showier early perennials such as oriental poppies or lupins.

Veratrum album

False Hellebore   Hardy perennial

A highly poisonous plant with large, oval, pointed basal leaves which are deeply indented with parallel pleats, especially when young. Tall, sparsely branched flower spikes develop during summer and bear large numbers of small, greenish white blooms.

Type: Hardy perennial
Soil preference: Any moist, but well-drained
Aspect: Shade, part shade.
Season of interest: Spring, summer, autumn
Height and spread: To 1.5m x 1m (5ft by 3ft 3in)

Companion plants: The bold, distinctive foliage contrasts dramatically with such other shade loving plants as hellebores, spring-flowering paeonies and the fussier leaves of *Aruncus dioicus*.

Hacquetia epipactis   Hardy perennial

In winter, bunched, ground-hugging buds gradually unfurl and produce blooms which consist of lobed, green collars with tightly packed tufts of bright golden florets at their centres. Rounded, slightly lobed foliage follows, eventually covering the developing seedheads. Understated but utterly charming. The white variegated form 'Thor' will suit some tastes.

Soil preference: Any, not too dry
Aspect: Shade, part shade
Season of interest: Flowers, spring, foliage in summer
Height and spread: 15cm x 20cm (6in by 8in)

Companion plants: A delight with spring bulbs, following on from winter aconites and snowdrops, and accompanying dwarf narcissus, hepaticas or wood anemones. Over-wintering ferns such as *Asplenium scolopendrium* or Polystichum also go well.

Epimedium grandiflorum   Barrenwort   Hardy perennial

A deciduous epimedium which, in early spring, produces thin stemmed, loose flower spikes with four-pointed flowers in white, pink or pale purple. The bronze-tinted leaves, which emerge soon after the flowers, form an attractive mound for the rest of summer, turning colour again in autumn. Garden selections include 'Rose Queen' and 'White Queen'.

Soil preference: Free-draining, humus-rich but not too dry
Aspect: Shade, part shade
Season of interest: Spring, summer
Height and spread: 30cm x 30cm (12in x 12in)

Companion plants: Attractive when teamed with such fellow Japanese species as Primula sieboldii or with hostas for their later foliage. Small spring bulbs, such as Leucojum vernum and low growing Narcissus varieties also make fine companions.

Liriope muscari   Lily Turf   Hardy perennial

A slow-spreading, clump-forming evergreen with dark green, strap-like leaves and, from early autumn, a long-lasting display of rigid flower spikes clustered with bead-like, violet-mauve flowers. Selected forms include 'Monroe White' (white blooms) and 'John Burch', whose leaves carry a yellow stripe. An indestructible plant, capable of surviving almost anywhere.

Soil preference: Any
Aspect: Sun, part shade, shade
Season of interest: Year round for foliage, autumn for flowers
Height and spread: 30cm x 45cm (12in x 1ft 6in)

Companion plants: Indispensable autumn flowers, useful for growing among shrubs, but striking if bedded, perhaps with colchicums, or set among autumn flowering chrysanthemums. Lovely when underplanted among hip-bearing roses such as *R. moyesii*.

Viola riviniana

Dog Violet, Wood Violet   Hardy perennial

Small evergreen plant with heart-shaped leaves and, in spring, non-scented but typical five-petalled 'violet' flowers. Unlike sweet violets, it lacks a running rootstock but is a prolific self-seeder. Colour varies from slaty blue-violet to pink or white. The form 'Purpurea' has dark leaves and deep violet blooms.

Soil preference: Any
Aspect: Shade, part shade
Season of interest: Spring, summer foliage
Height and spread: 15cm x 20cm (6in x 8in)

Companion plants: Pretty in lawn grass, seeding around in paving cracks, perhaps among *Alchemilla conjuncta*, or for naturalizing in wild or woodland gardens with primroses and wood anemones.

Anemone nemorosa

Wood Anemone   Hardy perennial

Creeping rhizomes from which stems emerge with divided foliage attached just below the single star-shaped flower in spring. Petal backs may be pinkish or purplish, opening in sun to reveal pure white interiors, which contrast with pale golden stamens. Garden selections are legion and include lilac-flowered 'Robinsoniana', blue-mauve 'Allenii' and 'Vestal', a semi-double white variety.

Soil preference: Humus-rich, not too dry
Aspect: Shade, part shade
Season of interest: Spring
Height and spread: To 20cm (8in), spreading

Companion plants: Woodland beauties, best allowed to form drifts among deciduous trees with bluebells, primroses and little wild daffodils.

Omphalodes verna

Blue Eyed Mary, Creeping Forget-me-not   Hardy perennial

Low-growing, European native from moist woodland habitats with oval, pleated, pointed leaves and from late winter, through spring, small sprays of vivid blue forget-me-not flowers, each with a white eye. The albino form 'Alba' has less vigour but pure white flowers.

Soil preference: Any, not too dry
Aspect: Shade, part shade
Season of interest: Spring
Height and spread: 15cm (6in), spreading

Companion plants: A carpeting plant in the right conditions, suitable as ground cover among spring shrubs or with other creeping plants such as *Euphorbia amygdaloides* var. *robbiae* or *Anemone nemorosa*.

Arctotis x hybrida   Half hardy perennial

South African plants with downy, sometimes silvery foliage and a constant succession of large daisy flowers, usually in hot colours. 'Flame' has fiery orange-red flowers; 'Red Devil' is scarlet, with dark petal bases; and 'Mahogany' has deep tan flowers. Easy to root from cuttings, but must be protected from winter frost.

Soil preference: Any free-draining
Aspect: Sun
Season of interest: Summer, autumn
Height and spread: 30cm x 30cm (1ft x 1ft)

Companion plants: Good companions on a hot, dry site would be silver artemisias, the closely related blue daisy *Felicia amelloides*, diascias and any Mediterranean shrubs or herbs.

Anaphalis margaritacea

Pearl Everlasting   Hardy perennial

Dark grey-green, oval foliage, whiter and more downy on the leaf undersides. In summer, tall stems carry flower clusters made conspicuous by the numerous pearly bracts that surround each bloom. Benefits from regular division.

Soil preference: Any free-draining
Aspect: Sun, partial shade
Season of interest: Summer, autumn
Height and spread: 75cm x 45cm (2ft 6in x 1ft 6in)

Companion plants: Best in a border where the silvery effect can contrast with the blues of delphiniums or campanulas, or with lush border phloxes or asters. Large sedums such as *Sedum spectabile* also make good association for later colour.

Cichorium intybus

Chicory, Succory   Hardy perennial

Long, lobed, basal leaves form a broad rosette from which grows a small number of main stems. These form branches as they mature, which carry a long run of stemless, many-rayed flowers usually in an intense sky blue. White and pink flowered forms also occur. Propagate regularly from seed to keep the stock young.

Soil preference: Any reasonably fertile
Aspect: Sun
Season of interest: Summer
Height and spread: To 1.5m x 30cm (5ft by 1ft)

Companion plants: The tall, gawky habit makes this a good background plant among more compact perennials such as gaillardias or heleniums in contrasting colours. Superb in a meadow planting with cranesbills, knapweeds and field scabious (Knautia).

Crambe cordifolia

Colewort   Hardy perennial

Huge, dark-green ruffled or puckered leaves develop in spring and are later joined by burgeoning flower stems, which explode into a cloud of tiny white, four-petalled blooms. These relatives of the cabbage are mildly fragrant when distant, but have a sickly aroma close-to. Easy to propagate from root cuttings.

Soil preference: Any free-draining
Aspect: Sun
Season of interest: Summer
Height and spread: 2m x 1m (6ft 6in x 3ft 3in)

Companion plants: The dramatic flower sprays are handy for creating a large scale, especially with similarly tall mulleins or *Verbena bonariensis*. Also superb as a focal point for an early summer climax among poppies, lupins, honesty or red valerian.

Asphodeline lutea

Yellow Asphodel, Jacob's Rod   Hardy perennial

Grass-like, sage-green basal foliage emerges in spring and as the rigid flower stems extend, these too are furnished with similar loosely twisting, narrow leaves. The flower buds crowd the top third of the stems and open to large, saffron yellow, six-petalled flowers, whose stamens are elegantly curved.

Soil preference: Any free-draining
Aspect: Sun
Season of interest: Summer
Height and spread: 1m x 30cm (3ft 3in x 12in)

Companion plants: Plants for an early summer mixed border, perhaps with oriental poppies or among such sun-loving shrubs as *Brachyglottis greyii* or, for later flowers, the blue Caryopteris or Perovskia.

Eryngium x oliverianum

Hybrid Sea Holly   Short-lived, hardy perennial

A bristling, spiny perennial with heart-shaped, prickly toothed leaves and blue-grey, branched stems whose many flowers sit in nests of star-shaped bracts, all with a silvery sheen, suffused with purplish blue. The individual florets are arranged in tight dome-shaped clusters. Despite resembling thistles, sea hollies belong to the carrot family.

Soil preference: Any free-draining
Aspect: Sun
Season of interest: Summer, autumn
Height and spread: 90cm x 50cm (3ft x 1ft 8in)

Companion plants: Plants for a dry border or a Mediterranean planting scheme, pretty when interspersed with brighter coloured Argyranthemums or Osteopermums, and with shrubs such as *Genista lydia* or with rock roses.

Crambe maritima

Sea Kale   Hardy perennial

A seashore plant, occurring in shingle beaches and banks, consisting of a long, durable tap root from which grow large, oval, glaucous grey-green leaves which are handsomely ruched. Sprays of off-white flowers, which have a muskily sweet smell, appear in early summer, followed by spherical, green seedheads.

Soil preference: Free-draining, poor soil preferred
Aspect: Sun
Season of interest: Spring, summer, autumn
Height and spread: 45cm x 75cm (1ft 6in x 2ft 6in)

Companion plants: Superb foliage plant for a dry setting. Lovely among perennial wallflowers, hardy annual poppies, euphorbias and small, Mediterranean shrubs.

Origanum laevigatum   Hardy perennial

A sparse-growing perennial with thin, woody branched stems and small, oval leaves. As summer advances, flower sprays form on the stems, carrying a long succession of tiny, rose-purple blossoms. Stems and leaf-backs are suffused with reddish purple. Easily established, especially in limy soils, where it self-seeds freely.

Soil preference: Dry, free-draining, limy
Aspect: Sun
Season of interest: Summer
Height and spread: 45cm x 45cm (1ft 6in x 1ft 6in)

Companion plants: A good plant for paving cracks or stony places, attractive with *Alchemilla mollis* or with *Verbena bonariensis*. Also interesting to plant with other oreganos, since they tend to hybridize and produce interesting seedlings.

Arctotis fastuosa

Cape Daisy, Monarch of the Veldt   Short-lived, tender perennial

Soft, hairy, deeply lobed, pale green leaves form a loose clump above which extending, but sometimes rather weak, stems hold the blooms just clear of the leaves. The flowers are large and showy, with pale white or yellow ray florets surrounding a deep blue to purple black central disc. 'Zulu Prince' is white, with a midnight blue centre.

Soil preference: Free-draining, fertile
Aspect: Sun
Season of interest: Summer
Height and spread: 45cm x 30cm (1ft 6in x 1ft)

Companion plants: Best planted near the front of a sunny flower border, where it can rub shoulders with such other bright plants as gazanias, diascias and, for late in the summer, Zauschneria.

Artemisia absinthium

Wormwood, Absinthe   Shrubby perennial

A shrubby plant with deeply divided, silvery green, filigree leaves and, in summer, small sprays of insignificant yellowish-green flowers. The foliage is soft to the touch and pleasantly aromatic. Selections include 'Lambrook Silver', a compact form with very silvery, lacy leaves. Cut back frequently to keep the plant young.

Soil preference: Any very dry, free-draining
Aspect: Sun
Season of interest: Spring, summer, autumn
Height and spread: To 90cm x 60cm (3ft x 2ft)

Companion plants: Classic candidate for the dry or Mediterranean border, beautiful with lavenders, rosemary and rock roses, especially when such summer bulbs as Gladiolus, Tigridia or Galtonia can bloom among them.

Lampranthus spectabilis

Half hardy, succulent perennial

A semi-trailing species with succulent leaves and branching stems forming low mounds which are covered, during the growing season, with masses of daisy-like flowers in pink, purple or crimson. Selected varieties include the purplish-flowered 'Tresco Brilliant' and the intensely coloured 'Tresco Red'. Protection from frost is essential.

Soil preference: Free-draining, dry
Aspect: Sun
Season of interest: Summer, autumn
Height and spread: 40cm x 50cm (1ft 4in x 1ft 10in)

Companion plants: Plants for a rock garden or a hot, sunny corner where their bright flower colour will show up well. Succulents such as Crassula, Aeonium, Opuntia and Echeveria make fitting companions.

Verbascum chaixii

Nettle-leaved Mullein   Hardy perennial

Basal rosettes of dark, deeply veined leaves from which arise successions of thin, erect stems bearing numerous small yellow flowers, each with a central boss of purple stamens. *Verbascum chaixii* 'Album' is lower growing with pure white flowers, which retain their purple centres. Longer lasting than most mulleins.

Soil preference: Free-draining, dry
Aspect: Sun
Season of interest: Summer
Height and spread: To 90cm x 45cm (3ft by 1ft 6in)

Companion plants: A lovely plant for enriching a dry border, either among annuals such as Cerinthe or poppies, with lacy artemisias, Helichrysum or Anaphalis for a foliage contrast.

Tanacetum coccineum   Pyrethrum   Hardy perennial

Feathery basal foliage develops in spring before the slender flower stems extend in early summer, carrying daisy blooms in shades of pink, white or crimson. Varieties include the wine red 'James Kelway', pale pink 'Eileen May Robinson' and 'Snow Cloud'. A popular cut flower a few years back. Wind-proof and easy to grow.

Soil preference: Any reasonably fertile
Aspect: Sun
Season of interest: Summer
Height and spread: To 60cm x 30cm (2ft x 1ft)

Companion plants: Classic plants to go near a border front. Effective with mid-height grasses or grass-like perennials or to contrast in shape and colour with campanulas or penstemons. Handsome when simply lined out with other 'cutting' flowers such as larkspurs and cornflowers.

Centranthus ruber

Red Valerian   Hardy perennial

Hairless foliage and branched, hollow stems develop rapidly during early summer and bear dense clusters of small pinkish red or white flowers, each with a tiny tail or spur. Seeds with downy parachutes disperse midsummer onwards and self-seeding is prolific. Cut back immediately after flowering to ensure second flushes of bloom.

Soil preference: Any, free-draining
Aspect: Sun
Season of interest: Summer
Height and spread: Up to 90cm x 45cm (3ft x 1ft 6in)

Companion plants: Excellent for very poor soil, at the base of a wall or on a dry bank where it blends attractively with *Euphorbia characias* or with *Alchemilla mollis*.

Osteospermum jucundum   Near hardy perennial

A mound-forming, hairless perennial with semi-prostrate stems and simple or lobed leaves. The large daisy flowers, which open in the sun, come in an almost constant succession through the growing season and may be mauve, pink or rich purple, always with a dark purple-blue central disc. Easy to multiply from cuttings.

Soil preference: Any free-draining, dry
Aspect: Sun
Season of interest: Summer, autumn
Height and spread: 30cm x 40cm (1ft by 1ft 4in)

Companion plants: Attractive at the edge of a hot border or in a sunny gravel scree with *Erigeron karvinskianus* or *Euphorbia myrsinites* and diascias or perennial nemesias.

Leucanthemum vulgare

Ox-eye Daisy, Moon Daisy   Hardy short-lived perennial

A meadow species which forms loose clumps of lobed basal leaves and sparsely branched stems carrying yellow centred, white daisy flowers. Best grown in harsh conditions or naturalized in grass to avoid coarse growth. A familiar wayside wilding throughout much of Europe.

Soil preference: Any
Aspect: Sun, part shade
Season of interest: Summer
Height and spread: 75cm x 30cm (2ft 6in x 1ft)

Companion plants: The ultimate meadow plant, lovely to follow from cowslips and snakeshead fritillaries and to associate with meadow cranesbill. In poor soil, team it with *Verbascum chaixii*, the origanums or honesty.

Malva moschata

Musk Mallow   Hardy perennial

Loose clumps of divided, rounded leaves and somewhat lax stems which carry a steady succession of large, saucer-shaped flowers in silvery pink, each with a fused central tower of stamens and stigma, from midsummer onwards. *Malva moschata* f. *alba* is a superb albino form, which comes true from seed.

Soil preference: Heavy, preferably calcareous
Aspect: Sun
Season of interest: Summer
Height and spread: To 90cm x 45cm (3ft x 1ft 6in)

Companion plants: A useful perennial to seed about in a mixed border. Lovely with hybrid achilleas such as 'Lachsschönheit' or 'Cerise Queen'.

Knautia macedonica   Hardy perennial

A loose, clump-forming perennial with sparse, divided, compound leaves and slender, branched stems which carry small to medium, blood-red, compound flowers with larger rays around their edges. Irresistible to bees and butterflies. Garden selections include 'Melton Pastels', which come in paler pink hues as well as deep crimson.

Soil preference: Any
Aspect: Sun
Season of interest: Summer
Height and spread: To 1m x 60cm (3ft 3in by 2ft)

Companion plants: Meadow plants, but equally beautiful in a colourful border, among tall cranesbills such as *Geranium pratense* or *G. psilostemon*, or with dahlias in a warm colour scheme, or blue campanulas and hardy summer salvias for a cooler effect.

Alstroemeria ligtu **hybrids**   Hardy perennial

Tall, slender stems, with simple, narrow leaves along their lengths, carry compact sprays of vividly coloured flowers in bright sunset hues – orange, yellow, ochre – often with contrasting stripes on their petals. Difficult to transplant, owing to a fragile root system, but easy to establish from carefully planted container specimens or from self-sown seed.

Soil preference: Free-draining, reasonably fertile
Aspect: Sun, but out of harsh winds
Season of interest: Summer
Height and spread: 1m x 30cm (3ft 3in x 1ft)

Companion plants: Best naturalized among informally planted perennials such as campanulas, cranesbills or scabious, where their hot colours make a cheerful contrast.

Anemonopsis macrophylla   Hardy perennial

A delicate woodland perennial from Japan, hardy but susceptible to wind damage. Clumps of two- or three-part leaves develop during spring, from among which the nodding flowers are borne on slender, dark stems. These have curved, pale lilac sepals, elegantly held above the smaller mauve petals. Slow to increase, but of surpassing beauty.

Soil preference: Humus-rich, fertile
Aspect: Shade or part shade, sheltered
Season of interest: Summer
Height and spread: 75cm x 30cm (2ft 6in x 12in)

Companion plants: Lovely to follow from earlier woodland species such as aquilegias, spring bulbs or oxlips, and to team with the berry-bearing *Actaea rubra*.

Argyranthemum **hybrids**

Marguerite   Shrubby tender perennial

Shrubby perennials, developed from a number of Madeiran and Canary Island natives, with hairless, lobed, divided leaves and many-branched stems which produce, throughout the growing season, masses of daisy flowers in colours varying from white, through pink or apricot shades to lemon or yellow.

Soil preference: Any, fertile, free-draining
Aspect: Sun, prefers shelter
Season of interest: Spring, summer, autumn
Height and spread: Variable to 90cm x 75cm (3ft x 2ft 6in)

Companion plants: Valuable container plants on their own or mixed with summer annual plantings, perhaps with contrasting salvia species or with pelargoniums.

Baptisia australis Blue False Indigo Hardy perennial

Sturdy, bushy perennial with fresh green, palmate leaves and an abundance of short racemes of intense blue pea flowers, often with cream or white markings on their petals. Handsome black pods follow the flowers and can be dried for indoor arrangements. The rootstock creeps, but at a sedate pace.

Soil preference: Any free-draining, not too dry
Aspect: Sun
Season of interest: Summer, autumn
Height and spread: 1m x 1m (3ft 3in x 3ft 3in)

Companion plants: A big, sturdy border plant, superb to team with tall white campanulas or to site among old roses such as striped pink *Rosa gallica* 'Versicolor' or the crimson 'Charles de Mills'.

Lobelia tupa Marginally hardy perennial

Massive perennial with broadly oval, pointed, felty-textured leaves with a touch of grey in their green. In summer, thick, erect flower spikes are furnished with large, hook-shaped flowers in brilliant scarlet or brick red. Needs protection, particularly from spring frosts. A stately, climactic plant for a large summer border.

Soil preference: Sandy, free-draining but not too dry
Aspect: Sun, part shade
Season of interest: Summer
Height and spread: 1.8m x 90cm (6ft by 3ft)

Companion plants: Wonderful to contrast with the equally distinctive spikes of *Ligularia* 'The Rocket' or *L.* 'Desdemona' and even more exciting among blue delphiniums.

Meconopsis grandis varieties

Himalayan Blue Poppies Perennials, some short-lived

Hoary leaves and fragile, sparsely branched stems, often covered with yellowish hairs, develop at the end of spring. The exquisite, four-petalled flowers unfurl to morning sun and are an intense sky blue with golden stamens at the centres. *M. grandis* has large, hanging blooms; other cultivars vary in colour from deep indigo to white.

Soil preference: Deep, humus-rich, lime-free
Aspect: Shade or part shade or some sun. Shelter essential
Season of interest: Early summer
Height and spread: Up to 1m x 45cm (3ft 3in x 1ft 6in)

Companion plants: At home in a moist, open woodland setting, where they are lovely to blend with white or pale-coloured foxgloves or with candelabra primulas. Good plants for following on include *Kirengeshoma palmata* and *Actaea matsumerae*.

Hostas

Hostas are eternally popular, not only because of the decorative nature of their foliage, but because of their growth habit. The shapely leaves arrange themselves well on the plants and are held almost horizontally, creating a shapely canopy over the ground. With such subtle colouration, from grey-green to emerald, and with a vast variety of different variegations available, it is hardly surprising that they have such a wide use.

But hostas are also cursed with some profound disadvantages. They are prone to mollusc damage and, once a leaf has been ruined, the plant is extremely slow to regenerate with new foliage. Indeed, most varieties produce but one leaf crop per season, so early damage is irreparable. Their season is also quite limited, for foliage plants, since the leaves do not unfurl until late spring and are ruined in early autumn. Finally, few plants die back so ungraciously as hostas. Their lank, rotting leaves and stems can ruin the looks of an otherwise well-planted garden.

1. **'Wide Brim'**
2. **'Sum and Substance'**
3. **'Snowden'**
4. H. sieboldiana **'Elegans'**
5. **'Patriot'**
6. **'Krossa Regal'**
7. **'Halcyon'**
8. **'June'**
9. **'Frances Williams'**
10. **'Hadspen Blue'**
11. **'Francee'**
12. **'August Moon'**

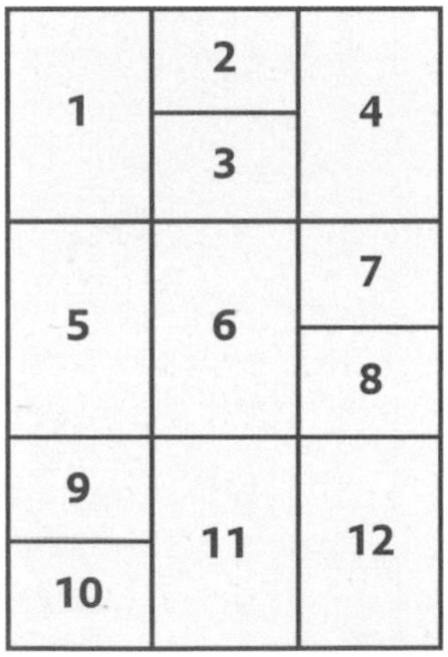

Agapanthus   Blue African Lily   Marginally tender perennials

Rounded clusters of flowers on tall stems. Hues range from midnight blue to pale, soft azure or white. *Agapanthus inapertus* has dark, hanging flowers which barely open; *A. africanus* has rounded, well-filled umbels of flowers with out-turned petals. Examples are 'Goliath' – huge, rounded heads in violet blue, 'Lilac time' with lilac blue flowers and 'Albatross', whose large flowers are white.

Soil preference: Any, free-draining
Aspect: Sun
Season of interest: Summer
Height and spread: Variable to 1.2m x 90cm (4ft x 3ft)

Companion plants: Superb coastal plants to site with such wind-resistant species as *Cordateria selloana* or the shrub *Hippophae rhamnoides*. Also excellent as container plants or to use as focal points for bedding schemes.

Centaurea cineraria   Dusty Miller   Hardy perennial

Grown mainly for its lobed and dissected, pinnate, downy leaves which, in mature plants, form a beautiful tumble of palest silver grey. In summer, the flower stems emerge from among the foliage and carry rose pink to crimson flowers with hard, rounded calyces. Not especially long-lived, so needs regular propagation from cuttings or by division.

Soil preference: Any free-draining
Aspect: Sun
Season of interest: Spring, summer, autumn
Height and spread: 60cm x 45cm (2ft x 1ft 6in)

Companion plants: Often used as silvery contrast plants in formal bedding schemes, but equally lovely in a border among Dianthus, particularly old-fashioned clove scented varieties. The silver also makes a striking contrast with the bronze of *Carex flagellifera* and blue-silver Eryngium species.

Eryngium alpinum   Eryngo, Sea Holly   Hardy perennial

Long-stemmed leaves, which are very spiny, deeply divided and which have a blue-grey caste. The flower stems are also well armed with prickly, metallic blue-grey leaves and carry large, narrowly dome-shaped flowers which are bedded on beautiful rosette-shaped, lacy ruffs.

Soil preference: Any free-draining, reasonably fertile, but not too dry
Aspect: Sun
Season of interest: Summer
Height and spread: 60cm x 60cm (2ft x 2ft)

Companion plants: One of the prettiest sea hollies, ideal for growing among dark varieties of *Astrantia major* such as 'Hadspen Blood' or with other glaucous leaved perennials such as pinks or between verbascums.

Fascicularia bicolor   Half hardy perennial

A bizarre-looking relative of the pineapple with rosettes of narrow, curved, creased leaves which are prickly along their margins and leathery to the touch. In summer, the centre of each rosette colours up to a brilliant scarlet red and surrounds a tightly packed, downy inflorescence from which tiny, pale blue flowers emerge.

Soil preference: Free-draining
Aspect: Sun
Season of interest: Summer
Height and spread: 30cm x 60cm (1ft x 2ft)

Companion plants: Not much of a companion to other plants, but stylish in a container and lovely to nestle into an old wall base or to establish on a bank, perhaps among succulents or with short grasses.

Limonium platyphyllum   Sea Lavender   Hardy perennial

A tough perennial with clumps of leathery, slightly downy, oval or spoon-shaped leaves and, in summer, many-branched, wiry stems carrying cloud-like sprays of tiny lavender-mauve flowers. After the flowers have fallen, the sun-bleached sepals continue to make a more modest display.

Soil preference: Any free-draining
Aspect: Sun
Season of interest: Summer
Height and spread: 75cm x 60cm (2ft 6ln x 2ft)

Companion plants: Useful for an exposed border, perhaps with *Armeria maritima*, feathery artemisias or low grasses.

Geranium sanguineum

Bloody Cranesbill   Hardy perennial

Clump-forming evergreen perennial with rounded, deeply lobed, shiny leaves, often turning reddish or bronze in cold autumn weather, and a long succession of relatively large, veined, magenta-purple flowers. The wild form, *G. s.* var. *striatum,* has very pale pink blooms with darker pink veining. Garden varieties include 'Alan Bloom' – deep magenta flowers, neat habit – and the albino form, 'Album'.

Soil preference: Any free-draining
Aspect: Sun
Season of interest: Summer, autumn
Height and spread: 20cm x 40cm (8in x 1ft 4in)

Companion plants: Too big for a small rock garden, but effective at the border front or at the base of a wall, perhaps among small grasses, with *Sisyrinchium striatum* and *Iris unguicularis*.

Alchemilla mollis

Lady's Mantle   Hardy perennial

An easily grown, free-seeding member of the rose family, with rounded, finely toothed leaves which have silvery undersides. Especially beautiful after rain, when each leaf holds a pearl-like drop at its centre. Sprays of tiny green flowers appear during summer. A prolific self-seeder, often invasive.

Soil preference: Any
Aspect: Sun or part shade
Season of interest: Spring, summer, autumn
Height and spread: 45cm x 45cm (1ft 6in x 1ft 6in)

Companion plants: Handy for furnishing the ground between shrub roses or for free-seeding among bulbs in a gravel garden, perhaps with annuals such as Iberis and Shirley poppies.

Artemisia stelleriana

Beach Wormwood, Old Woman   Hardy perennial

Fairly lax stems bearing deeply lobed leaves which are densely coated with silvery grey, felty down. The tiny yellowish flowers, which appear in midsummer, are insignificant. Favoured forms include 'Boughton Silver', which is prostrate and a much lighter colour than the typical species.

Soil preference: Dry
Aspect: Sun
Season of interest: Spring, summer, autumn
Height and spread: 45cm x 45cm (18in x 18in)

Companion plants: Good to contrast with Alchemilla in gravel, with such bronze sedges as *Carex buchananii* or in a mixed silver planting with verbascums, Helichrysum and lavenders.

Bupleurum falcatum

Sickle Leaved Hare's Ear   Hardy perennial

A slender, weedy perennial belonging to the carrot family, with narrow leaves, broadening towards their bases, and strange, yellow-green flowers held above paler bracts. Naturalizes readily in free-draining spots and has an understated beauty.

Soil preference: Any free-draining
Aspect: Sun
Season of interest: Summer
Height and spread: 60cm x 30cm (2ft x 1ft)

Companion plants: A plant that is best naturalised with other, more substantial species such as *Alchemilla mollis*, sea hollies and among low-growing, Mediterranean shrubs such as *Cistus x corbariensis* or *C. ladanifer*.

Zauschneria californica   Shrubby perennial

Over the summer, branched stems develop to form a
low-growing, rather straggling outline, but in late summer
the plant is transformed by masses of bright scarlet
orange flowers. These are tubular, with flared petals at
their ends. Selected forms include 'Dublin', with downy
foliage and red flowers. Z. c. subsp. *latifolia* has a
spreading habit and is less woody.

Soil preference: Any free-draining
Aspect: Sun
Season of interest: Late summer, autumn
Height and spread: To 60cm x 45cm (2ft x 1ft 6in)

Companion plants: Star plants of late
summer, ideal for the very dry garden,
perhaps with *Verbena bonariensis* above
them, and rubbing shoulders with sedums,
thymes and lavenders.

Sedum spectabile   Ice Plant   Hardy perennial

A clump-forming perennial with brilliant green, succulent
leaves, slightly toothed at their tips, which run up the rigid
stems as they extend. The flower buds appear in mid-
summer, formed in tight, flat-topped umbels, and open to
bright pink flowers as the days begin noticeably to shorten.
Irresistible to butterflies. In winter, the dead flowerheads
make beautiful outlines, especially when frosted. Annual
division prevents plants collapsing when in flower.

Soil preference: Any, not wet
Aspect: Sun
Season of interest: Summer, autumn, winter
Height and spread: To 60cm x 45cm (2ft x 1ft 6in)

Companion plants: Valuable extenders of
the summer flowering season and
harmonious with perennial asters,
Chrysanthemum rubellum and as a
foreground to many dahlia varieties.

Kniphofia caulescens   Red Hot Poker   Hardy perennial

A sub-tropical looking plant with durable, evergreen,
keeled foliage, which is an attractive blue-grey green. In
autumn, established plants produce rigid, thick stemmed
flower spikes, which carry tightly packed blooms in the
classic poker shape. These are a glowing coral hue, fading
to yellow as they mature.

Soil preference: Any well-drained; not wet
Aspect: Sun
Season of interest: Autumn
Height and spread: 1m x 1m (3ft 3in x 3ft 3in)

Companion plants: A focus plant, largely
for its distinctive foliage, good in a dry
garden in the company of Zauschneria,
tall-growing Colquhounia or with autumn
grasses.

Lotus berthelotii

Coral Gem, Parrot Beak   Tender, trailing perennial

Long, pliable, trailing stems are furnished along their length with tufts of soft, needle-shaped leaves in pale sea-green. The striking blood-red flowers, which appear in spring and continue into early summer, are held in pairs along the stems and are shaped like hooked parrot bills. A beautiful native of the Canary islands.

Soil preference: Any free-draining
Aspect: Sun, part shade
Season of interest: Year round
Height and spread: 20cm (8in), spreading

Companion plants: On its own in a hanging basket, this plant is sublime. Possible companions, if you must, include Sutera, trailing petunias, *Bidens ferulifolia* and Scaevola.

Osteospermum **Symphony Series**

Tender perennials

Modern hybrids of South African daisies (see page 152), which are well adapted for container use. Semi-lax stems, flowers in warm colours of orange, apricot and cream and a reasonably long flowering season make these a good choice for container use. However, most osteospermums have periods even in summer when flowering is interrupted. Flowers close in dull light.

Soil preference: Any fertile, free-draining
Aspect: Sun
Season of interest: Summer
Height and spread: 45cm x 45cm (1ft 6in x 1ft 6in)

Companion plants: Best teamed with constant blooming companions such as *Callibrachoa* 'Million Bells Terracotta' or with vivid blue, trailing lobelias.

Verbena **'Homestead Purple'**

Half hardy perennial

A superbly vigorous perennial with divided foliage and semi-prostrate, dark coloured, four-sided stems which, all summer long, carry sizeable umbels of bright purple flowers. The plant roots wherever a stem comes into contact with the ground, forming a spreading mat.

Soil preference: Any, reasonably fertile
Aspect: Sun
Season of interest: Summer, autumn
Height and spread: 45cm (1ft 6in), spreading

Companion plants: A brilliant container plant either on its own or with other vigorous plants such as yellow Bidens, for a colour contrast, or to harmonize with trailing petunias and perhaps a standard blue potato bush (*Solanum rantonetii*) or a yellow-flowered Abutilon as a focal point.

Glechoma hederacea   Ground Ivy   Trailing hardy perennial

A trailing plant, which roots wherever the stem is in contact with the ground. Small, paired, heart-shaped leaves occur along each stem accompanied in spring by small, blue, lipped flowers. For container use, the long trails of the cream- and green-leaved 'Variegata' make the most eye-catching display.

Soil preference: Any moist, well-drained
Aspect: Sun or part shade
Season of interest: Spring, summer
Height and spread: 20cm (8in), spreading

Companion plants: Useful as a trailing plant for more or less any container companions. Pelargoniums, Impatiens, antirrhinums, Sutera, lobelias, pansies – all make great associations.

Antirrhinum pulverulentum   Half-hardy perennial

A spreading, shrubby perennial with prostrate stems and paired, oval, grey-green leaves. The 'snapdragon' flowers, which are constantly produced through the growing season, are pinkish-white with diffuse yellow marking at the throat and lips. *A. sempervirens* is a similar species, but with dark pink pencil lines on the flowers.

Soil preference: Any free-draining
Aspect: Sun
Season of interest: Summer, autumn
Height and spread: 20cm x 45cm (8in x 1ft 6in)

Companion plants: Pretty as trailing plants for window boxes or other containers, especially when teamed with darker colours. Trailing Lobelia, Laurentia and Torenia would also team well.

Viola **Hybrid cultivars**

Pansies (see also pages 140–1 for small-flowered violas)   Hardy perennial

A diverse group of small plants with hairless, slightly lobed leaves and an almost constant succession of flowers whose five petals are arranged in the unmistakeable viola shape. Many varieties have markings that make the honey-scented flowers resemble faces. All colours other than pure pink and red, are represented, often in bewitching combinations.

Soil preference: Any, reasonably fertile, free-draining
Aspect: Sun, part shade. Not too hot
Season of interest: Year-round
Height and spread: To 20cm x 25cm (8in x 10in)

Companion plants: Universally popular, pansies go with absolutely anything! Winter and spring blooming pansies are perfect companions to bulbs, often flowering long after these have faded.

Dianthus species   Wild Pinks   Hardy perennials

Low growing, narrow leaved perennials, usually with disc-shaped flowers, often with pinked or fringed petal edges and usually fragrant. *Dianthus deltoides*, the Maiden Pink, has trailing stems and bright magenta flowers. The Cheddar pink, *D. gratianopolitanus*, has blue-green leaves and shell pink flowers. *D. superbus* has feathery, intensely fragrant flowers and is the forebear of most garden pinks. A precious group for limy gardens, happy even in poor soil.

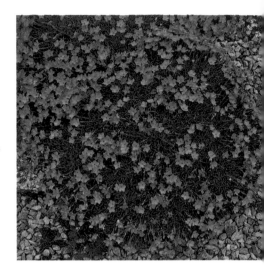

Soil preference: Any free-draining
Aspect: Sun
Season of interest: Spring, summer, autumn
Height and spread: Variable to 30cm x 30cm (1ft x 1ft)

Companion plants: These little perennials team beautifully with decorative thymes, sedums, Origanum species and helianthemums. With rosemary, Santolina and lavenders, they are also delightful.

Geranium renardii   Cranesbill   Hardy perennial

Grey-green, rounded, deeply veined leaves form low mounds from which spring the short-stemmed sprays of large flowers, which are soft white, pencilled with narrow but dark purplish lines. Slow to increase, but surprisingly drought tolerant.

Soil preference: Any free-draining
Aspect: Sun, part shade
Season of interest: Summer
Height and spread: 30cm x 30cm (12in x 12in)

Companion plants: As valued for its foliage as the flowers, this is a quiet companion for low-growing perennials such as *Antirrhinum hispanicum* in sun or some of the purple-leaved heucheras in semi-shade.

Roscoea cautleyoides   Hardy perennial

A member of the ginger family with hairless, narrowly oval pointed leaves and in early summer, erect flower spikes carrying creamy yellow, orchid-like flowers, each with a large, hanging lower petal. 'Kew Beauty' is an excellent garden form with larger flowers and there are also varieties with purple or white flowers.

Soil preference: Any free-draining
Aspect: Sun, part shade
Season of interest: Summer
Height and spread: To 45cm x 30cm (1ft 6in x 1ft)

Companion plants: An exotic-looking species which is effective when allowed to spring up among perennials with contrasting foliage, such as dicentras.

Sidalcea **hybrids**   False Mallow   Hardy perennials

Leaves of this American genus may be rounded or
palmate. The self-supporting flower spikes carry densely
packed, disc-shaped flowers in varying shades of pink.
'Little Princess' has large, tight clusters of shell pink
blooms; 'Rose Queen' has deeper, coppery pink blooms
and 'Monarch' grows taller, with smaller, more evenly
spaced blooms.

Soil preference: Any free-
draining
Aspect: Sun
Season of interest: Summer
Height and spread: 50cm x
60cm (1ft 8in x 2ft)

Companion plants: Gentle pinks for a
summer border, beautiful with *Campanula
lactiflora* or to follow on from Aquilegias or
to contrast their shapes with the foliage of
bearded irises.

Verbascum phoenicium

Purple Mullein   Hardy perennial

Lacking the usually felty mullein foliage, this plant has
dark green, hairless, veined leaves and through summer
produces several slender flower spikes bearing purplish,
pinkish or occasionally white blossoms, each with dark
purple stamens. Not a long-lived perennial, but a free-
seeder. Susceptible to attack by the mullein moth
caterpillar in some regions.

Soil preference: Reasonably
fertile, free-draining
Aspect: Sun
Season of interest: Summer
Height and spread: To 75cm x
30cm (2ft 6in x 1ft)

Companion plants: A smaller, less coarse
mullein than most, suitable for blending
with medium perennials such as
Catananche caerulea, herbaceous potentillas
or the creamy, salmon and terracotta-
coloured achilleas.

Potentilla recta

Upright Cinquefoil, Sulphur Cinquefoil   Hardy perennial

Handsome, palmate leaves with deeply toothed leaflets and
acutely branched stems which, in early and midsummer,
carry large numbers of five petalled, rose-like flowers in
bright golden yellow. The form *P. r.* var. *sulphurea* has paler
lemon flowers and is more desirable for softer colour
schemes. Short lived, but a copious self-seeder.

Soil preference: Any
Aspect: Sun
Season of interest: Summer
Height and spread: 60cm x
60cm (2ft x 2ft)

Companion plants: The lemon form
blends superbly with lilac mauve or purple
colour schemes and looks fetching with
Monarda fistulosa or with Limonium.
Penstemons make fine, contrasting flowers
for later in summer.

Arisaema candidissimum   Hardy perennial

A large, solitary, three-part leaf emerges in spring, with dark mottling on its thick stem. The flower consists of a bold spathe, curved like a question mark over the spadix or central spike, very dark in hue but marked with pale green and pink stripes. A bewitching, exotic-looking beauty for woodland planting.

Soil preference: Humus-rich, acid, not too dry
Aspect: Shade or part shade
Season of interest: Early summer
Height and spread: 30cm x 45cm (1ft x 1ft 6in)

Companion plants: Interesting to team with other members of the arum family or perhaps with Paris species. Also superb with more easily grown woodland plants such as *Epimedium grandiflorum* or to follow on from *Trillium grandiflorum*.

Celmisia spectabilis

Cotton Daisy, Cotton Plant   Marginally hardy perennial

Dense, sometimes spreading clumps of shining bright green, grass-like leaves are covered with silvery or beige coloured downy hairs. The conspicuous daisy flowers have bright yellow disc florets surrounded by brilliant white rays and are held on sturdy stems, well clear of the foliage. A handsome New Zealand native.

Soil preference: Humus-rich, not too dry
Aspect: Sun or part shade
Season of interest: Year round
Height and spread: 30cm x 45cm (1ft by 1ft 6in)

Companion plants: A popular plant for contemporary schemes, perhaps in gravel or grit, contrasting with dark leaved Ophiopogon or grown with aromatic Prostanthera and New Zealand sedges such as *Uncinia unciniata* or *U. rubra*.

Cornus canadensis

Creeping Dogwood, Bunchberry   Hardy, shrubby perennial

A creeping, spreading perennial with ground-covering foliage and in late spring, small green flowers each of which is surrounded, usually, by four brilliant white bracts. Red, edible fruits follow and in some years the foliage colours for autumn. Can be difficult to establish, but where happy, it can become invasive.

Soil preference: Moist, humus-rich, lime-free preferred
Aspect: Shade or part shade
Season of interest: Summer, autumn
Height and spread: 15cm (6in), spreading

Companion plants: A beautiful plant for lime-free woodland conditions, especially if grown with such fellow North Americans as Mertensia, *Smilacina racemosa*, *Uvularia grandiflora* and deciduous azaleas.

Iris Pacific Coast or Californian hybrids

Hardy perennials

Narrow-leaved, beardless irises developed from several western North American species, particularly the blue flowered *Iris innominata* and the variable *I. douglasiana*. Colours range from blue, through purple and reddish mauve to coral, apricot tints and yellow. Flower shapes are elegant, usually with broad, decorated falls.

Soil preference: Free-draining, acid or neutral
Aspect: Sun or part shade
Season of interest: Early summer
Height and spread: 30cm x 30cm (1ft x 1ft)

Companion plants: Superb in a late spring, early summer border, especially assembled in groups of their own kind or, perhaps, among hostas and, for later flowers, Tricyrtis or colchicums.

Meconopsis betonicifolia

Himalayan/Tibetan Blue Poppy   Hardy, short-lived perennial

Hoary, easily bruised foliage and in early summer, tall, branched stems carrying hairy buds from which the brilliant sky blue flowers unfurl, each with its contrasting golden stamens. Lime tolerant but flower colour is impure when grown on alkaline soils. Must be propagated regularly from seed.

Soil preference: Humus-rich, fertile
Aspect: Shade or part shade, moist atmosphere essential
Season of interest: Early summer
Height and spread: To 90cm x 45cm (3ft x 1ft 6in)

Companion plants: A beautiful plant to accompany developing hosta foliage, especially if there are some moisture-loving ferns nearby.

Myosotidium hortensia

Chatham Island Forget-me-not   Marginally hardy perennial

Large relative of the forget-me-not from New Zealand's cool and wet Chatham Island. Large, rounded, creased leaves are carried in thick stems and are joined in late spring and early summer by chunky sprays of forget-me-not flowers in vivid blue. This plant dislikes extremes of heat or cold and is difficult to establish, but well worth the effort.

Soil preference: Moist, humus-rich
Aspect: Part shade or shade
Season of interest: Summer
Height and spread: 30cm x 45cm (1ft x 1ft 6in)

Companion plants: Grow it wherever it is happy, regardless of companions. *Mimulus* 'Andean Nymph' looks pretty near the rhubarb-like leaves. Good container plant.

Alcea rugosa (syn. Althaea rugosostellulata)

Hollyhock   Short-lived hardy perennial

A tall perennial with rounded or sometimes, palmate leaves, hoary and rough to the touch. Flower spikes extend during summer and carry along their length large, disc-shaped flowers in a warm, primrose yellow. A free-seeder which hybridizes readily with the closely related *A. rosea* to produce interesting progeny. Susceptible to hollyhock rust.

Soil preference: Any free-draining
Aspect: Sun
Season of interest: Summer
Height and spread: 2m x 45cm (6ft 6in x 1ft 6in)

Companion plants: A striking alternative to tall mulleins at the back of a dry border. Superb with purple-flowered *Verbena bonariensis* and as beautiful against a grey stone wall as the more common pink hollyhock, *Alcea rosea*.

Anaphalis triplinervis   Pearl Everlasting   Hardy perennial

An Asian species of Pearl Everlasting, whose oval, pointed leaves and stems are coated in a grey-green down, which is denser and therefore whiter on the leaf undersides. The grey-white flowers appear in midsummer and are held in neat umbels. The compact garden form 'Sommerschnee' ('Summer Snow') has more silvery flowers and whiter stems.

Soil preference: Any free-draining
Aspect: Sun, part-shade
Season of interest: Summer
Height and spread: 75cm x 45cm (3ft by 1ft 6in)

Companion plants: Handy, in a dry border, for beefing up the silver content, especially when planted with anchusas, annual poppies, bergenias or grasses.

Armeria maritima   Thrift, Sea Pink   Hardy perennial

Compact, evergreen perennial forming rounded, loaf-like domes of soft, needle-like leaves. From late spring, thin, wiry stems extend from the basal rosettes and carry tight clusters of papery flowers. Colours, both in cultivars and wild stocks, vary from pale lilac pink, through deepening shades of mauve or white. Selections include intense pink 'Vindictive', the magenta 'Rubrifolia' and 'Alba'.

Soil preference: Very free-draining
Aspect: Sun
Season of interest: Spring, summer, autumn
Height and spread: To 30cm x 45cm (1ft x 1ft 6in)

Companion plants: Useful to establish in an old wall or on a bank, as well as in a dry border. Other maritime species such as *Glaucium flavum* and *Silene uniflora* make beautiful companions.

Carpobrotus edulis

Hottentot Fig   Near hardy, succulent perennial

Fleshy, fast-growing, trailing stems with paired, succulent, prism-shaped leaves cover large areas of ground. The daisy-like flowers open primrose yellow in summer, but turn pink as they mature. They are followed by reddish, edible fruits whose seeds, in their native South Africa, are often distributed by baboons.

Soil preference: Any free-draining
Aspect: Sun
Season of interest: Spring, summer, autumn
Height and spread: 20cm (8in), spreading

Companion plants: Plant with caution. If happy, this species is highly invasive! Effective for scrambling over low lying rocks or down banks, but difficult to associate with other plants because it tends to swamp them.

Cynara cardunculus

Cardoon   Hardy perennial

A huge perennial, surprisingly lush for the dry conditions in which it can grow. Huge, deeply divided, decorative leaves, silvery blue-grey in hue, form a vast, arching rosette from which grows a tall, thick, branched stem bearing artichoke-like flowerheads. whose tough, pointed scales surround a vivid purple-blue inflorescence.

Soil preference: Any free-draining
Aspect: Sun
Season of interest: Summer, autumn
Height and spread: 2m x 1.5m (6ft 6in x 5ft)

Companion plants: Superb for the back of a dry border with *Ruta graveolens*, artemisias, *Teucrium fruticans* and any of the drought-tolerant salvias, such as *S. involucrata*.

Gazania krebsiana   Half hardy perennial

Low-growing rosettes or mats of compound leaves whence, from midsummer onwards, short flower stems develop, curving upwards as this conspicuous daisy flowers. Buds open only to direct sunlight, staying closed during overcast or wet weather. Typical colours are blood red or ochre yellow, often with dark centres. Protection from frost is essential.

Soil preference: Any free-draining
Aspect: Sun
Season of interest: Summer
Height and spread: 20cm x 30cm (8in x 1ft)

Companion plants: Must share a sunny spot for the flowers to open; lovely teamed with dark leaved sedums, *Felicia amelloides* and Zauschneria.

Polemonium caeruleum

Jacob's Ladder   Hardy perennial

A clump-forming perennial with ladder-shaped basal leaves. Sparsely branched stems, also carrying leaves, extend in early summer and bear clusters of neat, rounded flowers in clear blue or white. The flowers have an acrid smell, only noticeable if they are cut and brought indoors. The variety 'Brise d'Anjou' has striking yellow-cream leaf margins.

Soil preference: Any free-draining
Aspect: Sun, part shade
Season of interest: Summer
Height and spread: To 75cm x 45cm (2ft 6in x 1ft 6in)

Companion plants: Emerging foliage makes an attractive foil for spring bulbs such as tulips, small narcissus or Muscari. Scabious and achilleas make lovely summer companions.

Solidago hybrids

Goldenrod   Hardy perennials

Vigorous North American perennials with simple, narrow leaves and erect flowering stems furnished with tiered branches in late summer, covered with tiny yellow-gold daisy flowers. 'Goldenmosa' has short, horizontal, tiered plumes; 'Golden Wings' is taller, with more arching panicles. Mildew-prone and with a brief flowering period, but superb when at their best.

Soil preference: Any fertile, free-draining
Aspect: Sun
Season of interest: Summer
Height and spread: To 1.25m x 75cm (4ft x 2ft 6in)

Companion plants: Effective sited with plants that bloom for longer, such as dahlias, asters and heleniums.

Helenium hybrid cultivars   Hardy perennials

Simple, narrowly oval leaves and branched flower stems. Stems are topped with daisy flowers whose central florets are arranged in narrow domes, surrounded by conspicuous ray florets in warm colours from yellow or orange to dark mahogany. The flowers resemble flights of large bumble bees. Striking varieties include the dusky orange-mahogany 'Moerheim Beauty', 'Butterpat' – bright yellow and the ochre and brown 'Wyndley'.

Soil preference: Fertile, free-draining but not too dry
Aspect: Sun
Season of interest: Late summer
Height and spread: Variable to 1m x 45cm (3ft 3in x 1ft 6in)

Companion plants: Mainstay of the late border, exciting with rudbeckias, echinaceas and dahlias, especially with burnishing foliage colours – such as from *Euphorbia palustris* – to provide warm autumn tints.

Helianthus **cultivars**

Perennial Sunflower   Hardy perennial

Vigorous, invasive plants with hoary foliage, darkish, sparsely branched stems and in late summer a heavy, long-lasting crop of all-yellow daisy flowers. 'Loddon Gold' has egg-yolk yellow, double flowers; 'Capenoch Star' has single yellow blooms; and 'Lemon Queen' has pale primrose rays.

Soil preference: Any
Aspect: Sun, part shade
Season of interest: Summer
Height and spread: To 2m (6ft 6in), spreading

Companion plants: Pushy perennials, best for a border back or to fill up an otherwise difficult spot between shrubs. The flowers contrast sweetly with purple or blue perennial asters, Vernonia or among hip-bearing shrub roses.

Aster novi-angliae   New England Aster   Hardy perennial

Tough, disease-resistant perennials which form tight clumps of erect stems, much branched at their tips and bearing daisy-like flowers in glowing hues of pink, purple or white. Fine cultivars include vivid cerise 'Andenken an Alma Pötschke', the much paler 'Harrington's Pink' and the white 'Herbstschnee'. Earlier to bloom than most other perennial asters.

Soil preference: Any, reasonably fertile
Aspect: Sun
Season of interest: Late summer
Height and spread: 1.5m x 45cm (5ft x 1ft 6in)

Companion plants: Useful for linking summer with autumn and effective if contrasted with bronze fennel, goldenrods or harmonized with later flowering asters such as *A. novi-belgii* or *A. lateriflorus*.

Agastache **hybrids**   Anise Hyssop   Hardy, short-lived perennials

Aromatic perennials with handsome, toothed, triangular foliage and branched spikes of tightly packed, lipped flowers in blue, white or shades of coral, apricot and mauve. 'Tutti-frutti' is cherry red with greyish foliage. *Agastache foeniculum* has smoky-blue flowers packed into greyish spikes.

Soil preference: Fertile, moist but free-draining
Aspect: Sun, part shade
Season of interest: Summer
Height and spread: To 1.2m x 45cm (4ft x 1ft 6in)

Companion plants: Sunny border companions for dark flowered *Scabiosa atropurpurea*, *Knautia macedonica* or to go with *Catananche caerulea*.

Aegopodium podagraria 'Variegatum'

Bishopweed, Ground Elder   Hardy perennial

Member of the carrot family with creeping rootstock and handsome, compound leaves. White flowers, borne on umbels, appear in early summer but are best removed to prevent self-seeding. In its green form, ground elder is a noxious weed, but the variegated form is said to be more easily contained for anyone daring enough to give it a try.

Soil preference: Any
Aspect: Sun, part shade, shade
Season of interest: Spring, summer
Height and spread: 60cm (2ft), spreading

Companion plants: Probably safer in a container than at large, but the soft green and cream foliage is fetching with such other ground covers as *Lamium galeobdolon* or *L. maculatum*.

Alcea rosea   Hollyhock   Short-lived, hardy perennial

Tall plants with coarse, rugose, rounded basal leaves and very tall, waving stems, decorated with saucer-shaped, single or double flowers for much of the summer. Colours range from purplish black to pink, yellow and through salmon shades and sunset hues. Seed series include 'Peaches and Dreams' (doubles in sunset shades) and the dark 'Nigra'. Susceptible to rust.

Soil preference: Free-draining, dry
Aspect: Sun
Season of interest: Summer
Height and spread: To 3m x 75cm (10ft by 2ft 6in)

Companion plants: A traditional cottage garden plant often grown against the house wall. Try them with climbing roses, such as apricot 'Lady Hillingdon' or the ivory-flowered rambler, 'Alberic Barbier'.

Arum italicum   Lords and Ladies   Hardy perennial

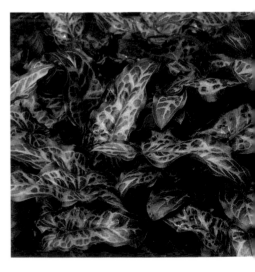

Large, arrow-shaped leaves emerge from the ground in late autumn and persist until the end of spring. These are frequently marked or marbled with paler lines or with contrasting leaf margins. 'Marmoratum' has cream lines along its leaf veins. In spring, green spathe flowers appear, followed in autumn by spikes of red berries.

Soil preference: Any free-draining
Aspect: Sun, part shade
Season of interest: Winter, spring, autumn
Height and spread: 30cm by 30cm (1ft by 1ft)

Companion plants: Grown mainly for the foliage which looks delightful with hardy cyclamen and spring bulbs such as crocus, muscari, scilla and dwarf narcissus. Also beautiful with pulmonarias, among *Dicentra formosa* or to replace hosta foliage which disappears in autumn.

Cardamine pratensis

Lady's Smock, Cuckoo Flower   Hardy perennial

A plant of damp meadows, having modest rosettes of compound leaves from which grow slender hairless stems carrying clusters of small, four-petalled flowers in pale lilac mauve. Garden forms include 'Flore Pleno', which has double flowers. Non-invasive and ideal for naturalizing in damp grassy areas.

Soil preference: Any, not too dry
Aspect: Sun, part shade
Season of interest: Spring
Height and spread: To 45cm x 30cm (1ft 6in x 1ft)

Companion plants: Beautiful companion to oxlips, snakeshead fritillaries or cowslips, either in dampish grass or a traditional orchard or wild garden.

Geranium pratense   Meadow Cranesbill   Hardy perennial

Non-creeping roots produce rosettes of rounded, deeply cut leaves. In summer, tall, branched stems carry masses of five-petalled, mid-blue flowers, each decorated with attractive darker veining. The ripening seed capsules resemble a bird's head and bill. Selections include pale grey-blue 'Mrs Kendall Clark', white *G.p.* var. *pratense* f. *albiflorum* and double 'Plenum Violaceum'.

Soil preference: Limy, free-draining
Aspect: Sun
Season of interest: Summer
Height and spread: To 90cm x 45cm (3ft x 1ft 6in)

Companion plants: Fine border plants to follow lupins and oriental poppies, perhaps sharing a bed with astrantias and achilleas. Also lovely naturalized among border grasses with knapweeds (Centaurea) and field scabious. May be a nuisance self-seeder.

Leucanthemum x superbum

Shasta Daisy   Hardy perennial

Tough perennials with dark green, slightly toothed foliage and in summer, big yellow-centred, white daisy flowers on long stems. 'Sonnenschein' has primrose yellow young flowers, fading to cream as they mature. 'Esther Read' has double white flowers and the blooms of 'Wirral Supreme' are anemone flowered.

Soil preference: Any, not too dry but reasonably free-draining
Aspect: Sun, part shade
Season of interest: Summer
Height and spread: To 1.2m x 60cm (4ft x 2ft)

Companion plants: Cool-coloured border plants to associate with dark summer monkshood *Aconitum napellus* or with delphiniums and Anaphalis for a silver and blue effect. Also beautiful beneath silvery leaved *Buddleja* 'Lochinch'.

Ajuga reptans   Bugle   Hardy perennial

Creeping perennial with rosettes of spoon-shaped or oval leaves, often attractively coloured, setting off showy spikes of lipped flowers in early summer. 'Catlins Giant' has large bronzed leaves and striking, dark blue flowers; variegated 'Burgundy Glow' has pink, purple, green and cream foliage; 'Pink Elf' has pink flowers.

Soil preference: Any moist
Aspect: Shade, part shade or sun
Season of interest: Spring, summer, autumn
Height and spread: To 30cm (1ft), spreading

Companion plants: Easy ground cover plants for a moist, shaded area; lovely in spring when dotted with *Narcissus cyclamineus* or interspersed with *Cardamine pratensis* 'Flore Pleno'. A pretty summer carpet, too, for neutral ground between shrubs or below trees. May be invasive.

Aquilegia hybrids   Columbines   Hardy perennial

Spurred hybrids, largely bred from American plants, with typically ferny columbine foliage and large flowers whose spurs are greatly extended. Many are two-coloured with such bewitching combinations as cream and blue, red and yellow or pink and white. Varieties include the old 'McKana' hybrids and more recently, much larger-flowered 'Songbird Series', whose colours are clean and bright.

Soil preference: Any fertile, free-draining, not too dry
Aspect: Sun
Season of interest: Spring, summer
Height and spread: Variable to 90cm x 45cm (3ft x 1ft 6in)

Companion plants: Border plants for early summer, delightful when allowed to drift among the developing leaves of later perennials, or among such low shrubs as daphnes, *Ceanothus thyrsiflorus* or deciduous azaleas. The 'Songbird' aquilegias are also excellent for containers in a conservatory.

Dicentra spectabilis

Bleeding Heart, Lady in the Bath, Lyre Flower   Hardy perennial

A striking perennial which produces thick but fragile stems, early in the season, which develop elegantly held, ferny foliage and arching sprays of hanging flowers whose heart-shaped petals are bright pink, partially enclosing a creamy white centre. A white form, 'Alba', and pale pink forms are also available. Susceptible to late spring frost damage.

Soil preference: Any free-draining, but not too dry
Aspect: Part shade or sun, but not too hot
Season of interest: Early summer
Height and spread: To 90cm x 45cm (3ft x 1ft 6in)

Companion plants: A spectacular plant for early summer, lovely with early peonies such as *P. mlokosewitchii* or *P. peregrina*. Also attractive when associated with *Aquilegia vulgaris* and *Brunnera microphylla* in semi-shade. Dies down completely by mid-summer.

Heuchera sanguinea   Coral Bells   Hardy perennial

Hard, twiggy rhizomes produce irregularly lobed basal leaves and in summer, thin-stemmed, elegant sprays of small, vivid red flowers. Varieties include 'Scintillation' (rich pink flowers), 'Splendens' (fiery red) and the white 'Alba'. This species is valued for its flowers, rather than foliage (see other Heucheras, pages 139). Divide regularly to keep plants young.

Soil preference: Rich in humus, not too dry
Aspect: Sun or part shade
Season of interest: Summer
Height and spread: To 60cm x 30cm (2ft x 1ft)

Companion plants: Attractive to associate with geums, in contrasting colours, low-growing geranium species such as *G. renardii* or *Ajuga reptans*. The flowers blend sweetly with other heucheras whose foliage may be more richly coloured.

Eryngium x tripartitum

Eryngo, Sea Holly   Hardy perennial

A sea holly (see pages 50 and 149) with more profusely branched stems than many, each carrying large numbers of small flowers, silvery but blue-flushed and held above beautiful but spiny collars. A hybrid of unknown origin which possibly first occurred wild, in the Mediterranean.

Soil preference: Free-draining
Aspect: Sun
Season of interest: Summer
Height and spread: 60cm x 45cm (2ft x 1ft 6in)

Companion plants: Perfectly at home in a Mediterranean garden with arid-loving shrubs and herbs or to grow among grasses and New Zealand sedges in a gravel garden.

Iris sibirica

Siberian Iris   Hardy perennial

Dark green, narrow, sword-shaped foliage and, in early summer, erect, hairless stems carrying a succession of iris blooms, each with three hanging petals (falls) and three upright ones. Prism-shaped, tan seedheads follow. Colours, mainly blue, also include violet, creamy yellow and white. 'Butter and Sugar' is white and yellow; 'Perry's Blue' is pale blue; and 'Caesar's Brother' is bright blue.

Soil preference: Moist, fertile
Aspect: Sun or part shade
Season of interest: Summer
Height and spread: To 1.25m x 75cm (4ft x 2ft 6in)

Companion plants: Superb plants for lush conditions to contrast in flower and foliage with *Ligularia dentata* or perhaps to team with hostas and Hemerocallis.

Tanacetum vulgare

Tansy   Hardy perennial

Vigorous perennial with a creeping rootstock and feathery, ferny foliage. The yellow button-like flowers, produced on large, showy umbels, are highly aromatic. Cautious planting is necessary, since the roots are highly invasive. *T. v.* var. *crispum* is a decorative form with crisp, curled leaves.

Soil preference: Any
Aspect: Sun, part shade
Season of interest: Summer
Height and spread: 90cm (3ft), spreading

Companion plants: Striking in a herb garden among vigorous mints, marjorams and sages. Also useful in a wild garden to accompany meadow flowers such as *Geranium pratense*, *Leucanthemum vulgare* or the burnets (Sanguisorba species).

Achillea ptarmica

Sneezewort   Hardy perennial

Vigorous perennial with a creeping root stock from which tall stems emerge, furnished with dark green, narrow, slightly toothed leaves and clusters of pure small, compound flowers whose greyish centres are surrounded by short, pure white rays. Garden forms include 'The Pearl', whose sterile flowers are double and pure white.

Soil preference: Moist but well-drained
Aspect: Sun, part shade
Season of interest: Summer
Height and spread: 1.25m x 1m (4ft x 3ft 3in)

Companion plants: Valuable for leavening colour, in a perennial border, especially when grown among blue campanulas or intensely coloured delphiniums. Also superb in a moist wild garden with purple loosestrife and, perhaps, rodgersias.

Lythrum salicaria

Purple Loosestrife   Hardy perennial

Beautiful riverside species with willow-like leaves and, in summer, long, showy spires of rich vibrant purple. Named because bunches were tied to horses' bridles to repel troublesome flies – hence 'loosing their strife'. Note: although trouble free and desirable in Europe, this species has become an invasive alien in parts of North America where it has been declared a noxious weed.

Soil preference: Moist, fertile
Aspect: Sun or part shade
Season of interest: Summer
Height and spread: To 1.75m x 1m (6ft x 3ft 3in)

Companion plants: Best among wetland plants such as *Iris sibirica*, Lysimachia and *Achillea ptarmica*.

Lysimachia ciliata   Loosestrife   Hardy perennial

A rapid-growing perennial with running roots, whose many branched stems carry diamond-shaped leaves and, from midsummer, many star-shaped, bright golden yellow flowers. The variety 'Firecracker' is especially dramatic, having dark bronze foliage, which makes a strong contrast with the bright flowers.

Soil preference: Moist, fertile but well-drained
Aspect: Sun or part shade
Season of interest: Spring, summer
Height and spread: 90cm x 90cm (3ft x 3ft)

Companion plants: A superb informal plant for a mixed border or lovely when drifting among such shrubs as rhododendrons, which have flowered earlier, or summer blooming Enkianthus and Desfontainia.

Tanacetum parthenium

Feverfew   Short-lived hardy perennial

Simple leaves, lobed and divided, are accompanied, during the growing season, by many small, white single or double daisy flowers. The plant has an astringent aromatic quality and is very bitter to taste, but is said to cure headaches. Many insects shun its odour. Named varieties include the gold-leaved 'Aureum' and 'Plenum', whose flowers are double.

Soil preference: Any
Aspect: Sun
Season of interest: Spring, summer, autumn
Height and spread: 60cm x 30cm (2ft x 1ft)

Companion plants: The gold-leaf form is useful as a foliage plant in bedding schemes or to bring brightness to an all green border. Also attractive to naturalize among other plants, such as Sweet William or Calendula, in a cottage-style border.

Melissa officinalis

Lemon Balm   Hardy perennial

A tough perennial with broadly oval, toothed, pointed leaves which are strongly lemon-scented. The flowers are small, off-white and uninteresting. Roots tend to creep and self seeding can be copious. Attractive forms include 'All Gold', which has gold foliage, and 'Aurea', whose leaves are flecked with yellow. The lemon scent helps to deter mosquitoes and midges.

Soil preference: Any
Aspect: Sun or part shade
Season of interest: Summer
Height and spread: To 1.25m x 60cm (4ft x 2ft)

Companion plants: Too invasive for a small herb garden but pleasant to grow next to a garden seat or along a pathway in a wild area. Try with the larger decorative tender salvias such as *S. guaranitica* or *S. involucrata*.

Acorus calamus

Sweet Flag   Hardy wetland perennial

A vigorous, rush-like member of the arum family with bold, arching, swordlike leaves and curious flowers which appear as rigid spikes emerging from a fold in the leaf. The white-striped 'Variegatus' is the most decorative garden form. The leaves are sweet-smelling, especially when crushed.

Soil preference: Wet
Aspect: Sun or part shade
Season of interest: Summer
Height and spread: 1m x 1m (3ft 3in by 3ft 3in)

Companion plants: Suitable for a large pond, in the company of yellow flags or *Iris ensata*, perhaps with *Ranunculus lingua*.

Chamaemelum nobile

Chamomile, Camomile   Hardy perennial

A richly aromatic perennial with vivid emerald green, feathery foliage and a ground-hugging character. The daisy flowers are warm white, single – with a greenish yellow central disc – or double. The variety 'Treneague' hardly ever flowers and is the best choice for a chamomile lawn.

Soil preference: Free-draining
Aspect: Sun
Season of interest: Year round
Height and spread: To 15cm x 30cm (6in x 1ft)

Companion plants: Romantic when grown as a lawn, but more interesting if teamed with creeping thymes, Pratia and other prostrate species. Also welcome in any herb garden where it will be best in front of marjoram, sages and bush-forming culinary thymes.

Clematis tubulosa (syn C. heracleifolia var. davidiana)   Shrubby, hardy perennial

A coarse, shrubby perennial with large, hoary, three-part leaves and from midsummer, a succession of small, four-sepalled, mid-blue flowers which have the fragrance of spring narcissus. The form 'Alan Bloom' is compact, and has good, clean flower colour. The dying leaves, in autumn can be unappealing, but the late summer fragrance is worthwhile.

Soil preference: Any, reasonably fertile, not too dry
Aspect: Sun or part shade
Season of interest: Late summer
Height and spread: 1m x 1m (3ft 3in x 3ft 3in)

Companion plants: Tuck this distinctly non-climbing clematis among big perennials which will neutralize its ugly foliage, but be sure to have access to enjoy its fragrance. Handy to plant in among big shrub roses, especially *R. moyesii*.

Convallaria majalis   Lily-of-the-valley   Hardy perennial

Much loved woodlander with a creeping root stock and large, paired, oval, pointed leaves. Short, stiff stems develop in spring and carry a dozen or so tiny, nodding, bell-shaped flowers which have an intense and sweet fragrance. The form *C. m.* var. *rosea* has dusky, purplish pink blooms and 'Variegata' gold and green striped leaves.

Soil preference: Humus-rich, well-drained
Aspect: Shade or part shade
Season of interest: Spring
Height and spread: 25cm (10in), spreading

Companion plants: Happiest when allowed to creep under deciduous trees with such other woodland plants as *Polygonatum odoratum*, bluebells and woodland anemones.

Mirabilis jalapa

Marvel of Peru, Four O'Clock Plant   Tender perennial

Fast-growing member of the bougainvillea family with a carrot-like tuberous root and bushy top-growth, with simple, diamond-shaped leaves. Delicate, fragrant, trumpet flowers are constantly produced, opening each afternoon, but lasting only until struck by morning sun. Colours may be pink, cerise, yellow or white.

Soil preference: Any reasonably fertile, free-draining
Aspect: Sun or part shade
Season of interest: Summer
Height and spread: 60cm x 45cm (2ft x 1ft 6in)

Companion plants: Lovely plants to tuck in among such other fragrance providers as Nicotiana, heliotrope or herbaceous daturas. Happy in pots.

Primula florindae

Giant Cowslip   Hardy perennial

Neat rosettes of large, toothed, spoon-shaped leaves develop in spring. From these, slender but self-supporting stems extend and carry generous umbels of nodding flowers whose calyces are dusted with a white indumentum and whose flowers are a pale but intense yellow. The fragrance of this Tibetan native is delicate, reminiscent of freesia, but less strong.

Soil preference: Moist, fertile, humus-rich
Aspect: Shade or part shade
Season of interest: Summer
Height and spread: 1m x 30cm (3ft 3in x 1ft)

Companion plants: Superb plants for a moist planting scheme, with blue Himalayan poppies, candelabra primulas, hostas and ferns.

Yellow doronicums with *Veronica gentianoides*

Centranthus ruber and *Euphorbia characias* subsp. *wulfenii*

Spring Perennials

(See picture above)

Perennials that flower reliably in the spring, especially during the early part, are less abundant than those which contribute to the summer and autumn glut. It is hardly surprising, therefore, that perennial-based planting schemes and mixed borders run the highest risk of losing floral momentum during the first months of the growing season. In the main picture above, any risk of a 'post bulb anticlimax' has been swept away by developing a bold drift of Doronicum whose golden daisy flowers make an exquisite contrast with the pale sky blue spikes of *Veronica gentianoides*. With the advancing months, the doronicums die away but although the veronica is short-lived in flower, it sustains tight mats of glossy green foliage throughout summer, giving background foliage to perennials when they flower later. The gentle colours – clean and bright for spring –

are picked up by the golden bamboo and pale flowered broom (Cytisus) in the background.

Centranthus ruber and Euphorbia

Continuity. The golden-green flowers of *Euphorbia characias* subsp. *wulfenii* will have shown their first colour in mid- to late winter, reaching a climax towards mid-spring. The red valerian, *Centranthus ruber*, takes over with its brighter, summer colour from late spring onwards. There is also a harmony between the shapes of the two inflorescences – bold, broad spikes – which make the plants look comfortable together. And, when the flowers are finally over, the young stems of the euphorbia, with their narrow, blue-green leaves, will make a pleasing feature for the remainder of the growing season, and on into winter.

Meconopsis grandis

Allium schubertii

Meconopsis mixture

Banking on fickle brilliance. Some perennials are so spectacular, when at their best, that short flowering periods, and other shortcomings, can be forgiven. Blue Himalayan poppies such as *Meconopsis grandis* are just such an example, dramatic and alluring during their late-spring or early summer glory, but offering nothing once flowering is over. Their foliage dies away or looks untidy and, unless grown in ideal conditions, they refuse to come up again another year!

The problem is tackled, in this scheme, in two ways. A different species, *Meconopsis napaulensis* – pink flowered here, but they can also be white or primrose yellow – gives a double display. Being biennial, it has a vegetative season, when bold rosettes of impressive leaves are formed, followed the next year by towering, branched flower spikes. And to back up the transient poppies, moisture-loving ferns have been planted. The season could be extended further by including such autumn plants as toad lilies (Tricyrtis) and a selection of trilliums or Paris for spring.

Allium schubertii and sedum

Relieving monotony. Late summer flowering plants such as *Sedum spectabile* produce mounds of foliage early in the year, but apart from a pleasant, neutral green, do little else for a planting scheme until the end of summer. Introducing more dramatic companion plants will help to relieve the uniformity of this without compromising the spectacular sedum display when it finally happens. For spring, the bizarre but beautiful onion species *Allium schubertii* gives the impression of an exploding firework, with its little flowers produced on variable stem lengths. The seed capsule will stay whole for much of summer.

Bergenia cordifolia

Elephant's Ears, Pig Squeak   Hardy perennial

Easily grown species with large, heart-shaped, leathery leaves. The flowers are bright pink, produced from plump basal buds in late winter and carried on stems which extend as they mature. Good leaf colour varieties include 'Purpurea', which turns coppery bronze in winter and 'Tubby Andrews', whose foliage is variegated.

Soil preference: Any
Aspect: Sun, shade, part shade
Season of interest: Year round
Height and spread: To 45cm (1ft 6in), spreading

Companion plants: Durable ground cover plants, also attractive for winter borders at the feet of Hamamelis, Chimonanthus and other winter-flowering shrubs.

Pulmonaria saccharata

Lungwort, Soldiers and Sailors   Hardy perennial

Bold, broad, hoary leaves are decorated with blotches or marks of pale greyish white. In early spring, bunched pink or blue flowers appear on short, branched stems. Selections include Argentea Group whose leaves are silver and the lovely albino 'Sissinghurst White'. Remove spent flower spikes and foliage in late spring, to encourage regeneration.

Soil preference: Humus-rich, not too dry
Aspect: Part shade, shade
Season of interest: Year round, spring
Height and spread: 30cm x 45cm (1ft x 1ft 6in)

Companion plants: Gems for a spring planting scheme with hardy cyclamen, bulbs, *Hacquetia epipactis* and hellebores. Also attractive to contrast with winter heathers.

Pulmonaria rubra   Lungwort   Hardy perennial

Large, bright green, unmarked leaves, which are slightly hoary, persist virtually all year. From midwinter, clustered buds begin to show coral red flowers and by spring, these will have extended into generous sprays. Garden forms include the variegated 'David Ward' and supremely early-flowering 'Redstart'.

Soil preference: Any, preferably humus-rich
Aspect: Shade, part shade
Season of interest: Year round
Height and spread: 45cm x 60cm (1ft 6in x 2ft)

Companion plants: Handsome when teamed with other lungworts whose marked leaves contrast. Also excellent for winter planting among trees with decorative bark – *Betula utilis*, for example, or *Prunus serrula* – or with hellebores, especially *H. foetidus*.

Euphorbia characias   Milkweed, Spurge   Hardy perennial

Resembling a shrub, rather than a herb, with stout evergreen, erect stems, often blushed pinkish, and furnished with narrow, sage-green leaves. From late winter large clusters of vivid lime-green to gold flowers develop and persist for several months. Fine forms include *E. c.* subsp. *wulfenii* and 'Lambrook Gold'.

Soil preference: Any free-draining
Aspect: Sun
Season of interest: Year round
Height and spread: To 1.5m x 1m (5ft x 3ft 3in)

Companion plants: Capable of growing between rocks, this is perfect for a wall base, or in a Mediterranean setting with *Helleborus argutifolius*, *Teucrium fruticans* and the tougher genistas such as *G. hispanica* or *G. lydia*.

Epimedium x versicolor   Barrenwort   Hardy perennial

A durable perennial with thin stems bearing three or five-part leaves which colour in the autumn. In early spring, frail flower stems extend, carrying sprays of small, pale yellow blossoms. Old leaves are best removed annually, just before spring, to enable the flowers to show. Varieties include bright yellow 'Sulphureum', and *E. v.* 'Versicolor', whose leaves are veined with coppery patterns.

Soil preference: Any, well-drained
Aspect: Part shade or shade
Season of interest: Year round
Height and spread: 30cm x 30cm (1ft x 1ft)

Companion plants: The spring flowers are lovely contrasted with blue-flowered bulbs such as scillas, Muscari or Chionodoxa. The foliage also harmonises well with ground cover plants such as pulmonarias, bergenias or *Lamium maculatum*.

Helleborus argutifolius

Corsican Hellebore   Hardy perennial

A sun-loving hellebore, native to Corsica, with compound, leathery leaves, prickly along their margin. From late winter, generous clusters of large, bright apple green flowers that last for months appear. Spent flower spikes are best removed in early summer, as soon as new growth is detected at the base of the plant. Some support may be necessary in rich soils.

Soil preference: Any free-draining
Aspect: Sun or part shade
Season of interest: Winter, spring
Height and spread: 75cm x 60cm (2ft 6in x 2ft)

Companion plants: A natural companion to *Euphorbia characias*, especially if the two are allowed to seed about. Also pretty with *Artemisia absinthium* and with *Alchemilla mollis*.

Brunnera macrophylla   Hardy perennial

Large, heart-shaped, slightly rough-textured leaves form a loose rosette which persists for most of the year. In mid-spring, generously branched sprays of tiny, intense blue forget-me-not flowers create a colourful mist. Variegated forms include 'Hadspen Cream' (cream leaf margin) and more palely marked 'Dawson's White'. *B. m.* 'Jack Frost' (pictured) has a silvery white patina on its bold foliage.

Soil preference: Humus-rich, not too dry
Aspect: Shade, semi shade
Season of interest: Spring, summer
Height and spread: 75cm x 60cm (2ft 6in x 2ft)

Companion plants: Woodland beauties to follow on from hellebores and to flower with Solomon's seal, white honesty, Smilacina and perhaps, yellow crown imperials.

Iris pallida   Dalmatian Iris   Hardy perennial

A bearded iris with stiff, erect, sword-like leaves and, in early summer, pale silvery-blue, fragrant iris flowers. The most desirable varieties are grown for their dramatic foliage. *I. p.* 'Argentea Variegata' has white and green striped leaves whereas *I. p.* 'Variegata' has yellow stripes. Divide clumps every few years, to sustain their youthfulness.

Soil preference: Any free-draining
Aspect: Sun, or part shade
Season of interest: Spring, summer, autumn
Height and spread: 75cm x 60cm (2ft 6in x 2ft)

Companion plants: Lovely punctuation marks, in a flowery border, bringing relief to the green of such developing perennials as young delphiniums, penstemons, asters and phloxes.

Symphytum x uplandicum 'Variegatum'
Variegated Comfrey   Hardy perennial

Very large, broadly oval, pointed basal leaves are decorated with a wide, creamy yellow margin. When the coarse, much-branched flower stems develop and extend, these also have creamy variegations. Small, tubular flowers hang in clusters and are pink, turning blue with age. Prone to mildew and inclined to revert to green.

Soil preference: Any not too dry
Aspect: Sun or part shade
Season of interest: Spring, summer
Height and spread: To 1.5m x 1m (5ft x 3ft 3in)

Companion plants: A striking companion for the blue flowers and contrasting foliage of *Iris sibirica* or when grown among such larger grasses as Miscanthus. Also very beautiful when leaves can contrast with those of *Baptisia australis*.

Valeriana phu 'Aurea' Valerian Hardy perennial

An easy perennial grown mainly for the golden basal foliage which emerges in early spring. The first leaves are simple, but as the plant matures and flower stems develop, they become compound. Sprays of tiny white flowers appear in midsummer. Foliage colour is more intense when plants are grown in full sun.

Soil preference: Any, not too dry
Aspect: Sun or part shade
Season of interest: Spring
Height and spread: 90cm x 45cm (3ft x 1ft 6in)

Companion plants: A bright perennial for bringing relief to an all-green border of such later developing perennials as lupin, oriental poppies, phloxes or campanulas. Also delightful when dotted with scarlet or crimson tulips, especially when forget-me-nots are also associated.

Filipendula ulmaria 'Aurea'

Golden Meadowsweet Hardy perennial

Creeping rhizomes produce stems, from early spring onwards, furnished with compound leaves which are attractively creased, when young, and are a bright golden green. Umbels of disappointing, off-white blooms appear in summer, but it is better to cut back stems before flowering, to encourage fresh foliage production.

Soil preference: Any moist
Aspect: Sun or part shade
Season of interest: Summer
Height and spread: 75cm (2ft 6in), spreading

Companion plants: Pretty waterside plants to associate with *Mimulus luteus* or to contrast with iris foliage, with water forget-me-nots or with reeds or rushes. Also handsome in a moist border with purple leaved heucheras.

Origanum vulgare 'Aureum'

Golden Marjoram, Golden Oregano Hardy herbaceous perennial

Gold form of the deliciously aromatic herb, having rounded, slightly puckered leaves on stems which, in maturity, carry small, irregular clusters of pale mauve flowers. Best cut back during summer, to promote new young stems. As a culinary herb, this form is as richly flavoured as common marjoram.

Soil preference: Any, free-draining
Aspect: Sun
Season of interest: Summer, autumn
Height and spread: 60cm x 60cm (2ft x 2ft)

Companion plants: Handsome to grow among coloured sages such as *Salvia officinalis* 'Purpurea' and with rosemary, lavender and assorted thymes. Also pretty with small flowered violas.

Tellima grandiflora **Rubra Group**

Fringe Cups   Hardy perennial

Rounded, lobed, hoary leaves form a carpet above which the narrow, erect stems extend and bear strange-looking, fringed flowers, often marked red at their edges. The Rubra group have reddish purple-edged leaves. Closely related to heucheras (see pages 139 and 175) and to Tiarella, the foam flowers.

Soil preference: Moist, humus-rich
Aspect: Shade or part shade
Season of interest: Spring, summer
Height and spread: 60cm x 60cm (2ft x 2ft)

Companion plants: Woodlanders with an understated beauty, attractive when grown with the related heucheras, tiarellas and Tolmeia to create interesting foliage blends.

Eupatorium rugosum **'Braunlaub'**

White Snakeroot   Hardy perennial

A shrub-like perennial with branched stems and large, handsomely toothed, leaves which, in this variety, are suffused with khaki-brown. Flattened clusters of flowers, like small, bronze-tinged white tufts, begin to emerge in mid autumn and persist until winter. The sombre foliage is at its darkest when young.

Soil preference: Reasonably fertile, humus rich
Aspect: Sun or part shade
Season of interest: Summer, autumn
Height and spread: To 1m x 50cm (3ft 3in x 2ft 6in)

Companion plants: A useful plant to tone down autumn colour, especially when teamed with rudbeckias, chrysanthemums or with late blooming penstemons. Great as a foliage contrast with *Valeriana phu* 'Aurea' or with the silvery *Anaphalis margaritacea*.

Ophiopogon planiscapus **'Nigrescens'**

Black Mondo Grass   Hardy perennial

Slow-growing, black, grass-like foliage and, occasionally, tiny, insignificant, dirty white flowers on short stems. Opinions are divided: some designers and enthusiasts love this plant for its dark colour and glossy texture; others find it charmless and boring. Shreds of black polyethylene would be as inpiring to this writer.

Soil preference: Any
Aspect: Sun or part shade
Season of interest: Year round
Height and spread: 30cm x 30cm (1ft by 1ft)

Companion plants: A good choice for a modernistic rocky gravel scree, perhaps with a Japanese maple nearby and, of course, some decking, almost certainly painted in some improbable colour, and at least one large, glazed ceramic pot.

Matthiola fruticulosa   Perennial Stock   Short-lived perennial

Shrubby plant with a woody main stem and branches carrying narrow, silvery grey, felty leaves and from late spring, spikes of fragrant, four-petalled flowers in white, cream, pink or lilac mauve. The plant thrives in very poor, free-draining conditions, where it will often produce self-sown seedlings.

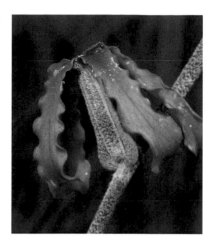

Soil preference: Very free-draining
Aspect: Sun
Season of interest: Spring, summer
Height and spread: 45cm x 30cm (1ft 6in x 1ft)

Companion plants: A plant for the dry garden, handsome with *Convolvulus cneorum* or among dwarf bearded irises. Also attractive growing in old walls with naturalised wallflowers and *Corydalis lutea*.

Mertensia virginica (syn. M. pulmonarioides)

Blue Bells, Virginia Cowslip   Hardy perennial

Vigorous, but fragile plant with glaucous hairless leaves and many branched stems bearing clusters of hanging, tubular flowers in an intense violet blue or sometimes white. Can be difficult to establish, but where happy, it will self-seed and naturalize. *Mertensia ciliata* is a close, taller relative, with longer leaves and clean blue flowers.

Soil preference: Humus-rich, preferably lime-free
Aspect: Shade or part shade
Season of interest: Spring
Height and spread: 45cm x 30cm (1ft 6in x 1ft)

Companion plants: Part of the North American woodland scene, where they might rub shoulders with trilliums and wild columbines. In a garden, add *Polygonatum multiflorum*, *Primula elatior* and *Epimedium grandiflorum* to broaden the picture.

Sanguinaria canadensis

Bloodroot   Hardy perennial

Distinctive member of the poppy family with rounded, lobed, blue-green leaves which emerge in early spring accompanied by flowers which are cup-shaped and either single or, in the form 'Plena', double. If the roots are wounded, they bleed a red sap. Prefers cool, moist conditions and may be slow to establish.

Soil preference: Moist, humus-rich, lime-free
Aspect: Shade or part shade
Season of interest: Spring
Height and spread: 15cm x 20cm (6in x 8in)

Companion plants: A fine New World woodlander to mix with the plants suggested as companions for mertensia. Broaden the mix further by adding *Leucojum vernum*, bluebells and ragged robin (*Lychnis flos-cuculi*).

Senecio pulcher   Marginally hardy perennial

Late-emerging rosettes of leathery, oblong leaves are joined, in late autumn, by stout stems which carry small numbers of flower buds held in loose corymbs. These open to conspicuous daisy flowers whose vivid yellow centres contrast with brilliant rose-purple outer ray florets. A sheltered spot is essential for this South American species, but it will take light frosts.

Soil preference: Rich but well-drained
Aspect: Sun
Season of interest: Autumn, winter
Height and spread: 45cm x 30 cm (1ft 6in x 1ft)

Companion plants: A bright gem for the autumn garden, blending well with the rich blue flowers and reddening foliage of *Ceratostigma plumbaginoides* or making a startling contrast with the yellow blooms of *Coronilla glauca*.

Bidens heterophylla   Hardy perennial

A vigorous species with thin but largely self-supporting, sparsely branched stems which carry thin, serrated leaves sometimes entire and sometimes lobed. The flowers, which appear from late summer throughout autumn, have broad, short outer ray florets in pale cream or bi-coloured acid yellow and white, usually with dusky gold centres.

Soil preference: Any, preferably rich but well-drained
Aspect: Sun or part shade
Season of interest: Summer, autumn
Height and spread: 1.5m x 1m (5ft x 3ft)

Companion plants: Superb late border plant to accompany the kingfisher blue *Salvia uliginosa* or the taller growing *Leucanthemella serotina*. Also handy to include among shrubs for added autumn interest.

Chrysanthemum rubellum 'Mary Stoker'

Hardy perennial

One of the hardiest and easiest of the outdoor chrysanthemums with the aromatic 'oak-leaf' divided or lobed foliage and sprays of buds which stay green and tight until early autumn. The flowers are single, with greenish yellow centres and ray florets in a soft apricot to beige, with a dash of pale salmon in some lights. A superb cut flower.

Soil preference: Any fertile, reasonably well-drained
Aspect: Sun
Season of interest: Autumn
Height and spread: 1m x 1m (3ft x 3ft)

Companion plants: Wonderful with such other chrysanthemums as 'Clara Curtis' (pink) 'Peterkin' (bright bronze to apricot) and 'Mei Kyo' which is double, purplish pink. Also pretty with large, dark leaved dahlias such as 'Bishop of Llandaff'.

Schizostylis coccinea   Hardy cormous perennial

A pretty South African species whose sword-like foliage forms decorative clumps during spring and summer, and from which stiff stems emerge, towards the end of the year, bearing bright pink or coral red flowers which open in succession. Garden selections include the carmine flowered *S. c.* 'Major,' and the vigorous shell pink 'Jennifer.'

Soil preference: Any moist, but free-draining
Aspect: Sun
Season of interest: Autumn, winter
Height and spread: 40cm x 60cm (1ft 4in x 2ft)

Companion plants: A fine plant to use where hotter colours of Crocosmia might clash. With the soft lilac, mauve, violet and blue of perennial asters, these plants look superb, but they also look well at the base of a wall furnished with *Parthenocissus tricuspidata*.

Coreopsis 'Limerock Beauty'

Marginally hardy perennial

A delicate perennial with highly divided, filamentous foliage. Throughout summer, a succession of bright wine pink or ruby flowers are carried on thin, wiry stems. The petals (outer ray florets) are broad, slightly pleated and are serrated at their tips. Not hardy in sustained frost, but easy to propagate from cuttings or division.

Soil preference: Any fertile, free-draining but not too dry
Aspect: Sun
Season of interest: Summer.
Height and spread: 60cm x 30 cm (2ft x 1ft)

Companion plants: This is a pretty summer companion for the low growing, pink evening primrose *Oenothera* 'Siskiyou Pink' or for paler pink *Corepsis rosea*.

Primula Candelabra types   Hardy perennials

Large, handsome rosettes or oblong, puckered, serrated leaves create an initial display before the flower spikes begin to emerge in late spring, to flower in early summer. The flowers are produced in whorls around the stems at intervals, new whorls developing through summer as the flower spikes gain height. Dark wine red and pink species include *Primula japonica* and *P. pulverulenta*; *P. cashmiriana* and *P. bulleyana* come in warm orange and gold hues.

Soil preference: Moist, humus-rich
Aspect: Dappled shade or sun
Season of interest: Early summer
Height and spread: 1m x 30cm (3ft x 1ft)

Companion plants: The perfect bog garden plant, lovely to follow on from Lysichiton and to accompany water irises or moisture loving ferns such as Osmunda or *Matteuccia struthiopteris*.

The Autumn Climax

Every natural flora has an easily identified seasonal rhythm or cycle. During winter, flowering is sparse for obvious reasons: pollinating insects are few and far between. Spring brings a rush of short-lived, highly conspicuous blooms which, with interim ebbing and flowing, leads to a floral climax around the longest day. Then, as the majority of plants that have flowered run to seed, colour becomes scarcer. But as nights begin to lengthen, the short-day plants perk up and begin to perform. In well planned, skilfully planted gardens, these are of immense value. They may hold their buds tight for months, while their neighbours flower copiously, but the accelerating change in day length, can result in a spectacular reprise of colour, texture and fragrance in the closing months of the year. And in the softer, more golden light of autumn, when foliage is also firing up with warm tints before falling, vivid flowers like those in the illustration give the feeling that winter will never come.

The three main plant types, deployed here, are perennial asters, which bring lavender, mauve and blue shades, outdoor spray chrysanthemums, whose hot tones include brick red, maroon, orange and paler yellow and penstemons, whose main season is over but which, if cut back strategically, in mid-summer, would come back to bloom profusely for late summer. Subsidiary plants, but still making strong contributions are Schizostylis in the foreground and a backdrop of wind-breaking shrubs.

To achieve such a strong autumn display, it would be necessary to reduce the number of summer flowering plants, or, to use summer annuals for stop-gap early colour, and to grow the chrysanthemums on in pots, plunging these into the spaces left by the spent annuals at flowering time. For that, you need space to stand the pots, where the display plants can be allowed to develop, and to have a good sense of timing.

With careful planning and skilful planting, you can produce a display of breathtaking colour and drama to round off the season.

groundcover

Groundcover for sun, year round

Groundcover for shade, year round

Groundcover for hot and dry sites, year round

Groundcover for poor soil, year round

Artemisia ludoviciana

Silver Wormwood, Western Mugwort   Hardy herbaceous perennial

Tough perennial with a creeping rootstock and stems whose slightly lobed leaves are so densely covered with fine, short down that they look almost white. The flowers are small, greenish yellow and insignificant, so it is best to cut the stems back as they mature to encourage new foliage. Best varieties include 'Silver Queen', whose leaves are more divided and the broader leaved 'Valerie Finnis'.

Soil preference: Any free-draining
Aspect: Sun
Season of interest: Spring, summer, autumn
Height and spread: 90cm x 90cm (3ft x 3ft)

Companion plants: A superb plant for spreading a silver coat over a sunny border, especially when teamed with such other grey plants as *Anaphalis margaritacea* or with other wormwoods. Lovely too with hot coloured dahlias or penstemons.

Bergenia hybrids   Pig Squeak   Hardy evergreen perennial

Bold, leathery, rounded leaves which emit a squeaking sound when tweaked, cover a network of thick, weed-suppressing rhizomes. In late winter tight, rounded buds burst to release dense clusters of pink or white flowers whose stems gradually extend as spring progresses. Fine cultivars include 'Abendglut', whose flowers are purple-red; 'Silberlicht', whose pale pink buds open to white blooms; and the purple-pink flowered 'Morgenröte', whose leaves are purple tinged.

Soil preference: Any
Aspect: Sun or part shade
Season of interest: Year round
Height and spread: 45cm (1ft 6in), spreading

Companion plants: A valuable group for impenetrable ground cover, best when carpeting under such spring shrubs as Ribes, forsythias, Corylopsis or to soften the edges of paved areas.

Cerastium tomentosum

Snow-in-Summer   Hardy perennial

A highly invasive perennial, belonging to the pink family and closely related to chickweed, whose silvery grey-white leaves and stems form dense, spreading mats, smothering all in their path. In early summer, the pure white flowers are a bonus, but the spreading habit is relentless!

Soil preference: Any
Aspect: Sun
Season of interest: Year round, early summer
Height and spread: 30cm (1ft) and spreading

Companion plants: Excellent for covering areas of ground below such structures as pillars or walls. Difficult to team with other plants, but silvery colour makes a pleasant contrast with lawn grass or with paving.

Diascia hybrids Twinspur Marginally hardy perennials

Mat-forming perennials with creeping stems from which spring erect shoots bearing spikes of distinctive flowers, with an open snapdragon shape and twin spurs projecting from the rear. Diascias offer shades of pink and mauve and varieties include 'Lilac Belle', 'Coral Belle', 'Salmon Supreme' and the trailing form 'Twinkle', which has dark stems and purplish pink flowers.

Soil preference: Well-drained, but not too dry
Aspect: Sun
Season of interest: Summer, autumn
Height and spread: 30cm (1ft), spreading

Companion plants: Beautiful with fellow South African natives such as perennial Nemesia or with other medium or low-growing ground cover plants such as catmint or *Campanula carpatica*.

Nepeta x faassenii Catmint Hardy perennial

A clump-forming perennial producing many arching or semi-lax stems furnished with toothed, nettle-like leaves and an almost constant run of big, generous spikes bearing small, hazy blue, lipped flowers. Cats find the plants' aroma irresistible. Other garden forms include the taller *Nepeta* 'Six Hills Giant', whose foliage is silvery grey green and *N. racemosa*, which is lower growing.

Soil preference: Any, well-drained
Aspect: Sun or part shade
Season of interest: Spring, summer, autumn
Height and spread: 60cm x 1m (2ft x 3ft 3in)

Companion plants: The classic companion to roses, often used to edge borders in a rose garden. But also superb as ground cover with other creeping perennials such as diascias, among bergenias or as a companion to medium-sized grasses.

Trifolium repens (ornamental forms)

Creeping Clover Hardy herbaceous perennial

A tough, meadowland perennial with creeping, prostrate stems furnished with short leaf stalks and, usually, three lobed compound leaves which are heart-shaped and form the familiar trefoil or shamrock outline. Garden forms include 'Purpurascens Quadrifolium', whose lucky four-leaf clovers are suffused with dark purple-brown, and the grey, green and cream 'Harlequin'.

Soil preference: Any
Aspect: Sun
Season of interest: Spring, summer
Height and spread: 20cm (8in), spreading

Companion plants: Delightful for covering small areas, especially when bulbs such as Crocus, Chionodoxa, Scilla, Muscari or *Hermodactyla* are encouraged to grow among them.

Lamium galeobdolon

Yellow Archangel   Hardy herbaceous perennial

A vigorous, invasive woodland perennial with toothed, nettle-like leaves which may be green, or silver striped. Spikes bearing whorls of butter yellow, lipped, deadnettle flowers develop in early summer. 'Hermann's Pride' has leaves streaked with silvery marks; 'Silver Angel' is more generously netted with silver-grey, but lacks vigour.

Soil preference: Any
Aspect: Shade
Season of interest: Year round
Height and spread: 45cm (1ft 6in), spreading

Companion plants: A useful woodlander for dry conditions, excellent with *Euphorbia amygdaloides* subsp. *robbiae*, and to follow bluebells and wood anemones.

Lysimachia nummularia

Creeping Jenny   Trailing hardy perennial

A creeping, semi-evergreen perennial whose long, lax stems root wherever they come into contact with the ground. The rounded, shiny leaves are produced in pairs along the stem and, in the growing season, bright yellow, five-petalled flowers appear in a steady succession. The form 'Aurea' has golden foliage.

Soil preference: Any not too dry
Aspect: Shade or part shade
Season of interest: Spring, summer
Height and spread: 6cm (2.5in), trailing

Companion plants: A valuable, weed-suppressing ground cover for sharing a shady spot with blue-flowered *Omphalodes verna* or any of the bugles (Ajuga).

Geranium macrorrhizum   Cranesbill   Hardy perennial

Mature plants form mats of creeping underground stems from which rise handsome, rounded, lobed, partly toothed leaves which are strongly apple-scented and which colour up to reds and russets in autumn. Flower stems, produced in late spring, carry pale pink blossoms, set off by dark calyces and prominent stamens. Richer coloured forms include 'Bevan's', which is bright pink, and 'Czakor', whose flowers are deeper magenta.

Soil preference: Any
Aspect: Any
Season of interest: Spring, summer, autumn
Height and spread: 50cm (1ft 8in) x 60cm (2ft), spreading

Companion plants: One of the very best groundcovers, superb with other cranesbills or furnishing the ground below shrub roses, rhododendrons or in the relatively dry shade thrown buy mature trees.

Polygonatum x hybridum (syn P. multiflorum)

Hardy perennial

Fleshy rhizomes produce plump shoots in spring which gradually unfurl to carry paired, oval leaves all the way along their arching length. Small clusters of bell-shaped, waxy greenish white flowers hang from each leaf axil in spring. Other pretty species include the smaller, *Polygonatum odoratum* which, in turn, has a prettily variegated form 'Striatum'.

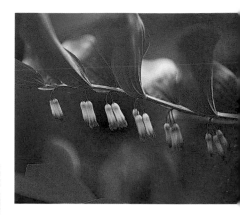

Soil preference: Any, not too wet
Aspect: Shade or part shade
Season of interest: Spring
Height and spread: 90cm x 60cm (3ft x 2ft), spreading

Companion plants: Lovely with ferns and other shade ground covers such as epimediums or lamiums and with its close relative, *Smilacina racemosa*, whose flowers stems are topped with creamy tufts.

Vinca minor

Lesser periwinkle   Creeping woody plant

A vigorous trailer with thin, woody stems and paired, oval, shiny, sometimes faintly marbled leaves. Each spring, flushes of pale blue, white or purple flowers grow from the leaf joints and thereafter flowering continues sporadically. Choices include 'Bowles Variety' (pale blue flowers), 'Gertrude Jekyll' (white) and such variegated forms as 'Argenteovariegata' (silvery cream) and 'Illumination' (gold).

Soil preference: Any
Aspect: Shade, part shade or sun. Not too hot
Season of interest: Year round
Height and spread: 15cm (6in), spreading

Companion plants: An invasive plant, best planted singly furnishing the feet of shrubs, or the base of a shady wall. An excellent foil for dwarf daffodils or try with carpeting *Lysimachia nummularia* or *Persicaria vacciniifolia*.

Persicaria vacciniifolia

Knotweed   Near woody, trailing perennial

A creeping plant from the Himalaya which forms mats of thin, wiry stems bearing small, pointed leaves which fire up for autumn colour, before falling. The flowers appear in late summer as a profusion of pale pink, tapering rat tails.

Soil preference: Any not too dry, nor too wet
Aspect: Shade, part shade
Season of interest: Summer, autumn
Height and spread: 15cm (6in), spreading

Companion plants: Beautiful for trailing over a bank and when allowed to thread itself among winter heathers. Good folllowing on from *Lithodora diffusa*.

Sedum **medium-sized hybrids**

Stonecrop   Hardy perennials

Robust perennials with rounded, fleshy leaves, often dark in colour and arching or prostrate stems, usually terminating in colourful clusters of flowers. *Sedum* 'Bertram Anderson' has dark purple to black foliage and dark wine pink flowers, 'Vera Jameson' also has purplish foliage but paler dusky rose pink flowers and 'Ruby Glow' has greenish purple foliage and brooding maroon to pink flowers.

Soil preference: Any free-draining
Aspect: Sun
Season of interest: Year round
Height and spread: 10–30cm x 30–45cm (4–12in x 12in–1ft 6in)

Companion plants: When massed at a sunny border front, these plants mix well with late summer perennials such as penstemons or with lower growing grasses. *Festuca glauca* and *F. amethystina* make a striking contrast with the purplish sedum leaves.

Sedum kamtschaticum

Stonecrop   Hardy perennial

Creeping rhizomes result in loose, slowly expanding mats of fleshy foliage on low growing plants which are topped in summer by flattened clusters of golden yellow flowers. The cream and green leaved form 'Variegatum' has the added bonus of attractive foliage, throughout the growing season.

Soil preference: Any free-draining
Aspect: Sun
Season of interest: Spring, summer
Height and spread: 15cm x 60cm (6in x 2ft)

Companion plants: Pretty weaving among other low growing, sun-loving plants such as aubretias, arabis and such other stonecrops as *Sedum acre* or *S. hispanicum*.

Thymus serpyllum

Wild Thyme   Woody, creeping perennial

Densely growing, mat-forming plants with criss-crossing prostrate stems covered with tiny, aromatic, rounded leaves. In early summer, the foliage is completely hidden by a carpet of brightly coloured flowers. Colours vary from rich purple through the rosy hues of 'Annie Hall' to shell pink in 'Pink Chintz' and pure white in *T. s.* var. *albus*.

Soil preference: Any free-draining
Aspect: Sun
Season of interest: Spring, summer, autumn
Height and spread: To 10cm (4in), spreading

Companion plants: Striking when grown as a lawn, or in cracks in paving along with other species of thyme such as *Thymus praecox* or with garden forms such as the gold and green 'Doone Valley' or *T. citriodorus* cultivars.

Tropaeolum majus   Nasturtium (trailing kinds)   Hardy annual

Familiar annual with large, hairless, rounded leaves carried along fleshy, prostrate stems and interspersed from midsummer onwards with vividly coloured, spurred flowers. The best trailing varieties include 'Jewel of Africa' (yellow, reds and peachy sunset hues – pictured), 'Climbing Mixed' and 'Tall Single Mixed'.

Soil preference: Free-draining, not too rich
Aspect: Sun
Season of interest: Summer, autumn
Height and spread: 30cm (1ft), spreading

Companion plants: Great for scrambling over a dry bank or for furnishing an old tree stump. The vivid colours and unruly growth make this plant a poor team player.

Buglossoides purpurocaerulea

Purple Gromwell   Hardy perennial

An invasive member of the forget-me-not family which produces erect stems, in spring and early summer, bearing flower clusters which are purplish in bud but turn an intense deep blue when fully open. When the flowers fade, the stems become prostrate and extend by 1m (3ft 3in) or more before touching the ground and taking root.

Soil preference: Any free-draining
Aspect: Sun
Season of interest: Summer
Height and spread: 30cm (1ft), spreading

Companion plants: Superb perennials for early summer but rampantly invasive. Beautiful with red valerian and with tall, late sedums to follow.

Erigeron karvinskianus

Mexican Daisy   Marginally hardy perennial

Not a weed-suppressing ground cover, but a free-seeding perennial which forms drifts and is capable of growing in the poorest of soils – even in the mortar of a brick wall! The small simple leaves are unremarkable but each plant produces masses of thin, wiry stems which carry several small pink-flushed white daisy flowers.

Soil preference: Any free-draining, preferably poor
Aspect: Sun
Season of interest: Spring, summer, autumn
Height and spread: 30cm x 45cm (1ft x 1ft 6in)

Companion plants: Whether as part of a rock garden, or grown in gravel or allowed to colonize old masonry, these little daisies are natural companions to sedums, sempervivums and alpine cranesbills.

Geranium x cantabrigiense   Hardy perennial

A hybrid, sometimes naturally occurring, between *G. macrorrhizum* and the much smaller *G. dalmaticum*. Neat, rounded, lobed, mildly aromatic foliage (redolent of mature apples) lasts from spring through to late autumn. The flowers are held just clear of the leaves and may be pinkish or white. The best known wild form has the variety name 'Biokovo', relating to where it was discovered in Dalmatia. 'Cambridge' (pictured) has smaller, neater, pink flowers.

Soil preference: Any
Aspect: Any
Season of interest: Spring, summer
Height and spread: 25cm (10in), spreading

Companion plants: A lovely ground cover among shrubs, especially if blended with such spring bulbs as *Narcissus cyclamineus* or crown imperials (*Fritillaria imperialis*). This hybrid also looks pretty grown with both its parents. Somewhat invasive.

Euphorbia amygdaloides var. robbiae

Mrs Robb's Bonnet   Hardy evergreen perennial

One of the best garden spurges, despite its invasiveness. Broad, oval leaves which resemble those of laurel, encircle the emerging stems which are topped from late winter with crozier-shaped spikes which straighten as the golden green flowers emerge. A vigorous, creeping root system ensures a dense cover of weed-proof vegetation.

Soil preference: Any, free-draining
Aspect: Shade or part shade
Season of interest: Winter, spring, summer
Height and spread: To 60cm (2ft), spreading

Companion plants: A striking woodlander, when grown in broad drifts with vivid red tulips such as *Tulipa sprengeri* or bright golden daffodils or yellow doronicums to go with the lime-green flowers. Solomon's seal and taller umbellifers such as *Anthriscus sylvestris* 'Ravenswing' make more subdued companions.

Trachystemon orientalis

Russian Borage   Hardy perennial

A thug, but a charming one, whose rootstock spreads in all directions with startling vigour. The small, pale blue and white flowers emerge first in early spring and are on short stems with narrow, swept-back petals and pointed stamens resembling shooting stars. The big, oar-shaped leaves come later, crowding together to form a weed-proof carpet.

Soil preference: Any, not too dry
Aspect: Shade or part shade
Season of interest: Spring, summer
Height and spread: 60cm (2ft), spreading

Companion plants: Allow this plant to spread in drifts, in dry shade, perhaps with epimediums, low-growing Mahonia species and with annual honesty *Lunaria annua* to provide extra height.

Persicaria microcephala 'Red Dragon' Hardy perennial

A vigorous species of which the cultivar 'Red Dragon,' is the best for garden use. Narrow, erect, jointed stems extend during spring and summer and carry leaves shaped like a Zulu warrior's *assegai* (spear). Their ground colour is a rich dusky purple, suffused with pewter and deep chocolate markings. The irregular sprays of small, white flowers are anticlimactic.

Soil preference: Moist, fertile
Aspect: Part shade or sun
Season of interest: Summer, autumn
Height and spread: 1.2m (4ft), spreading

Companion plants: The open habit of this plant makes is a good candidate for blending with others such as grasses, late-flowering lilies or colourful late perennials such as asters, Tricyrtis or heleniums.

Lamium maculatum

Dead Nettle   Hardy perennial

Easy, ubiquitous and a free seeder, this European wild plant has triangular, toothed leaves which are streaked or striped with silvery grey and held on stems which are square in section. The lipped flowers, produced in whorls at each leaf joint, may be shades of pink or white. 'Beacon Silver' has all-grey leaves and pink flowers. 'White Nancy' is similar but albino.

Soil preference: Any rich, well-drained but moist
Aspect: Sun or part shade
Season of interest: Year round
Height and spread: 30cm x 60cm (1ft by 2ft)

Companion plants: The fresh foliage and neat clumps of the young plants are beautiful with later flowering hellebores, some tulips, or among perennial wallflowers. Cut back several times for a fresh flush of growth.

Rodgersia aesculifolia

Hardy perennial

Stems rear up directly from the ground, bearing huge palmate leaves which resemble those of a horse chestnut (*Aesculus*). In summer, tall flower stems carry big panicles of creamy white blooms. Other Rodgersias worth growing include *R. podophylla* and *R. pinnata* 'Superba'.

Soil preference: Rich, deep but free-draining
Aspect: Sun or part shade
Season of interest: Summer
Height and spread: 1m x 1.5m (3ft 3in x 5ft)

Companion plants: Plants for a big planting on a bold scale. With tall growing plume poppies, Bocconia, they are superb, perhaps along with *Cortaderia selloana* or with a giant salvia such as *S. guaranitica* or *S. confertiflora*.

Juniperus conferta

Shore Juniper   Hardy prostrate shrub

A superb and dependable ground cover plant which, in good soil, roots as it goes, creating dense, weed-proof mats of spiky evergreen foliage. Easy to keep under control, but the spiky foliage can be quite painful when handled. Various garden forms include 'Emerald Sea,' 'Blue Lagoon' and the cream-blotched 'Sunsplash.'

Soil preference: Any
Aspect: Sun or part shade
Season of interest: Year round
Height and spread: 30cm (1ft), spreading

Companion plants: Good choice for covering a bank and pretty when loosely underplanted with short-season bulbs for a little extra spring colour.

Ophiopogon japonicus   Marginally hardy perennial

Grassy perennial whose dense growths of soft, loosely curled leaves are its main feature. In summer, small, off-white to dirty lilac flowers are produced, but are unremarkable. Marginally tender, in cold regions where it could be substituted with the hardier *O. planiscapus*, the natural, green-leaved form of the popular plant usually prized – by all those gardeners that like such things – for its unusual black foliage.

Soil preference: Any
Aspect: Sun, part shade
Season of interest: Year round
Height and spread: 10cm (4in), spreading

Companion plants: A lawn substitute, useful for furnishing a steep bank, for edging formal plantings or for covering space between other garden objects. Neutral, and therefore companionable to anything.

Hemerocallis   Day Lily   Hardy perennial

A huge group of versatile and beautiful perennials which can be grown individually, or masses as ground cover. The leaves are big, bold and grass or reed-like; the large, showy flowers are produced in generous sprays and resemble lilies. Colours range through yellow hues to mahogany, dusky pink, orange and salmon. Fine varieties include 'Golden Chimes' (pictured) the smaller flowered 'Corky,' 'Neyron Rose' and 'Pink Damask.'

Soil preference: Moist but well-drained, fertile
Aspect: Sun, part shade
Season of interest: Summer
Height and spread: Variable to 1m x 1m (to 3ft x 3ft)

Companion plants: Day lilies are great to mass with hostas, in moist conditions, and with later-flowering Ligularia or with earlier spuria irises.

Symphoricarpus x chenaultii 'Hancock'

Hardy shrub

A deciduous, creeping self-layering plant which quickly invades a large area, forming a network of prostrate or semi-prostrate stems with shiny, rounded leaves and, in summer, clusters of small, insignificant white flowers which are followed by small, white, pink-flushed fruits. Invasive and troublesome, but a fine ground cover where space is plentiful.

Soil preference: Any
Aspect: Sun, part shade, shade
Season of interest: Year round
Height and spread: 75cm, (2ft 6in) spreading

Companion plants: A fine plant for covering a difficult bank. Let it fight with *Hypericum calycinum* or any of the trailing cotoneasters for an interesting vegetative blanket.

Lonicera pileata   Hardy evergreen shrub

A slowly spreading shrub with small, triangular, glossy leaves arranged neatly along the stems. The creamy flowers are small and insignificant, and are followed by pale purple fruit, also insignificant. Can be clipped like a hedge, or left to develop into an attractive, low mound.

Soil preference: Any
Aspect: Sun or shade
Season of interest: Year round
Height and spread: 6ocm (2ft), spreading

Companion plants: A dense, but slow-growing ground cover plant, weed-proof and lovely to contrast with berry–bearing cotoneasters, blue-flowering *Ceanothus thyrsiflorus* var. *repens*.

Pachysandra terminalis

Japanese Spurge   Hardy, creeping shrub

Short, erect stems bear simple, evergreen leaves toothed or serrated at their tips. The flowers, produced in terminal clusters, are small, insignificant and greenish white. Probably the most uninteresting plant in cultivation, but it will grow in the densest shade, even where roots from other plants provide intense competition, and forms a neutral, green ground cover.

Soil preference: Any
Aspect: Shade
Season of interest: Year round
Height and spread: 30cm (1ft), spreading

Companion plants: Team with Vinca, *Helleborus foetidus*, bergenias or drought-tolerant ferns such as *Polypodium vulgare*.

Groundcover Schemes

Uniform, single species groundcover can be effective in creating a pleasant-looking, weed-suppressing surface. However, a skilfully composed mixture of plants usually has more impact and can sustain interest for longer. Groundcover can be the same height without being dull, if there is plenty of leaf and flower variety among the plants. Two schemes here demonstrate just what potential there can be, even with relatively humble plants.

Combining colour, texture and shape

Despite the area being rather limited in size, a rich mix of plants brings together some exciting combinations of colour, texture and shape in the main picture. The strongest contrast is between the dark-leaved clover, *Trifolium repens* 'Purpurascens Quadrifolium' and the *Thymus vulgaris* 'Silver Posie' whose leaves have a pale cream edge. That silvery theme is picked up behind by the beautifully marked fern, *Athyrium niponicum* var. pictum and, as an extra bonus, *Erigeron karvinskianus* produces its little pink-flushed white daisy blooms for much of the year.

All these plants are easy to maintain. The thyme needs to be trimmed back, preferably in mid- to late summer, to foster new growth; the clover is invasive, so its spread should be restricted and the Erigeron will self-seed copiously. Simply pull out unwanted seedlings before they become large enough to be troublesome.

Stunning evergreen groundcover

Rich contrasts in both colour and texture are obvious in this delightful composition (below) where the golden-leaved form of creeping Jenny, *Lysimachia nummularia* 'Aurea', merges with the dark, purple-leaved bugle, *Ajuga reptans* 'Atropurpurea'. Both plants love moist conditions in slightly dappled shade, and each has enough vigour to avoid being overrun by the other. At flowering time, in early summer, the bugle produces short but conspicuous spires of Oxford-blue, lipped flowers which go perfectly with the bright gold of the creeping Jenny, whose bright yellow flowers are all but lost among the vivid gold foliage.

This groundcover is just about evergreen, but both species benefit from re-planting every few years. There is no need to buy new plants, for this, but it is desirable to remove all old clumps, to gather rooted segments or runners from the most vigorous growths and to re-plant them.

Mixing dark-leaved *Trifolium repens* 'Purpurascens' with the silvery *Thymus vulgaris* 'Silver Posie' makes this area of groundcover really stand out.

This contrasting, evergreen combination of *Ajuga reptans* 'Atropurpurea' to the left and the golden-leaved *Lysimachia nummularia* 'Aurea' shows off nature's painting palette at its very best.

grasses

Carex flagellifera

Weeping Brown New Zealand Sedge   Evergreen grass-like perennial

A shimmering, tussock-forming sedge with narrow leaves which are surprisingly strong but extremely flexible. Flowers are unremarkable except that they are produced on prostrate stems that gradually extend for seed dispersal. Leaf colour varies from beige-green to gingery-brown in better selections.

Soil preference: Free-draining but not too damp
Aspect: Sun or part shade
Season of interest: Year round
Height and spread: 50cm x 50cm (1ft 8in x 1ft 8in)

Companion plants: Attractive mingling with flowering perennials in dusky hues or to contrast with broad-leaved plants like blue hostas and glossy bergenias. Also pleasing with silverlings in gravel.

Carex buchananii

Leatherleaf Sedge Grass   Evergreen grass-like perennial

Bold eruptions of thin, arching, whippy leaves which are reddish brown. The flowers, which develop during summer, are borne on arching stems which lengthen to more than 1m (3ft 3in), thus distributing seed near, but not too near, the parent plant. The colour is more intense in full sun. Not hardy in extremes of frost.

Soil preference: Free-draining in winter
Aspect: Sun
Season of interest: Year round
Height and spread: 60cm x 45cm (24in x 18in)

Companion plants: Beautiful rising up between other low growing green or variegated grasses and sedges. Handsome with bold spring bulbs or with Mediterranean shrubs like Artemisia and lavender.

Chasmanthium latifolium

Sea Oats, Spangle Grass   Perennial grass

An upright grass with broad, flat leaves carried on thin, cane-like stems which end in panicles of showy, flattened flowers. Throughout autumn, the leaves gradually turn yellow and the oat-like seedheads hold their shape well into winter. An excellent plant for cutting to use as dried arrangements.

Soil preference: Fertile, free-draining, but not too dry
Aspect: Sun or part shade
Season of interest: Summer, autumn
Height and spread: 90cm x 45cm (3ft x 1ft 6in)

Companion plants: A handy companion to late flowering perennials, particularly rudbeckias and heleniums. The erect stems and strange flowers make an interesting contrast, too, with Ratibida or perennial asters.

Festuca glauca   Blue Fescue   Hardy evergreen grass

A neat, tussock-forming grass with thin, needle-like leaves which, in full sun, are a striking blue-green, almost with a lustre. In summer, pale, silvery green flower stems develop and carry small, but attractively feathered flowers which turn buff with age.

Soil preference: Any dry
Aspect: Sun
Season of interest: Year round
Height and spread: To 30cm x 30cm (1ft x 1ft)

Companion plants: Delightful when bedded semi-formally with other 'texture' plants such as *Euphorbia myrsinites*, *Ophiopogon planiscapus* 'Nigrescens' or the sedges described above.

Oryzopsis miliacea

Smilo Grass   Hardy perennial grass

A big, waving, graceful species from arid western North America, with bold but narrow, gently arching leaves. Throughout summer, thin flower stems emerge from the loose tussock and bear light, airy panicles of tiny flowers. Although these stems move in the slightest breeze, they do not collapse.

Soil preference: Any, but not wet
Aspect: Full sun
Season of interest: Year round
Height and spread: 1.5m x 1m (5ft x 3ft 3in)

Companion plants: A superb grass for bringing a little lushness to a hot, dry spot. Fine among Mediterranean style plants such as Californian poppies, Lampranthus or helichrysums.

Hordeum jubatum

Foxtail Barley, Squirreltail Barley   Perennial grass

Vivid green leaves and stems are joined, in late spring, by paler green or purple-flushed flowers which nod, and whose long, crowded awns make a squirrel tail effect. As they ripen, the flowers and stems turn gradually to pale beige, contrasting with all the greenery around them.

Soil preference: Any reasonably fertile and well-drained
Aspect: Sun
Season of interest: Spring, summer
Height and spread: 60cm x 30cm (2ft x 1ft)

Companion plants: A lovely plant to crowd in with mixed hardy annuals such as poppies and cornflowers, or to surround such early perennials as oriental poppies and lupins. Also striking when planted with *Verbascum chaixii* or where it can ripen among midsummer penstemons or Tagetes.

Agrostis canina 'Silver Needles'

Velvet Bent   Hardy perennial grass

A low, mat-forming grass with narrow, softly spiky leaves and, through summer, slender, feathery flowerheads held 10cm (4in) above the dense foliage. An understated perennial, but the soft, tactile mats are particularly attractive when produced by 'Silver Needles' which has thin, white margins to the foliage. Deadhead to prevent seeding.

Soil preference: Any, not too dry
Aspect: Sun or part shade
Season of interest: Year round
Height and spread: 6cm x 30cm (2.5in x 1ft)

Companion plants: A pretty grass to spread on a scree or low-growing scheme, with thymes and carpeting heathers or with shade tolerant alpines like mossy saxifrages and violas.

Carex morrowi 'Evergold'   Evergreen grass-like perennial

Squat clumps of stiffly arching, glossy leaves which are boldly striped along their lengths with green and yellow-gold. Small panicles of brownish flowers are produced in late spring, but the plant is most valued for its durable evergreen foliage. Leaf tips may brown during bad weather and should be trimmed to improve appearance.

Soil preference: Any moist
Aspect: Part shade
Season of interest: Year round
Height and spread: 30cm x 35cm (1ft x 1ft 1in)

Companion plants: Useful to blend with moisture or part-shade loving flowers such as Trollius or blue *Aconitum napellus*. The narrow leaves contrast well, in spring, with those of *Brunnera macrophylla* whose lacy sprays of forget-me-not flowers also make a foil for the golden hue of the sedge.

Deschampsia caespitosa

Tufted Hairgrass or Tussock Grass   Hardy perennial grass

Large grass which forms bold but compact tussocks of narrow, mid green, silky foliage. Height comes from the tall, wiry flower stems. Height comes from the narrow, wiry flower stems which wave gracefully in the breeze. The flowers form cloud-like sprays which are especially beautiful when they are spangled with dew and catch the light. 'Bronzeschleier' (Bronze Veil) is an improved form with bronze-tinted flowers.

Soil preference: Any not too dry
Aspect: Part shade or sun
Season of interest: Year round
Height and spread: 1.5m x 1m (5ft by 3ft 3in)

Companion plants: Lovely with herbaceous subjects such as geums, campanulas or poppies in a border or in more sparse planting among rocks or gravel. Also, try in a meadow-planting scheme with wild flowers.

Deschampsia flexuosa 'Tatra Gold'

Wavy Hair Grass   Evergreen grass

A neat, tussock forming grass with very fine but soft, needle-like leaves in a bluish green colour. 'Tatra Gold' has fluorescent green leaves and from late spring. From late spring golden flower stems emerge and soon erupt into feathery blooms. The flowers persist until late summer but are best removed when fully faded.

Soil preference: Moist, acidic
Aspect: Sun, part shade or shade
Season of interest: Summer
Height and spread: 70cm x 30cm (2ft 6in x 1ft)

Companion plants: Lovely in a naturalistic setting, among ferns and such flowers as epimediums, primroses or anemones. Could also be contrasted with bold leaved perennials such as bergenias or pulmonarias.

Holcus mollis 'Albovariegatus'

Perennial grass

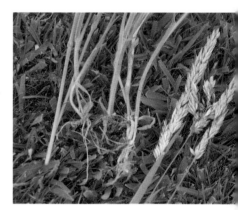

A brightly variegated grass with a creeping root stock and loose mats of narrow velvety leaves which are sage green with bold, white to cream margins. The flower stems, often sparse in number, carry small, dense panicles of blooms which turn buff as they age. Regular division and re-planting, will help this plant to retain vigour.

Soil preference: Any, not too dry
Aspect: Sun or part shade
Season of interest: Spring or summer
Height and spread: 30cm x 45cm (1ft x 1ft 6in)

Companion plants: The colourful spring mats make a bright relief from the monotonous green of emerging summer perennial foliage such as that of lupins and oriental poppies. It also creates a pretty foil for blue- and pastel-coloured spring bulbs.

Luzula sylvatica

Greater Wood Rush   Hardy grass-like evergreen

A rush which forms clusters of rosettes, each composed of stiff, broad leaves with a pale margin and deeper green midribs. In spring, small clusters of dark rusty brown flowers are held on short stems. The form 'Aurea' has bright yellow-green leaves and 'Aureomarginata' has narrow, cream margins to its leaves.

Soil preference: Any reasonably moist with high humus content
Aspect: Part shade or shade
Season of interest: Year round
Height and spread: To 45cm x 45cm (1ft 6in x 1ft 6in)

Companion plants: An attractive woodlander, at home with wood anemones, hardy cyclamen, and other shade loving species. Particularly effective carpeting the bases of old trees, especially among ferns.

Giant grasses

Larger grasses have great architectural value and will help to bring character to planting schemes. Dense kinds such as pampas grasses are most effective when sited among shrubs or given plenty of space, but the more graceful species, whose flower stems may nod and wave in the breeze, can be used to augment herbaceous plantings, where they bring a softer texture.

1. Cortaderia selloana
The familiar Pampas grass, a native of South America, whose plumes appear in early autumn.

2. Miscanthus sinensis
Commonly known as Elephant Grass. This is an Asian deciduous species which forms vast tussocks, often with silver-lined stems, and comes into flower late in the season.

3. Spartina pectinata
A vigorous North American wetland species, which can grow up to 3m (10ft) high.

4. Carex pendula
Wood Sedge, a shade-loving European species with curved, pleated leaves and stately flower stems held 2m (6ft 6in) high, whose female blooms hang like catkins.

5. Eragrostis curvula
Commonly known as African Love Grass. A large but graceful grass with arching stems and long, feathery inflorescences produced during late summer.

6. Phragmites australis
A widespread wetland grass, known as the Common Reed, whose broad, blue-green leaves and tall stems are topped with dark, pendulous tassels of flower late in summer. Ecologically important in marsh or reed-bed habitats.

1	2	3
4	5	6

Arundo donax var. versicolor

Giant Reed   Near hardy perennial grass

Not a true reed, but a giant Mediterranean grass producing thick, flexible canes furnished along their length by broadly strap-shaped, blue-green leaves (white-striped in *A. d.* var. *versicolor*). In mild areas, each stem will terminate, in autumn, with a feathery, silky inflorescence. Used as hedging or screen material in some temperate regions.

Soil preference: Any
Aspect: Sun, shelter from extreme frost
Season of interest: Year round
Height and spread: To 3m (10ft), spreading

Companion plants: An architectural accent for a border planted for sub-tropical effect or near a big pond where its tall stems can arch over the water. Interesting as a container plant, as well.

Carex comans   Evergreen grass-like perennial

A tussock-forming sedge with very narrow, flexible, hair like leaves usually sold as a bronze-tinted selection. The flowers are insignificant and as with so many New Zealand sedges, their stems extend beyond the dimensions of the plant. 'Frosted Curls' has silvery green leaves. Cut back in spring for fresh, tidy tussocks.

Soil preference: Any
Aspect: Sun or part shade
Season of interest: Year round
Height and spread: 30cm x 30cm (1ft x 1ft)

Companion plants: A charming and wind-resistant ingredient for cottage-style plantings of coast-loving perennials such as erigerons, osteospermums, pinks or taller sedums. Also attractive as container plants.

Elymus hispidus (E. glaucus of gardens)

Hardy perennial grass

An eye-catching grass with a creeping, rhizomatous rootstock and bold, strap-shaped leaves of an intense blue-green. The flower spikes are carried on 60cm (2ft) stems in mid-summer. Though it spreads, this grass is seldom invasive in a garden.

Soil preference: Free-draining, sandy
Aspect: Sun
Season of interest: Summer
Height and spread: 60cm (2ft), spreading

Companion plants: Beautiful with other coastal plants such as the glaucous leaved *Crambe maritima* or with red annual poppies and the tougher euphorbias.

Lagurus ovatus   Hare's Tail Grass   Hardy annual grass

Soft, pale green, grassy foliage develops in autumn or spring, and is joined in early summer by flower stems held just clear of the leaves. The broad, bluntly pointed flower spikes are pale in colour, turning silvery as they mature, and are soft and furry to the touch.

Soil preference: Any free-draining
Aspect: Sun
Season of interest: Summer, autumn
Height and spread: To 45cm x 15cm (1ft 6in x 6in)

Companion plants: A pretty but somewhat invasive annual, common on roadsides in temperate regions, and best mixed with flowering annuals, or allowed to naturalise on sandy coastal soils with sea hollies, sea campion and sea kale.

Elegia capensis   Fountain Reed

Marginally tender grass-like perennial

A restio, i.e. one of a group of exclusively Southern African rush-like perennials. Tall, bottle green, canes produce dense, fluffy clusters of foliage at their joints, giving the impression of a huge mare's tail. The brownish tan flowers are produced in showy clusters.

Soil preference: Moist but free-draining
Aspect: Sun
Season of interest: Year round
Height and spread: 2m x 1.5m (6ft 6in x 5ft)

Companion plants: A very large plant for a sheltered, mild spot, perhaps with such other African natives as crocosmias, Agapanthus and for autumn, *Amaryllis belladonna*. Also at home complementing bamboos and other large grasses.

Briza maxima

Greater Quaking Grass   Marginally hardy annual grass

Soft, pale green foliage emerges from dispersed seeds in autumn or spring. In early summer, flower stems extend and branch into wiry filaments, each of which carries hanging, scaled, heart-shaped flowers. These shake and tremble in the slightest breeze, and persist on the plants long after the foliage has yellowed and died back. Can be invasive.

Soil preference: Any
Aspect: Sun or part shade
Season of interest: Summer, autumn
Height and spread: 45cm x 20cm (1ft 6in x 8in)

Companion plants: Pretty if allowed to self-seed among low Mediterranean shrubs such as lavenders or among old fashioned roses, perhaps with nigellas.

Alopecurus lanatus

Woolly Foxtail Grass   Hardy perennial grass

A little gem from rocky slopes of the Mediterranean, perfect for a well-drained spot. Narrow, hairy or woolly, silvery blue-green leaves form tiny, neat tussocks. The flowers are produced sparsely, on small, densely packed spikes. One of the few truly woolly grasses, but challenging to grow.

Soil preference: Free-draining but not too dry
Aspect: Sun
Season of interest: Summer
Height and spread: 10cm x 12cm (4in x 5in)

Companion plants: Really best in an alpine trough or treasured in an alpine house and very beautiful with the small *Artemisia schmidtiana* 'Nana', with cushion saxifrages or among small, Mediterranean bulbs.

Festuca amethystina

Large Blue Fescue   Hardy perennial grass

A glaucous grass whose very narrow, cylindrical leaves form bold but tidy evergreen tussocks. Almost interchangeable with *Festuca glauca* which is slightly smaller and more refined. In early summer, short spikes appear bearing zigzag panicles of flowers.

Soil preference: Any, well-drained
Aspect: Sun
Season of interest: Year round
Height and spread: 45cm x 25cm (1ft 6in x 10in)

Companion plants: A fine team mate for *Festuca glauca*, which is slightly smaller and more refined and a fine team mate for other grass-like plants with contrasting foliage. *Carex buchananii* or *Ophiopogon planiscapus* 'Nigrescens' would also go well, perhaps with a backdrop of airy *Verbena bonariensis*.

Leymus arenarius

Blue Lyme Grass   Hardy perennial grass

A grass of coastal sand dunes with a creeping rootstock from which spring tillers bearing broad, strap-shaped, vivid blue-green leaves. In summer, the stems lengthen but stay stiff and erect, carrying long, narrow flower spikes.

Soil preference: Any, well-drained
Aspect: Sun
Season of interest: Summer
Height and spread: 1m (3ft 3in), spreading

Companion plants: This bold grass is good on a sunny bank, with sun-loving shrubs and herbaceous plants such as *Romneya coulteri*, *Stachys byzantina* or with summer bulbs such as *Galtonia candicans*.

Pennisetum alopecuroides

Fountain Grass Near hardy perennial grass

A big, bold grass originating from eastern Asia, with soft, arching foliage and flexible flower stems. The broad, bushy, foxtail flowers are silvery with purplish or bronze suffusions, and held on fairly lax stems creating a fountain effect. Good varieties include the more compact, earlier flowering 'Hameln' and 'Moudry', which has dark purple flowerheads.

Soil preference: Any fertile, free-draining
Aspect: Sun
Season of interest: Summer
Height and spread: 1m x 60cm (3ft 3in x 2ft)

Companion plants: Beautiful near a border front, or when cascading over a bank, particularly planted with strongly coloured perennials such as asters, dahlias or, earlier in the summer, delphiniums.

Stipa gigantea

Giant Feather Grass, Golden Oat Hardy evergreen grass

Big evergreen tussocks of dark green leaves which are flat and soft to the touch grow to about 75cm (30in). Each spring, wand-like flower stems emerge and extend, eventually creating a firework display of loose panicles of papery flowers which, when lit from behind, appear as bright, translucent gold.

Soil preference: Any free-draining
Aspect: Sun
Season of interest: Spring, summer
Height and spread: To 2m x 1m (6ft 6in x 3ft 3in)

Companion plants: Though very tall, this is a great plant to feature near the front or middle of a border. Tulips are blooming when the wands extend, but the mature, drying flowers are wonderful as a foil for mulleins, tall campanulas, *Onopordon nervosum* or sunflowers.

Poa labillardierei

Silver/Blue Tussock Grass Marginally hardy perennial grass

A dense, tussock forming plant with fairly upright, silvery green leaves and stems which arch outwards slightly as they age. The flowers, which have a deeper blue-green hue, are borne in panicles on long, slender, arching stems in summer. Happy in an exposed spot, but needs protection from sustained deep frost.

Soil preference: Any free-draining
Aspect: Sun
Season of interest: Year round
Height and spread: 1m x 75cm (3ft 3in x 2ft 6in)

Companion plants: The tall, but flexible blue-green leaves are lovely among pink flowers of Sidalcea, or among penstemons and would make a dreamy combination with equally blue-green eryngiums.

Acorus gramineus   Japanese Rush   Medium evergreen perennial

Surprisingly, these belong to the arum family but resemble sedges. Narrow, tough, sword-shape leaves grow from a network of rhizomes to form dense fan-shaped tussocks. The flower spikes jut out at angles but are not very conspicuous. Variegated forms are the most decorative. 'Ogon' has yellow-green and cream striping and is similar to 'Variegatus'. 'Hakuro-nishiki' is more compact with yellow-green foliage.

Soil preference: Any, especially damp or boggy
Aspect: Sun or part shade
Season of interest: Year round
Height and spread: 40cm x 90cm (1ft 4in x 3ft)

Companion plants: A gently coloured but conspicuous asset to any bog planting scheme, particularly among the broader leaves of such hostas as 'Golden Prayers', 'Halcyon' or *H. sieboldiana*.

Carex riparia 'Variegata'

Great Pond Sedge   Large grass-like perennial

An invasive perennial with a creeping rootstock and incredible toughness, but strikingly beautiful if kept under control, or grown where the spread is unlikely to cause problems. The bold gold and green variegations contrast in early summer with the dark female flowers.

Soil preference: Any wet or boggy or aquatic
Aspect: Any
Season of interest: Spring, summer
Height and spread: 1.5m (5ft) high, spreading

Companion plants: Hardly a team player, but plant it with *Ranunculus lingua* greater spearwort, and you can expect a dual between two thuggish plants.

Juncus effusus f. spiralis

Corkscrew Rush   Large, grass-like perennial

Form of the familiar clump-forming rush which has dark green, narrow, shiny stiff leaves and rusty brown flower tufts in late summer. The aptly named corkscrew rush has a hormone disorder which causes it to grow bizarre spring-like leaves. A curio, rather than an object of beauty, but it adds interest to a moist garden.

Soil preference: Any damp
Aspect: Sun or part shade
Season of interest: Year round
Height and spread: 1.2m x 75cm (4ft x 30in)

Companion plants: Fun to plant among margin species such as kingcup (*Caltha palustris*) and water forget-me-not – *Myosotis scorpioides*, where its odd foliage makes a twisted contrast.

Miscanthus sinensis   Chinese Silver Grass   Large grass

A bold grass with arching, narrowly strap-like leaves up to 3cm (1in) across, each with a silver central line along its length. In late summer or autumn, the tall, erect stems erupt to produce silky tassel flowers. Stems and leaves turn beige in autumn, but remain decorative for most of the winter. There are many varieties of Miscanthus, but most are big and bold. 'Silberfeder' has silvery pink flowers, 'Morning Light' pale leaf margins and 'Variegatus' has striped white and green leaves.

Soil preference: Any fertile and moist
Aspect: Sun or part shade
Season of interest: Summer, autumn
Height and spread: 2m x 1m (6ft 6in x 3ft 3in)

Companion plants: Big plants like these need big companions. Try with large-flowered hydrangeas and bold-leaved perennials such as such as Rodgersia or Ligularia.

Panicum virgatum

Switch Grass   Hardy perennial grass

An upright but waving grass whose young leaves may be tinged with purple, and which turn yellow-gold as they age, late in autumn. The flowers, produced during late summer and early autumn, come in large, nodding panicles. Fine garden forms include 'Heavy Metal', whose leaves have a pewter sheen and 'Strictum', whose narrow, upright foliage colours well in autumn.

Soil preference: Moist but free-draining
Aspect: Sun
Season of interest: Summer, autumn
Height and spread: 1m x 75cm (3ft 3in x 2ft 6in)

Companion plants: Best used among late perennials in a mixed border. Rudbeckias, heleniums, monardas and dahlias all make beautiful companions.

Uncinia unciniata

New Zealand Hook Sedge   Grass-like perennial

An understated but gently attractive sedge which forms slow-growing, tightly packed clumps of rhizomes from which narrow, leathery, rust-coloured leaves and stems grow. These hold their colour all year and in late summer are joined by dark brown flower spikes. Protect from extremes of frost.

Soil preference: Moist but free-draining
Aspect: Sun or part shade
Season of interest: Year round
Height and spread: 25cm x 30cm (10in x 1ft)

Companion plants: A fine plant to blend with contrasting, silvery foliage, as supplied by *Salix lanata* or *S. helvetica*. Also pretty with spring perennials such as *Omphalodes verna* or with such blue spring bulbs as *Muscari armeniacum* or *Scilla sibirica*.

Chusquea culeo

Clump/Clumping Bamboo   Bamboo

A graceful New World bamboo with tall, erect canes of olive to bottle green, with which the pale, papery leaf sheathes contrast. Clusters of leaves develop at the stem joints giving a bottle-brush impression and on mature stems, when the foliage dies, twiggy clusters of secondary stems remain. Not for a small garden.

Soil preference: Humus-rich, not too dry
Aspect: Sun or part shade, sheltered
Season of interest: Year round
Height and spread: To 6m (20ft), usually less, spreading

Companion plants: A fine plant for the woodland edge, either grown with other bamboos or among trees with handsome trunks – *Prunus serrula*, *Arbutus unedo* or Stewartia would be examples.

Pleioblastus viridistriatus

Dwarf Greenstripe   Semi-dwarf bamboo

A low growing, gently suckering bamboo with thin, jointed, sometimes branched stems which are deep green. The broad, hanging leaves are vividly striped green and gold. If grown as an herbaceous perennial, i.e. cut to ground level each spring, the young stems are fresher and the foliage more vibrant than in unpruned specimens.

Soil preference: Any
Aspect: Sun or part shade
Season of interest: Summer
Height and spread: 1.5m x 1.5m (5ft x 5ft)

Companion plants: A valuable plant for gold foliage which does not scorch in sun. Superb with contrasting intense blues of *Anchusa* 'Loddon Royalist' or Ceratostigma, or with the vivid red of such dahlias as 'Bishop of Llandaff'.

Phyllostachys aurea

Fishpole Bamboo, Golden Bamboo   Tall bamboo

A vigorously suckering bamboo from China, with thick stems which are olive green when young, maturing in sun, to a rich gold. The dark green leaves contrast well. The tendency for forming dense thickets needs to be curbed by thinning out annually. Remove weedy growth and some of the oldest stems at ground level, leaving an open distribution of graceful stems. Take off unwanted new shoots as they appear.

Soil preference: Any free-draining, not too dry
Aspect: Sun or part shade
Season of interest: Year round
Height and spread: To 8m (26ft), spreading

Companion plants: A fine feature plant on its own or standing by water, perhaps with dark stemmed bamboos such as *P. nigra* or large-leaved perennials.

Phyllostachys nigra   Black Bamboo   Tall bamboo

One of the most dramatic of the large bamboos because of its thick, attractively jointed, black stems which contrast so strongly with the fresh, green leaves. Young stems are green, but gradually become mottled with darker blotches before turning black. Remove the thin suckers on mature plants to sustain an open habit.

Soil preference: Any, not too dry
Aspect: Sun or part shade
Season of interest: Year round
Height and spread: 8m (26ft), spreading

Companion plants: Good in a container, while young, so perfect for bringing height to a small area such as a roof garden. The dark stems are handsome against the golden or glaucous leaves of hostas.

Sasa veitchii

Kuma zasa   Medium-sized bamboo

A Japanese bamboo with a creeping rootstock and numerous slender green canes whose foliage forms a dense, weed-suppressing groundcover. The leaves are broader and shorter than those of most bamboos and turn beige at their margins in winter, creating a variegated effect.

Soil preference: Any
Aspect: Shade or part shade
Season of interest: Year round
Height and spread: 1.5m (5ft), spreading

Companion plants: Too invasive to be inter-planted, but handy for dense shade, or for a woodland floor, perhaps at the feet of such blossom-bearing trees as cherries, Malus or Aesculus.

Thamnocalamus crassinodus

Merlyn   Hardy bamboo

A stately bamboo from Nepal which is reliably hardy in mild areas, but which will not tolerate penetrating frost. The beauty is in the stems, whose bluish patina, when young, contrast with the beige colour of the maturing bracts. The variety 'Merlin' has taller, more elegant stems with smaller leaves than the typical species. Thinning the stems, from time to time, will enhance the beauty of this plant.

Soil preference: Any free-draining
Aspect: Sun or part shade
Season of interest: Year round
Height and spread: 5m x 3m (16ft x 10ft)

Companion plants: A fine companion to other bamboos, but best viewed where the light is able to shine through the clump. Under plant with bold-leaved plants such as hostas, or with a mixture of ferns.

Hakonechloa macra 'Aureola'

Japanese Forest Grass, Golden Hakone   Hardy deciduous grass

Graceful, soft textured, Japanese species which forms loose, soft textured tussocks of cascading stems furnished with tapering, ribbon-like leaves. The flowers are in fine, open panicles. In autumn, the leaves become suffused with russet and last well into winter. Garden forms include 'Aureola', which is gold-striped.

Soil preference: Any, humus-rich, not too dry
Aspect: Sun or part shade
Season of interest: Summer
Height and spread: 60cm x 60cm (2ft x 2ft)

Companion plants: The gentle texture and cascading habit make this a fine companion for other contained plants like blue-leaved specimen hostas and ferns or to team with a Japanese maple.

Anemanthele lessoniana
(syn. Stipa arundinacea)   Hardy evergreen grass

A handsome perennial grass from New Zealand with lax, gracefully arching stems and leaves which are green, with reddish suffusions and big, floppy panicles of flower which create a shimmering, silvery effect whenever they catch the light.

Soil preference: Any not too dry
Aspect: Sun or part shade
Season of interest: Summer
Height and spread: 1m x 45cm (3ft 3in x 1ft 6in)

Companion plants: A fine container plant, best grown on its own, so that it can cascade over the sides of the pot. Combine with pots of lilies in summer or dwarf asters and chrysanthemums in autumn.

Zea mays   Indian Corn, Maize   Annual grass

The familiar crop, grown since prehistoric times in North and Central America makes an unusual ornamental for containers. Thick, erect stems are furnished with broad, flag-like leaves and terminate in showy flower 'tassels'. Ornamental varieties include 'Quadricolor', whose leaves are striped pink cream and green, and 'Indian Summer', whose cobs bear coloured kernels.

Soil preference: Any fertile and well-drained
Aspect: Sun
Season of interest: Summer, autumn
Height and spread: 2m x 45cm (6ft 6in x 1ft 6in)

Companion plants: Useful as focal points, in containers, bringing height to sub-tropical plant groupings, including plants like Solenostemon (coleus) and morning glory.

Imperata cylindrica 'Rubra'

Japanese Blood Grass   Tender perennial grass

A distinctive grass whose erect, flattened leaves, in the variety 'Rubra', take on a striking red hue in the right conditions. Flower spikes carry long, thin panicles but the plant seldom blooms in colder regions. Will not tolerate frost.

Soil preference: Fertile, not too dry
Aspect: Sun or part shade
Season of interest: Summer
Height and spread: 45cm x 30cm (1ft 6in x 1ft)

Companion plants: A striking grass, but not easy to cultivate in the cold. Good in a container when contrasted with rich greens of other grasses such as *Deschampsia flexuosa* or with foliage plants such as Solenostemon (coleus) or bergenias.

Pennisetum setaceum 'Rubrum'

Purple Fountain Grass   Marginally tender perennial grass

An African and Asian native which forms big clumps from which cascade bold, curving leaves and arching flower stems carrying generous foxtail inflorescences. In the form 'Rubrum' (sometimes sold as 'Atrosanguineum') the leaves and stems are suffused with deep purple red. The paler flowers are tinted dusky rose.

Soil preference: Rich, well-drained
Aspect: Sun
Season of interest: Summer
Height and spread: 1m x 75cm (3ft 3in x 2ft 6in)

Companion plants: A superb container plant to place near bright flowers – orange or red nasturtiums, perhaps, or to make a contrast with such potted succulents as Echeveria or *Aeonium* 'Zwartkop'.

Cymbopogon citratus

Lemon Grass   Tender perennial

The familiar culinary herb, native in southern India and Sri Lanka. The tall, relatively straight, grassy foliage is strongly aromatic, smelling of ripe lemons and makes a lovely container plant, but only for summer use outdoors in cold climates. The flowers consist of loose panicles, but these seldom appear on greenhouse-raised plants.

Soil preference: Any fertile
Aspect: Sun
Season of interest: Year round
Height and spread: 1m x 30cm (3ft 3in x 1ft)

Companion plants: Try this as a fragrant addition to a containerised herb collection, growing it among rosemary, thymes, sage, tarragon and bay.

Carex pendula

Pendulous Sedge   Hardy grass-like perennial

Huge, bold, thrusting sedge species common in moist European woodland. The arching, evergreen leaves have a central pleat and, when the flower stems emerge in summer, these are also arching, carrying catkin-like female flowers and tan male ones. A large but elegant, free-seeding plant.

Soil preference: Any, not too dry
Aspect: Part shade or shade
Season of interest: Year round
Height and spread: 2m x 1.5m (6ft 6in x 5ft)

Companion plants: Wonderful in woodland when set about with ragged robin (*Lychnis flos-cuculi*), bluebells, *Euphorbia amygdaloides* in all its forms and woodland primula species.

Helictotrichon sempervirens

Blue Oat Grass   Hardy evergreen grass

Narrow, blue-green leaves form neat evergreen tussocks from which spring tall, slender, arching flower stems which carry panicles of paler green to beige flowers. *H. s.* var. *pendulum* produces heavier, more nodding flower stems. The long-lived tussocks are a haven for over-wintering invertebrates. From the Mediterranean.

Soil preference: Any free-draining
Aspect: Sun, partial shade
Season of interest: Year round
Height and spread: 1m x 1m (3ft 3in by 3ft 3in)

Companion plants: A striking feature plant when set among perennials such as salvias or achilleas, or between low shrubs such as *Teucrium chamaedrys* or Ceratostigma, so that it can arch its flower stems above them.

Phalaris arundinacea 'Picta'

Gardeners' Garters   Hardy perennial grass

An invasive but beautiful grass with creeping rhizomes and stems bearing keeled leaves which are striped white and green, flushed pinkish when very young. The soft flower spikes appear in late summer and quickly turn beige. Delay cutting back until spring to maximise shelter for wintering wildlife.

Soil preference: Any
Aspect: Any apart from deep, dense shade
Season of interest: Spring, summer
Height and spread: To 1.5m (5ft), spreading

Companion plants: A classic border grass, at home with summer flowers like dahlias, lupins, big poppies or campanulas. Also very beautiful among old fashioned roses such as *Rosa* 'Fantin-Latour', *R.* 'Charles de Mills' or *R. gallica* 'Versicolor'.

Stipa calamagrostis Hardy deciduous perennial grass

Tuft-forming foliage makes this grass a neat grower from which spring generous supplies of flower stems bearing big, breezy panicles of flowers which are as attractive cut for indoors as when left on the plant. The foliage matures early and turns beige brown, but the inflorescences continue to add interest all winter.

Soil preference: Light, free-draining
Aspect: Sun
Season of interest: Summer
Height and spread: 1m x 60cm (3ft 3in x 2ft)

Companion plants: Good to blend with prairie perennials such as gaillardias, *Verbena bonariensis*, scabious and later in the season, Vernonia (ironweed).

Stipa tenuissima

Hardy perennial grass

An American species which forms neat clumps of upstanding, narrow, almost hair-like stems and, in summer, soft, feathery, plume-like flowers which gradually become pendulous, as they mature, and turn beige, contrasting with the sage-green of the foliage.

Soil preference: Well-drained, dies over winter if ground too soggy
Aspect: Sun or part shade
Season of interest: Summer, autumn
Height and spread: 60cm x 30cm (2ft x 1ft)

Companion plants: The soft, biscuit colour of the late summer plants makes a fitting complement to very dark coloured flowers such as *Scabiosa atropurpurea* 'Chile Black' or to set among the purple leaved *Persicaria* 'Red Dragon'.

Calamagrostis x acutiflora

Feather Reed Grass Hardy perennial grass

A tall, tussock forming grass with long, arching leaves and big, feathery inflorescences which turn tan soon after flowering. A natural, sterile hybrid between *C. arundinacea* and *C. epigejos* which occurred in Europe. Garden forms include 'Overdam', which has silver variegations, the upright 'Stricta' and pink-flowered 'Karl Foerster'.

Soil preference: Not too dry
Aspect: Sun or part shade
Season of interest: Summer, autumn
Height and spread: 2m x 45cm (6ft 6in x 1ft 6in)

Companion plants: Best blended with very large perennials such as Ligularia, perennial forms of Helianthus or the massive, red flowered *Lobelia tupa*.

Briza media

Common Quaking Grass, Totty Grass   Hardy perennial

A common meadow grass of northern Europe with typical, 1cm-thick leaves and, from late spring, long stems which carry panicles of hanging, cone-shaped flowers, suspended on wire-like stalks which quake and shimmer in the slightest breeze. Though perennial, the plants are not long-lived and should be allowed to seed.

Soil preference: Any, humus-rich, not too dry
Aspect: Sun
Season of interest: Summer
Height and spread: 60cm x 45cm (2ft x 1ft 6in)

Companion plants: Best in a mixed grass meadow, but also pretty when grown in a border with summer perennials such as campanulas, cranesbills or *Betonica officinalis*.

Carex siderostica

Hardy grass-like perennial

A deciduous sedge which produces relatively broad, pleated leaves during summer and spreads slowly to form a broad clump. The variegated forms are best, particularly *C. s.* 'Variegata' (cream striped) and *C. s.* 'Kisokaido'.

Soil preference: Any, not too dry
Aspect: Shade
Season of interest.: Summer
Height and spread: 30cm x 40cm (1ft x 1ft 4in)

Companion plants: Not as vigorous as most sedges and in need of care while establishing. Happy in the company of hostas, heucheras with hellebores for winter, and epimediums for spring.

Eragrostis curvula

African Love Grass   Hardy perennial grass

A lax, waving, willowy grass with narrow leaves, very long, thin, floppy stems and large feathery panicles so ethereal in appearance that one can see straight through them. Despite its lush appearance and rapid growth, this is a plant for a hot, dry spot. Severe frost may prove destructive.

Soil preference: Any
Aspect: Sun
Season of interest: Summer, autumn
Height and spread: To 75cm x 1m (to 2ft 6in x 3ft)

Companion plants: A fine grass to include in a Mediterranean planting with Coronilla glauca, *Euphorbia characias*, and *Brachyglottis greyii*.

Carex testacea   Hardy evergreen perennial

A New Zealand sedge with upright but arching, creased, narrow leaves whose colour is a subtle blend of green and khaki, turning orange at the leaf tips. The flower stems are unremarkable, but as the seed begins to mature, they lengthen and, when blown by the wind, are inclined to dump their seed a metre or so from the parent plant.

Soil preference: Any, not too dry but free-draining
Aspect: Sun or part shade
Season of interest: Year round
Height and spread: 60cm x 60cm (2ft x 2ft)

Companion plants: A handsome sedge to form interestingly hued clumps against flowers in the purple range – centaureas, perhaps – or to harmonise with dark-leaved dahlias and such hot-coloured perennials as gaillardias or heleniums.

Carex trifida

Tataka, Muttonbird Sedge   Hardy evergreen perennial

A robust, vigorous sedge with broad, pleated leaves whose undersides are paler blue-green. The upright flower spikes produce rusty brown flowers in late summer. A remarkably hardy plant which grows deep in the southern hemisphere and is found in New Zealand, and southern South America.

Soil preference: Any, not too dry
Aspect: Sun
Season of interest: Year round
Height and spread: 1m x 1 m (3ft x 3ft)

Companion plants: A tough alternative to the less hardy New Zealand sedges and lovely when interplanted with naturalistic perennials such as *Crocosmia* 'Lucifer,' *Euphorbia griffithii* or *E. palustris*, Cephalaria and Centaurea as well as big grasses such as Miscanthus.

Glyceria maxima

Reed Sweet Grass   Hardy perennial grass

A large, rank-growing grass found wild growing in water courses. The ribbon-like leaves grow rapidly in spring and are soon joined by bronze or purple-tinted panicles. In gardens the form 'Variegata' is the best choice, having pale cream and green striped leaves. Handsome, but invasive and hungry for space.

Soil preference: Any not too dry
Aspect: Sun or part shade
Season of interest: Summer
Height and spread: 80cm (2ft 6in), spreading

Companion plants: One for the bog garden, pretty with yellow flag irises, and even grown as an aquatic with pickerel weed, or with other reeds and sedges.

Grasses Scheme

A wetland planting whose main feature plant is one of the very finest sedges in cultivation, *Carex elata* 'Aurea' or Bowles' golden sedge, named after the great early 20th century plantsman E. A. Bowles. In moist soil – or even in shallow water for that matter – this plant reaches its full potential, a mature specimen growing almost a metre high, with its gracefully arching, golden leaves spreading a metre or more across. The golden leaved form of meadowsweet, *Filipendula ulmaria* 'Aurea' picks up a similar colour, but provides a subtle contrast with its slightly winkled, toothed compound leaves and, behind, a similar contrast works between the ferns and narrow leaved Siberian irises which, briefly, bring an extra dimension with their flowers.

This association is long-lasting, but not year-round, and will call for some maintenance. The sedge, though it turns a pleasant beige colour in winter, needs to be cut hard back just before spring begins, so that the curious flowers and brand new, emerging foliage can be enjoyed. The irises, which sustain their beauty through summer and autumn with foliage and tan-coloured seed capsules, must also be cut down at winter's end.

Cascading leaves of Bowles' golden sedge form a focal point in this wetland planting, with the iris blooms providing a complementing colour.

ferns

Asplenium ceterach

Rusty Back Fern   Tiny fern

A tiny fern which will happily naturalise in a wall or a rock crevice but is also at home in an alpine container. The triangular, lobed, tapering fronds are mid-green on their upper surfaces but have undersides coated in a mealy, rust-coloured material – hence the colloquial name.

Soil preference: Any very free-draining
Aspect: Shade or part shade
Season of interest: Year round
Height and spread: 5cm x 20cm (2in x 8in)

Companion plants: Pretty with such other wall ferns as maidenhair spleenwort (*Asplenium trichomanes*) or among shade-tolerant alpines and dwarf bulbs.

Polystichum setiferum

Soft Shield Fern   Large evergreen fern

The evergreen fronds grow from a woody base and are lacy and soft in texture. Fresh green, newly emerged foliage contrasts with the rusty, scaly stems and rachis (central axis of the frond). Grows naturally in moist woodland but is quite tolerant of dry conditions and is easy to establish. Forms such as *P. s.* 'Divisilobum Group' are collectable.

Soil preference: Well-drained, leafy or humus-rich
Aspect: Shade or part shade
Season of interest: Year round
Height and spread: 45cm x 60cm (18in x 2ft)

Companion plants: Solomon's seal, epimediums and cranesbills make fine companions in a shady border, or plant among shrubs to add off-season interest. Bluebells or wild daffodils are also excellent companions along with *Dryopteris filix-mas* and forms.

Polypodium vulgare

Common Polypody   Small to medium evergreen fern

A spreading, though non-invasive rootstock enables this fern to form drifts of semi-upright, lobed fronds, borne on thin stems which sometimes run along wall tops and will even establish in moss along the main branches of old trees. Very drought tolerant and, though commonest on acid soils, it is relatively lime tolerant.

Soil preference: Any free-draining
Aspect: Shade or part shade. Also tolerant of direct sunlight
Season of interest: Year round
Height and spread: Up to 30cm (12in), spreading slowly

Companion plants: Attractive in a dry woodland garden or scrambling among rocks with shade tolerant *Saxifraga* x *urbium* or *S. fortunei*, or with the limestone species *Geranium robertianum* for an interesting textural contrast.

Asplenium trichomanes Maidenhair Spleenwort Tiny fern

Slender, dark wiry stems up to about 20cm (8in) long, carry neat, oblong or rounded pinnate leaves. The roots spread especially well through the soft mortar of old walls, as the ferns colonize their habitat, but they do not appear to cause much damage to building structures.

Soil preference: Very free-draining
Aspect: Shade or part shade
Season of interest: Year round
Height and spread: 15cm (6in) spreading

Companion plants: To many, the spleenworts are weeds but they soften hard outlines and lend an impression of age to building fabric. Encourage them to blend with Rusty back ferns, Wall Rue, *Asplenium ruta-muraria* and such other wall plants as *Sedum acre* or ivy-leaved toadflax.

Blechnum spicant Hard Fern Medium evergreen fern

A neat, clump-forming, evergreen fern, very shade tolerant, with long, gently curving fronds furnished with narrow, dark green leaflets. The outer leaves are sterile but surround more erect stems carrying spiky, spore-bearing organs. Equally happy in damp or dry conditions, but dislikes alkaline soils.

Soil preference: Lime-free soil, well-drained
Aspect: Shade or part shade
Season of interest: Year round
Height and spread: 45cm x 30cm (1ft 6in x 1ft)

Companion plants: A beautiful companion to early shrubs such as camellia or rhododendrons whose interest wanes in summer when the ferns are at their best. The hart's tongue fern, *Asplenium scolopendrium*, makes a lovely foil with its tongue-like leaves.

Asplenium scolopendrium

Hart's Tongue Fern Medium evergreen fern

The least fern-like of garden ferns, but as alluring as any. Glossy, tongue-shaped leaves spring from a broad rosette. Mature leaves develop a fishbone pattern of spore-bearing organs on their undersides. The wild form is simplest but there are also selected forms such as Crispum Group (undulating leaf margins), 'Kaye's Lacerated' (irregularly lobed) and Cristatum Group (divided fronds).

Soil preference: Any well-drained, leafy or humus-rich
Aspect: Shade or part shade
Season of interest: Year round
Height and spread: 30cm x 30cm (1ft x 1ft)

Companion plants: An asset to any dark border. New spring foliage contrasts well with *Viola riviniana* Purpurea Group (syn. *V. labradorica*) or *Anemone nemorosa* and Solomon's seal (Polygonatum).

Athyrium filix femina

Lady Fern   Medium to large fern

Tall, elegant fronds, with slender arching stems and pinnate leaves which are themselves further divided. New 'fiddlehead' growths emerge each spring but by early autumn all the top growth withers and turns brown. A moisture-loving species but it will also grow in relatively dry conditions.

Soil preference: Moist, leafy, humus-rich soil
Aspect: Shade or part shade
Season of interest: Spring, summer
Height and spread: 60cm x 60cm (2ft x 2ft)

Companion plants: Stately species for a moist, shaded summer border, with hostas, ligularias or Rodgersia, or between dark evergreen shrubs such as rhododendrons and camellias.

Athyrium niponicum var. pictum

Japanese Painted Fern   Medium to large fern

Slowly creeping rhizomes from which grow dark purplish red stems carrying boldly coloured fronds with silvery pewter and maroon suffusions. In winter the foliage persists long after that of the lady fern has withered, making this a useful foliage plant for a damp situation. Leaf colour is better in semi-shade than in deep gloom.

Soil preference: Moist, humus-rich
Aspect: Part shade or shade
Season of interest: Summer, autumn
Height and spread: 60cm x 30cm (2ft x 1ft)

Companion plants: The feathery fronds contrast sweetly with the bolder leaves of hostas or Veratrum species.

Matteuccia struthiopteris

Ostrich Plume Fern   Large fern

From neat crowns, the erect stems rise up to form the impression each spring of huge green shuttlecocks. Their intense green hue and distinctive outline make a strong statement among emerging vegetation in wet places but by late summer the colour loses its freshness and the leaves die back in autumn.

Soil preference: Moist, leafy soil
Aspect: Part shade, shade or sun – though not too hot
Season of interest: Spring, summer
Height and spread: 1m x 60cm (3ft x 2ft)

Companion plants: Enchanting with such spring bog plants as kingcup (*Caltha palustris*), Cuckoo flower (*Cardamine pratensis*) but also striking with other big leaf moisture lovers.

Osmunda regalis   Royal Fern   Large fern

A big, bold fern which develops a large, raised, woody rootstock from which long stems with coppery brown fiddleheads shoot each spring. The fronds, when they unravel, carry pale green, pinnate leaves which are quite unfern-like! Rusty brown, fertile spore-bearing stems develop later in the summer. Rich autumn tints.

Soil preference: Moist, lime-free. Can also be aquatic
Aspect: Sun, part shade or shade
Season of interest: Summer
Height and spread: 1.25m x 1m (4ft x 3ft)

Companion plants: A fine waterside plant, beautiful with *Iris pseudacorus* or with Japanese moisture loving irises such as *I. ensata*, or to place among such bold sedges as *Carex undulata* or *C. elata*.

Onoclea sensibilis

Sensitive Fern   Spreading fern

An American native fern, happiest when allowed to spread its rhizomes beneath trees in moist woodland. The big, wide fronds are borne on arching stems and are rich green during summer, but at the first touch of frost, take on a vivid russet hue. Fine ground cover, but too invasive for a small garden.

Soil preference: Any moist
Aspect: Shade or part shade
Season of interest: Summer, autumn
Height and spread: 45cm (18in) spreading

Companion plants: An excellent choice to naturalize with bog primulas such as *Primula cashmeriana*, *P. pulverulenta* and *P. florindae*.

Dryopteris wallichiana

Wallich's Wood Fern   Large fern

A large, handsome deciduous fern which, with age, develops a short bole like a tree fern. The young fronds are particularly striking in spring, when they glow yellow-green in the sunshine. They are borne on strong slightly arching stems which are clothed with soft, dark brown scales.

Soil preference: Moist
Aspect: Shade or part shade
Season of interest: Spring, summer
Height and spread: 1.5m x 1m (5ft x 3ft)

Companion plants: One of the finest species, for a woodland or shaded garden, looking magnificent with larger sedges such as *Carex pendula* or at the feet of mature trees among Epimedium or the blue flowered *Corydalis flexuosa*.

Polystichum aculeatum

Hard Shield Fern, Prickly Shield Fern   Hardy evergreen fern

An elegant, glossy evergreen with a loose shuttlecock frond formation. The individual leaflets are finely cut and lacy, held along a slightly prickly stem, clothed in rust coloured scales. Young fronds are pale golden green in early spring, deepening in colour as the year advances.

Soil preference: Humus-rich, not too dry
Aspect: Part shade or shade
Season of interest: Year round
Height and spread: 60cm x 90cm (2ft x 3ft)

Companion plants: Lovely either in a container on its own, or planted with a broad-leaved companion such as *Hosta ventricosa* or perhaps a broad leaved bergenia.

Polystichum polyblepharum

Japanese Tassel Fern   Hardy, evergreen fern

A loose, rosette-forming evergreen fern whose elegant, lacy foliage stays fresh-looking throughout the year. The unfurling stems and leaf bases are clothed with soft, rusty scales and the individual leaves are etched and toothed, making an intricate outline.

Soil preference: Humus-rich, not too dry
Aspect: Shade or part shade
Season of interest: Year round
Height and spread: 75cm x 90cm (2ft 6in x 3ft)

Companion plants: When grown in a container, try underplanting with early spring bulbs such as *Narcissus* 'Peeping Tom' or 'Jack Snipe', or associate with *Saxifraga* x *urbium*, (London Pride).

Dryopteris affinis

Golden Male Fern   Semi-evergreen fern

A large, vigorous fern with upright fronds which form a narrow, shuttlecock shape. The leaf colour is pale golden green, in early spring, when the stems are clothed with soft, brownish scales, but by mid-summer, the fronds darken and coarsen. A good alternative is *D. erythrosora* (copper shield fern) with coppery red new growth and glossy leaves.

Soil preference: Humus-rich, moist
Aspect: Shade or semi-shade
Season of interest: Spring, summer
Height and spread: 90cm x 90cm (3ft x 3ft)

Companion plants: Worth planting in a shady container scheme with Japanese maples such as *Acer palmatum* Dissectum Atro purpureum Group or with a fragrant daphne such as *D. bholua*.

Asplenium nidus   Bird's Nest Fern   Half hardy evergreen fern

A large, evergreen, pan-tropical fern with broad, oar-shaped leaves in a rich, iridescent green. As the fronds mature, spore bearing organs appear in parallel lines across the leaves, creating a fishbone pattern. Old fronds should be removed to sustain a fresh appearance. Protect from frost, or over-winter this plant indoors.

Soil preference: Humus-rich
Aspect: Shade or part shade
Season of interest: Year round
Height and spread: To 1.5m x 1m
(5ft x 3ft)

Companion plants: A solo container plant, but lovely to stand near potted maples, such as *Acer palmatum* or small shrubs, where its dramatic foliage can create a bold contrast.

Cyrtomium falcatum

Japanese Holly Fern   Hardy fern

A distinctive fern whose fronds have a dark central stem (rachis) and large, dark green, glossy leaflets which are oval and toothed and so resemble soft holly leaves. As they mature the leaves arch gracefully, but in harsh conditions the plant is likely to die right back to ground level for winter.

Soil preference: Humus-rich, not too dry
Aspect: Shade or part shade
Season of interest: Year round
Height and spread: 60cm x 90cm (2ft x 3ft)

Companion plants: Pretty if underplanted with spring bulbs such as *Narcissus* 'Jack Snipe' or with trailing, shade tolerant plants such as *Lysimachia nummularia* or sweet violets (*Viola odorata*).

Blechnum discolor

Crown Fern, Piupiu   Near hardy evergreen fern

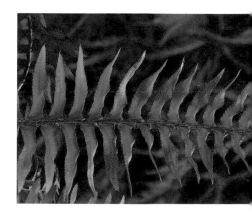

Neat, symmetrical rosettes of fronds with simple leaflets which are pale green when new, darkening to a rich glossy green as they mature. The previous year's foliage makes a beautiful contrast with new leaves unfurling at the rosette's centre. Needs a warm, sheltered spot in deep shade.

Soil preference: Humus-rich, lime free
Aspect: Shade
Season of interest: Year round
Height and spread: 40cm x 40cm (1ft 4in x 1ft 4in)

Companion plants: For container use, best on its own, so the neat growth habit can be admired, but lovely if its pot is sited near such other shade-loving plants as tellimas or tiarellas.

Blechnum chilense   Hardy evergreen fern

A tough, leathery-textured evergreen fern whose fronds develop from hard, fibrous, slowly creeping rhizomes. The leaflets (pinnae) are entire but toothed or serrated at their edges. In very favourable conditions, this plant can grow considerably taller, with much longer fronds than the typical dimensions given.

Soil preference: Humus-rich, free-draining but not too dry
Aspect: Shade, part shade
Season of interest: Year round
Height and spread: 1m x 1 m (3ft x 3ft)

Companion plants: A vigorous and stately woodlander, attractive when interplanted with other ferns, hostas, winter-flowering hellebores or epimediums.

Athyrium otophorum   Hardy semi-evergreen fern

An Asian clump-forming fern whose pale green bi-pinnate fronds contrast well with the dark reddish brown midribs. Fronds are broad, creating a triangular outline when fully extended. The form *A. o.* var. *otokanum* has much paler, yellow-green fronds with dark, purple-red midribs.

Soil preference: Any humus-rich, moist but well-drained
Aspect: Shade
Season of interest: Year round
Height and spread: 45cm x 30cm (1ft 6in x 1ft)

Companion plants: Beautiful under trees where attractive summer foliage is called for after the spring rush of bluebells, wood anemones or primroses.

Adiantum venustum

Himalayan Maidenhair   Hardy evergreen fern

A tough maidenhair fern, variable in its size, with thin, dark stems and lacy fronds consisting of much branched, wiry stalks carrying triangular, vivid green leaflets. The creeping rootstock allows this plant to spread into a drift in time.

Soil preference: Any, humus-rich
Aspect: Shade, part shade
Season of interest: Year round
Height and spread: 40cm x 60cm (1ft 4in x 2 ft), variable

Companion plants: A beautiful and delicate-looking fern to naturalise among rhododendrons or between camellias in a woodland garden, or to create infill in a shaded border with such perennials as trilliums, Cardiocrinum, hostas and pulmonarias.

Equisetum hyemale

Dutch Rush, Rough Horsetail   Hardy non-flowering plant

Not a fern, but a more primitive, non-flowering plant related to the horsetail weed which plagues so many gardeners, but not nearly so invasive. Tall bottle green, non-branched stems give the impression of rushes, but with dark and light bands round each joint all the way up the stem. Dark cones form at the tops of the stems in summer.

Soil preference: Wet – a bog plant
Aspect: Sun or part shade
Season of interest: Year round
Height and spread: 1.25m x 45cm (4ft x 1ft 6in)

Companion plants: A wetland beauty to share with *Hottonia palustris*, moisture-loving iris species and, perhaps, candelabra primulas.

Dicksonia antarctica

Tree fern   Half hardy fern

The familiar giant fern, native to Australasia where it inhabits cool, moist, forested regions. From a dense, fibrous 'trunk' come huge fronds which can extend, in good conditions, to two metres (six feet) or more across. Moist atmosphere is preferred and shelter from wind is essential. A very untidy plant, when stressed, and unsuitable for hot, cold or exposed sites.

Soil preference: Any humus-rich
Aspect: Shade
Season of interest: Year round
Height and spread: To 3m x 2m (to 10ft x 6ft)

Companion plants: Only truly attractive when grown in shade and shelter, preferably among similar woodland species such as rhodoendrons, or among deciduous trees. Also superb along a water course.

Polystichum munitum

Sword Fern   Hardy fern

An evergreen fern with broad fronds bearing simple leaflets whose margins are toothed. Fronds grow around a central bud, making a shuttlecock shape and fertile or spore-bearing fronds are blunt ended, rather than tapering to a point.

Soil preference: Any, humus-rich
Aspect: Shade, part shade
Season of interest: Year round
Height and spread: 1m x 1.5m (3ft x 5ft)

Companion plants: Attractive anywhere, but especially effective when set to contrast with broad-leaved foliage plants such as *Rodgersia tabularis*, or hostas.

Planting Scheme Using Ferns

With their tolerance of shade, lasting beauty and their ability to thrive for years with very little attention, ferns can form the mainstay of many an excellent planting scheme. It is important to select the species which best suits the habitat – some prefer moist conditions, others are drought tolerant – and to understand that hardiness varies.

In this wetland scheme, the Royal Fern, *Osmunda regalis*, acts as anchor, preceding the flowering of Asiatic candelabra primulas and Siberian irises, with their vivid, fresh green foliage, and continuing long after they have died. In summer, rusty brown spore-bearing stems are produced among the green leaves and in autumn the foliage runs through yellow to rusty brown, allowing the small evergreen shrubs, in this group, to become more conspicuous. In the background, more familiar ferns such as Polystichum and Dryopteris provide more feathery fronds which are longer lasting and, in favourable conditions, sustain their colour through winter.

A wetland habitat planted with Royal Fern whose fresh new foliage makes a bright contrast with groups of Asian candelabra primulas. As summer advances, the colours subside through greens and golds, eventually turning to russet for autumn.

climbers

Solanum crispum Sprawling shrub or climber

A vigorous and fast-growing, straggling shrub or climber with long, lax stems furnished with narrow, simple leaves. From early summer onwards, a constant succession of lavender-blue flowers is produced, each having a conspicuous yellow centre. The selection 'Glasnevin'(pictured) is more floriferous than most. Protect from extremes of frost.

Soil preference: Any free-draining
Aspect: Sun
Season of interest: Summer, autumn
Height and spread: 2.5m x 3m (8ft x 10ft)

Companion plants: Though it needs to be kept in check, the luxuriant stems and blue flowers harmonise well with crimson or blush roses, or with the brighter flowers of *Eccremocarpus scaber*.

Campsis radicans Hardy climber

A vigorous, woody, deciduous climber with decorative, compound leaves and, from late summer, clusters of flowers whose tubular buds resemble lobster claws, as they extend, but which open to trumpet flowers in dark orange or, in the case of *C. r.* 'Flava' pale yellow. The hybrid *C.* x *tagliabuana* is similar and the variety *C.* x *t.* 'Madame Galen' more robust.

Soil preference: Any free-draining
Aspect: Sun
Season of interest: Summer, autumn
Height and spread: 5m x 5m (15ft x 15ft)

Companion plants: When teamed with spring flowering wisterias, the season of colour is extended, but if morning glories are persuaded to weave through the summer stems, the effect can be sensational.

Rosa banksiae

Banksian Rose Marginally hardy deciduous climber or scrambler

A rampaging rambler whose lax, thornless stems carry pinnate leaves typical of most roses and which, in mid- to late spring, is covered with generous clusters of small, white or pale yellow, faintly fragrant flowers. The hardiest and most popular variety is *R. banksiae* 'Lutea', whose primrose yellow flowers are double. *R. b.* 'Lutescens' bears single, yellow blooms.

Soil preference: Any free-draining
Aspect: Sun or part shade
Season of interest: Spring, early summer
Height and spread: 10m (33ft), spreading

Companion plants: Charming if the blooms can be mixed with Chinese wisteria, but also an interesting climber to grow up into a large, vigorous tree such as an old apple, or pear.

Eccremocarpus scaber   Chilean Glory Vine

A fast growing climber which clings by tendrils and whose ferny, compound leaves make a dark green contrast with the dense clusters of orange, red, pink or yellow, tubular flowers. Though susceptible to frost, this plant will tolerate mild winters and is a free self-seeder. Some suppliers offer named seed strain strains such as 'Tresco Cream' or 'Tresco Mixed.'

Soil preference: Moist but well-drained
Aspect: Sun
Season of interest: Summer, autumn
Height and spread: 4m x 3m (13ft x 10ft)

Companion plants: Handy for covering an unsightly object, or for growing with annual climbers as a temporary display. Effective with blue morning glories, or with the bright yellow *Tropaeolum peregrinum* (Canary creeper.)

Billardiera longiflora

Climbing Blueberry, Purple Appleberry   Marginally hardy climber

A relatively slow-growing native of Tasmania and south-eastern Australia with slender, twining stems and simple leaves. Tubular, greenish flowers are produced during summer and are followed by oblong berries which are usually deep purple but which may be pink, red or white. Must be protected from frost and cold winds.

Soil preference: Humus-rich, lime-free, well-drained
Aspect: Sun
Season of interest: Summer, autumn
Height and spread: 2m x 1m (6ft x 3ft)

Companion plants: An elegant plant, for shelter, perhaps teamed with Lapageria or trained through a more robust wall plant such as *Sophora* 'Sun King.'

Cobaea scandens

Cathedral Bell   Tender climber

A vigorous perennial climber from Mexico which clings by branched tendrils and has compound leaves. The large, bell-shaped flowers are produced all summer long and are greenish when young, turning purple or white as they age. Conspicuous sepals, at the bases of the bells give the impression of cups and saucers. Papery fruits follow.

Soil preference: Any fertile, free-draining
Aspect: Sun, part shade
Season of interest: Summer, autumn
Height and spread: to 10m (33ft), spreading

Companion plants: Usually grown as an annual, in cold regions, where it makes a good companion to Eccremocarpus or to twine among climbing roses or clematis.

Rosa 'Albertine'   Hardy climbing rose (Rambler)

Technically a rambling rose, with thorned, coppery stems and compound leaves and in summer, brick-red buds which open to gently fragrant, light salmon pink flowers. In bloom for a long period, but does not repeat flower. Alternative choices are 'François Juranville' (salmon blush) 'Claire Jacquier' (salmon buff to yellow) and 'Félicité et Perpétue' (pink buds opening flushed white).

Soil preference: Moisture-retentive, fertile
Aspect: Sun
Season of interest: Summer
Height and spread: 4m (12ft), spreading

Companion plants: Clematis, especially late flowering varieties derived from *C. viticella*, will help extend the season. The deep violet-blue flowered *C.* 'Polish Spirit' or paler blue *C.* 'Prince Charles' create interesting contrasts with the rose colours.

Rosa 'Albéric Barbier'   Hardy climbing rose (Rambler)

Dark, glossy, near evergreen foliage, on this vigorous rambling rose, makes a strong contrast with the lemon buds, which open to soft white, gently fragrant flowers. The main flush lasts for weeks in mid-summer, but flowers are produced sporadically through the rest of the growing season. Comparable varieties include 'Climbing Iceberg' and 'Madame Alfred Carrière'.

Soil preference: Any, not too dry
Aspect: Sun or part shade
Season of interest: Summer
Height and spread: To 6m (20ft) and spreading

Companion plants: Wonderful companions for late summer clematis. 'Madame Julia Correvon' (red) or the cerise flowered *C.* 'Etoile Rose' will blend with the pale rose colours, but the yellow *C.* 'Bill Mackenzie' also makes an interesting companion.

Clematis montana   Hardy climber

A strong, vigorous species with bronze suffusions in the young foliage and, in late spring, masses of mid-sized, showy flowers in shades of pink or white, each with central bunches of pale yellow stamens. Best of the whites is *C. spooneri* because of its broad petals. Pinks include the pale 'Elizabeth' and deeper pink 'Tetrarose'. *Clematis montana* var. *wilsonii* flowers a month later than the rest with fragrant blossoms.

Soil preference: Any, not too dry
Aspect: Sun or part shade
Season of interest: Spring
Height and spread: To 8m (25ft), spreading

Companion plants: These clematis are difficult to team since their vigour makes them likely to swamp other climbers but they are excellent for growing into large trees to cascade through the branches.

Clematis **late flowering hybrids**   Hardy climbers

Plants with twisting leaf petioles and large, colourful flowers in shades of blue, purple, mauve and red – though never scarlet. Easiest and best known of the dark blues is *Clematis* x *jackmanii* (pictured). 'Comtesse de Bouchaud' has deep, dusky pink flowers and 'Niobe' is deep maroon red. The late clematis flower on new wood and so are best pruned each winter or spring.

Soil preference: Fertile, not too dry, cool
Aspect: Sun or part shade but must have cool roots
Season of interest: Summer, autumn
Height and spread: Up to 4m (12ft), spreading

Companion plants: Excellent companions to large flowered roses, or to blend on a wall with fragrant honeysuckles, particularly *Lonicera periclymenum* and varieties such as 'Graham Thomas'.

Lonicera periclymenum

Woodbine, Honeysuckle   Hardy, twining climber

Twisting, woody stems and simple, oval leaves, joined in summer by clusters of elongated tubular flowers with gaping petals. Tight clusters of bright red berries follow, along with a sporadic succession of further blooms. Fine varieties include the lemon-petalled 'Graham Thomas'; 'Belgica' or 'Early Dutch' which flowers remarkably early and the later-flowering 'Serotina' which begins in late summer.

Soil preference: Any free-draining, not too dry
Aspect: Sun or part shade
Season of interest: Summer, autumn
Height and spread: To 7m (23ft), spreading

Companion plants: Good wall or trellis plants, happy to scramble with golden hops, clematis or such herbaceous climbers as everlasting pea (*Lathyrus latifolius*).

Parthenocissus tricuspidata, P. quinquefolia

Boston Ivy and Virginia Creeper   Hardy, self-clinging climbers

Rampant relatives of the grape, with large, three-lobed leaves (Boston Ivy) or palmate, five lobed leaves (Virginia Creeper). The greenish flowers and small black fruits are insignificant, but the plants acquire magnificent autumnal hues – fiery red, in the case of Virginia Creeper; crimson purple for Boston Ivy.

Soil preference: Not too dry
Aspect: Sun or part shade
Season of interest: Summer, autumn
Height and spread: Spreading. Could cover a battleship

Companion plants: Best as loners, because of their invasiveness, but could harmonise with wisteria, bringing hot autumn colour to the wisteria's gold-green.

Hedera helix   English Ivy   Hardy self-clinging climber

Ultimately rapid growing, invasive climber which attaches itself with adventitious roots. The juvenile evergreen leaves are three-pointed or three-lobed, shiny green, often marbled or variegated. The green flowers, on adult growth, come out in autumn, followed by berries which ripen during winter and early spring. Many decorative cultivars include 'Adam' – leaves marbled white and creamy yellow – and the bright yellow centred 'Oro di Bogliasco' ('Goldheart').

Soil preference: Any
Aspect: Any
Season of interest: Year round
Height and spread: Almost indefinite

Companion plants: Too invasive for weak companions, but beautiful interwoven with honeysuckles or with climbing roses such as red-flowered 'Scharlachglut' or salmon 'Albertine'. May be slow growing for first two years.

Hedera colchica; Hedera canariensis

Bullock's Heart Ivy; Canary Island Ivy   Hardy or near-hardy, self-clinging climber

Vigorous climber with huge, evergreen leaves, often heart-shaped or slightly lobed, curling outwards as they age. Mature plants produce stiff, twiggy flower-bearing stems. Green flowers in autumn precede black winter berries. Outstanding varieties include *H. c.* 'Sulphur Heart' and *H. c.* 'Dentata Variegata'. The less hardy *H. canariensis* 'Gloire de Marengo' (pictured) has irregularly shaped leaves with cream margins.

Soil preference: Any
Aspect: Shade or part shade
Season of interest: Year round
Height and spread: Almost unlimited. Would cover a barn

Companion plants: Best on their own, covering unsightly objects, or growing over ugly walls. Blend with vigorous honeysuckles or *Clematis montana* for spring interest. Slow growing for first two years.

Hydrangea anomala subsp. petiolaris

Climbing hydrangea   Hardy, self-clinging climber

A native of north eastern Asia, with tan-coloured, flaking stems, vibrantly fresh green leaves in spring and umbels of creamy white, lace cap flowers in summer. Not troublesome, but will, ultimately grow very large, particularly in rich soil in part shade.

Soil preference: Any not too dry, but well-drained
Aspect: Sun or part shade
Season of interest: Year round
Height and spread: To 10m x 7m (35ft x 22ft)

Companion plants: Not an easy plant to team, but attractive with late flowering clematis such as *C. montana* and forms growing through the foliage. A superb plant to train up a mature, tall tree, so that the flowers furnish the trunk.

Euonymus fortunei   Self-clinging climber or bushy groundcover

Green, form-hugging stems are furnished with small, evergreen, oval leaves. Insignificant greenish-yellow flowers appear in summer. Well marked varieties include 'Emerald Gaiety' whose leaves are margined white and are pink-tinged in cold weather and the larger 'Silver Queen,' whose leaf margins are yellow.

Soil preference: Any
Aspect: Sun or part shade
Season of interest: Year round
Height and spread: 30cm x 3m (1ft x 10ft) and spreading

Companion plants: Useful at any scale, whether accompanying perennials in winter containers or scaling walls. The variegated forms team sweetly with such clematis as *C. alpina* 'Helsingborg,' (dark blue) 'Frances Rivis' (lighter blue) or *C. macropetala* 'Markham's Pink'.

Jasminum nudiflorum

Winter Jasmine   Lax wall shrub or ground cover

Deep green, slightly ribbed stems are furnished with three-part leaves in summer, but retain their green colour when naked in winter. From late autumn to winter's end, bright yellow flowers open in pairs along young stems. A classic plant, native to Northern China and a garden essential, but care needed in training the lax stems.

Soil preference: Any
Aspect: Sun, part shade or shade
Season of interest: Winter
Height and spread: 3m x 3m (10ft x 10ft)

Companion plants: Beautiful trained on a wall, with honeysuckles such as 'Hall's Prolific' for summer colour and fragrance, but also attractive when woven through evergreen hedges, such as laurel, osmanthus or euonymus.

Lonicera japonica

Japanese Honeysuckle   Hardy semi-evergreen climber

A semi-evergreen with twining stems bearing paired, oval leaves and, from mid-summer onwards, intensely fragrant flowers, also paired with short, flared tubes. Small black berries follow. Flowers appear on the side shoots of the main climbing stems. Good varieties include 'Halliana' and 'Hall's Prolific'.

Soil preference: Any cool soil, not too wet
Aspect: Part shade or shade
Season of interest: Summer
Height and spread: Up to 5m x 5m (15ft x 15ft)

Companion plants: A fine climber to blend with other, more flamboyant honeysuckles, or with *Jasminum officinale*, for a rich cocktail of scents. Also useful to bring an extra dimension to ivy-clad supports.

Clematis

This versatile and popular plant genus offers such a broad range of species and varieties that it is possible to have clematis of one sort or another in flower at almost any time of the year. Culture of most varieties, given reasonably fertile soil and protection from the worst of the wind, is straightforward.

1. **Clematis cirrhosa 'Wisley Cream'**
A vigorous form of the Mediterranean species whose winter flowers are soft primrose.

2. **Clematis 'Perle d'Azur'**
Mid- to late summer flowers, on current year's growth, are a warm powder blue with textured surfaces. One to prune hard back each year.

3. **Clematis montana var. rubens 'Tetrarose'**
Vigorous and early flowering, this variety has strong flower colour and young leaves and stems suffused with purplish bronze.

4. **Clematis montana var. 'Grandiflora'**
One of the best forms of *C. montana* with good vigour, a long flowering season and relatively large blooms in stark white.

5. **Clematis armandii**
An early evergreen climber with large, handsome leaves and pure white, waxy-looking flowers which are sweetly scented.

6. **Clematis serratifolia**
A late flowering Asian species whose lemon-beige flowers have subtle fragrance. The flowers are followed by conspicuous, fluffy seed heads which last all winter.

7. **Clematis 'Burford White'**
A spring-flowering species whose elegant, nodding blooms retain their clean whiteness until the sepals (petals) are ready to drop.

8. **Clematis 'Helsingborg'**
Vigorous and dependable, this early spring-blooming variety has dark stems and deep purple-blue flowers.

9. **Clematis 'Etoile Rose'**
Climbing herbaceous species like this can be cut to ground level each winter. The fast-growing stems carry a long succession of intense, rosy pink, lantern shaped flowers.

1	2	3
4	5	6
7	8	9

Clematis 2

For late spring and summer colour, large flowered clematis hybrids have universal appeal. Their colours range through purples, blues and pinks to crimson or white, with considerable variation in flower shape. Early varieties such as 'Lasurstern', which flower on previous year's growth, have the largest blooms, but those which begin to flower after the longest day flower the most persistently.

1. Clematis **'Countess of Lovelace'**
Large flowered double or varieties like this produce fully double blooms in late spring, followed by a second flush of simple flowers in late summer.

2. Clematis **'Marie Boisselot'**
An early variety of great value. Huge pure white blooms appear in late spring or early summer, followed by fewer, slightly smaller flowers in late summer.

3. Clematis **'Lasurstern'**
Large early blooms in soft pastel hues are followed, in favourable conditions, by sporadic repeat flowers later in the season.

4. Clematis **'Jackmanii Superba'**
The toughest and most dependable variety with royal blue or purple blue flowers produced on current season's growth from mid-summer onward.

5. Clematis **'Niobe'**
A deep purple-red variety of moderate vigour flowering through summer.

6. Clematis **'Carnaby'**
Pink flowers with a deeper pink bar down the middle of each petal. The dark green foliage makes a great contrast with the flower colour.

7. Clematis **'Hagley Hybrid'**
Pink flowers with slightly pointed sepals to give a starry effect and chocolate brown stamens make this a distinctive variety for mid-summer.

8. Clematis **'Markham's Pink'**
One of several good forms of the multi-petalled *Clematis macropetala*. The flowers open in early spring.

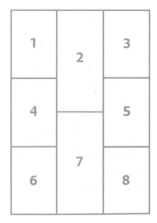

Wisteria floribunda   Japanese Wisteria   Hardy climber

Woody deciduous climber whose mature stems are twisted
and gnarled. Bronze-tinted, eventually pale green pinnate
leaves emerge in late spring, just ahead of the long
racemes of gently scented violet-blue pea flowers.
Gardenworthy varieties include 'Multijuga' – with its 1m-
long (3ft-long) racemes – 'Alba', with long white racemes
and the pink flowered 'Kuchi-beni'.

Soil preference: Any free-
draining
Aspect: Sun
Season of interest: Spring
Height and spread: More than
10m (30ft), spreading

Companion plants: Herbaceous climbers
such as morning glories, *Tropaeolum
peregrinum* or *Eccremocarpus scaber* can be
woven through to relieve summer dullness.

Rosa 'Alister Stella Gray'

Hardy climber (Noisette rose)

Vigorous climbing rose with coppery coloured stems and
young foliage and sprays of small, double blooms which
are egg-yolk hue in bud, opening to pale lemon, but with
darker yellow centres. Not a repeating rose, but with a
longish flowering season and sweetly fragrant.

Soil preference: Heavy, not too
dry
Aspect: Sun
Season of interest: Summer
Height and spread: To 5m (15ft),
spreading

Companion plants: Useful to team with a
blue clematis such as *Clematis* 'Jackmanii'
or *C.* 'Perle d'Azur'.

Vitis vinifera 'Purpurea'   Purple Grape Vine   Hardy climber

A vigorous grape vine which clings by tendrils and
produces flexible wands whose bark turns tan when
mature, furnished with beautiful lobed, sculpted leaves.
The emerging foliage in spring is downy, blue-green with
purple suffusions, deepening to sombre purple when
mature. In autumn the leaf colour intensifies. Small, sour
black grapes are also produced.

Soil preference: Any
Aspect: Sun
Season of interest: Summer,
autumn
Height and spread: 5m x 5m
(16ft x 16ft)

Companion plants: Vibrant red roses such
as 'Parkdirecktor Riggers' or 'Guinée' contrast
well with the purple foliage, but the single
flowered *Rosa* 'Scharlachglut' has the added
bonus of large, orange-red hips in autumn,
when the vine colour becomes even richer.

Trachelospermum jasminoides

Star Jasmine   Marginally tender, evergreen climber

Vigorous, but cold-hating evergreen with simple, oval, pointed leaves and, through summer and early autumn, a succession of small sprays bearing intensely fragrant, five-petalled, star-shaped white or pale cream flowers. A member of the periwinkle family from China and Japan, ideal for a warm, sunny balcony or a well-lit terrace.

Soil preference: Free-draining
Aspect: Sun
Season of interest: Summer
Height and spread: To 5m (15ft) and spreading

Companion plants: The soft white of the flowers enables them to blend sweetly with almost any hue. Equally effective with roses, passiflora or with purple grape vine.

Lonicera x tellmanniana   Hardy deciduous climber

Deciduous climber with woody, twining stems and simple, oval, paired leaves and clusters of tubular flowers with divided, flared lips. The coppery-orange colour effect is caused by a mottled blend of scarlet and golden yellow on the petals. One of the brightest coloured honeysuckles but devoid of fragrance.

Soil preference: Any free-draining but not too dry
Aspect: Sun or part shade. Roots must be cool
Season of interest: Summer
Height and spread: 3m x 1.5m (10ft x 5ft)

Companion plants: Effective when blended with more fragrant honeysuckles such as *Lonicera periclymenum*, which bring perfume as well as gentler colours. Also useful to contrast with the a rich blue clematis such as 'H.F. Young'.

Forsythia suspensa

Golden Bell   Hardy deciduous climber or lax shrub

A lax plant with long, thin, roughened, drooping stems which need tying in to their support. The foliage is undistinguished, though it colours yellow in autumn, but in early spring, pale yellow flowers appear on naked branches. A tough native of China, capable of surviving a cold or exposed position.

Soil preference: Fertile, not too dry
Aspect: Sun, part shade or shade
Season of interest: Early spring
Height and spread: 3m x 3m (10ft x 10ft)

Companion plants: Blends well with golden hop, which brings summer interest, or to weave through with decorative leaved forms of *Euonymus fortunei*.

Maurandya barclayana

Herbaceous climber/tender annual

Thin twining stems with slightly lobed leaves and, from mid-summer onwards, tubular, trumpet-shaped flowers in deep violet purple, pink or white. Dark coloured flowers have paler throats. Though technically perennial, this Central American native is more usually grown as a tender annual.

Soil preference: Any fertile
Aspect: Sun
Season of interest: Summer
Height and spread: 2m (6ft), spreading

Companion plants: A weed but a very pretty one, especially when blended with such climbers as the flame *Ipomoea lobata* or *Tropaeolum peregrinum*.

Lathyrus rotundifolius

Persian Everlasting Pea   Herbaceous climber

A handsome but non-fragrant relative of the sweet pea with flat stems, clinging tendrils and rounded, two-lobed leaves. Clusters of showy, brick-red pea blossoms are produced through much of summer. The deep roots inhibit transplanting so mature plants should be left in situ. New plants are easy to raise from seed.

Soil preference: Any free-draining
Aspect: Sun
Season of interest: Summer
Height and spread: 1m x 45cm (3ft x 1ft 6in)

Companion plants: Very pretty, on a small frame or obelisk, when its reddish flowers are able to contrast with the dwarf golden leaved hop, *Humulus lupulus* 'Golden Tassels'.

Lophospermum erubescens (syn. Maurandya erubescens)

Creeping Gloxinia   Herbaceous climber/tender annual

Triangular, slightly hairy, toothed leaves are carried on twining stems. The bold, rosy pink, tubular, foxglove-like flowers appear from mid-summer and keep coming as long as the plant is in growth. Technically a perennial but usually grown in cold regions as a tender annual. Very quick and easy from seed.

Soil preference: Fertile, free-draining
Aspect: Sun
Season of interest: Summer
Height and spread: To 3m (10ft)

Companion plants: A good plant to mix with other annual climbers, such as tropaeolums or Lathyrus.

Lathyrus odoratus Sweet Pea Annual climber

One of the world's most loved annuals with paired leaves and tendrils, flattened main stems and large, cleanly coloured, intensely fragrant pea flowers. The wild species, which comes from Sicily, is reddish purple and violet. Cultivated varieties range from red or pink, through violet, mauve and white.

Soil preference: Fertile, moisture retentive and slightly alkaline
Aspect: Sun
Season of interest: Summer
Height and spread: To 3m x 45cm (10ft x 1ft 6in)

Companion plants: Though enchanting on their own up pea stick wigwams, sweet peas are valuable when mixed with other twining plants on frames, such as squashes or gourds, in the kitchen garden.

Ipomoea tricolor

Morning Glory Annual climber

An annual with twining stems and big, heart-shaped leaves which from mid-summer onwards have huge saucer-shaped flowers with primrose throats. The flowers open before dawn but remain only until the sun has shone directly onto them. 'Heavenly Blue' is the best cultivar.

Soil preference: Fertile, moisture-retentive but free-draining
Aspect: Sun
Season of interest: Summer
Height and spread: To 3m (10ft), spreading

Companion plants: A good plant to weave through wisteria, on a hot wall, or to mix with white, cream or yellow roses, to create a startlingly cool effect. Also combines effectively with the flame *Ipomoea lobata*.

Tropaeolum peregrinum

Canary Creeper Annual climber

Twining, fleshy stemmed climber from South America with small, glaucous green, palmate or deeply lobed, rounded leaves and garlands of small, bright yellow blossoms whose petals are divided like the teeth of a coarse comb. Can be very vigorous.

Soil preference: Fertile, well-drained
Aspect: Sun
Season of interest: Summer
Height and spread: To 2.5m x 45cm (7ft 6in x 1ft 6in)

Companion plants: The yellow sits comfortably with hot-hued plants, in a mixed annual border, or can contrast with the purple blue of *Maurandya barclayana* or as a foil for blue morning glories.

Clematis viticella   Hardy deciduous climbers

Small and medium flowered clematis varieties which flower on current season's growth from mid-summer onwards. The full clematis colour range is represented with excellent examples, including 'Minuet' (white with purple veining), 'Royal Velours' (dark maroon), 'Alba Luxurians' (white with green tips) and 'Venosa Violacea' (deep violet with paler veining). Cut back hard in late winter.

Soil preference: Cool, fertile, moist but well-drained
Aspect: Sun or part shade (roots must be cool)
Season of interest: Summer
Height and spread: Up to 3m (10ft), spreading

Companion plants: These are happy companions to grow through robust evergreens such as medium sized or ground-covering conifers. The less vigorous varieties can also be trained into spring flowering shrubs, such as lilacs or ceanothus.

Tropaeolum tuberosum var. lineamaculatum
'Ken Aslet'   Herbaceous perennial climber

A relative of the familiar nasturtium with five-lobed, rounded leaves and from mid-summer attractive, spurred red or orange and yellow flowers. The tubers from which this Andean native grows are edible. Susceptible to mollusc damage in spring.

Soil preference: Fertile, well-drained, cool
Aspect: Sun or part shade
Season of interest: Summer
Height and spread: Up to 3m (10ft), spreading

Companion plants: One of the best herbaceous climbers for weaving through small or medium shrubs whose interest wanes after spring, including Spiraea, Weigela, Philadelphus and Viburnum. The Chilean Glory Vine (*Eccremocarpus scaber*) is similar in effect.

Tropaeolum speciosum

Flame Creeper   Herbaceous climber

A delicate-stemmed but vigorous climber bearing garlands of small lobed or palmate leaves and elegantly spurred flowers through summer and autumn. Their colour is startling vermilion, but later, glistening blue-black fruit form in reddish calyces. Slow to establish but will self-seed freely when happy. The roots must be cool but the flowers look best in semi-shade or dappled sunlight.

Soil preference: Fertile, humus-rich, not too dry
Aspect: Shade or part shade
Season of interest: Summer
Height and spread: Up to 3m (10ft), spreading

Companion plants: Especially good through evergreens such as clipped yew or *Osmanthus delavayi*, where the scarlet blooms show against the dark foliage.

Aconitum hemsleyanum

Climbing Monkshood   Herbaceous perennial climber

A moderately vigorous, perennial from China with twining stems and handsome, lobed, toothed leaves. In summer, short racemes of dark, rather dusky violet-blue, helmet-shaped flowers appear and persist until autumn. Sometimes confused with *A. volubile*, another less vigorous climbing species with paler, greenish blue flowers in late summer.

Soil preference: Fertile, moist but free-draining
Aspect: Sun or part shade
Season of interest: Summer
Height and spread: 2m x 45cm (6ft x 1ft 6in)

Companion plants: The dusky flowers are effective when blended with the brighter tints of a climbing rose such as purplish pink 'Zéphirene Drouhin', or when trailing over pale leaved evergreens such as *Juniperus pfitzeriana* 'Aurea.'

Dicentra scandens

Herbaceous perennial climber

A quick-growing climber with frail coppery-coloured stems and delicate, ferny, deeply lobed foliage. From early summer, a long succession of tightly clustered, yellow or cream flowers runs. Though vigorous, the stems are easily damaged and the plants sometimes succumb to late frost.

Soil preference: Any fertile, not too dry
Aspect: Sun or part shade, sheltered spot
Season of interest: Summer
Height and spread: 1m (3ft), spreading

Companion plants: A low-growing climber, ideal to train over small shrubs such as winter-flowering heathers, cotoneasters or ground cover conifers, where it will bring extra interest.

Clematis x jouiniana 'Praecox'

Semi-herbaceous perennial climber

A cross between the climbing European *Clematis vitalba* and the Asian upright perennial *C. heracleifolia*. Lax stems with dark green, rather glossy compound leaves and, from late summer, sprays of small, narrow sepalled, pale blue flowers. A trailer rather than a climber, ideal to drape over a bank or down the side of a retaining wall.

Soil preference: Any fertile, preferably alkaline
Aspect: Sun or part shade
Season of interest: Summer, autumn
Height and spread: 2m (6ft), spreading

Companion plants: On a steep bank, this plant looks superb with colchicums growing through the pale flowers. Also impressive when allowed to scramble through other perennials in a late autumn border.

Honeysuckle

Honeysuckle (Lonicera) is one of the easiest groups of climbers to grow. Many are sweetly fragrant and most come in attractive colours. Train them on a wall or fence, or into a large shrub or tree.

1. Lonicera henryi
A fast-growing evergreen climber with leathery, oblong leaves, dark tinted stems and, in summer, groups of small, purplish pink flowers followed by glossy black fruits.

2. Lonicera x brownii 'Dropmore Scarlet'
A fast growing, semi-evergreen honeysuckle whose scentless, brilliant scarlet, trumpet blooms have orange throats. Red berries follow.

3. Lonicera japonica 'Halls Prolific'
One of several outstanding Japanese honeysuckle varieties with semi-evergreen foliage and an almost constant run, from mid-summer, of pale straw yellow, intensely fragrant flowers which deepen in colour as they mature.

4. Lonicera periclymenum 'Graham Thomas'
A selected wild honeysuckle whose fragrant, tubular flowers are creamy at first, turning parchment yellow as they age. A heavy crop of scarlet berries follows.

5. Lonicera periclymenum 'Belgica'
One of the earliest European honeysuckles to bloom, with a heavy crop of blossoms in mid-spring.

6. Lonicera periclymenum 'Sweet Sue'
A more sedate honeysuckle which blooms on shorter stems.

7. Lonicera caprifolium
The Italian honeysuckle whose intensely fragrant, tubular flowers have pinkish exteriors and soft creamy to primrose yellow interiors.

8. Lonicera x tellmanniana
The flower clusters appear to be orange but closer examination reveals a bright yellow background colour, to the petals, subtly marbled with scarlet. Sadly, no fragrance, but a spectacular climber, all the same.

1	2	3
4	5	6
7	8	

Akebia quinata   Hardy climber

Vigorous, fast-growing climber from Japan with thin wiry stems and pretty, palmate leaves. In spring, small, purplish maroon, spicily vanilla-scented, three-petalled blooms appear in clusters, sometimes followed by cylindrical fruits.

Soil preference: Any
Aspect: Sun or part shade
Season of interest: Year round
Height and spread: To 5m (16ft)

Companion plants: A rampant climber, so difficult to team with anything less vigorous. Blending a late flowering clematis such as *Clematis* 'Jackmanii' or varieties of *C. viticella* will help to relieve summer monotony.

Jasminum officinale

Summer Jasmine, Jessamine   Hardy, woody climber

Vigorous climber with greenish, flexible stems and compound leaves. From mid- to late summer, sprays of small, white, intensely fragrant flowers appear and persist until the first winter frosts. Ageing stems should be pruned out and vigorous, young stems trained in their place.

Soil preference: Any, free-draining
Aspect: Sun
Season of interest: Summer, autumn
Height and spread: Climbing to 5m (16ft)

Companion plants: The perfect patio climber, especially if it can blend its sweet perfume with that of honeysuckles like *Lonicera japonica*, the rich purple-pink, fragrant rose 'Zephirine Drouhin' or apricot 'Compassion'.

Schisandra chinensis

Hardy climber

A deciduous climber with simple, glossy dark green, toothed leaves and a long run of small, sweetly fragrant cup-shaped pink flowers. Female plants carry clusters of fleshy red or pink fruits, but specimens of both sexes are required for that, and two examples of this giant plant might be hard to accommodate in most gardens.

Soil preference: Moist but well-drained
Aspect: Shade or part shade
Season of interest: Spring, summer
Height and spread: Climbing to 10m (33ft)

Companion plants: A fine pergola plant, perhaps in the company of clematis or honeysuckles, or in a woodland setting, growing into medium or large trees.

Wisteria sinensis   Hardy, woody climber

Fast growing climber whose mature stems form interesting, twisted, gnarled shapes. Hanging racemes of fragrant blue-mauve pea flowers appear before the leaves emerge, the latter opening coppery and gradually turning golden green. *W. s.* 'Alba' is white and 'Prolific' is two-tone lilac and blue. Summer pruning is advised to enhance free flowering.

Soil preference: Any, free-draining
Aspect: Sun
Season of interest: Spring
Height and spread: To 8m (26ft) and spreading

Companion plants: Try this with the pale yellow-flowered *Rosa banksiae* 'Lutea' or with a *Campsis radicans* woven through for late summer flowers.

Buddleja auriculata

Weeping Sage   Marginally hardy, lax shrub, suitable as a wall shrub

A weak-stemmed shrub from South Africa with gangling habit and narrow, pointed leaves, deep green on top but with silvery grey undersides. From early autumn sprays of tiny, off-white, yellow centred flowers appear and are sweetly scented. Protection from extremes of frost is essential.

Soil preference: Free-draining
Aspect: Full sun
Season of interest: Autumn, winter
Height and spread: To 2.5m (9ft)

Companion plants: Fun to grow with bright summer climbers such as Lophospermum, *Rhodochiton atrosanguineus* or *Eccremocarpus scaber*.

Holboellia latifolia

Marginally tender climber

Evergreen climber (potentially vigorous in a warm spot) with compound palmate leaves which are leathery and dark green and in spring, clusters of intensely fragrant flowers, the male ones being greenish white and the females purplish. Occasionally sausage-shaped, purplish fruits form.

Soil preference: Humus-rich, moist but well-drained
Aspect: Sun or part shade
Season of interest: Spring
Height and spread: Climber to 5m (16ft)

Companion plants: Blend this climber with other shelter-loving plants. Either *Lapageria rosea* or *Lonicera hildebrandiana* combines well in a frost-free spot.

Itea ilicifolia

Near hardy lax shrub, trained as a climber

A sedate but densely covering evergreen climber with glossy, holly-like leaves – but smaller, softer prickles – and, in summer, a long-lasting display of long, narrow, golden green catkins. Susceptible to extreme frost.

Soil preference: Any fertile
Aspect: Sun or part shade
Season of interest: Summer
Height and spread: To 2m (6ft 6in) and spreading

Companion plants: Best if allowed to flower without other climbers woven through, but very beautiful grown alongside colourful climbers with which it can contrast. The beige-yellow rose 'Gloire de Dijon' goes well, as does summer jasmine.

Acacia pravissima

Oven's Wattle   Frost-sensitive lax shrub, suitable as a climber

Vivid, glaucous grey-green, triangular leaves clothe the gracefully arching stems of this lax wall plant. From late winter, pale yellow, fragrant mimosa ball flowers emerge and persist for many weeks. Though marginally hardy, a sheltered spot in sun will enable this plant to survive all but severe frosts.

Soil preference: Very free-draining
Aspect: Sun
Season of interest: Year round
Height and spread: To 3m (10ft)

Companion plants: Striking if planted next to a dark leaved Caeanothus, such as 'Trewithen' or 'Puget Blue', whose azure flowers will make a delicious contrast with the blue-grey foliage.

Pileostegia viburnoides

Marginally hardy evergreen climber

Simple, glossy, dark green leaves set the big creamy umbels of flowers off to perfection when they appear in late summer on this vigorous, self-clinging plant. An excellent climber to scale a large, mature tree, but also beautiful on a part shaded wall, preferably where it receives afternoon sun.

Soil preference: Humus-rich, moist but free-draining
Aspect: Sun or part shade
Season of interest: Late summer, autumn
Height and spread: Climber to 6m (20ft)

Companion plants: Lovely grown on a building with such other climbers as *Ampelopsis brevipedunculata* or *Parthenocissus henryana*.

Lonicera henryi   Henry's Honeysuckle   Vigorous climber

A vigorous, twining, evergreen honeysuckle with leathery, oblong leaves and rust-coloured stems. In summer, small, dusky pink to purplish double-lipped flowers are produced in clusters and are followed, in autumn, by small, black, glossy berries. Not a seductively beautiful plant but a good, vigorous, screen-forming climber.

Soil preference: Any
Aspect: Sun, shade or part shade
Season of interest: Year round, but low key
Height and spread: To 7m (20ft) and climbing

Companion plants: Relieve the dullness by working other, more vigorous climbers through the leathery leaves. Golden hop is useful for this or you could blend with spring flowering *Clematis armandii*.

Clematis cirrhosa   Climber

A variable Mediterranean native with long, scrambling stems and divided, dark green, semi-evergreen foliage. Flowers may be pale greenish parchment or primrose yellow, often marked with freckles or rust-coloured spots. 'Wisley Cream,' pictured, carries paired, bell-shaped flowers in pale greenish-yellow; *C. c.* var. *purpurea* 'Freckles' has flowers with densely rust-flecked interiors.

Soil preference: Any, not too dry
Aspect: Sun or part shade
Season of interest: Winter, spring
Height and spread: 3m (10ft), spreading

Companion plants: This valuable winter climber looks attractive on its own, or blended with varieties of *Clematis viticella* for summer interest. Contrasts well with Chaenomeles, but prune the clematis to prevent it overcrowding the wall shrub.

Passiflora caerulea   Blue Passion Flower   Near hardy climber

Tendril climber with palmate leaves, purplish stems and, from late summer onwards, a steady production of distinctive blossoms. These consist of circles of pale green sepals, surrounding bright purple-blue, filamentous petals with three central stigmas shaped like nails. Tasteless amber coloured fruits follow. Can be cut hard back.

Soil preference: Any
Aspect: Sun or part shade
Season of interest: Summer, autumn
Height and spread: To 6m (20ft)

Companion plants: The young stems need unfettered sun to develop flower buds, so weaving other climbers through may inhibit that. Lovely alongside summer jasmine or when grown through a heat-loving wall shrub such as *Cytisus battandieri* or with *Solanum laxum* 'Album' (*S. jasminoides* 'Album').

Hedera helix   English Ivy   Hardy, self-clinging climber

A rapid, evergreen which roots wherever it comes into contact with the ground. The three-lobed leaves on running stems are quite different from the smaller, diamond-shaped ones which occur on mature, twiggy, flower-bearing growths. If controlled, wall-trained ivy provides the best shelter for wildlife and also sustains many species with late nectar and winter berries.

Soil preference: Any
Aspect: Any, even dense shade
Season of interest: Year round
Height and spread: More or less unlimited!

Companion plants: The handsome, sometimes marbled leaves make a fine setting for flowers of honeysuckles and of vigorous climbing roses such as 'Albertine' or 'Scharlachglut'.

Actinidia kolomikta

Hardy deciduous climber

A vigorous, leafy climber whose main attributes are the bold splashes of white or purplish pink which appear on the maturing foliage. The leaves are simple, oval and pointed and in early summer clusters of small, fragrant flowers appear. Though tolerant of shade, the leaves colour best in sun.

Soil preference: Any well-drained, not too dry
Aspect: Sun
Season of interest: Spring, early summer
Height and spread: To 5m (15ft), spreading

Companion plants: Fine blended with such other climbers as *Jasminum officinale*, or perhaps the purple grape, especially when planted partly to create wildlife cover.

Parthenocissus henryana

Silver Vein Creeper   Near-hardy, self clinging, deciduous climber

A vigorous climber with five-lobed, palmate leaves with purple leaf-backs and green upper surfaces marbled with pewter-coloured veining when grown in shade. In autumn, the foliage fires up to vivid crimson. Needs protection from extremes of frost.

Soil preference: Rich, well-drained
Aspect: Part shade, shade
Season of interest: Summer, autumn
Height and spread: To 10m (30ft), spreading

Companion plants: At its most spectacular when furnishing walls on its own, but also effective blended with other Parthenocissus species, or to make a contrast with ivies.

Clematis armandii   Near hardy evergreen climber

A rampaging but very beautiful Chinese species with glossy, evergreen, compound leaves and fast-growing stems. In spring each leaf joint carries bold sprays of waxy white, fragrant blossoms. *C. a.* 'Apple Blossom' has pink buds, opening white. Invasive, but easily controlled if pruned very hard immediately after flowering.

Soil preference: Fertile and cool, but well-drained
Aspect: Sun or part shade
Season of interest: Spring. Wildlife cover in summer
Height and spread: 7m (23ft) and spreading

Companion plants: Difficult to grow with other climbers, which it tends to smother, but pretty when blended with a grape vine, grown as an ornament rather than for its fruit, or trained into a strong tree.

Schizophragma hydrangeoides

Hardy deciduous, self-clinging climber

A species from Japan and Korea with oval, pointed, serrated leaves and, in summer, flat-topped, clusters of lace-cap flowers whose fertile components are surrounded by showy, oblong, sterile florets in creamy white. The form 'Roseum' has pale pink sterile florets which darken as they mature. Ultimately vigorous, but can be slow to establish.

Soil preference: Humus-rich, fertile but free-draining
Aspect: Part shade
Season of interest: Summer
Height and spread: To 9m x 3m (30ft x 9ft)

Companion plants: Loveliest when allowed to furnish the trunk of a mature tree but also fine on a wall with such climbers as *Clematis viticella* or with moderately vigorous honeysuckle varieties.

Vinca major

Greater Periwinkle   Perennial evergreen trailing plant

Trailing stems which carry glossy, oval, dark green leaves making a beautiful foil for the sky blue flowers which are produced almost constantly. A nuisance in the wrong place, for it roots wherever a stem tip touches the ground, but an excellent wildlife-supporting cover. Periwinkle will climb up into shrubs or other supports.

Soil preference: Any
Aspect: Shade, part shade
Season of interest: Year round
Height and spread: 45cm (1ft 6in), spreading

Companion plants: A handy background plant to cover between shrubs, or to grow at the base of a shaded wall.

Hydrangea seemannii

Near hardy evergreen climber

An evergreen woody climber which clings to its support or host tree by means of short, aerial roots. The leaves are leathery, slightly toothed and elliptical, deep on their upper surfaces, and the greenish white flowers, produced in corymbs, are surrounded by more showy, white sterile florets.

Soil preference: Any
Aspect: Part shade
Season of interest: Year round
Height and spread: 10m (30ft)

Companion plants: Happiest when trained up a large, mature tree so that it can furnish the trunk. Also effective on a wall, perhaps with *Tropaeolum speciosum* woven through.

Jasminum mesnyi

Primrose Jasmine   Marginally tender deciduous climber

A beautiful but tender climber or lax shrub with long, green-barked, flexible stems and deep green compound leaves. The non-fragrant flowers, which appear in spring and summer, are semi-double, large and bright golden yellow. Perfect for a sheltered spot, in a warm climate, but will only survive a light frost.

Soil preference: Any fertile, free-draining
Aspect: Sun
Season of interest: Spring and early summer
Height and spread: To 3m (to 10ft)

Companion plants: Interesting to blend with *Trachelospermum jasminoides* or with summer jasmine to extend the season. In mild areas, good for blending with *Jasminum polyanthum*.

Jasminum polyanthum

Marginally tender evergreen or semi-evergreen climber

A very vigorous but not very frost hardy jasmine with pretty, divided leaves and green barked stems. From late winter, in warm conditions, sprays of light pink buds open to starry, white flowers whose fragrance is so intense as to be almost cloying at close quarters. A touch of frost is tolerable, but not a freeze up.

Soil preference: Any reasonably fertile, not too dry
Aspect: Part shade, sun or shade
Season of interest: Winter, spring, summer
Height and spread: To 3m (to 10ft)

Companion plants The perfect conservatory plant, or to grow in a sheltered courtyard where the rich fragrance can blend with that of *Clematis armandii*. Blending this plant with the hardier *Jasminum officinale* could provide extra protection and guarantee later summer to autumn blooms.

Solanum jasminoides

Potato Vine   Marginally hardy climber

A vigorous and potentially invasive climber which clings by means of buckled leaf petioles. The simple leaves are dark when young, and accompanied from late spring onwards by loose, open clusters of small but conspicuous flowers which are deep blue in bud opening pale powder blue, fading almost white. The form 'Alba' (pictured) has white flowers. Sustained frost will cut this plant back to its roots.

Soil preference: Any
Aspect: Sun
Season of interest: Spring, summer, autumn
Height and spread: 10m x 10m (30ft x 30ft)

Companion plants: A rampaging but beautiful climber, probably safest on its own, but capable of sharing a wall with the equally vigorous *Rosa banksiae*.

Holboellia latifolia

Climber

A strong growing climber from the Himalayas whose deep green, compound leaves are evergreen. In spring, male (pale green) and female (purple) flowers are produced on hanging racemes. A distinctive and interesting climber which will readily cover a wall, but not hardy in exceptionally cold regions.

Soil preference: Any
Aspect: Sun or part shade
Season of interest: Spring, summer, autumn
Height and spread: 5m x 5m (15ft x 15ft)

Companion plants: Probably best grown on its own, on a sheltered wall, or with a non-invasive, herbaceous clematis such as *C. texensis* 'Etoile Rose' trained through its stems.

Berberidopsis corallina

Coral Plant   Marginally hardy climber

A beautiful climber from Chile whose twining stems carry narrow, oblong leaves and, from late summer through to autumn, clusters of cherry red, rounded flowers which hang gracefully along the stems on thin, red stalks. Protection from cold winds is essential.

Soil preference: Humus-rich
Aspect: Part shade or sun
Season of interest: Summer, autumn
Height and spread: 5m x 5m (15ft x 15ft)

Companion plants: Fine by itself on a sheltered wall, but even more beautiful if grown into a tree so that it can furnish the branches with bright red garlands.

Climbers Scheme

Beautiful walls benefit from being furnished with modest-growing climbers, rather than having their fabric blotted out by a dense cover of vegetation. The rose selected for this period building is 'Kathleen Harrop,' an intensely fragrant Bourbon variety which produces a long run of blooms after the main flush, and which, conveniently, is totally thornless. The young growths are a coppery pink, so they also harmonise with the greys and duns of the oölitic limestone.

Other climbers would probably be superfluous, since the intention is to enhance the beauty of the setting, rather than to hide an eye-sore, but an imaginative planter would probably be tempted to weave a soft blue clematis such as C. 'Prince Charles' or 'Perle d'Azur' among the rose stems.

The *Centranthus ruber* in the foreground gives a cheerful early summer display, seeding itself around liberally to provide later colour, too. But when its main display is done, the small, silvery leaved willow, *Salix helvetica*, makes a pleasing foil to the light pink flowers.

Matching colours to man-made structures can be difficult, particularly where the building materials have a distinctive hue. The grey of the limestone is kind to most flower colours, but is particularly beautiful with pastel hues, whether they contrast or harmonise. The soft mauve-blue of wisteria, for example, and the warm yellow of *Rosa banksiae* 'Lutea' blend sweetly, not only with each other, but also with the weathered wall.

Harsher building colours, such as modern red brick, might work better with warm salmon, deep red or orange flowers, particularly if richly coloured foliage can be introduced to tone things down. The purple vine, for example, looks striking on modern brickwork of almost any hue and, in turn, contrasts magnificently with crimson or scarlet roses such as *Rosa* 'Scarlet Fire,' 'Danse du Feu' and 'Soldier Boy' or with the subtle apricot blooms of *Rosa* 'Lady Hillingdon.'

The climbing Bourbon rose 'Kathleen Harrop' and pink valerian create a pleasing cottage ambience in the author's garden.

shrubs

Large shrubs for full sun, winter and spring

Large shrubs for full sun, summer and autumn

Large shrubs for partial sun, all year

Large shrubs for shade, all year

Magnolia stellata

Star Magnolia   Hardy shrub or small tree

A densely twiggy shrub whose bare stems carry a heavy crop of velvet-sheathed buds which each spring break into starry blooms with narrow white petals. Simple oblong, oval leaves emerge as the flowers fade. Fully lime-tolerant, unlike a number of magnolias, but the early blooms are susceptible to night frost.

Soil preference: Any, free-draining
Aspect: Sun or part shade
Season of interest: Early spring
Height and spread: 3m x 3m (10ft x 10ft)

Companion plants: A feature shrub for early spring, handsome among such evergreens as *Osmanthus delavayi* or with hollies whose dark leaves contrast with the whiteness of the blooms.

Ribes sanguineum   Flowering Currant   Hardy deciduous shrub

An aromatic, suckering shrub from North America with hanging racemes of pink or red flowers which emerge simultaneously with the bright green, three or five-lobed leaves. Small, blue-grey fruits follow. Worthwhile cultivars include gold leaved 'Brocklebankii', whose flowers are carmine, red flowered 'Pulborough Scarlet' and a clean-coloured 'Tydeman's White'.

Soil preference: Any
Aspect: Sun, part shade
Season of interest: Spring
Height and spread: 2.5m x 2m (8ft x 6ft 6in)

Companion plants: Useful as a barrier, especially if blended with other hedging plants. Traditionally used to contrast with yellow forsythias but also lovely for gracing a woodland edge, among such taller trees as alders, birches or sorbus.

Syringa vulgaris   Common Lilac   Hardy deciduous shrub

Vigorous, sometimes suckering shrubs with diamond-shaped leaves and, in late spring, bold panicles of fragrant blossoms. Typical hues are lilac, blue or white, but breeding has extended this range through purples to wine red. Excellent white varieties are the single flowered 'Vestale' and double 'Madame Lemoine'. Dark colours include deeper purple 'Charles Joly', the reddish 'Monge' and 'Sensation', whose purple flowers have white petal edges.

Soil preference: Any, well-drained
Aspect: Sun or part shade
Season of interest: Late spring
Height and spread: Variable to 5m x 4m (16ft x 12ft)

Companion plants: Lovely grouped to create big screens at the back of a planting scheme or to form a backdrop, especially if big shrub roses such as *R. moyesii* or *R.* 'Nevada' are there to follow.

Philadelphus 'Beauclerk' Mock Orange Hardy deciduous shrub

Large shrub with fast-growing, arching canes whose second-year side shoots bear trusses of intensely fragrant, large, single, white flowers whose centres are lightly flushed with purple pink markings. Best of a large range of fragrant varieties but other good hybrids include the more upright, double-flowered 'Virginal' and the gracefully arching 'Belle Etoile'.

Soil preference: Any
Aspect: Sun or part shade
Season of interest: Spring, early summer
Height and spread: 2.5m x 3.5m (8ft x 11ft)

Companion plants: Big sprawlers for a mature shrubbery, delightful in the company of early roses, such as 'Maigold' or 'Highdownensis' or to precede later flowering buddlejas. The blended scents of mock orange and wild honeysuckle make a very heady cocktail.

Viburnum farreri (syn. V. fragrans)

Winter Viburnum Hardy semi-evergreen shrub

An upright, deciduous, suckering shrub with simple, toothed leaves which turn reddish before falling. From autumn onwards small clusters of sweetly fragrant pink or white blooms appear, sometimes followed by scarlet berries. A pure white variety is 'Candidissimum'; the dwarf 'Nanum' grows to 75cm (30in), but only flowers when very mature. Daintier in flower than the popular *Viburnum* x *bodnantense*.

Soil preference: Any, not too dry
Aspect: Sun, part shade, shade
Season of interest: Autumn, winter
Height and spread: 2.5m x 2.5m (8ft x 8ft)

Companion plants: A superb winter bloomer to blend with such deciduous trees as maples, or to associate with spring and summer shrubs such as Forsythia, Cotinus or its own evergreen relative, *Viburnum tinus*.

Weigela garden hybrids

Hardy deciduous shrubs

Upright shrubs whose mature branches arch gracefully. The simple, oval, pointed leaves are joined, in late spring, by a fulsome peppering of small, funnel-shaped flowers in pink, white or red. Some, such as W. 'Praecox Variegata' or 'Foliis Purpureis', have coloured foliage. 'Bristol Ruby' has red blooms; 'Carnaval' [sic] has both pale and dark pink flowers on the same plant.

Soil preference: Any
Aspect: Sun, part shade
Season of interest: Late spring
Height and spread: Up to 3m x 2.5m (10ft x 8ft)

Companion plants: Fine contributors to a mixed border, where they can preside over such perennials as *Campanula lactiflora*, sidalceas and pink oriental poppies.

Abutilon vitifolium   Near hardy deciduous shrub

A rather brittle, fast growing, short-lived shrub with open habit and large, vine-like leaves and masses of saucer shaped flowers, in a rich, lavender mauve. Selections include 'Veronica Tennant', pinkish mauve flowers and 'Tennant's White'. The hybrid *Abutilon* x *suntense* is similar but with larger flowers, particularly in the clone 'Jermyns', whose blossoms are vibrant mauve.

Soil preference: Any, free-draining
Aspect: Full sun
Season of interest: Summer
Height and spread: 4m x 2.5m (13ft x 8ft)

Companion plants: Fine choice for a sunny spot, against a wall or free standing, with such other sun lovers as *Coronilla valentina* or perhaps to follow wisterias or to precede *Buddleja fallowiana* or *B.* 'Lochinch'.

Berberis dictyophylla

Hardy deciduous shrub

A strong growing shrub whose young stems are decorated with a pale bluish grey bloom. The small, dark green leaves conceal needle-like thorns and in spring are joined by pale yellow flowers which hang in pairs. The berries follow turning red, along with the foliage, in autumn.

Soil preference: Any free-draining, not too dry
Aspect: Sun or part shade
Season of interest: Year round
Height and spread: 2m x 1.5m (6ft x 5ft)

Companion plants: An attractive enough shrub to stand on its own, in grass, or to associate with other Berberis species such as *B. darwinii* or *D. thunbergii*. Maples and sorbus varieties which colour well in autumn also make fine companions.

Buddleja davidii   Butterfly Bush, Buddleia   Hardy deciduous shrub

A large Chinese shrub with brittle wood, grey-green, downy foliage and from mid-summer, fragrant, tapering panicles of densely crowded mauve flowers, each with a pinprick orange centre. Garden forms include 'Pink Beauty', the deep purple 'Black Knight', the red-magenta 'Royal Red', and 'Dartmoor', which produces multiple, mauve panicles. Irresistible to butterflies. Prune very hard each spring. See also page 298 for smaller varieties.

Soil preference: Any free-draining
Aspect: Sun
Season of interest: Summer
Height and spread: Variable to 6m x 3m (20ft x 10ft)

Companion plants: A fine border centre plant for mid-summer, especially when presiding over perennials in the mauve, purple or gold and yellow range. Try with Solidago, Phlox, Rudbeckia, Dahlia and Aster.

Ceanothus x delileanus 'Gloire de Versailles'

California Lilac   Marginally hardy, deciduous shrub

A moderately slow-growing shrub with mid-sized, dark green, toothed leaves which are held on greenish stems. From mid-summer onwards, airy clusters of tiny, pale smoky blue flowers are produced in generous quantities. The variety *C. x pallidus* 'Perle Rose' is similar in habit and form, but has dusky pink flowers.

Soil preference: Fertile, well-drained
Aspect: Sun
Season of interest: Summer, autumn
Height and spread: 1.5 m x 1.5m (5ft x 5ft)

Companion plants: The late flowers make inspiring company for the creamy-flowered *Hydrangea paniculata* or to add late season colour to groups of spring shrubs such as mock orange or forsythia.

Cytisus scoparius

Common Broom   Hardy deciduous shrub

A largely erect, somewhat ungainly shrub with dark evergreen stems and, in summer, small, three-lobed leaves, silvery at their margins. In late spring or early summer a mass of pea flowers open along the stem. Typically, these are buttercup yellow, but rusty red, lemon, orange and bi-coloured forms also grow. *Cytisus nigricans* is a close relative which flowers in late summer.

Soil preference: Free-draining, acidic, not too fertile
Aspect: Sun
Season of interest: Early summer
Height and spread: To 1.75m x 1.5m (6ft x 5ft)

Companion plants: Taller varieties are ideal frothing over from the back of a border planted with late spring and early summer shrubs and perennials or to lift dark evergreens.

Kolkwitzia amabilis   Beauty Bush   Hardy deciduous shrub

A big sprawling, suckering shrub with small, oval, tapering leaves and from early summer, great clouds of small, trumpet shaped flowers, pink on their outsides and pale pink to white inside with rust coloured speckles at their throats. The variety 'Pink Cloud' is a slightly deeper pink than the species.

Soil preference: Any reasonably fertile
Aspect: Sun
Season of interest: Early summer
Height and spread: 3.5m x 3.5m. (12ft x 12 ft)

Companion plants: A natural successor in mixed shrub plantings to mock orange, lilacs and the spring viburnums. Also lovely when encouraged to fall over a low wall, perhaps at the back of a mixed border with deep violet blue irises or delphiniums to make a colour contrast.

Hamamelis x intermedia

Witch Hazel   Hardy, deciduous shrub

Sedate shrub with spreading branches and large, slightly toothed leaves which colour richly in autumn. From mid-winter, yellow or rusty red, fragrant flowers with spidery petals emerge and persist for some weeks. 'Arnold Promise' has mid-yellow, 'Diane' rusty red and 'Pallida' pale primrose blooms. 'Jelena' (pictured) has a spreading habit with almost horizontal branches.

Soil preference: Humus-rich, well-drained, reasonably fertile
Aspect: Partial shade
Season of interest: Winter, autumn
Height and spread: Variable to 4m x 3m (13ft x 10ft)

Companion plants: Sublime when underplanted with winter blooming hellebores and snowdrops.

Hydrangea macrophylla

Hortensia, Garden Hydrangea, Florists' Hydrangea   Hardy deciduous shrub

From mid-summer, inflorescences develop at the stem tips which may be rounded, with many sterile florets (mop head) or consist of umbels with fertile flowers at their centres and showy sterile florets around the edges (lace cap). Flower colour varies according to variety and to soil type. Acid soils tend to produce blue flowers; alkaline pink.

Soil preference: Any fertile, not too dry
Aspect: Sun, but not too hot, or semi-shade
Season of interest: Summer, autumn
Height and spread: Variable to 2.5m x 2m (8ft x 6ft)

Companion plants: Hot coloured crocosmias such as *Crocosmia* 'Solfatare,' *C. masoniorum* and *C.* 'Lucifer' can be surprisingly effective partners and in woodland gardens, hydrangeas are valuable for bringing late colour to groups of otherwise boring rhododendrons.

Ligustrum lucidum

Glossy Privet   Hardy evergreen shrub

Large shrub or small tree with oval, pointed, glossy leaves, dark green above and paler below. In late summer and early autumn, mature specimens carry numerous, large panicles of pure white flowers which resemble those of lilac. Decorative forms include 'Tricolor' which has cream, green and silvery variegations.

Soil preference: Any
Aspect: Sun, shade or part shade
Season of interest: Summer
Height and spread: 6m x 5m (20ft x 16ft)

Companion plants: Valuable for late season colour, among mixed shrubs and beautiful with hip-bearing shrub roses or with such plants as *Euonymus europaeus* 'Red Cascade' or Fothergilla whose reddening foliage makes a strong contrast.

Lonicera x purpusii

Winter Honeysuckle   Hardy deciduous shrub

A vigorous shrub with simple, oval, pointed leaves and tan stems. During mild spells in winter, small, paired cream flowers emerge at the leaf axils. These are intensely fragrant and are produced severally throughout winter and early spring. Vigorous annual pruning, after flowering will ensure re-growth of strong, flowering stems.

Soil preference: Any free-draining, not too dry
Aspect: Sun, part shade or shade
Season of interest: Winter
Height and spread: 3m x 2.5m (10ft x 8ft)

Companion plants: An essential addition to a winter planting, beautiful with *Mahonia japonica*, Hamamelis and *Daphne laureola* for a rich mix of winter fragrances, perhaps with hellebores and snowdrops for underplanting, and early narcissus to follow.

Photinia x fraseri   Hardy evergreen shrub

Member of the rose family with waxy, oval leaves which are bright red when very young, maturing to sombre green. Off-white flowers appear as umbels, but it is the bright young foliage for which the plant is largely grown. Good varieties include 'Red Robin', a related hybrid 'Redstart', and 'Birmingham'. Regular pruning or clipping ensures abundant red growth.

Soil preference: Any reasonably fertile
Aspect: Sun or part shade
Season of interest: Year round
Height and spread: 4.5m x 4m (15ft x 13ft)

Companion plants: Excellent as a hedging plant, where the bright young leaves are so abundant but also dramatic as a structure shrub for a mixed border with hot-coloured or red plants such as oriental poppies, dahlias, sunflowers and cannas.

Rubus 'Benenden'   Hardy deciduous shrub

Thornless relative of the blackberry whose arching stems have attractive, peeling winter bark and bear bright green, three or five-lobed leaves in spring and summer. Large flowers appear along the stems in late spring and are single and rose-like with white-petals surrounding a central bunch of gold stamens.

Soil preference: Any
Aspect: Sun or part shade
Season of interest: Late spring; winter
Height and spread: 3m x 3m. (10ft x 10 ft)

Companion plants: A big, sprawling shrub ideal for filling an empty corner and for masking unsightly objects. The white blossoms are best savoured without competition, but buddlejas or *Ligustrum lucidum* would make handsome companions for foliage contrast and later flowers.

Cornus mas   Cornelian Cherry   Hardy deciduous shrub

A large shrub or small tree with stiff, twiggy branches whose bark is green when young. The simple leaves are oval, pointed and colour up well in autumn. Clusters of tiny yellow flowers open in winter, followed in late summer by small, oblong, edible red fruits. Decorative varieties include the gold leaved 'Aurea' and the cream and green 'Variegata'.

Soil preference: Any
Aspect: Sun, part shade or shade
Season of interest: Year round
Height and spread: 6m x 4.5m
(20ft x 15ft)

Companion plants: Amenable to clipping, therefore useful for structure planting in a formal garden, interplanted with perennials or bedding. If planted with spring shrubs such as lilacs and mock orange, *Cornus mas* adds an autumnal dimension and provides a shapely outline.

Corylopsis pauciflora

Winter hazel   Hardy deciduous shrub

A spreading shrub with loose, bushy habit and, in late winter and spring, hanging racemes of pale yellow flowers which resemble large catkins. The hazel-like leaves emerge as flowering concludes and, in autumn, woody fruits may form. Other useful species include *Corylopsis sinensis* and *C. glabrescens* whose foliage colours yellow in autumn.

Soil preference: Humus-rich, preferably lime free
Aspect: Shade or partial shade
Season of interest: Year round
Height and spread: 1.5m x 2m. (5ft x 6ft)

Companion plants: Shrubs for a woodland planting which look striking with magnolias, camellias and early flowering rhododendrons.

Corylus maxima

Filbert, Red Filbert   Hardy deciduous shrub

A bold, suckering shrub with erect stems and large, rounded, toothed leaves which turn ochre yellow before falling and, in winter, hanging golden catkins. Large, well-flavoured hazel nuts form in the autumn.

Soil preference: Any
Aspect: Sun, part shade or shade
Season of interest: Year round
Height and spread: Up to 6m x 4.5m (20ft x 15ft)

Companion plants: Pollarded plants of 'Purpurea' (pictured) produce the best foliage which makes a handsome backing for summer flowers, particularly those in the peachy salmon colour range. Roses such as 'Just Joey' and 'Perle d'Or' are especially lovely against the bronzed foliage.

Cornus alternifolia
Hardy deciduous shrub or small tree

An elegant shrub valued mainly for its distinctive outline. Branches grow horizontally from the main stem forming shapely tiers of foliage which is neutral green in summer but turns reddish in autumn. The starry little flowers produced along the tops of the branches are cream. There is an enchanting white variegated form, 'Argentea'.

Soil preference: Humus-rich, not too dry
Aspect: Part shade, shade or sun
Season of interest: Year round
Height and spread: 6m x 6m (20ft x 20ft)

Companion plants: A key plant for the garden's outline, best placed for an uninterrupted view of the tiered branches. Low-growing shrubs or perennials – dwarf willows, bergenias and Siberian iris – would grow prettily at its feet.

Mahonia lomariifolia

Marginally hardy evergreen shrub

Erect stems carry large whorls of prickly, compound leaves. In winter and spring spikes of small, bright yellow, fragrant flowers emerge from the stem tips. Susceptible to deep frost and cold winds. The hardier *Mahonia* x *media* (pictured), a cross between *M. japonica* and *M. lomariifolia*, has excellent cultivars including the fragrant *M.* 'Charity' and the autumn flowering *M.* 'Winter Sun'.

Soil preference: Any reasonably fertile, free-draining but not too dry
Aspect: Sun or part shade
Season of interest: Year round
Height and spread: 3m x 2m (10ft x 6ft)

Companion plants: The rather gaunt stems are probably better partially disguised by lower, mound-forming shrubs such as mop-head hydrangeas, Enkianthus or *Aucuba japonica*.

Osmanthus delavayi

Evergreen shrub

A member of the olive family with small, oval, glossy leaves carried in pairs along arching stems. In late winter and early spring, clusters of small, sweetly fragrant flowers appear and remain beautiful for several weeks. A pretty alternative is *O.* x *burkwoodii* which is slightly more compact, with more erect stems and very fragrant blooms.

Soil preference: Any not to dry, well-drained
Aspect: Shade or part shade
Season of interest: Spring; year round
Height and spread: 3m x 3m (10ft x 10ft)

Companion plants: The little white flowers are a delight to back up spring displays of wallflowers, tulips or narcissus while the dark foliage tones down the vividness of such spring shrubs as forsythia or *Ribes sanguineum*.

Lilacs

A much loved range of spring-flowering shrubs most of which are remarkably hardy, versatile and easy to grow. They will tolerate poor or sandy soils, but are also happy on heavy clay and can be kept compact by regular pruning or allowed to grow into medium-sized, suckering trees. Colours range through lilac, mauve to deep crimson-purple or pure white. Most are richly fragrant.

1. Syringa vulgaris 'Sensation'
A moderately vigorous lilac whose spring panicles of large, dusky purple flowers are edged with white, making a distinctive display.

2. Syringa vulgaris
Typical lilac bears cone-shaped panicles of fragrant blooms in pale lilac or mauve.

3. Syringa vulgaris 'Fall Baltyku'
Conical-shaped panicles of fragrant, rich purple flowers during late spring.

4. Syringa 'Massena'
A common lilac cultivar with rich, reddish purple flowers held in medium-sized, broad panicles.

5. Syringa vulgaris 'Pol Robson'
Dense panicles of medium-sized, fragrant flowers in rosy mauve-purple.

6. Syringa vulgaris 'Firmament'
An outstanding variety with good vigour and large, loosely packed panicles whose flowers open soft lilac which matures to pale, pearly-mauve.

7. Syringa x josiflexa 'Bellicent'
Dark stems and longer, narrower leaves distinguish this hybrid from more familiar lilacs. The individual, tubular flowers open to show four small petals opening shell pink, fading to pink blush.

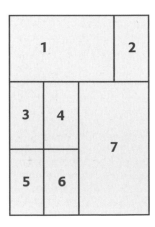

Abelia x grandiflora

Near hardy, evergreen shrub

Shrub of moderate vigour with slender, arching canes and small to medium-sized leaves, dark green in summer, but colouring bronze in winter. The small, trumpet-shaped pink flowers are fragrant and are produced from mid-summer through autumn. Varieties include the yellow and green leaved 'Francis Mason' and 'Confetti'.

Soil preference: Humus-rich, free-draining but not too dry
Aspect: Sun, part shade, sheltered
Season of interest: Summer
Height and spread: 2m x 2m (6ft x 6ft)

Companion plants: Valuable for late colour, especially when teamed with late perennials such as penstemons, asters in the blue and mauve range or with bold drifts of late lilies such as *Lilium auratum*.

Callistemon citrinus

Crimson Bottlebrush   Half-hardy evergreen shrub

Large shrub or small tree with tan bark and many narrow, leathery leaves. Young emerging shoots have a silvery, feathery appearance and the flowers, which develop as cylindrical whorls behind emerging shoots, have bright red, very prominent stamens which give the appearance of a glass or bottle-cleaning brush.

Soil preference: Any free-draining
Aspect: Sun, in a sheltered spot
Season of interest: Spring and early summer
Height and spread: 3m x 3m (10ft x 10ft)

Companion plants: In cooler regions, best grown as a wall plant, perhaps with *Acacia pravissima*, *Teucrium fruticans* or *Cytisus battandieri* as companions.

Carpenteria californica

Bush/Tree Anemone   Near hardy, evergreen shrub

A beautiful native of California with oblong, glossy, evergreen leaves and, in early summer, clusters of large white, single flowers whose centres carry generous bunches of golden stamens. Susceptible to fungal leaf spot in cold, wet climates and vulnerable to cold winds. Best grown on a wall in cool regions since it will not survive sustained frost.

Soil preference: Any free-draining, not too moist
Aspect: Sun
Season of interest: Summer
Height and spread: 2m x 2m (6ft 6in x 6ft 6in)

Companion plants: Superb on a wall with other marginally hardy plants such as bottlebrushes, *Lonicera hildebrandiana* or *Clianthus puniceus*.

Cordyline australis

New Zealand Cabbage Palm   Near hardy evergreen shrub or tree

A slow growing plant whose large rosettes of long, narrow, fiercely pointed leaves grows atop lengthening, erect, naked stems. On mature plants, large sprays of fragrant but tiny blossoms are produced, followed by clusters of grey-white berries. Selected forms include 'Torbay Red (reddish leaves) and the variegated 'Torbay Dazzler'.

Soil preference: Any free-draining
Aspect: Sun or part shade
Season of interest: Year round
Height and spread: To 6m x 2m (20ft x 6ft)

Companion plants: Useful seaside or town garden plant – for example, as a dot plant in summer bedding schemes, especially those planted for sub-tropical or Mediterranean effect. Distinctive as mature plants with other architectural specimens and grasses or as a solitary tree.

Spartium junceum

Spanish Broom   Near hardy shrub

A distinctive shrub with massed, whip-like, deep green stems and, in summer, small numbers of narrow, dark green leaves. Through summer, bright yellow, richly scented pea flowers are crowded on the stems, followed in autumn by flattened, blackening pods which burst open audibly in late sun.

Soil preference: Any free-draining
Aspect: Sun
Season of interest: Late summer
Height and spread: 3m x 3m (10ft x 10ft)

Companion plants: A gaunt, leggy thing, best tucked among dense, lower growing shrubs such as *Caryopteris* x *clandonensis*, Cistus or lower growing Ceanothus varieties.

Ulex europaeus 'Flore Pleno'

Gorse, Whin, Furze   Hardy shrub

Viciously armed shrub with sharp thorns sticking out in all directions. Even the rigid leaves take the form of sharp spines. Green stems, silvery when young, carry masses of bright yellow, double flowers from late winter onwards. These are strongly scented, smelling of coconut confections. The species is a noxious weed in some regions, but the double form 'Flore Pleno' is sterile.

Soil preference: Any free-draining
Aspect: Sun, exposed
Season of interest: Year round
Height and spread: 2m x 2m (6ft x 6ft)

Companion plants: A useful shrub for a rugged, windswept spot, perhaps grown with *Cytisus scoparius*, *Euonymus alatus* and the tougher kinds of grass and heather.

Abutilon megapotamicum

Trailing Abutilon   Tender evergreen shrub

A lax, sprawling shrub. Oval, pointed, toothed leaves and a constant succession of elegantly hanging flowers whose calyces are bright red, contrasting with the mustard yellow, mallow-like flowers. Selected varieties include 'Variegatum' whose leaves are stippled and blotched in yellow.

Soil preference: Any free-draining
Aspect: Sun
Season of interest: Summer
Height and spread: 2.5m x 2.5m (8ft x 8ft)

Companion plants: Best on a wall, in cold areas, perhaps blended with *Teucrium fruticans* or used as a central dot plant in bedding schemes with warm colours – with Tagetes, perhaps, or with *Salvia* x *superba*.

Acca sellowiana

Feijoa, Pineapple Guava   Tender evergreen shrub

A distinctive member of the myrtle family with dark green, glossy leaves, pale grey on their undersides and pinkish red flowers whose petals curve curiously on themselves, revealing pale pinkish backs. The flower centres consist of bold bunches of pink stamens. Large, edible fruits follow.

Soil preference: Any free-draining
Aspect: Sun
Season of interest: Year round
Height and spread: 3m x 3m (10ft x 10ft)

Companion plants: As handsome in a conservatory as outdoors, happiest with other heat-lovers such as mimosas, *Eriobotrya japonica* or with related myrtles.

Hibiscus syriacus

Hardy Hibiscus   Hardy deciduous shrub

Rigid-stemmed shrub with grey bark and slightly lobed, toothed leaves. From mid- to late summer, a long succession of large, saucer-shaped flowers is produced, each having a central tower of stamens. Colours vary through blue-mauve of such varieties as 'Oiseau Bleu' to the pinks of 'Boule de Feu' or 'Hamabo' (pale). 'Red Heart' has red-centred white blooms.

Soil preference: Any free-draining
Aspect: Sun
Season of interest: Summer
Height and spread: To 2.5m x 2m (8ft x 6ft)

Companion plants: Important providers of late summer colour and useful among such spring-flowering shrubs as Philadelphus or Deutzia to extend the flowering season. Also beautiful teamed with buddleias or Hoheria.

Laurus nobilis   Bay Laurel   Near hardy evergreen shrub or tree

Large shrub or small tree with waxy, leathery simple leaves and small, tufty beige-yellow flowers in early summer, followed by small black berries. Ancient Greeks revered this classic plant; Romans adorned themselves with it during festivities and cooks have valued its aromatic qualities for millennia.

Soil preference: Any, free-draining
Aspect: Sun, shade, part shade
Season of interest: Year round
Height and spread: 3m plus x 2m (10ft x 6ft)

Companion plants: Ideal for clipping into formal shapes, for hedging or growing naturally as part of a herb garden among sages, thymes and rosemary; attractive used formally in a rose garden or to bring structure to a mixed border of perennials.

Myrtus communis subsp. tarentina

Small-leaved Myrtle   Near hardy, evergreen shrub

A small leaved form of common myrtle. Densely growing shrub with small, glossy, dark green diamond-shaped leaves which are sweetly aromatic when crushed. The flowers, produced in summer and autumn, are creamy white with pinkish stamens. *Myrtus communis* subsp *tarentina* 'Microphylla Variegata' has creamy white leaf margins.

Soil preference: Any free-draining
Aspect: Sun
Season of interest: Year round
Height and spread: 1.5m x 1.5m. (5ft x 5 ft)

Companion plants: A fine hedging plant, for a sheltered garden and effective when backing bright summer flowers such as New World salvias, Arctotis, silver leaved plants or tender annuals.

Olearia x haastii

Daisy Bush   Hardy evergreen shrub

A dense-growing, twiggy shrub with small, oval leaves mid-green on their upper surfaces with paler grey undersides. In summer, masses of small, white, daisy flowers are produced and last for some weeks. A naturally occurring hybrid from the South Island of New Zealand.

Soil preference: Any free-draining
Aspect: Sun
Season of interest: Summer
Height and spread: 1.75m x 1.5m (6ft x 5ft)

Companion plants: Vigorous but compact shrub for a hot, dry spot, attractive with *Genista hispanica*, whose yellow blooms come before, or with the Mount Etna broom, *Genista aetnensis*. Fellow New Zealand shrubs such as Corokia also associate well.

Rhododendron

Although there are many hundreds of rhododendrons in cultivation, every one of them is a lime hater, so only gardens with acid soils are suitable. Smaller species of rhododendrons or azaleas make excellent container plants, however, if grown in ericaceous compost and watered with lime-free water. Almost all rhododendrons flower during the first half of the year.

1.   Rhododendron yakushimanum
A dwarf species from Japan which has been used to develop a wide range of excellent garden hybrids. Young shoots and the undersides of the leaves are coated with a tan felting or indumentum; flowers are a clean, clear pink.

2.   Rhododendron 'Hydon Dawn'
A compact, variety with oblong, medium sized leaves and tight trusses of bright pink flowers which turn paler as they mature.

3.   Rhododendron 'Percy Wiseman'
Compact variety seldom exceeding two metres in height with large, showy clusters of cream and pink flowers produced in late spring.

4.   Rhododendron 'Blue Diamond'
A small-leaved, evergreen rhododendron with rounded outline and a heavy crop, each spring, of showy, mauve-blue flowers.

5.   Rhododendron 'Golden Torch'
A neat-growing, upright evergreen with medium sized leaves and masses of salmon pink buds which open to soft, creamy yellow flowers.

6.   Rhododendron 'Loder's White'
A tall rhododendron growing 3 metres or more high, producing, in late spring, large trusses of fragrant, white blooms.

7.   Rhododendron yunnanense
Natives of Tibet and Western China, these large plants grow to 3 metres or more in height and across. Flowers, produced in late spring, are in the pink range, often richly speckled or stippled.

8.   Rhododendron 'Silver Jubilee'
A compact variety with medium sized leaves and large flowers which open white, from pink buds, and have conspicuous red centres.

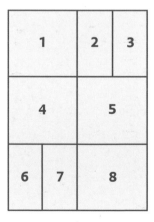

Prunus lusitanica

Portugal Laurel   Hardy evergreen shrub

A robust, many-branched shrub with reddish young stems and glossy dark blue-green, oval leaves. In late spring, racemes of almond-scented five-petalled white blossoms precede fruits which resemble small cherries and which turn glossy black. *P. l.* 'Variegata' has somewhat irregularly shaped, cream margined leaves.

Soil preference: Any
Aspect: Sun, part shade, shade
Season of interest: Year round
Height and spread: 6m x 4m
(20ft x 15ft). Grows larger in certain conditions

Companion plants: Valuable shrub, either for formal clipping, perhaps as part of a mixed border or for composing windproof screens where it could be blended with hollies such as *Ilex aquifolium* 'Madame Briot' or *I. a.* 'Handsworth New Silver' for a sumptuous leaf contrast.

Prunus laurocerasus

Cherry Laurel   Hardy evergreen shrub

A fast growing, robust, much branched shrub with big, oval, pointed, leaves, whose vibrant bottle green is enhanced by a glossy cuticle. Short spikes of white flowers precede black berries which resemble ripe olives. Useful garden forms include *P. l.* 'Castlewellan' (syn. 'Marbled White') whose leaves are stippled with white markings.

Soil preference: Any
Aspect: Sun, shade, part shade
Season of interest: Year round
Height and spread: To 6m x 6m
(20ft x 20ft). More in favourable conditions

Companion plants: Hedging material, either on its own or blended with other evergreens for a thick, wind-proof, sound-suppressing screen. Relieve the dullness by interplanting with big shrub roses such as *Rosa* 'Arthur Hillier' or *Rosa* 'Frühlingsgold' or weave winter jasmine through the branches.

Buxus sempervirens

Common Box, Boxwood   Hardy evergreen shrub

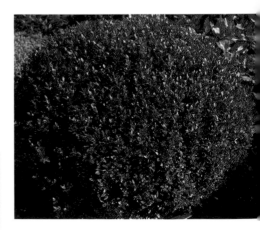

A slow-growing, dense shrub or small tree with characteristic odour, subtly reminiscent of tom cat, but less unpleasant. The small, oval or rounded leaves are thickly crowded making a dense screen. Dwarf forms, suitable for low hedging, are 'Suffruticosa' and taller 'Elegantissima' whose leaf margins are white.

Soil preference: Any
Aspect: Sun, part shade or shade
Season of interest: Year round
Height and spread: To 5m x 2m
(16ft x 6ft)

Companion plants: The perfect plant for low hedging, as in knot gardens, or for growing tall as screens. Large flowered perennials or roses – particularly *Rosa gallica* 'Versicolor' or the red 'Charles de Mills' – look lovely associated with box.

Eunoymus japonicus

Japanese Spindle   Near hardy evergreen shrub

Dense growing shrub with somewhat brittle stems which are almost completely hidden by the huge crop of simple, oval, dark green, glossy leaves. Flowering is sparse and unusual, the blooms being small and insignificant, followed by tiny orange fruits. 'Ovatus Aureus' is a variegated form. Subject to mildew unless grown in an airy spot.

Soil preference: Any free-draining
Aspect: Sun, shade or part shade
Season of interest: Year round
Height and spread: 3m x 2m (10ft x 6ft)

Companion plants: A fine, deep green background, useful for keeping the wind off more interesting shrubs such as daphnes, Edgeworthia or camellias.

Pittosporum tenuifolium

Kohuhu   Near hardy, evergreen shrub

A highly variable New Zealand native with slender branches, black bark and simple, narrowly oval, curled or waved leaves, often with interesting colour suffusions. The tiny dark brown flowers are insignificant. Selected varieties include grey-green, variegated 'Silver Queen', 'Tom Thumb', whose leaves are purple-brown and the stipple-leaved 'Irene Paterson'.

Soil preference: Humus-rich and fertile
Aspect: Full sun
Season of interest: Year round
Height and spread: Up to 6m x 4m (20ft x 14ft)

Companion plants: Often used by florists to accompany bouquets. The undulating curves on the leaves gives them a special sheen; lovely with roses, rhododendrons or other large flowered shrubs. Also beautiful grown in groups among bamboos.

Ligustrum ovalifolium

Oval-Leaved Privet   Hardy evergreen or semi-evergreen shrub

The classic privet, used *ad nauseam* in suburban hedging in the last century. Glossy green, oval leaves, dense enough to block out the view and in summer, panicles of pure white, unpleasant-smelling flowers. Golden privet, *L. o.* 'Aureum', has bright yellow leaf margins. Responds well to clipping. Susceptible to honey fungus.

Soil preference: Any
Aspect: Sun, part shade or shade
Season of interest: Year round
Height and spread: 3.5m x 3.5m (12ft x 12ft)

Companion plants: Best grown as a backdrop to colourful flowers and especially good behind dahlias, chrysanthemums. Quite fun to grow as a mixed hedge, blended with *Ribes sanguineum*.

Cotoneaster lacteus

Hardy evergreen shrub

A tall, rangy shrub with mid-sized, oval, pointed leaves, bright green on their upper sides, silvery in reverse and from autumn onwards a heavy crop of berries hanging in clusters. The white blossoms in late spring provide an extra bonus. Performs well even in an exposed spot, so useful for creating a decorative windbreak.

Soil preference: Any free-draining, not too dry
Aspect: Sun or part shade
Season of interest: Year round, autumn winter
Height and spread: 3m x 3m (10ft x 10ft)

Companion plants: A tough shrub, attractive among *Viburnum rhytidophyllum*, big lilacs, Sambucus and other shelter-creating shrubs.

Elaeagnus x ebbingei

Hardy evergreen shrub

A densely branched, vigorous shrub whose oval leaves are deep green and glossy above and pale grey beneath and, in autumn, conceal small but highly fragrant flowers. The variety 'Limelight' has subtle gold-green and primrose suffusions and leaf margins of 'Gilt Edge' are daffodil yellow.

Soil preference: Any
Aspect: Sun or part shade
Season of interest: Year round
Height and spread: To 3m x 3m (10ft 9in x 10ft 9in)

Companion plants: The ideal screen shrub, excellent for setting off cotoneasters, gold leaf *Philadelphus coronarius* or for contrasting with floriferous subjects such as *Hypericum* 'Hidcote'.

Rhododendron ponticum

Common Rhododendron   Evergreen shrub

A large, invasive shrub with glossy, dark green, oval, pointed leaves and, in late spring and early summer, clusters of bright magenta flowers with rusty speckles at their throats. Less vigorous garden forms include 'Silver Edge', which has white leaf margins and the cream variegated 'Variegatum'. This has become a noxious weed in some regions.

Soil preference: Any lime-free
Aspect: Sun, part shade or shade
Season of interest: Early summer
Height and spread: To 6m x 6m (20ft x 20ft)

Companion plants: Useful as a nurse shrub for other, more choice rhododendrons in a woodland planting, or as a windproof screen. Not suitable for a large wild garden because of dangers of spreading.

Phlomis fruticosa   Jerusalem Sage   Hardy evergreen shrub

A small shrub with open habit, whose paired leaves, stems and flower buds are densely downy, giving a silvery appearance when young. From late spring, tight whorls of bright, mustard yellow, lipped flowers appear, attracting bees with a fruity scent. Other choices include mauve bloomed *P. italica* and *P. purpurea*.

Soil preference: Any free-draining
Aspect: Sun
Season of interest: Late spring, summer
Height and spread: To 1.5m x 1m (5ft x 3ft)

Companion plants: Natural companion in the wild, to rosemary, lavenders, thymes, sages and therefore excellent to include in a dry Mediterranean garden.

Potentilla fruticosa

Shrubby Cinquefoil   Hardy deciduous or semi-evergreen shrub

A sub-arctic species, capable of thriving in harsh conditions. The small, compound leaves are silvery when unfolding and make an attractive foil for the five-petalled flowers which appear constantly through the growing season. The flowers are yellow, but garden varieties include pink 'Daydawn', flame 'Red Ace' and the white 'Abbotswood'.

Soil preference: Any, not too dry
Aspect: Sun or part shade
Season of interest: Spring, summer, autumn
Height and spread: To 1.5m x 1m (5ft x 3ft)

Companion plants: Handy shrubs to bring substance to a mixed border or to site with dwarf willows and small evergreens such as *Juniperus rigida* subsp. *conferta* or *Ilex crenata* in an exposed spot.

Rubus cockburnianus

Hardy deciduous shrub

Rampantly invasive, thorny, suckering shrub whose canes are coated with a pale grey bloom, attractive in winter. The compound leaves are puckered when young and mid-green. The form *R. c.* 'Goldenvale' has much paler stems, superb in winter, and bright golden yellow foliage which holds its colour well through summer.

Soil preference: Any, not too dry
Aspect: Any
Season of interest: Year round
Height and spread: 2.5m (8ft), spreading

Companion plants: A fine shrub for a winter garden, if kept under control, pretty with mahonias, *Cornus alba* when pollarded for winter twigs and large hellebores such as *Helleborus argutifolius* and *H. foetidus*.

Hydrangea

Hydrangeas come from a very large genus comprising many excellent garden plants. They are grown chiefly for their flowers, which are carried in large heads and come in a wide range of pinks, mauves, blues and whites.

1. Hydrangea macrophylla 'Ayesha'
A curious form of the common mop-head hydrangea in which the sterile florets have inward-curling edges creating a distinctive effect. Can be blue or pink.

2. Hydrangea paniculata 'Unique'
A valuable and easily grown species whose large, oblong panicles of creamy flowers appear in late summer. This variety is *H. p.* 'Unique'.

3. Hydrangea macrophylla 'Altona'
A popular mop-head with huge blossoms which colour up, when young, to deep pink and gradually take on purple hues as they age.

4. Hydrangea arborescens 'Annabelle'
A vigorous species with bright emerald green, toothed leaves and, in summer, large, rounded heads of pure white flowers.

5. Hydrangea macrophylla 'Lanarth White'
A lacecap variety whose fertile flowers, at the centres, are blue but surrounded by white sterile florets.

6. Hydrangea quercifolia
The oak leaved hydrangea. Large, deeply lobed leaves which colour richly in the autumn and in late summer, terminal panicles of creamy flowers.

7. Hydrangea 'Preziosa'
A lacecap variety whose fertile flowers are pink and surrounded with sterile floret which begin white but soon become flushed with vivid pink. Superb autumn colour.

8. Hydrangea serrata 'Bluebird'
A compact 'serrata' variety with flat-topped, lace cap flowers whose centres are deep blue, surrounded by paler blue sterile florets.

1		2
3	4	5
6	7	8

Cornus alba   Red-barked Dogwood   Hardy deciduous shrub

A spreading, suckering shrub with reddish young stems and simple leaves which tend to colour gold in autumn. Flowers appear as flat topped umbels, in summer, followed by white autumn berries. The best stems are seen on *C. a. sibirica* (red) and *C. a.* 'Kesselringii' (purple-black). The form 'Elegantissima' has white variegated leaves and red stems; *C. a.* 'Spaethii' (pictured) has gold variegated leaves and 'Aurea', all yellow.

Soil preference: Any, preferably moist
Aspect: Sun or part shade
Season of interest: Winter, summer
Height and spread: 2m x 3m (6ft x 10ft)

Companion plants: Precious winter garden shrubs, for teaming with small to medium willows, particularly *Salix daphnoides*, *S. irrorata* and for summer, with such shrub roses as *Rosa* 'Mrs Anthony Waterer' or *Rosa* 'Marguerite Hilling'.

Forsythia hybrids   Hardy deciduous shrubs

Popular shrub with simple leaves, sometimes coloured purplish when young, or before falling, and four-petalled, bright yellow flowers crowded on the early spring stems. Dependable varieties include 'Lynwood Variety' (vivid gold flowers), 'Karl Sax' (yellow blooms with dark leaves) and the dwarf *Forsythia viridissima* 'Bronxensis', which seldom exceeds 75cm (30in) height. See also *Forsythia suspensa* on page 255.

Soil preference: Any
Aspect: Sun, part shade
Season of interest: Spring
Height and spread: Variable to 3m x 2m (10ft x 6ft)

Companion plants: Valued for its brief, bright display, effective among later flowering shrubs such as lilacs and Philadelphus. Also useful in a mixed border above such spring perennials as *Brunnera macrophylla* and emerging peony foliage.

Acacia dealbata

Mimosa, Silver Wattle   Near hardy evergreen shrub

A gangling shrub or tree with widely spaced branches and feathery, compound leaves which are silky to the touch and a pleasing dark blue-green. In late winter, fragrant blossoms resembling small, yellow, fluffy balls last for several weeks. The Cootamundra wattle, *Acacia baileyana*, is more compact, with smaller leaves and paler flowers.

Soil preference: Any free-draining
Aspect: Sun
Season of interest: Late winter, spring
Height and spread: To 5m x 5m (16ft x 16ft) and more

Companion plants: Better used as a wall plant in cold areas and a handsome companion for other Acacia species or to precede *Abutilon megapotamicum* and *Carpenteria californica*.

Ceanothus   Californian Lilac   Near hardy evergreen shrubs

Lax shrubs with small, creased, glossy evergreen leaves and green stems. In spring, masses of intense blue flowers, produced in dense, rounded clusters, creates a startling display which lasts for weeks. 'Topaze' and 'Puget Blue' have the richest intensity of colour; 'Concha' (pictured) is a vivid dark blue and *C. thyrsiflorus* var. *repens* is a low-growing, trailing species with pale grey-blue flowers.

Soil preference: Free-draining, but fertile
Aspect: Sun
Season of interest: Spring
Height and spread: Variable to 3m x 3m (10ft x 10ft)

Companion plants: Shrubs to contrast with intense yellow of *Fremontodendron californicum*, especially if grown on a wall, or to group with spring flowering broom species.

Coronilla valentina subsp. glauca

Yellow Crown Vetch   Marginally hardy evergreen shrub

A lax shrub from the Mediterranean with blue-green, hairless, pinnate leaves whose lobes are attractively rounded. Crown-shaped clusters of small, golden yellow, fragrant, pea flowers are produced in profusion through winter and spring, and sporadically during the rest of the year. The form 'Citrina' (pictured) has lemon yellow blooms.

Soil preference: Any free-draining
Aspect: Sun
Season of interest: Winter; year round
Height and spread: To 1.5m x 1.5m (5ft x 5ft)

Companion plants: Best protected by a sunny wall – beautiful on old, red brick, perhaps beneath wisterias, *Solanum laxum* 'Album' or with a low-growing ceanothus.

Sophora

Kowhai   Evergreen marginally hardy shrub

Handsome member of the pea family with stiffish, branching stems and long, narrow, deep green pinnate, somewhat ferny leaves. In spring, leathery buds open to bright golden yellow, elongated pea flowers. Excellent trained on a wall, but also lovely free-standing.

Soil preference: Any free-draining
Aspect: Sun
Season of interest: Spring, year round
Height and spread: To 5m x 3m (16ft x 10ft)

Companion plants: Contrast the leaves of this plant with *Abutilon* x *suntense* or with the broader foliage of the purple vine. The flowers would be dramatic with *Ceanothus* 'Concha' or fellow New Zealander, the red flowered Clianthus.

Buddleja davidii var. nanhoensis

Butterfly Bush   Hardy deciduous shrub

Medium to small shrubs with lax, arching stems, grey-green leaves and panicles of deep blue-mauve flowers. Nanho varieties include *B. d.* 'Nanho Blue' (indigo panicles), the brighter coloured 'Nanho Purple' and 'Nanho White'.

Soil preference: Any free-draining
Aspect: Sun
Season of interest: Summer
Height and spread: To 1.5m x 1.5m (5ft x 5ft)

Companion plants: Blends well in a mixed border, backing such perennials as tall phloxes, penstemons and Madonna lilies.

Ceanothus Autumn-flowering varieties

Hardy or near hardy, evergreen shrubs

Shrubs with arching stems and with small, glistening, oblong leaves. In autumn, dense panicles of intense blue flowers appear for several weeks, often with a floral reprise in spring. 'A. T. Johnson' has the most intensely blue flowers, 'Autumnal Blue' has paler blue blossoms and 'Burkwoodii', one of the hardier forms, flowers in both summer and autumn.

Soil preference: Any free-draining
Aspect: Sun
Season of interest: Autumn, spring
Height and spread: Variable to 3m x 3m (10ft x 10ft)

Companion plants: Valuable for their double display, the autumn blooms team well with yellow clematis such as *C.* 'Bill MacKenzie' or *C. tibetana*. The evergreen foliage also makes an attractive foil for paler leaves of, say, *Cytisus battandieri* or *Acacia pravissima*.

Cistus ladanifer

Ladanum, Gum Rock Rose   Hardy evergreen shrub

A loose-limbed shrub whose oblong, dark green leaves are sticky to the touch. Large but shortlived white flowers, each with a purple blotch at the petal base, appear during summer. The plant exudes a musky, balsamic odour and is the source of the fragrant gum, 'Ladanum' – not to be confused with the opiate drug, Laudanum!

Soil preference: Very free-draining
Aspect: Sun
Season of interest: Summer
Height and spread: 1.5m x 1.5m (5ft x 5ft)

Companion plants: Perfect for a hot, sunny spot along with smaller flowered Cistus species or with Phlomis, lavenders or to front pruned buddleias.

Indigofera heterantha   Indigo   Hardy, deciduous shrub

A much-branched shrub with flexible, arching stems furnished with bright fluorescent green, glossy, pinnate leaves and through summer, lots of short racemes of pinkish red pea flowers. These are held upright along the branches making them charmingly conspicuous. Sustained hard frost may damage this plant, but regeneration often occurs from the roots.

Soil preference: Well-drained but not too dry
Aspect: Sun
Season of interest: Summer
Height and spread: 2m x 2m (6ft 6in x 6ft 6in)

Companion plants: Valuable among mixed shrubs for its summer flowers, but superb in a sunny border among such mid-summer perennials as sidalceas, achilleas, astrantias or to contrast its vivid green leaves with bronze fennel.

Lavatera x clementii

Tree Mallow   Hardy shrub or sub-shrub

Fast-growing shrubs with three-lobed leaves and a long succession of frail, funnel-shaped or saucer-shaped flowers in shades of pink or white, sometimes with darker centres. *L.* 'Barnsley' has carmine centred, flush white blooms, 'Rosea' has bright pink flowers and 'Ice Cool' is white. Prune hard back each spring for best results.

Soil preference: Any free-draining
Aspect: Sun
Season of interest: Summer
Height and spread: 2m x 2m (6ft 6in x 6ft 6in)

Companion plants: Great for extending the height of a border with such perennials as phloxes, asters or large campanulas in the foreground.

Alyogyne hueglii   Blue Hibiscus   Tender shrub

From Australia, a lax, rangy shrub with long, rather weak stems and pubescent, divided, palmate leaves. Throughout summer, large, pale-centred, lavender blue, saucer flowers appear, each centred with pale yellow stamens. The variety 'Santa Cruz' has blue-mauve flowers without the pale centres. Pinch back repeatedly to encourage bushiness and protect from frost.

Soil preference: Free-draining
Aspect: Sun
Season of interest: Summer
Height and spread: To 2m x 1.5m (6ft x 5ft)

Companion plants: Ravishing on its own in a big container or contrasted with the bright golden flowers of Euryops or among osteospermums or big-flowered hypericums. Also harmonizes sweetly with heliotropes or *Solanum rantonetii* in a summer display.

Piptanthus nepalensis

Marginally hardy evergreen shrub

A suckering shrub with glossy, bottle green stems and palmate leaves which, when young, are coated with silver down. From early summer, clusters of vivid yellow pea flowers appear in a generous first flush, followed by more sporadic blooming. Though evergreen, cold winter weather may cause this plant to lose its leaves.

Soil preference: Any well-drained, but moist
Aspect: Sun or part shade
Season of interest: Spring, summer
Height and spread: 2m x 1.5m (6ft x 5ft)

Companion plants: The dark stems and young silvery leaves make this an admirable companion to harmonize with *Teucrium fruticans* or to precede Abutilon.

Prunus x cistena

Purpleleaf Sand Cherry   Hardy deciduous shrub

A slow-growing, compact cherry with upright habit, forming a broadly columnar outline. The medium sized, oval, serrated leaves are dark purplish red, making a contrast with the pinkish white blossoms which flower among the newly emerging foliage. The leaves darken in colour as the year advances.

Soil preference: Any, free-draining, not too dry
Aspect: Sun, part shade
Season of interest: Spring
Height and spread: 2.5m x 1.5m (8ft x 5ft)

Companion plants: Useful for bringing strong leaf colour to a small planting scheme and dramatic when contrasted with the gold foliage of *Philadelphus coronarius* 'Aureus' or *Physocarpus opulifolius* 'Dart's Gold'.

Ribes odoratum

Buffalo Currant   Hardy deciduous shrub

A suckering, branching shrub with thin somewhat weak stems and attractively lobed, simple leaves. From early spring, hanging racemes of buttercup yellow blooms open and fill the air, on still days, with their sweet, spicy fragrance. The hybrid *R.* x *gordonianum* is an intriguing alternative whose deep salmon flowers are suffused with pale yellow.

Soil preference: Any
Aspect: Shade, part shade or sun
Season of interest: Spring
Height and spread: To 2m x 2m (6ft x 6ft)

Companion plants: More valuable for fragrance than colour or habit, but charming when blended with other spring shrubs or set in a woodland garden, flowering above bluebells and anemones.

Salix hastata   Hardy deciduous shrub

An upright willow with shiny, dark mahogany bark which makes a strong contrast in late winter with the silvery, furry catkins which are held erect and very close to the stems. Pale grey-green leaves emerge as the catkins mature and gradually subside to plain green for summer, turning yellow before falling in autumn.

Soil preference: Any, moist
Aspect: Sun, part shade, shade
Season of interest: Winter, spring
Height and spread: 1m x 1m (3ft 3in x 3ft 3in)

Companion plants: A beautiful winter companion for snowdrops, oriental hellebores and early narcissus. Summer ground cover plants such as creeping Jenny, *Lysimachia nummularia*, *Ajuga reptans* and *Lamium maculatum* also associate well.

Camellia   Camellia   Hardy evergreen shrub

Universally popular shrubs with medium or large, oval, glossy green leaves and in winter or spring, large showy flowers whose petals have a distinctive, satin texture. Blooms may be single, semi-double, 'anemone centred' or fully double in colours ranging from cream or white, through shades of pink to deep red. The *C.* x *williamsii* hybrids – *C. japonica* crossed with *C. saluenensis* – have excellent garden vigour. Among hundreds of varieties, 'J. C. Williams' is single pink, 'Miss Universe' is double white, 'Freedom Bell' is red.

Soil preference: Lime-free, not too dry
Aspect: Part shade, sun or shade
Season of interest: Winter, spring
Height and spread: Variable to 5m x 2.5m (16ft x 8ft)

Companion plants: Plants of the woodland margin. Use to form a beautiful link between taller trees, such as Cercidiphyllum or Zelkova and such understorey plants as Narcissus, Brunnera or Polygonatum.

Chimonanthus praecox   Wintersweet   Hardy deciduous shrub

A moderately vigorous, upright shrub with simple, mildly aromatic leaves. In mid- to late winter, the intensely fragrant, curiously star-shaped flowers, with beige, semi-translucent petals and dark purplish centres, appear along stems which have matured during the previous growing season. Desirable varieties include 'Luteus' (pictured) which has yellow blossoms and larger flowered 'Grandiflorus'. Susceptible to coral spot fungal disease.

Soil preference: Any, free-draining
Aspect: Sun, part shade
Season of interest: Winter, spring
Height and spread: 3m x 2.5m (10ft x 8ft)

Companion plants: Valued almost exclusively for its fragrance, but lovely, in spring with witch hazels, underplanted with *Iris reticulata* or with Muscari.

Hypericum x inodorum

Hardy, semi-evergreen shrub

An upright, shapely shrub with broad, oval leaves, dark when young, and from mid- to late summer, clusters of small, five petalled flowers with conspicuous central stamens. Pointed fruits which ripen to pinkish-red, appear in late summer and continue to develop through autumn. The variety 'Elstead' has rusty red fruits.

Soil preference: Any, not too dry
Aspect: Sun or part shade
Season of interest: Summer, autumn
Height and spread: 1.25m x 1.25m (4ft x 4ft)

Companion plants: Superb shrub for autumn colour, especially when contrasted with lavender or blue-coloured asters, penstemons.

Leycesteria formosa

Himalayan Honeysuckle   Hardy, deciduous shrub

A suckering, wand-forming shrub with erect or arching stems and longish green leaves which are slightly toothed or sometimes lobed. The flowers hang in clusters, rather like catkins, and are white held in purplish pink bracts. The fruit ripens purple-black, still held in the bracts whose colours deepen to purplish pink.

Soil preference: Any
Aspect: Shade, part shade or sun
Season of interest: Summer, autumn
Height and spread: To 2.5m x 2m (8ft x 6ft)

Companion plants: Useful for dense thickets of cover, or as a background for herbaceous plants which benefit from shelter. Annuals such as Agrostemma, Chrysanthemum and flowering grasses associate well.

Nandina domestica

Heavenly/Sacred Bamboo   Marginally hardy, evergreen shrub

A cane-forming shrub with attractive pinnate leaves, tinged reddish when young, and sprays of small, white, starry flowers which in autumn develop into loose, large clusters of vivid red berries. In winter, the foliage becomes suffused with bronze or purplish hues. Garden selections include 'Richmond,' a heavy cropper and dwarf 'Fire Power'.

Soil preference: Moist but well-drained
Aspect: Sun or part shade
Season of interest: Summer, autumn
Height and spread: 1.5m x 1.5m (5ft x 5ft)

Companion plants: The glossy hue of the leaves looks beautiful with contrasting foliage of real bamboos, especially *Pleioblastus viridistriatus*.

Phormium tenax   New Zealand Flax   Hardy shrub-like perennial

Huge plants with long, semi-rigid, strap-shaped leaves whose fibres are exceptionally strong and which may grow nearly 2m (6ft) long. When mature, tall flower spikes appear, carrying rusty red flowers which are followed by distinctive black fruits. Phormium hybrids include the cream edged 'Variegatum', the bronze leaved Purpureum Group and pink-striped 'Sundowner'.

Soil preference: Any not too dry
Aspect: Sun or part shade
Season of interest: Year round
Height and spread: Variable to 3m x 2m (10ft x 6ft)

Companion plants: Good solo plants, especially in contemporary designs among hardscaping, or growing in gravel. In a large border, they make sumptuous contrasts with such vigorous shrubs as buddlejas, tall shrub roses or can harmonize with yuccas and big grasses.

Spiraea japonica   Japanese Spiraea   Hardy deciduous shrub

Upright or mound-forming shrubs with simple, toothed leaves and flat-topped umbels of densely packed, pink flowers in late spring or early summer. Many forms have been raised among which 'Anthony Waterer' has wine-red flowers. Valued for foliage, 'Goldflame' has unique orange-hued leaves and 'Golden Princess' pure gold. Pruning the foliage varieties hard in spring stimulates new growth and improves the leaf quality.

Soil preference: Any free-draining
Aspect: Sun or part shade
Season of interest: Spring, summer
Height and spread: Variable to 1.75m x 1.25m (6ft x 4ft)

Companion plants: The late spring leaves make delightful companions to early perennials such as oriental poppies and lupins but the gold leaf kinds are magnificent with the bronze *Carex buchananii*.

Berberis x bristolensis

Hardy evergreen shrub

A dome-forming shrub with oval, prickle-edged leaves, some of which turn a striking red in winter. During late spring, a scattering of small yellow flowers shows up brightly against the darkness of the leaves. Small, oval, black fruits which develop in late summer and autumn are coated with a pale grey bloom.

Soil preference: Any free-draining, not too dry
Aspect: Part shade or sun
Season of interest: Year round
Height and spread: 1.5m x 2m (5ft x 6ft)

Companion plants: The autumn colours harmonize well with *Geranium wallichianum* 'Buxton's Variety' or with autumn gentians and with *Ceratostigma plumbaginoides*.

Aucuba japonica

Japanese Laurel, Spotted Laurel   Hardy evergreen shrub

A dome-shaped or rounded shrub with glossy, oval or pointed leaves and stems which are sea-green. Many forms have spotted or decorated leaves and female plants bear large, red berries. Decorative varieties include the female, speckle-leaved 'Crotonifolia' (pictured), 'Picturata' whose leaves have bold yellow centres and narrow-leaved 'Salicifolia'.

Soil preference: Any
Aspect: Shade or part shade
Season of interest: Year round
Height and spread: To 2.5m x 2m (8ft x 6ft)

Companion plants: Not stirringly beautiful but handy for growing in dense, even dry shade and harmonious with *Helleborus foetidus*, *Mahonia aquifolium* and a ground cover of Vinca.

Mahonia japonica   Hardy evergreen shrub

A distinctive, suckering shrub with naked, stiff stems topped with prickly rosettes of stiff, leathery pinnate leaves. Buds on long, curving racemes are formed at the centres of the rosettes in autumn and through winter, the primrose yellow, intensely fragrant flowers open. Blue-black berries ripen in mid-summer. Plants in the Bealei Group have olive green leaflets.

Soil preference: Any free-draining, not too dry
Aspect: Shade, part shade or sun
Season of interest: Winter, year round
Height and spread: 2m x 2m (6ft x 6ft)

Companion plants: Beautiful in the company of winter-flowering daphnes such as *D. bholua*, *D. odora* or with equally fragrant winter honeysuckle, *Lonicera* x *purpusii*.

Stachyurus praecox

Hardy deciduous shrub

A shapely plant with open branches and simple leaves which are sometimes bronze tinted when young. In late winter or early spring, hanging racemes of pale yellow flowers develop, resembling catkins, and persist until the leaves begin to emerge. *Stachyurus chinensis* has similar flowers. The form 'Magpie' has pinkish and cream variegations.

Soil preference: Lime-free, not too dry
Aspect: Part shade or sun
Season of interest: Winter, spring
Height and spread: 2m x 2m (6ft x 6ft)

Companion plants: A fine shrub for a spring border, in a sheltered spot, perhaps underplanted with winter blooming heathers.

Viburnum tinus   Laurustinus   Hardy evergreen shrub

A dense-growing, shrub with oval, pointed, slightly glossy leaves and an almost continuous run – even through winter – of flat-topped umbels carrying small, fragrant flowers. Though sometimes pinkish in bud, these usually open white. Attractive selections include the pink budded 'Eve Price', 'Gwenllian' and 'Purpureum', whose young leaves are suffused with bronze.

Soil preference: Any
Aspect: Any
Season of interest: Year round
Height and spread: 2.5m x 2m (8ft x 6ft)

Companion plants: Excellent as a hedge, or a background plant, where the dark leaves make a pleasant foil for summer perennials and a good winter outline. Also responds to formal clipping, perhaps to accompany roses or as a feature for herb gardens.

Garrya elliptica

Silk Tassel, Catkin Bush   Hardy evergreen shrub

A fast-growing, densely branched shrub whose mid-sized oval leaves are dark green on their upper surfaces and grey-green below. In winter, on male plants, catkins extend to hang up to 30cm (12in) long, shedding clouds of pollen. Female forms have shorter, thicker catkins followed by purplish fruit. The variety 'James Roof', male, has extra long tassels.

Soil preference: Any, not too dry
Aspect: Sun, part shade, shade
Season of interest: Winter
Height and spread: 3m x 2m (10ft x 6ft)

Companion plants: A useful winter garden plant, attractive with jasmine, or as a dark leaved contrast to witch hazels in flower. Charming as a summer host plant through which pale flowered varieties of *Clematis viticella* can be encouraged to climb.

Kerria japonica

Hardy suckering shrub

A thicket-forming shrub with bottle green stems and pleated, toothed leaves. In late winter and early spring, bright golden yellow flowers begin to emerge with blooming continuing into late spring. The most widely grown variety is a double 'Pleniflora' but a more fetching variety is 'Golden Guinea', whose flowers are single and very large.

Soil preference: Any
Aspect: Shade, part shade or sun
Season of interest: Spring
Height and spread: 2m x 1.5m (6ft x 5ft)

Companion plants: Brings brightness, in early spring, to a mixed border, and lovely behind wallflowers, tulips, forget-me-nots or leafy perennials which have yet to flower.

Callicarpa bodinieri

Beauty Berry   Hardy deciduous shrub

Simple leaves, bronze tinged when young, green when mature, turning golden yellow before they fall in autumn. The flowers, produced in summer, are lilac mauve but unremarkable. They are followed by a heavy crop of bright violet berries which persist to late autumn. The form *C. b.* var. *giraldii* 'Profusion' carries the heaviest berry crop.

Soil preference: Any, fertile, moist but well-drained
Aspect: Sun, part shade, shade
Season of interest: Autumn
Height and spread: 2.5m x 2m (8ft x 6ft)

Companion plants: The berries contrast richly with autumn tints from maples, berberis or *Fothergilla major*, as well as with the bright daisy flowers of Ligularia and Helianthus. Startling, too, with the white fruits of *Sorbus cashmiriana*.

Enkianthus campanulatus   Hardy deciduous shrub

A spreading, sprawling shrub with slightly toothed, simple, dull green leaves which turn fiery red in autumn. The flowers, which appear in generous clusters from late spring and last into summer, are cream lined with pink veins and shaped like tiny bells. *Enkianthus deflexus* has darker veined flowers and *E. cernuus* f. *rubens* has reddish flowers.

Soil preference: Humus-rich, moist but well-drained, acid or neutral
Aspect: Part shade or sun
Season of interest: Summer, autumn
Height and spread: To 3.5m x 3.5m (11ft x 11ft)

Companion plants: Delightful companions for such other shrubs of open woodland as *Magnolia sieboldii*, Fothergilla, Camellia and later flowering hydrangeas.

Fothergilla major

Hardy deciduous shrub

A north American member of the witch hazel family, forming an upright, loosely dome-shaped shrub with oval or rounded, attractively veined leaves which, in autumn, become vivid orange, red and yellow. In spring, the conspicuous tufts of creamy flowers, soft and silky to the touch, appear just before the new leaves begin to emerge.

Soil preference: Lime-free, humus-rich
Aspect: Part shade or shade
Season of interest: Spring, autumn
Height and spread: 2m x 1.5m (6ft x 5ft)

Companion plants: A superb woodland plant, at home among maples, Enkianthus and magnolias. Also pretty when underplanted with *Liriope muscari* whose autumn flowers contrast with the leaves.

Paeonia delavayi   Tree Peony   Hardy deciduous shrub

An open habited, rather ungainly shrub with stiff, upright stems and deeply divided, lobed leaves. New herbaceous growth is rapid in spring, when each shoot terminates in a single, intensely fragrant, goblet-shaped flower whose petals are a rich blood maroon. The two subspecies *P. delavayi* var. *ludlowii* and *P. d.* var. *lutea* have yellow flowers.

Soil preference: Any
Aspect: Sun, shade or part shade
Season of interest: Late spring
Height and spread: 2m x 1.5m
(6ft x 5ft)

Companion plants: Though shortlived in flower, these plants are spectacular when underplanted with spring and early summer perennials such as *Lamium maculatum* 'White Nancy' with camassias or epimediums with decorative foliage such as *E. versicolor* or with lilies, particularly *L. speciosum*, *L. candidum* and *L. auratum*.

Sambucus nigra

Common Elder, Elderberry   Hardy deciduous shrub

A coarse-growing, rank smelling shrub with compound leaves and in early summer, flattened umbels of creamy flowers. These are followed by clusters of glossy black berries. Garden forms include *S.* 'Gerda' (syn. 'Black Beauty', pictured), the lacy, dark leaved *S.* 'Eva' and gold leaved *S. n.* 'Aurea'. Can be regularly pollarded, or allowed to develop into a small tree.

Soil preference: Any
Aspect: Sun, part shade or shade
Season of interest: Summer, autumn
Height and spread: 5m x 5m
(16ft x 16ft)

Companion plants: The dark leaves of 'Gerda' provide a rich backdrop, not only to its own flushed flowers, but teams superbly with big shrub roses, or with later flowering buddlejas. Common green elder is wildlife-friendly and lovely to follow from hawthorn.

Skimmia x confusa

Hardy evergreen shrub

A fresh-looking, compact, dome shaped shrub whose dark green, broadly oval, pointed leaves are glossy and whose dense clusters of off-white male flowers, produced in late winter and early spring, are intensely fragrant. The form 'Kew Green' has cones of pale yellowish green flowers.

Soil preference: Any not too dry, but free-draining
Aspect: Part shade, sun or shade
Season of interest: Year round
Height and spread: 1.5m x 1m
(5ft x 3ft)

Companion plants: Beautiful fragrance to blend with that of *Daphne laureola* or to plant alongside the berry-bearing *S. japonica* subsp. *reevesiana*.

Teucrium fruticans

Shrubby Germander   Near hardy, evergreen shrub

A semi-trailing shrub whose lax stems and small, simple leaves are coated with a fine, greyish white down and whose distinctively shaped flowers have a curiously lobed, extended lower lip. In the typical species they are a soft grey-blue, but the variety 'Azureum' has rich cobalt blue blossoms which contrast with the grey foliage.

Soil preference: Any free-draining
Aspect: Sun
Season of interest: Year round, spring
Height and spread: To 2m x 2m (6ft x 6ft)

Companion plants: A beautiful shrub to train over a low wall, to blend with *Ceanothus thyrsiflorus* 'Repens' or to contrast with the yellow flowers of *Coronilla valentina* subsp. *glauca* or its lemon-coloured form 'Citrina'.

Raphiolepis umbellata

White or Pink Indian Hawthorn   Hardy evergreen shrub

Tough but slow growing member of the rose family with simple, leathery leaves, usually dark green and in spring, clusters of pink tinged or white, fragrant flowers. Black fruits follow in autumn. The hybrid *R.* x *delacourii* has pinkish flowers and deep purple berries in autumn.

Soil preference: Any free-draining
Aspect: Sun
Season of interest: Year round
Height and spread: 2m x 2m (7ft x 6ft)

Companion plants: Increasingly popular plant for mixed shrub borders, or for planting in a gravel garden where it brings evergreen 'body' to such grasses or sedges as Oryzopsis or *Carex buchananii*.

Rosmarinus officinalis

Rosemary   Hardy or near-hardy evergreen shrub

Aromatic Mediterranean shrub with a stiff, twiggy habit, whether prostrate or upright. The woody stems are clothed with short, very narrow, ginger-scented leaves and, in late winter and spring, small blue-grey or violet-grey hooked flowers appear. Garden forms include 'Miss Jessopp's Upright', the lax stemmed 'Severn Sea' and intense blue, narrow leaved 'Sissinghurst Blue'.

Soil preference: Any free-draining
Aspect: Sun, part shade
Season of interest: Year round
Height and spread: To 1.5m x 1m (5ft x 3ft)

Companion plants: Essential for every herb garden, along with thyme, parsley, sage, lavender and marjoram (oregano). Also lovely as a small formal hedge, perhaps enclosing small beds of annuals or groundcover plants.

Pinus mugo   Mugo Pine, Swiss Mountain Pine   Hardy evergreen shrub

A small pine with shrubby, spreading habit, seldom reaching its potential height except in favourable conditions. The needle leaves are arranged in pairs along upright, rigid stems which are attractively gnarled when grown in hard conditions. Garden forms include the diminutive 'Mops' and smaller 'Mops Midget' and slowly spreading Pumilo Group.

Soil preference: Any free-draining
Aspect: Sun
Season of interest: Year round
Height and spread: 6m x 2m, usually smaller

Companion plants: A mainstay of the classic 'Heather and Conifer' planting scheme and none the worse for that. Delightful in a dry garden with such colourful companions as Zauschneria, Eschscholzia, Helianthemum or taller *Verbena bonariensis*.

Myrtus communis

Myrtle   Marginally hardy evergreen shrub

A Mediterranean evergreen shrub with simple, oval, pointed deep green leaves which are sweetly aromatic when moist or crushed. In summer and autumn creamy white flowers open with big central tufts of conspicuous stamens. Protect from severe frost and from damaging winter winds.

Soil preference: Any, free-draining
Aspect: Sun or part shade
Season of interest: Year round
Height and spread: 3m x 3m (10ft 9in x 10ft 9in)

Companion plants: Lovely to contrast with the grey foliage of fellow Mediterranean olives or to train on a wall with *Carpenteria californica* for early flower, or to contrast with late blooming Ceanothus varieties such as 'Autumnal Blue'.

Corokia x virgata   Marginally hardy evergreen shrub

A sparsely clothed shrub with rounded leaves, dark green above but paler below, borne on zigzagging branches. The yellow star-like flowers appear in late spring and are followed by orange or yellow fruits. A naturally occurring hybrid between *C. cotoneaster* (the 'wire netting' bush) and *C. buddlejoides*. Varieties include 'Bronze Lady' – dark leaves and reddish fruit – and the golden fruit-bearing 'Yellow Wonder'.

Soil preference: Any free-draining
Aspect: Sun
Season of interest: Year round
Height and spread: To 2m x 2m (6ft x 6ft)

Companion plants: An attractive wall plant for colder areas, especially if grown with *Acacia pravissima*. If grown free-standing in a sheltered corner, it can be grouped with the purple-flowered *Olearia* 'Master Michael'.

Berberis darwinii

Hardy evergreen shrub

A vigorous species with upright or stiffly arching stems and small, prickly, glossy leaves. Masses of bright orange flowers hang in small clusters during spring followed, in late summer, by blue-grey fruits. Occasional blooms also appear in autumn. The variety 'Flame' has flowers of a more intense orange than the species.

Soil preference: Any
Aspect: Sun or part shade
Season of interest: Year round
Height and spread: Up to 3m x 3m (10ft x 10ft)

Companion plants: A robust plant, lovely for an informal screen, perhaps with other big berberis, or with winter viburnums and summer buddleias – particularly *Buddleja* x *weyeriana* – for an extended display.

Cytisus x kewensis

Hardy deciduous shrub

A prostrate broom with spreading, curving, pale green branches which, in spring, carry a heavy crop of creamy primrose pea flowers. The small leaves open silvery but turn greener as the plant ages. One of the parents of this hybrid, *C. multiflorus*, Portuguese Broom, has similar, creamy flowers on taller plants.

Soil preference: Any free-draining
Aspect: Sun
Season of interest: Spring
Height and spread: 45cm x 1.5m (1ft 6in by 5ft)

Companion plants: A superb ground-cover broom, lovely in spring, with dark tulips growing through, or alongside blue forget-me-nots or to share a sunny bank with Perovskia or Caryopteris.

Euonymus alatus

Winged Spindle   Hardy deciduous shrub

A dense growing shrub whose stems, as they mature, develop strange 'wings' or protuberances which run continuously down four sides. The dark green, glossy leaves turn brilliant red in autumn before falling and in mature specimens reddish purple fruits split to display orange seeds. The form 'Compactus' is smaller in all its parts.

Soil preference: Any free-draining
Aspect: Sun, part shade
Season of interest: Autumn; year round
Height and spread: 2m x 2.5m (6ft x 8ft)

Companion plants: Excellent for providing autumn colour to a mixed border, with late flowering perennials such as Chrysanthemums or *Aconitum carmichaelii* or with shrubs like Forsythia, Ribes or Philadelphus, relieving any autumn boredom.

Griselinia littoralis   Broadleaf   Borderline hardy evergreen shrub

Vigorous shrub with an upright, then spreading habit and handsome, broad, leathery leaves which are pale green contrasting with paler, straw-coloured stems. The variegated form 'Dixon's Cream' (pictured) is a colourful alternative. A magnificent, wind-proof hedging species for coastal areas, but not capable of surviving sustained frost.

Soil preference: Any free-draining
Aspect: Sun
Season of interest: Year round
Height and spread: 6m x 5m (20ft x 16ft)

Companion plants: Handy as an evergreen specimen, to back up such flowering shrubs as hydrangeas, Kolkwitzia or Abelia but most useful as a light coloured hedge.

Juniperus x pfitzeriana

Pfitzer Juniper   Hardy evergreen shrub

A vigorous and hardy conifer with tiered branches held at an acute angle to the ground, making it almost flat-topped. The leaves are tiny and pointed and only male flowers are produced. Selected forms include the golden 'Pfitzeriana Aurea' and neater, smaller 'Pfitzeriana Compacta'. Prettiest when young and difficult to prune without ruining the shape.

Soil preference: Any
Aspect: Sun, part shade
Season of interest: Year round
Height and spread: 1m x 3m (3ft 3in x 10ft 9in)

Companion plants: Difficult to team with anything, but these junipers are capable of thriving in harsh conditions and therefore useful to furnish a windswept bank, with other tough conifers.

Pyracantha hybrids   Firethorns   Hardy deciduous shrubs

Familiar shrubs with simple, entire leaves, vicious spines and twiggy habit. In spring, creamy blossoms appear in sprays followed, in autumn, by coloured berries hanging in fulsome clusters. Yellow berried varieties include 'Soleil d'Or' and 'Golden Dome'; 'Teton' has orange yellow berries; whereas 'Watereri' and 'Mohave' have red fruits. Excellent winter feed for wild birds, particularly migrant thrushes and waxwings.

Soil preference: Any
Aspect: Sun, part shade
Season of interest: Spring, autumn
Height and spread: To 3m x 2m (10ft 9in x 6ft)

Companion plants: As wall plants, firethorns mix beautifully with summer-flowering clematis and with Chaenomeles. As hedge plants, they help to enrich a tapestry of holly, berberis, privet and hawthorn.

Abelia x grandiflora

Glossy Abelia   Marginally hardy, evergreen shrub

A moderately vigorous shrub with arching stems and small, dark green leaves which become suffused with coppery redness in autumn. The flowers, which are mauve-pink, have a sweet scent. Varieties include 'Confetti' whose leaves are variegated, 'Sunrise', also variegated with excellent autumn colour and the lower growing 'Sherwoodii'. Protect from severe weather.

Soil preference: Free-draining, fertile
Aspect: Sun
Season of interest: Year round, summer
Height and spread: 2m x 2m (6ft x 6ft)

Companion plants: Lovely arching over a summer border with mixed perennials or annuals, or for filling a warm corner as backdrop for summer bulbs such as Gladiolus, Ixia, Galtonia and lilies.

Buddleja fallowiana

Marginally hardy deciduous shrub

A delicate species, with an open, airy habit. Simple leaves are borne on thin, lax stems which, in summer, terminate with panicles of tiny, fragrant, soft lilac-mauve flowers. Leaves, stems and flower buds are clothed with pale, silvery-grey down. The form *B. f.* var. *alba* has white flowers and is equally or even more desirable.

Soil preference: Any free-draining
Aspect: Sun
Season of interest: Summer
Height and spread: 3m x 3m (10ft 9in x 10ft 9in)

Companion plants: A beautiful, dreamy summer companion to shrubs with bigger, bolder blooms such as shrub roses, Abutilon, Eucryphia or Hypericum. Also striking when underplanted with hot-coloured Crocosmia.

Daphne odora

Winter Daphne   Hardy evergreen shrub

An understated, low growing shrub with broadly oval leaves and bearing, from late winter, tight groups of four petalled flowers, pinkish on their outer petals and pale pink to flush white when open. Despite their small size, the flowers are intensely fragrant. The form 'Aureomarginata' (pictured) has gold leaf edges. Not vigorous and prone to virus, but lovely for a sheltered corner.

Soil preference: Fertile, humus-rich and well-drained
Aspect: Part shade
Season of interest: Winter, spring
Height and spread: 1m x 1.5m (3ft x 5ft)

Companion plants: Like many daphnes, this species benefits from sheltering shrubs nearby and is charming when underplanted with small winter bulbs such as *Iris reticulata*, dwarf narcissus, snowdrops or scillas.

Erica arborea   Tree Heather   Marginally hardy evergreen shrub

A vigorous shrub whose main stems, when old, become quaintly gnarled and twisted and consist of remarkably durable timber. Growth is dense, forming cloud-like masses of tiny, needle-like foliage and, in late spring, a vast crop of small, fragrant, off-white flowers which are adored by bees. 'Estrella Gold' (pictured) has yellowish foliage; *E. a.* var. *alpina* is compact with cylindrical flower stems.

Soil preference: Any free-draining, humus-rich
Aspect: Sun
Season of interest: Year round
Height and spread: 4m x 3m (13ft x 10ft)

Companion plants: In a favoured spot, this species makes a striking specimen to stand alone, perhaps in a bed, underplanted with Liriope or colchicums, for autumn, or with smaller heathers for a colour contrast.

Leptospermum scoparium

Tea Tree, Manuka   Near hardy, evergreen shrub

A vigorous shrub with branches becoming pendulous with age and tiny, dark green, needly leaves. The small but conspicuous, white, five-petalled flowers are produced in profusion during early summer. Garden varieties have flower colours ranging through pink to rich red and include double 'Red Damask', semi-double, pink 'Gaiety Girl' and purplish red 'Ruby Glow'.

Soil preference: Free-draining, fertile. Not too dry
Aspect: Sun
Season of interest: Spring, summer
Height and spread: 2m x 2m (6ft x 6ft)

Companion plants: In a sheltered garden, these are superb 'top layer' plants which would associate interestingly with olearias, Cordyline or phormiums, for an interesting southern hemisphere effect, perhaps with the waving, arching stems of restios.

Pericallis lanata

Tender evergreen sub-shrub

A lovely native of the Canary islands with broad, slightly lobed, grey-green, woolly coated leaves and, from late winter onwards, a succession of fragrant, lilac-mauve daisy flowers whose centres are deeper purple, contrasting with paler sterile rays. A delicate, easily damaged shrub but outstandingly beautiful.

Soil preference: Fertile, free-draining
Aspect: Sun, part shade, sheltered
Season of interest: Winter, spring
Height and spread: 1m x 1m (3ft x 3ft)

Companion plants: A lovely container subject for a sheltered courtyard or cool conservatory perhaps with the companionship of fellow Canary islanders such as *Euphorbia mellifera*, *Lotus berthelotii* or the Madeiran *Geranium maderense*.

Roses

Roses have been subject to breeding and selection for many centuries and the number of varieties available to gardeners runs into thousands. Worldwide, the rose is still one of the most widely grown genera and it is well beyond the scope of this book to provide detail on any but a tiny sample. Rather than trying to cover every type, colour, size and habit, the object of these few pages is to introduce a small selection of roses which are desirable for particular qualities.

1.   Rosa 'Alberic Barbier'
A old and dependable rambler whose semi-evergreen foliage retains a dark, healthy looking gloss throughout the growing season. Lemon buds open to ivory double flowers, whitening with age. Suitable for unfavourable sites, including semi shade.

2.   Rosa 'Claire Jacquier'
A vigorous rambler with coppery new growth and deep salmon buds which open to produce flowers whose apricot centres harmonize with rich cream outer petals. Faintly fragrant and lovely to climb into a tree.

3.   Rosa 'Scharlachglut' (syn. 'Scarlet Fire')
Can be grown as a climber or a big, sprawling shrub. Deep green foliage sets off the large, vivid scarlet, single blossoms to perfection. A heavy crop of bright orange hips follows in autumn and will persist all winter.

4.   Rosa 'Blairi Number 2'
A heavily floriferous but non-repeating climber with good vigour.

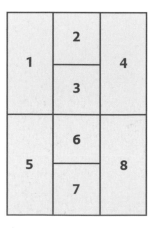

The double flowers are a striking pink, with intensely cerise centres and paler outer petals. The fragrance is rich and heady.

5.   Rosa 'Madame Gregoire Staechelin' (syn. 'Spanish Beauty')
A characterful climber which, though once-flowering, has a satisfying crop of heavy, coral red hips. The big, semi-pendulous flowers have loosely packed, mid-pink petals and are rich with fragrance.

6.   Rosa canina (Dog rose)
A common hedgerow plant in Europe whose faintly scented, five-petalled pink or white blooms appear at the end of spring. The heavy crop of bright scarlet hips which follow each autumn have great widlife value. Can be used as a climber, as hedging or as a free standing shrub.

7.   Rosa 'Marguerite Hilling' (syn. 'Pink Nevada')
A vigorous and dependable shrub rose whose long, slightly arching stems are covered, in early summer, by deep pink, single or semi-double flowers. After the main flush, sporadic blooms are produced during the rest of summer.

8.   Rosa moyesii
A big, bold, fast-growing shrub whose thick wands are viciously armed with curved thorns and whose foliage is ferny and fresh green, colouring well in autumn. The single flowers are, typically geranium red but may also be pink or white, and are followed by elongated hips which persist throughout winter.

Roses

A few examples of the different types of roses are highlighted here. These include the repeat flowering Hybrid Tea roses, the compact China and Polyantha types, roses which are perfect for the patio or as groundcover and Old Roses, which are able to survive adverse conditions.

Hybrid Teas

1. **Rosa 'Tequila Sunrise'**
One of the most vividly coloured modern roses with well-shaped, pointed buds, good vigour and flowers which display fiery crimson on the petal uppersides, with yellow undersides. A startling variety which needs careful siting.

2. **Rosa 'Warm Wishes'**
A hybrid tea with warm but gentle flower colour which might harmonize well, in a mixed border, especially when planted near dark foliage of *Corylus maxima* 'Purpurea' or could contrast with the purples and blues of perennials asters.

China and Polyantha

3. **Rosa 'Gruss an Teplitz'**
An old China hybrid with rather lax stems and a summer-long run of rich crimson red, intensely fragrant blooms which are as attractive when blown and fading as when in bud. Not the easiest to grow but well worth the effort.

4. **Rosa 'Perle d'Or'**
One of the most dependable of the old polyantha varieties whose small, pointed buds are salmon pink in bud, opening to a salmon beige. Almost constantly in flower from early summer until hard frost.

Patio and Groundcover

5. **Rosa 'Bonica'**
A sprawling rose, suitable as a groundcover plant with long, lax stems and semi-double, shell pink flowers whose centres reveal bunches of yellow-gold stamens.

6. **Rosa 'Newly Wed' (syn. 'Mummy')**
A small, compact variety which is ideal for container culture on the patio or terrace. The flowers are produced in loose sprays and are ivory white, semi-double with attractively contrasting stamens. Constant deadheading keeps this variety productive.

Old Roses

7. **Rosa 'Tuscany Superb'**
A 19th Century gallica hybrid which flowers just once a season. The rounded buds open to flat, richly fragrant, dark crimson blooms centred with gold stamens. One of the best of the old roses.

8. **Rosa 'Agnes'**
An old hybrid developed from the dune rose *R. rugosa* whose bristling stems and mid-green, roughened foliage is accompanied, through summer but the sweet smelling, pale yellow, double flowers.

	2	
1		4
	3	
	6	
5		8
	7	

Abeliophyllum distichum

White Forsythia   Hardy deciduous shrub

A lax, semi-trailing shrub from Korea, ideal for training up a warm wall. The dark stems contrast with pink buds which, in early spring, open as white, four-petalled flowers. Simple, oval leaves emerge soon after the flowers and are dark green in summer, sometimes taking on a purplish hue before falling. The form *A. d.* Rosea Group has pink flowers.

Soil preference: Any, not too dry
Aspect: Sun
Season of interest: Spring; year round
Height and spread: 1.5m x 2m (5ft x 6ft)

Companion plants: Pretty on a wall with winter foliage nearby, perhaps from *Itea illicifolia* or with *Euonymus myrianthus*.

Robinia hispida

Rose Acacia, Bristly Locust   Deciduous shrub or tree

A fast-growing shrub with spreading, brittle branches and attractive, pinnate leaves with rounded or oblong leaflets. Buds and young stems have bristles or coarse hairs. In early summer, racemes of bright deep pink flowers hang among the foliage. *R. kelseyi* has brighter rose pink flowers and 'Hillieri', pictured, is pale pink.

Soil preference: Any free-draining
Aspect: Sun
Season of interest: Spring, summer and autumn
Height and spread: 2.5m x 2.5m (8ft x 8ft)

Companion plants: Loosely attached to a wall, this would be an interesting companion to the more rampant *Rosa banksiae* 'Lutea'. Non-vigorous forms of summer-flowering clematis could also be encouraged to twine among the branches for later colour.

Hoheria glabrata

Lacebark   Marginally hardy, deciduous shrub or tree

Really a tree, rather than a shrub, but it can be grown by a wall in a sheltered spot. The large, toothed, diamond-shaped leaves are pale green in summer, turning butter yellow in autumn. During late summer, a generous crop of white blossoms are borne singly on short stems along the branches. *Hoheria lyallii* is a similar species.

Soil preference: Fertile, free-draining
Aspect: Sun or part shade
Season of interest: Summer, autumn
Height and spread: 5m x 5m (16ft x 16ft)

Companion plants: Best given room to flower freely and beautiful when part of a late summer display, perhaps with dahlias, tall grasses and phloxes nearby.

Ficus carica   Fig   Hardy deciduous shrub or tree

A magnificent fruiting tree with immense ornamental value. Big, palmate or lobed leaves are borne on thick, rigid stems which also carry an almost constant crop of small, fruit-like green flower 'pods', which never open. These figs ripen in late summer, developing their fullest flavour and turning soft and luscious just before falling. 'Brown Turkey' and 'Brunswick' (pictured) are reliable outdoor croppers.

Soil preference: Any free-draining, dry
Aspect: Sun
Season of interest: Spring, summer, autumn
Height and spread: Variable to 6m x 6m (20ft x 20ft)

Companion plants: Best trained on a wall on their own, but a superb backdrop for Mediterranean style garden plants such as Leptospermum, rosemary, *Teucrium fruticans* and Santolina.

Clethra delavayi

Marginally hardy deciduous shrub

An imposing shrub with oblong, dark blue-green leaves. In late summer, semi-upright racemes of small, white, bell or cup-shaped flowers emerge, their colour contrasting with the coppery pink of the sepals and flower stems. Though it benefits from the warmth and shelter of a wall, this plant needs protection from strong, direct sunlight.

Soil preference: Lime-free, fertile
Aspect: Part shade or sun
Season of interest: Year round, late summer
Height and spread: 3m x 3m (10ft x 10ft)

Companion plants: A difficult plant to place, since it needs shelter and warmth, but dislikes strong sun. Happiest with partial shade from such light canopied trees as *Robinia pseudoacacia* 'Frisia', small leaved birches or even a well-pruned, tall apple.

Acacia pravissima

Oven's Wattle   Near hardy evergreen shrub

A handsome foliage shrub, ideal for growing on a hot wall. The stems, though weak, arch gracefully and are furnished with distinctive, triangular leaves in a soft, hairless blue-green. The gently fragrant, fluffy-looking, yellow mimosa flowers begin to emerge in late winter and last for much of the spring.

Soil preference: Any free-draining
Aspect: Sun
Season of interest: Year round
Height and spread: 3m x 5m (10ft x 16ft)

Companion plants: Beautiful sharing a wall with contrasting foliage. The purple vine, for summer, would go well, as would the pale blue-flowered *Solanum laxum* whose young leaves and stems are purplish.

Chaenomeles x superba   Hardy deciduous shrub

A dense, twiggy shrub with simple, oblong leaves which are glossy when young. From late winter, clusters of large, mainly five-petalled, goblet-shaped blossoms appear in colours ranging through pink and salmon to intense crimson, with conspicuous yellow stamens. Red flowered varieties include 'Crimson and Gold', 'Rowallane' and 'Knap Hill Scarlet'; 'Pink Lady' has shell pink blooms.

Soil preference: Any reasonably fertile, free-draining
Aspect: Sun, part shade
Season of interest: Winter, spring
Height and spread: 1.5m x 2m (5ft x 6ft)

Companion plants: More compact than some Japanese quinces, and yet with larger flowers, these hybrids are superb for a low or mid-height wall, with such climbers as *Clematis alpina*, *Euonymus radicans* or the orange *Rosa* 'Warm Welcome'.

Chaenomeles speciosa

Japonica, Japanese Quince, Flowering Quince   Hardy deciduous shrub

A vigorous species with simple, oval, pointed leaves, glossy when young and, from winter to spring, clusters of goblet-shaped flowers followed, in autumn by edible quince-like fruits. Desirable varieties include the double-flowered salmon 'Geisha Girl', white 'Nivalis' and 'Moerloosei', whose flowers are greenish white when young, maturing pink.

Soil preference: Any, free -draining, reasonably fertile
Aspect: Sun or part shade
Season of interest: Late winter, spring
Height and spread: 3m x 3m (10ft 9in x 10ft 9in)

Companion plants: Excellent winter shrub for sharing a wall with *Forsythia suspensa*, winter jasmine, *Chimonanthus praecox* or *Garrya elliptica*. Also attractive as a free-standing shrub with spring shrubs.

Cotoneaster horizontalis   Hardy deciduous shrub

A distinctive and universally popular shrub whose stiff branches form a semi-rigid, fishbone outline. On the ground they form overlapping layers, but grown against a wall, these become shapely, near vertical tiers. The leaves are tiny and glossy, the late spring blossoms small and pink and the crop of small, scarlet-orange berries is heavy. Autumn foliage colours well, too.

Soil preference: Any
Aspect: Any
Season of interest: Year round
Height and spread: 1m x 2m (3ft 3in x 6ft), higher on a wall

Companion plants: A perfect companion plant, on a wall, for such climbers as *Clematis viticella* – in any variety – Maurandya, Lophospermum and Eccremocarpus. Also a handy wall plant to grow alongside Ceanothus or Fremontodendron.

Prunus triloba

Flowering Almond, Flowering Plum   Hardy deciduous shrub

A compact shrub with straight branches and simple leaves which are often three-lobed. In spring, pink, semi-double or double flowers appear along the stems before the leaves emerge and are sometimes followed, in autumn, by a crop of reddish fruits. Susceptible to die-back disease but worth growing for the earliness of the flowers.

Soil preference: Any free-draining, not too dry
Aspect: Sun or part shade
Season of interest: Spring
Height and spread: 2m x 2m (6ft x 6ft)

Companion plants: A striking focal point for a small-scale spring planting scheme, especially when underplanted with white or lemon flowers of such narcissi as 'Charity May' or 'Dove Wings', or with the deep blue *Brunnera macrophylla*.

Ribes speciosum

Fuchsia-flowered Currant   Marginally hardy, deciduous shrub

A bristling and thorny shrub with lobed, toothed leaves and, in late spring, blood red flowers which hang along the stems. Their shape, with long, protruding stamens and stigma, recall the flowers of *Fuchsia magellanica*. Hairy, dark red fruits follow later in summer. Susceptible to late frost but elegant when fan-trained on a wall.

Soil preference: Reasonably fertile, free-draining
Aspect: Sun or part shade
Season of interest: Spring
Height and spread: 3m x 3m (10ft 9in x 10ft 9in)

Companion plants: Best grown on its own but also lovely with contrasting wall plants such as *Acacia pravissima*, with deep blue Ceanothus or perhaps with the evergreen *Itea ilicifolia*.

Poncirus trifoliata

Japanese Bitter Orange   Hardy deciduous shrub

A thorny shrub with three-lobed, intensely aromatic leaves. In late spring and, to a lesser extent, in autumn, richly fragrant, creamy white flowers appear along the stems. Bright orange fruits form for autumn and winter which, though non-poisonous are extremely bitter. Frequently used as grafting rootstock for edible citrus fruits including lemons and oranges.

Soil preference: Any free-draining
Aspect: Sun
Season of interest: Year round
Height and spread: 3m x 3m (10ft 9in x 10ft 9in)

Companion plants: An excellent winter garden plant, where the greenish, thorned stems and fruits can set off hellebores, bergenias, and such shrubs as Edgeworthia and daphnes.

x Fatshedera lizei Hardy evergreen shrub

An intergeneric hybrid of ivy, probably *Hedera hibernica* and *Fatsia japonica*, with large, glossy, five lobed leaves, resembling those of ivy, and an upright or semi-upright habit. Sprays of greenish cream to white flowers are produced in autumn but are sterile. Garden forms include 'Annemieke', whose leaves are yellow-green variegated and the white margined 'Variegata'.

Soil preference: Any, not too dry but free-draining
Aspect: Shade, part shade
Season of interest: Year round
Height and spread: 2m x 3m (6ft x 10ft)

Companion plants: Useful for a difficult, dark wall, especially if the big, glossy leaves can contrast with winter jasmine or with *Euonymus fortunei*.

Prunus cerasus 'Morello'

Morello Cherry, Bitter Cherry Hardy deciduous shrub or tree

A culinary tree, with oblong, toothed, simple leaves which turn gold in autumn. The blossoms are pure white, held on stems about 3cm (1in) long. In late summer, blood red cherries begin to develop, turning dark maroon as they become fully ripe. Their flavour is both sharp and sweet, making them highly desirable for preserve making.

Soil preference: Any, not too dry but free-draining
Aspect: Any
Season of interest: Spring, late summer
Height and spread: Depends on root stock

Companion plants: A popular culinary cherry variety, lovely grown as an ornamental, perhaps with honeysuckle or climbing hydrangea species nearby.

Camellia saluenensis

Hardy evergreen shrub

A Chinese camellia with dense branches bearing glistening, oval, toothed leaves and, during late winter and spring, a succession of medium sized, single, pink, white or red flowers. One of the parents of the *C.* x *williamsii* hybrids, but especially capable of living on a dark wall provided it is protected from severe, sustained frost.

Soil preference: Lime-free, fertile, rich in humus
Aspect: Shade or part shade
Season of interest: Winter, spring
Height and spread: 3m x 3m (10ft 9in x 10ft 9in)

Companion plants: A fine camellia to liven up groups of *Aucuba japonica* or sharing a wall with Fatshedera, evergreen Euonymus or, in less gloomy surroundings, *Garrya elliptica*.

Euonymus fortunei 'Kewensis'

Winter Creeper   Prostrate, evergreen shrub

A mat-forming, ground-covering variety of 'Winter Creeper' with prostrate, green-barked stems with a widely spreading habit. The flowers are insignificant, but the myriad tiny, oval leaves are subtly marbled and rather pretty. Easily persuaded to scale a wall. *E. f.* 'Minimus' is similar.

Soil preference: Any
Aspect: Shade, part shade
Season of interest: Year round
Height and spread: 10cm (4in) – much more on a wall – and spreading

Companion plants: Useful for softening hard structures, where light levels are low. Pretty when contrasting with ivies or with other Euonymus varieties.

Rosa

Rose (varieties)   Hardy deciduous shrubs or climbers

Certain climbing or rambling roses will furnish a shaded wall and even produce flowers. Examples include the rich scarlet-flowered 'Parkdirektor Riggers', ivory white 'Albéric Barbier', thornless, mauve-pink 'Zéphirine Drouhin' (pictured) and the curious two-coloured *Rosa* x *odorata* 'Mutabilis'. None will perform as well as in sun, but all will tolerate shade.

Soil preference: Fertile, moisture retentive but not waterlogged
Aspect: Sun, part shade or shade
Season of interest: Summer
Height and spread: Variable to 5m x 3m (16ft x 10ft)

Companion plants: Blend these plants with such truly shade-loving evergreens as *Parthenocissus henryana*, decorative ivies or *Camellia saluenensis*.

Azara microphylla   Vanilla Tree   Hardy evergreen shrub

Vigorous shrub with medium and small, shiny, oval leaves held on slightly pendulous branches. In late winter and spring, greenish yellow, tufted blossoms appear along the yearling stems. These are fragrant, smelling of vanilla or to some, chocolate. In favourable conditions, reddish fruit may follow.

Soil preference: Any, free-draining, not too dry
Aspect: Part shade or shade
Season of interest: Winter, spring
Height and spread: To 6m x 2m (20ft x 6ft)

Companion plants: Harmonize the distinctive foliage with climbing hydrangeas in a darkish corner, or enjoy the yellow flowers alongside the tassels of *Garry elliptica*. Azara is also pretty, in a better lit spot, with summer jasmine, or with the more sedate species of honeysuckle.

Prunus laurocerasus 'Otto Luyken'

Hardy evergreen shrub

Low-growing variety of cherry laurel. The leaves are narrow, long and pointed, accompanied in spring by erect spikes of small, white, almond scented flowers and followed in late summer by blue-black fruits. *P. l.* 'Otto Luyken' (pictured) is compact with semi-erect stems in a 'shuttlecock' outline; 'Zabeliana' has a wide, spreading habit.

Soil preference: Any
Aspect: Shade, part shade or sun
Season of interest: Year round
Height and spread: 1m x up to 3m (3ft x up to 10ft)

Companion plants: The dark green foliage makes a striking contrast with such gold leaved plants as *Philadelphus coronarius* 'Aureus' or *Choisya ternata* 'Sundance'. 'Otto Luyken' is useful for providing formal shapes, if replicated at a border edge or even used for hedging.

Mahonia aquifolium

Oregon Grape   Hardy evergreen shrub

A slowly spreading, suckering shrub with short, stiff, twiggy stems and pinnate, leathery leaves with prickly edges. These are glossy green in summer, taking on bronze hues in winter. Dense clusters of vivid yellow flowers bloom in spring, followed by small, black berries. The variety 'Smaragd' is very compact; 'Atropurpurea' has purple winter foliage.

Soil preference: Any
Aspect: Shade, part shade, sun
Season of interest: Year round
Height and spread: 1m x 1.5m (3ft x 5ft)

Companion plants: An indestructible shrub, ideal in a shaded area with Aucuba, Osmanthus or underplanted with epimediums, pulmonarias or *Lamium galeobdolon*.

Clethra alnifolia

Sweet Pepper Bush   Hardy deciduous shrub

A thicket-forming shrub with upright stems and medium to large, oval leaves which are slightly toothed. At summer's end, elegant, upright spikes of buds develop, lengthening to almost 15cm (6in) before the fragrant white flowers open. Benefits from wind protection.

Soil preference: Lime-free, humus-rich, moist
Aspect: Shade or part shade
Season of interest: Summer, autumn
Height and spread: 2m x 2m (6ft x 6ft)

Companion plants: A delightful woodlander, valuable for its late blooms, especially when planted with Enkianthus, or to contrast with hydrangeas. Also lovely interplanted with late lilies or Tricyrtis.

Daphne tangutica   Hardy, evergreen shrub

A neat, dome-forming, densely branched shrub with small, glossy, oval leaves which are dark green above and paler on the reverse. From spring onwards, clusters of small, purplish pink buds open to form four-petal flowers which are pink-flushed white and intensely fragrant. Dark red berries sometimes follow and yield viable seed.

Soil preference: Any, well-drained but not too dry
Aspect: Sun, shade or part shade
Season of interest: Spring, summer
Height and spread: 1m x 1m (3ft 3in x 3ft 3in)

Companion plants: A beautiful spring companion to the lower growing dicentras, with *Polygonatum odoratum* and with other daphnes such as *D. serica* Collina Group and *D. tangutica* Retusa Group.

Hebe large-flowered hybrids

Near hardy evergreen shrubs

Dense-growing, dome shaped shrubs with glossy simple leaves and pliable stems. Flower spikes are produced almost continuously, and are closely packed with small flowers in the white, blue, purple or pink range. Varieties include 'Great Orme' (pink flowers), 'Eveline' (long, purple spikes) and *H.* x *franciscana* 'Blue Gem'.

Soil preference: Any free-draining
Aspect: Sun
Season of interest: Year round
Height and spread: Variable to 1.5m x 1.5m (5ft x 5ft)

Companion plants: Many varieties form structural dome shapes, ideal for formal use with most perennials, or to line up as informal hedging. Compact varieties are attractive with *Brachyglottis greyii* or in a general Mediterranean scheme with artemisias and other grey-leaved plants.

Rhododendron yakushimanum

Hardy evergreen shrubs

A compact species with leathery oblong leaves, covered with rusty felting (indumentum) when young. Big clusters of bright pink buds open to pale rosy pink flowers in late spring. 'Yak' hybrids of worth include 'Renoir' (Rose pink with white throats), 'Golden Torch' (Yellow), 'Titian Beauty' (red) and a number named after the Snow White dwarves – 'Grumpy', 'Doc' etc.

Soil preference: Lime-free, not too dry
Aspect: Sun, part shade
Season of interest: Early summer
Height and spread: To 1m x 1m (3ft x 3ft)

Companion plants: Popular rhododendrons for containers or for small-scale planting schemes with heathers, particularly Daboecia, or with ferns and alpines in a large-scale rock planting.

Fuchsia

With literally thousands of varieties in cultivation, one is spoilt for variety choice! All fuchsias prefer mild but cool conditions, in sun or partial shade and all are susceptible to damage by vine weevil. Propagation is easy from cuttings and plants benefit from being pinched back to promote dense, bushy growth.

1. Fuchsia 'Thalia'
Member of the 'Triphylla' group with dark foliage, erect habit and small elongated, tubular flowers whose sepals and petals are scarlet.

2. Fuchsia magellanica
One of the hardiest fuchsia species from southern Chile and Argentina. Slender, deep red sepals and plummy purple petals. Used as hedging material in mild areas. *F. m.* var. *molinae* (pictured) has pale flowers.

3. Fuchsia 'Lady Thumb'
Upright in habit, with masses of small to mid-sized flowers whose sepals are wine red surrounding white petals.

4. Fuchsia 'Annabel'
One of the best white forms, with large, pure white petals, pink stamens and flush white sepals. Upright habit.

5. Fuchsia 'Marinka'
A free flowering, trailing variety with rounded buds opening to reveal dark red petals. The sepals are also red, but slightly paler than the petals.

6. Fuchsia 'Dark Eyes'
Upright variety with mid-sized flowers whose sepals, which are deep red, curl fully back and contrast with the damson-coloured petals.

7. Fuchsia 'Red Spider'
A free flowering, trailing variety with red sepals and narrow, red petals.

8. Fuchsia 'Swingtime'
An old favourite with loosely upright habit and masses of double flowers whose sepals are red and whose ruched white petals resemble ballet skirts.

Caryopteris x clandonensis

Blue Spiraea   Hardy deciduous shrub

Dome or mound-forming shrub with simple greyish-green leaves. From late summer onwards the flower stems extend, bearing dense clusters of bright blue flowers along their lengths and at their tips. The gold-leaf form 'Worcester Gold' sets off its blue flowers pleasingly and 'Arthur Simmonds' has purplish blue flowers.

Soil preference: Any free-draining
Aspect: Sun
Season of interest: Summer, autumn
Height and spread: 1m x 1m (3ft 3in x 3ft 3in)

Companion plants: Strong contributors to hot, dry schemes and beautiful with silver leaved artemisias or with dark leaved *Teucrium chamaedrys* or spiky *Genista hispanica* to contrast.

Artemisia abrotanum

Lad's Love, Old Man, Southernwood   Hardy evergreen sub-shrub

An intensely aromatic, silky leaved shrub which begs to be grown where one can touch the foliage and enjoy the aroma. The greyish-green leaves are a deeply divided filigree and borne on erect stems which, by late summer, extend into spikes bearing rather uninteresting, greenish yellow flowers.

Soil preference: Any free-draining
Aspect: Sun
Season of interest: Spring, summer, autumn
Height and spread: 1m x 1m (3ft 3in x 3ft 3in)

Companion plants: A valuable ingredient, not only for the herb garden among lavenders, santolinas, thymes and sages, but also to play a supporting role with cottage or mixed border plants such as pinks, antirrhinums, gaillardias or penstemons.

Santolina chamaecyparissus

Cotton Lavender   Hardy evergreen shrub

Small, mound-forming shrubs whose aroma, redolent of an overstocked chicken shed, has not dented their popularity. Feathery, grey-green leaves are joined, in mid-summer, by large numbers of yellow or cream button-like flowers. The paler flowered *S. pinnata* 'Edward Bowles' is also desirable. Prune hard to keep plants compact.

Soil preference: Any free-draining
Aspect: Sun
Season of interest: Spring, summer, autumn
Height and spread: 6ocm x 1m (2ft x 3ft 3in)

Companion plants: A fine plant for making low hedges, alternating with lavenders or even growing with dwarf box. The flowers are attractive with brightly coloured campanulas or with other 'spike' plants such as lupins or kniphofias.

Convolvulus cneorum   Marginally hardy evergreen shrub

A compact shrub from the Mediterranean with narrow, flat, silvery leaves which gleam like real metal in certain light conditions. Medium-sized, saucer-shaped flowers appear in constant succession in summer, opening white from pale pink buds. This plant, though reasonably hardy, tolerates neither wet conditions, nor sustained frost.

Soil preference: Free-draining
Aspect: Sun
Season of interest: Spring, summer
Height and spread: 60cm x 75cm (2ft x 2ft 6in)

Companion plants: An arid-loving gem whose pale foliage makes a beautiful foil for brightly coloured, sun-loving flowers such as Lampranthus, or such summer bulbs as Brodiaea. A fine container plant, too, for standing beside purple heliotrope.

Helichrysum splendidum   Hardy evergreen shrub

Upright shrub which forms a loose dome with semi-rigid, sharp-angled branches whose stems are covered with white to grey down. The small, simple, downy leaves are also silvery-grey and, in late summer or autumn, a medium to heavy crop of tiny, mustard yellow, button flowers appears and persists for some weeks.

Soil preference: Any free-draining
Aspect: Sun
Season of interest: Summer, autumn
Height and spread: To 1.25m x 1m (4ft to 3ft)

Companion plants: A useful bringer of structure, with its upright, then rounded habit, to an arid planting of artemisias, cotton lavenders and *Euphorbia myrsinites*. Also pretty underplanted with old world annual poppies, particularly red field poppies.

Ceratostigma willmottianum

Chinese Plumbago   Hardy deciduous shrub

Suckering shrub, or woody-based perennial, with thin, wiry branches and simple leaves which emerge from coppery red buds. From mid-summer, stems extend above the leaves, bearing groups of small, disc-shaped flowers in an intense mid-blue. Later, the foliage takes on rich reddish autumn hues.

Soil preference: Well-drained, but not too dry
Aspect: Sun
Season of interest: Summer, autumn
Height and spread: 1m x 1.5m (3ft x 5ft)

Companion plants: The intense blue of the flowers makes a lively contrast with orange, either with Eschscholzia or Calendula. The turning foliage also teams sweetly with outdoor spray chrysanthemums, particularly in the pale pink, bronze or yellow range.

Betula nana

Dwarf Birch   Hardy deciduous shrub

A dwarf birch with tan stems and small, rounded, toothed leaves which are fresh green in spring, and turn yellow in autumn before falling. New stems emerge from underground runners, but the plant is neither troublesome nor invasive. Remarkably hardy, growing wild near the Arctic circle, but not a good choice for warm regions.

Soil preference: Any, not too dry
Aspect: Sun, shade, part shade
Season of interest: Spring, summer, autumn
Height and spread: 60cm x 1.2m (2ft x 4ft)

Companion plants: Once popular as a rock garden or alpine plant, dwarf birch brings a little height and body when placed among such low-growing species as Androsace, small primulas, cushion saxifrages and Cassiope.

Calluna vulgaris

Heather, Ling   Hardy evergreen shrub

A low-growing, heathland shrub with semi-prostrate stems which form cushions of springy growth. Small, nectar-rich flowers, borne on maturing current season's growth, appear in late summer and last into autumn. Garden forms are legion and include double pink 'Annemarie', golden leaved 'Beoley Gold' and 'Wickwar Flame', whose foliage fires up for winter.

Soil preference: Lime-free, well-drained
Aspect: Sun
Season of interest: Summer, autumn
Height and spread: 60cm x 75cm (2ft x 2ft 6in)

Companion plants: Heathers are best with their own kind. Blend with Erica, Daboecia and such associated moorland species as Vaccinium, or low-growing, sun-tolerant rhododendrons.

Erica carnea, Erica x darleyensis

Winter Flowering Heather; Darley Dale Heath   Hardy evergreen shrubs

Spreading, lime-tolerant shrubs with thin stems and tiny, needle-like leaves, creating dark green mats. From mid-winter, these are spangled with flowers in white, pink or purple shades. *E. carnea* varieties include: 'Pink Spangles', 'Springwood White' and the gold-leaved 'Foxhollow'. *E.* x *darleyensis* varieties include: 'Darley Dale' (pink), 'Silberschmelze' (white) and 'Ghost Hills', whose leaves are cream tipped.

Soil preference: Lime tolerant, but best in well-drained, humus-rich soil
Aspect: Sun or part shade
Season of interest: Winter
Height and spread: 30cm x 60cm (1ft x 2ft)

Companion plants: Excellent with other heathers, these also team well in mixed borders with early bulbs such as snowdrops, crocus, dwarf narcissus or winter perennials such as Pulmonaria and *Arum italicum*.

Grindelia chiloensis

Rosin Weed, Gum Plant   Marginally hardy sub-shrub

A strange member of the daisy family from whose woody-based herbaceous stems lengthen and terminate in late summer with the flowers. These are heavily protected, when in bud or newly opening by a deposit of excessively sticky white resin. The big daisy flowers, when they finally emerge, are bright golden yellow.

Soil preference: Any free-draining
Aspect: Sun
Season of interest: Summer
Height and spread: 1m x 1m (3ft 3in x 3ft 3in)

Companion plants: Valuable for the luxurious colour they bring to a hot, dry planting, especially among plants which begin to flag in late summer. Lovely contrasted with *Verbena bonariensis* or with the chocolate cosmos (*Cosmos atrosanguineus*).

Juniperus procumbens

Bonin Island Juniper   Hardy evergreen conifer

A slow-spreading, prostrate or procumbent species with tiny scale-like, sharp pointed leaves. Over many years, a single plant will develop a dense, weed-suppressing mat of green. The variety *J. p.* 'Nana' forms neater, denser, lower-growing mats than would an unselected seedling.

Soil preference: Any free-draining, not too dry
Aspect: Sun or part shade
Season of interest: Year round
Height and spread: 60cm (2ft), spreading

Companion plants: Ideal for furnishing an otherwise boring bank, or for creating a durable ground cover. Planting non-vigorous viticella clematis varieties such as *C.* 'Pagoda' or *C.* 'Etoile Rose' to scramble over the mats can help to relieve the monotonous colour.

Yucca filamentosa   Adam's Needle   Hardy evergreen shrub

Big rosettes of sword-like, dark green leaves, each with a sharp pointed tip and thread-like filaments at their sides, grow to about 75cm (30in). Flower spikes extend from the centre of mature rosettes in late summer or autumn, sometimes to 2m (6ft) carrying numerous, large, creamy-white bell flowers. 'Bright Edge' (pictured) is yellow variegated.

Soil preference: Any free-draining
Aspect: Sun or part shade
Season of interest: Late summer; year round
Height and spread: To 2m (6ft)

Companion plants: Superbly spiky plants for enhancing a tropical flavour in a cold region. Phormiums, large grasses and hardy bananas such as *Musa basjoo* blend well, but in warmer areas, agaves and aloes could also be added.

Daphne bholua   Hardy evergreen or deciduous shrub

An upright shrub, evergreen or semi-deciduous depending on its provenance, whose leaves are glossy, oblong and pointed. The flowers, appearing in small clusters from late winter through early spring, are pale or deep pink and intensely perfumed. *D. b.* var. *glacialis* 'Ghurka' is deciduous, *D. b.* 'Jacqueline Postill' is more evergreen, but a tougher variety than either is *D. b.* 'Darjeeling'.

Soil preference: Any free-draining, humus-rich, not too dry
Aspect: Sun or part shade
Season of interest: Winter, spring
Height and spread: 2.5m x 1.5m (8ft x 5ft)

Companion plants: Lovely winter garden shrubs to team with the coloured stems of *Cornus alba* or *Rubus cockburnianus* 'Goldenvale' and to underplant with hellebores, early daffodils or bergenias.

Daphne laureola   Spurge Laurel   Hardy evergreen shrub

A lowly European evergreen with oblong or oval, shiny green leaves. In late winter trusses of semi-pendant, green, sweet scented flowers are all but lost among the leaves. Later, green fruits ripen glossy black. Being surprised by its sweet fragrance on a still afternoon, is one of the joys of winter gardening. The subspecies *philippi* is more compact.

Soil preference: Any free-draining, preferably alkaline, humus-rich
Aspect: Shade, part shade
Season of interest: Winter; year round
Height and spread: 1m x 1.5m (3ft x 5ft)

Companion plants: A quiet but desirable woodlander to grow above violets, *Convallaria majalis* or pulmonarias. Also happy in a container, perhaps with snowdrops and winter aconites, in a dark courtyard.

Pieris formosa   Marginally hardy, evergreen shrubs

Chinese evergreens with dark green, shiny leaves and generous panicles of little pink buds which open to small, lantern-shaped, creamy white or pink flowers. The young shoots of *P.* 'Forest Flame' are bright red at first, fading flamingo pink before turning green. Other outstanding cultivars include 'Jermyns' whose habit is more spreading and the wine-red flowered 'Valley Valentine'.

Soil preference: Neutral or lime-free, humus rich
Aspect: Part shade or shade
Season of interest: Spring, year round
Height and spread: Variable to 3m x 2m (10ft x 6ft)

Companion plants: Striking companions for medium sized and large rhododendrons, and for *Kalmia latifolia*. Associating them with magnolias and Corylopsis would also ensure early season interest.

Cotoneaster radicans   Hardy evergreen shrub

A tough, fast-growing, prostrate evergreen whose stems wander indefinitely, rooting as they go to form a dense, contour-hugging ground cover. In late spring, small, white five petalled flowers are dotted among the tangled branches and later, these develop into attractive red berries. A native of eastern China.

Soil preference: Any, free-draining
Aspect: Sun or part shade
Season of interest: Year round
Height and spread: 20cm (8in), spreading

Companion plants: A useful plant to scramble over a low wall, bank, or to conceal unattractive ground features. Though weed proof, such bulbs as narcissus, Leucojum or Camassia can be persuaded to grow up through the branches.

Salix lanata

Woolly Willow   Hardy deciduous shrub

A compact, tidy willow with thick stems, interestingly gnarled when old, and pale grey-green, rounded, downy or hairy leaves which emerge at the same time as the erect, golden catkins. *Salix helvetica*, a pretty alternative, has narrower grey-green leaves and grows slightly taller.

Soil preference: Any, not too dry
Aspect: Sun or part shade
Season of interest: Year round
Height and spread: 1m x 2m (3ft x 6ft)

Companion plants: The gnarled, stubby outline brings small scale structure and is attractive with grasses, or with sparse plantings of herbaceous subjects – *Lathyrus vernus*, for example, or violas and pansies with low tulips.

Sarcococca hookeriana var. humilis

Christmas Box, Sweet Box   Hardy evergreen shrub

A ground-covering shrub which forms dense, low thickets with very shiny, curled, triangular leaves and, in mid-winter, small, off-white flowers which, despite being little more than bunches of filaments, give off a sweet and persistent honey fragrance. Related varieties include *S. h.* var. *digyna*, which has narrower leaves and *S. h.* var. *digyna* 'Purple Stem'.

Soil preference: Any free-draining, not too dry
Aspect: Part shade, shade
Season of interest: Winter
Height and spread: 45cm (1ft 6in), spreading

Companion plants: Charming for its mid-winter fragrance and greenery, making a lush background for winter blooms of *Iris reticulata* or *Leucojum vernum*. In summer, the foliage makes a great back-drop to Impatiens or fuchsias.

Helianthemum nummularium

Sun Rose, Rock Rose   Hardy evergreen shrub

Small, lax shrubs with simple, narrow leaves that are bright green or grey-green. The stems end in drooping clusters of buds which, during late spring and summer, open to reveal frail, five-petalled flowers which only last a day. Double-flowered kinds have slightly more durable blooms. Varieties include orange 'Ben Heckla', double red 'Mrs C. W. Earle', 'Wisley Primrose' and the pink and white 'Raspberry Ripple'.

Soil preference: Any free-draining
Aspect: Sun
Season of interest: Spring, summer
Height and spread: To 20cm x 45cm (8in x 1ft 6in)

Companion plants: Perfect for a dry bank or a hot rock garden where they blend well with *Euphorbia myrsinites*, Anthyllis, Sedums and *Antirrhinum hispanicum*.

Cistus x corbariensis

Sun Rose, Rock Rose   Hardy evergreen shrub

A dense-growing shrub with bright green, wavy edged leaves whose surfaces are rough to the touch and, from mid-summer onwards, a succession of large but short-lived, snow white flowers which emerge from attractive, reddish buds. Not especially long-lived, so best propagated from cuttings every few years.

Soil preference: Any free-draining
Aspect: Sun
Season of interest: Summer
Height and spread: 1m x 1.5m (3ft 3in x 5ft)

Companion plants: A fine plant for a hot, sunny bank in association with such other rock roses as *Cistus ladanifer* or *C. laurifolius*.

Genista hispanica

Spanish Gorse   Borderline hardy shrub

A slow-growing, very spiny shrub which forms a low, neat mound of well-armed stems which stay green all winter. During spring, tiny green leaves appear and short flower stems develop, terminating in groups of bright golden yellow flowers. Small, dark brown seed pods follow.

Soil preference: Any free-draining
Aspect: Sun
Season of interest: Spring, summer
Height and spread: 75cm x 1.5m (2ft 6in x 5ft)

Companion plants: A charming shrub for small but sculptural statements, perhaps among the softer outlines of helianthemums or to grow with later flowering sedums and other succulents.

Artemisia arborescens   Wormwood   Hardy, evergreen shrub

A silvery grey shrub or sub-shrub with silky, filigree foliage produced on fast-growing stems and, in summer, sprays of small, yellowish green, uninteresting flowers. Good garden forms include 'Powis Castle'. Flowers are best removed, during mid-summer pruning, to rejuvenate the foliage.

Soil preference: Free-draining
Aspect: Sun
Season of interest: Year round
Height and spread: 1.5m x 1.5m (5ft x 5ft)

Companion plants: Mainstay of a dry garden, bringing soft, silvery lushness, lovely to contrast with the green leaved cotton lavender, *Santolina rosmarinifolia* 'Primrose Gem' or with the bottle green domes of *Genista hispanica*.

Phlomis fruticosa

Jerusalem Sage   Hardy evergreen shrub

A common Mediterranean shrub with downy stems, square in section, and felty, grey-green oval leaves. The late spring flower buds develop in tight whorls around the stems where the paired leaves also join them and open to present hook-lipped, mustard-yellow flowers with a fruity aroma. Bees adore this relative of true sages.

Soil preference: Any free-draining
Aspect: Sun
Season of interest: Spring, summer
Height and spread: 1m x 1.5m (3ft 3in x 5ft)

Companion plants: A fine plant for bringing freshness to a hot spot, lovely with such arid-loving bulbs as *Anemone* x *fulgens*, Crocus, Mediterranean fritillaries, ixias or wild tulip species.

Thymus vulgaris

Common Thyme, Culinary thyme   Hardy evergreen shrub

Deliciously aromatic, dwarf shrub with masses of wiry stems furnished with small, oval leaves and, in summer, pale mauve flowers. Decorative forms, which are just as good for cooking as the plain green include 'Silver Posie', whose leaves are silver-edged and 'Aureus' (recently renamed *T. pulegioides* 'Goldentime'), which has gold-suffused leaves. Prune hard to promote new growth.

Soil preference: Any free-draining
Aspect: Sun
Season of interest: Year round
Height and spread: 30cm x 60cm (1ft x 2ft)

Companion plants: Pretty anywhere, whether with other thymes and mixed herbs or edging a kitchen garden border, or in gravel with decorative Origanum species and sedums.

Heathers

Winter flowering varieties, derived from *Erica carnea* or its hybrid *E.* x *darleyensis*, are lime tolerant but the majority of heathers prefer acid, free-draining soils. Although heathers occur worldwide, the great majority of species – more than 600 – are native to South Africa. Most benefit from light pruning immediately after flowering.

1. Erica x darleyensis 'Kramer's Rote'
Also known as 'Kramer's Red', a winter or spring flowering variety with bronzed winter leaves and reddish purple flowers.

2. Erica x darleyensis 'Silberschmelze'
Winter-blooming heather with white flowers and needly foliage which is cream-tipped in spring, when fresh.

3. Erica arborea 'Albert's Gold'
A shrub growing to 2m (6ft), but seldom flowering. The golden foliage consists of tiny needly leaves. Flowers, when produced, are white.

4. Erica vagans 'Mrs D. F. Maxwell'
A variety of Cornish or Wandering Heath, whose summer flowers are deep pink.

5. Calluna vulgaris
Native to Britain but less common elsewhere in the world, heather or 'ling' has tiny pink – or rarely, white – flowers in late summer, on short shrubs with tiny, scale-like leaves.

6. Calluna vulgaris 'Spring Cream'
A white flowered form of heather or ling, whose new shoots are tipped with cream, darkening to green as they age.

7. Erica carnea 'Springwood Pink'
Alpine Heath. A winter flowering variety whose flowers are clear, shell pink, contrasting with the deep green foliage.

8. Erica carnea 'Myretoun Ruby'
Long-lasting winter flowering variety with dark green foliage and flowers which open flush pink but which deepen as they age.

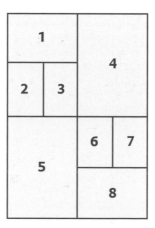

Genista lydia

Dwarf Genista   Hardy deciduous shrub

A small shrub whose constantly green stems arch in semicircles to create a distinctive mound, often with a cloud effect. Tiny, narrow, dark green leaves emerge along the curved branches in spring and are soon followed by short sprays of buds which open to create a vivid yellow display. Small, flat pods form in late summer.

Soil preference: Any free-draining
Aspect: Sun
Season of interest: Late spring, summer
Height and spread: 60cm x 90cm (2ft x 3ft)

Companion plants: A useful plant for furnishing a windswept spot and popular with large-scale landscapers. Team it with blue flowers of *Ceanothus* 'Blue Mound' or *C. thyrsiflorus* var. *repens*.

Teucrium chamaedrys

Germander   Hardy evergreen sub-shrub

A slowly spreading, evergreen sub-shrub or woody-based perennial with small, oval toothed leaves which are dark, glossy green, and spikes bearing numerous purplish-pink, lipped flowers arranged in whorls. The plants flower best if cut back, like herbaceous perennials, each winter or spring. Irresistible to bees.

Soil preference: Any free-draining
Aspect: Sun
Season of interest: Summer
Height and spread: 60cm x 60cm (2ft x 2ft)

Companion plants: A popular plant in Elizabethan-style planting schemes, often used with cotton lavender, lavender and rosemary. The plants can also be used for very low hedges in a knot garden.

Berberis thunbergii

Barberry   Deciduous hardy shrub

Compact, variable, thorny shrub with oval leaves which may be green, gold or purple. Yellow flowers open in spring and are followed by small, oblong red fruits. Foliage colours in autumn, before falling. Compact forms for small places include the dark leaved 'Atropurpurea Nana', the upright 'Helmond Pillar' and very neat 'Bagatelle'.

Soil preference: Any not too dry, free-draining
Aspect: Sun or part shade
Season of interest: Spring, summer, autumn
Height and spread: Variable to 2m x 2m (6ft x 6ft)

Companion plants: The autumn hues of these barberries are superb with blue autumn gentians, or blue perennial asters. Silver foliage, perhaps from *Salix helvetica* or in drier conditions from *Artemisia* 'Powis Castle' would also contrast well.

Lavandula angustifolia   Lavender   Hardy evergreen shrub

A neat-growing shrub whose woody base becomes gnarled with age. The stiff, upright stems are concealed by narrow, simple, pale grey-green leaves. Naked flower stems grow from the tips of these and carry short, densely packed spikes of intensely fragrant flowers in blue, white, mauve, purple or deep violet. Loved forms include the dwarf, dark blue-flowered 'Hidcote', paler 'Munstead', 'Loddon Pink' and tiny white 'Nana Alba'.

Soil preference: Any free-draining
Aspect: Sun or part shade
Season of interest: Spring, summer, autumn
Height and spread: Variable to 1m x 1m (3ft 3in x 3ft 3in)

Companion plants: Lavenders go with anything. As a baseline for roses they are superb; they bring extra grace and fragrance to a mixed planting of herbs and, in formal bedding, as dot plants or to make border hedges, they are also delightful.

Hypericum 'Hidcote'

Saint John's Wort   Hardy semi-evergreen shrub

Tough, dome shaped shrub with simple, oval leaves which are bright green and moderately shiny. Through summer and into autumn, there follows a constant run of large, five-petalled, bright golden yellow flowers. A worthy alternative, with darker yellow flowers, is *Hypericum* 'Rowallane'.

Soil preference: Any reasonably fertile, not too dry
Aspect: Any
Season of interest: Summer
Height and spread: 1.5m x 1.5m. (5ft x 5ft)

Companion plants: The strident yellow can be difficult to harmonize subtly, but for a strong contrast, try them with the reds of certain roses – 'Parkdirektor Riggers' or 'Scharlachglut'. Lovely with purple-coloured *Buddleja davidii* cultivars.

Ligustrum vulgare

Common Privet   Hardy semi-evergreen shrub

A tough species with arching branches, narrow, curved leaves and, in mid- to late summer, generous panicles of white flowers which resemble those of a skinny lilac and which smell unpleasant, to some, at close quarters. Clusters of small black fruits follow. Tolerant of a wide range of conditions. The golden form 'Aureum' (pictured) has yellow leaves.

Soil preference: Any, free-draining
Aspect: Sun, part shade, shade
Season of interest: Year round
Height and spread: 3m x 3m (10ft 9in x 10ft 9in)

Companion plants: Useful for planting where little else will grow. Can be used as hedging or a vehicle for honeysuckles or late-summer clematis of moderate vigour.

Argyranthemum frutescens

Marguerite   Tender shrub or sub-shrub

Woody based plants with many-branched, fragile stems and lobed or finely dissected leaves often with a bluish tinge. An almost constant succession of single or double daisy flowers is delivered throughout the growing season. The wild species is white but the numerous garden hybrids, tall and dwarf, now come in white, yellow, pink and crimson with intermediate hues. 'Mary Wooton' is a double pink and 'Butterfly' a yellow.

Soil preference: Any fertile, free-draining
Aspect: Sun or part shade
Season of interest: Summer, autumn
Height and spread: 90cm x 90cm (3ft x 3ft)

Companion plants: Sublime container plants, beautiful with fuchsias, heliotrope or in a bed, perhaps with New World salvias.

Salvia microphylla

Marginally hardy deciduous shrub

A soft-stemmed Mexican shrub with small, dark green, triangular leaves and purplish or pinkish-red, hooked flowers whose lower lips are flared and showy. Selections include 'Pink Blush' and 'Coral'. The form *S. m.* var. *microphylla* has brighter green leaves and scarlet or cherry red flowers. Needs protection from sustained frost.

Soil preference: Any, free-draining, not too dry
Aspect: Sun
Season of interest: Summer, autumn
Height and spread: 1m x 1m (3ft 3in x 3ft 3in)

Companion plants: A bright and dependable shrub, lovely among other sages such as *Salvia patens* or culinary sage, or with artemisias, helichrysums or more or less any Mediterranean shrub.

Phygelius aequalis

Cape Fuchsia   Marginally hardy shrub or sub-shrub

A suckering shrub or woody perennial with a slowly creeping rootstock. Broadly oval, toothed leaves are carried in pairs on stems which terminate with spikes of gracefully hanging, tubular flowers in red or salmon hues, often with a contrasting throat colour. The form 'Yellow Trumpet' has pale primrose blooms.

Soil preference: Any free-draining, not too dry
Aspect: Sun or part shade
Season of interest: Summer
Height and spread: 1m x 1m (3ft 3in x 3ft 3in)

Companion plants: Lovely grown among perennials, especially when bringing gentle colour to hostas or Heuchera, or to extend the season of the earlier campanulas.

Ceanothus thyrsiflorus var. repens

Trailing, evergreen shrub

A ground-covering shrub which forms dense mats of green branches furnished with small, glossy, oval leaves and in spring, an abundance of compact panicles of small flowers whose colour wavers between pale blue and a very light grey. Blossoms are susceptible to late frost damage.

Soil preference: Any free-draining
Aspect: Sun or part shade
Season of interest: Spring, summer
Height and spread: 45cm (1ft 6in), spreading

Companion plants: A valuable ground cover plant to team with such perennials as *Geranium macrorrhizum* or *Euphorbia myrsinites*, or with creeping cotoneasters and, for later blooms, *Teucrium chamaedrys*.

Prostranthera cuneata

Mint Bush   Doubtfully hardy, evergreen shrub

An intensely aromatic shrub from Australia with stocky growth habit and small, crinkled leaves held on thin, twiggy stems. In early summer, small but distinctively shaped flowers, looking like tiny pansies, smatter the branches and are soft white with darker violet markings.

Soil preference: Any free-draining
Aspect: Sun
Season of interest: Summer, year round
Height and spread: 1m x 1.5m (3ft 3in x 5ft)

Companion plants: Supreme choice for a garden hot spot, perhaps with such fellow Southern Hemisphere treasures as *Grevillea rosmarinifolia*, Plumbago or scented-leaf pelargoniums.

Heliotropium arborescens

Heliotrope, Cherry Pie   Tender shrub

Popular shrub since Victorian times, with dark green, rugose foliage and large, tight clusters of buds which resemble unfurling fiddleheads as they expand and open their deep purple flowers. The vanilla-scented blossom brings extra value. Choice varieties include a compact form, 'Marine', the richly scented 'Chatsworth' and paler flowered 'Lord Roberts'.

Soil preference: Any reasonably fertile, free-draining
Aspect: Sun
Season of interest: Summer
Height and spread: 1m x 75cm (3ft 3in x 2ft)

Companion plants: Traditionally used as dot plants in old-style bedding schemes but also magnificent as container plants when trained as standards or teamed with purples and pinks of fuchsias, pastel-hued petunias or white argyranthemums.

Hippophae rhamnoides

Sea Buckthorn   Hardy, deciduous shrub or small tree

A large, spreading shrub or small tree with narrow, grey-green leaves and, in spring, inconspicuous greenish flowers. Male specimens bear only pollen, but on females a heavy crop of densely packed, orange berries develops through late summer and persists through much of winter. Resists the strongest gales, even when salt-laden, and thrives in sandy soils.

Soil preference: Any free-draining
Aspect: Sun
Season of interest: Year round
Height and spread: 5m x 5m (16ft x 16ft)

Companion plants: A tough plant with the colouring of an olive tree, beautiful to contrast with dark leaved Escallonia or to team with Lavetera for extra flower power.

Tamarix ramosissima

Tamarisk   Hardy deciduous shrub

A dense growing shrub with many slender branches bearing minute leaves and shoots making them soft to the touch. In summer extensive, hanging clusters of tiny pink flowers appear and last for several weeks. A pretty alternative is *Tamarix gallica*, whose foliage has a blue-green hue. Ideal for coping with salt-laden winds.

Soil preference: Any free-draining
Aspect: Sun, part shade
Season of interest: Spring, summer
Height and spread: 5m x 3m (15ft x 10ft)

Companion plants: The classic seaside shrub, lovely teamed with big hebes, Griselinia and *Hippophae rhamnoides*.

Bupleurum fruticosum

Shrubby Hare's Ear   Hardy evergreen shrub

Dense, bushy shrub with moderately glossy, oblong, pointed leaves which have dark blue to grey-green upper surfaces and paler undersides. From early summer, umbels of bright yellowish green flowers are held just clear of the young stems. Though not capable of taking sustained frost, this species revels in a windy, seaside location. Propagate from seed.

Soil preference: Any free-draining, not too wet
Aspect: Sun
Season of interest: Year round
Height and spread: 2m x 1.5m (6ft x 5ft)

Companion plants: A charming maritime plant to blend with perennial wallflowers such as *Erisymum* 'Bowles Mauve' or with Mediterranean shrubs such as *Teucrium fruticans*, *Phlomis fruticosa* or rock roses.

Atriplex halimus   Tree Purslane   Near hardy, evergreen shrub

A distinctive, sprawling shrub with triangular to oval, hairless leaves which are a brilliant metallic silvery grey, particularly while young and fresh. The flowers are insignificant and seldom produced in cool climates. Will not tolerate waterlogging at the root, but copes well with severe maritime weather.

Soil preference: Any free-draining, especially sandy
Aspect: Sun
Season of interest: Year round
Height and spread: 2m (6ft)

Companion plants: The pale, silvery foliage makes a delightful foil for dark foliage of such shrubs as Poncirus, *Prunus lusitanica* or to set off bright summer flowers such as gazanias, Arctotis or poppies.

Lupinus arboreus

Tree Lupin   Hardy, semi-evergreen sub-shrub

A lax, short-lived shrub with typical lupin leaves, i.e. palmate with five to seven narrow leaflets per stem, and in summer, short, erect spikes of showy, pale yellow, blue or bicoloured pea flowers. Not long-lived, so essential to propagate from seed or cuttings, but a lovely shrub to allow to naturalize in sandy, coastal soils.

Soil preference: Any free-draining ·
Aspect: Sun
Season of interest: Summer
Height and spread: 1m x 1m (3ft 3in x 3ft 3in)

Companion plants: Handy for placing with large or small grasses in a naturalistic setting, but also beautiful as a climax plant in a summer mixed border where pastel hues dominate. Try it with big *Campanula lactiflora* or with achilleas.

Yucca gloriosa

Spanish Dagger   Hardy evergreen shrub

A big, brash American native whose wide rosettes of spiky, sword-shaped leaves are held on thick trunks which slowly extend, with age, to heights of a metre or more, but whose flower spikes grow considerably higher. These mature during summer and produce thick spires of large, creamy white flowers which resemble pendulous tulips.

Soil preference: Any free-draining
Aspect: Sun, part shade
Season of interest: Year round, summer, autumn
Height and spread: 2m x 2m (6ft x 6ft)

Companion plants: A fine constituent for an 'exotic' border with cannas, phormiums, bananas, and, if climate permits, agaves and aloes. Makes a bold centre piece for sparsely planted rock and gravel or as the centre of a dry planting scheme.

Rhododendron

Dwarf Rhododendron, Azaleas   Hardy evergreen or near-evergreen shrubs

Small-leaved shrubs of compact habit developed from a variety of origins, but always small enough to flourish in permanent containers. Colours range from deep crimsons or scarlet, through pinks and purples, salmons and peachy cream to white. Varieties include *Kurume* azaleas such as 'Hinode-giri' (crimson pink) and 'Hino-crimson', and 'Azuma-kagami', whose 'hose-in-hose' flowers are bright pink.

Soil preference: Lime-free, not too dry
Aspect: Sun or part shade
Season of interest: Spring
Height and spread: Variable to 1m x 1m (3ft 3in x 3ft 3in)

Companion plants: Best in containers of their own, but attractive when assembled with ferns, hostas or for later colour, potted lilies.

Camellia   Tender or hardy evergreen shrubs

Mid-sized, oval, glistening dark green foliage makes a superb foil for the brightly coloured, disc-shaped flowers which may be single, semi-double, 'anemone centred' or fully double. Forms of the tender *Camellia reticulata* have the largest, most sensational flowers. Examples are 'Dark Jewel' (crimson) and the pink 'Arch of Triumph'. *C. japonica* varieties include 'Lovelight' (white), 'Lavinia Maggi' (pictured) and the upright, red-flowered 'Miss Charleston'.

Soil preference: Lime-free, humus-rich
Aspect: Part shade, shade
Season of interest: Winter, spring
Height and spread: Variable to 3m (10ft)

Companion plants: In large containers, small narcissus can be planted at their feet, but these are also excellent solo container plants.

Forsythia viridissima 'Bronxensis'

Hardy deciduous shrub

A beautiful miniature version of the familiar spring shrub with tan-barked stems and in early spring, masses of four petalled, yellow blossoms which are in full bloom before the simple, toothed leaves emerge. The growth habit is compact and twiggy, old specimens developing great character. Easy to propagate from cuttings or even divisions.

Soil preference: Any
Aspect: Sun, part shade
Season of interest: Spring
Height and spread: To 75cm x 50cm (2ft 6in x 2ft)

Companion plants: Lovely for playing a key role in a big Alpine trough, perhaps with *Primula marginata*, small bulbs such as *Crocus sieberi* or *Iris reticulata* and *Corydalis solida*.

Rosa   Patio Roses   Hardy deciduous shrubs

Small, shrubby rose varieties with compound leaves, thorny stems and single or double flowers, often fragrant, in a variety of colours. Disease resistant 'Flower Carpet' roses, though technically ground cover types, make excellent container plants and come in shades of pink, white and soft yellow. Other patio roses include the orange 'Darling Flame' (pictured), pink 'Queen Mother' and 'Festival', which is red.

Soil preference: Any fertile, free-draining but not too wet
Aspect: Sun
Season of interest: Summer
Height and spread: Variable to 1m x 75cm (3ft 3in x 2ft 6in)

Companion plants: Attractive with summer plantings of petunias, Torenia, Sutera and such silver foliage plants as *Senecio cineraria* and *Helichrysum petiolare*.

Sorbus reducta

Hardy deciduous shrub

A slow-growing, suckering dwarf willow which, in time forms a loose thicket of stems whose winter bark is dark tan. The pinnate leaves are slightly toothed, mid-green and turn rich gold and russet in autumn. Creamy spring blossoms, held in tight umbels, give way to blood red or scarlet orange berries in autumn.

Soil preference: Any, not too dry, preferably lime-free
Aspect: Sun, part shade, shade
Season of interest: Year round
Height and spread: To 1m x 1m (3ft 3in x 3ft 3in)

Companion plants: A characterful shrub, lovely in a container with such autumn-flowering gentians as *Gentiana farreri* or the more intense blue *G. sino-ornata*.

Solanum rantonnetii

Blue Potato Bush   Tender, deciduous or evergreen shrub

A lax, fast-growing shrub or semi-climber whose arching stems carry simple, oval, pointed leaves and throughout the growing season, a succession of saucer-shaped, crinkly textured, pale blue flowers, each with a small, yellow centre. Red berry-like fruits follow. Useful garden forms include the purple-blue 'Royal Robe' (pictured). Must be pinched back to promote bushiness.

Soil preference: Any, not too damp
Aspect: Sun
Season of interest: Summer
Height and spread: 2m x 2m (6ft x 6ft)

Companion plants: A refreshing alternative to the ubiquitous standard fuchsia in container displays, harmonizing well with heliotrope or contrasting with pink, primrose or white *Chrysanthemum frutescens*.

Choisya 'Aztec Pearl'

Mexican Orange Blossom   Hardy evergreen shrub

A neat-growing but rather large shrub with palmate leaves whose slender 'finger' leaflets make an attractive outline for the clusters of fragrant, five petalled blossoms which open in late spring and early summer. The flowers are rusty pink in the bud, opening soft white with yellow stamens. The foliage is gently aromatic.

Soil preference: Any free-draining
Aspect: Sun, part shade
Season of interest: Year round
Height and spread: 2.5m x 2m (8ft x 6ft)

Companion plants: A handsome evergreen which performs best in full light, perhaps with buddlejas – particularly *Buddleja* 'Lochinch', Cotoneaster or, for companion blooms, evergreen forms of Ceanothus.

Cotoneaster conspicuus 'Decorus'

Hardy evergreen or semi-evergreen shrub

Stiff but gracefully arching stems are furnished with small, oval or rounded, glossy dark green leaves which burnish – and sometimes fall – in cold winter weather. The five petalled, pearly white flowers are small but showy in spring and are followed by brilliant scarlet-orange, glistening autumn berries. A shrub of quiet – but lasting – beauty.

Soil preference: Any, free-drained but not too dry
Aspect: Sun
Season of interest: Year round
Height and spread: 1.25m (4ft), spreading

Companion plants: A superb host shrub through which to grow non-invasive *Clematis viticella* and *texensis* hybrids such as 'Etoile Rose', 'Gravetye Beauty' or 'Purpurea Plena Elegans'.

Lespedeza thunbergii

Hardy, deciduous sub-shrub

A woody perennial or sub-shrub whose lax, arching branches carry fluorescent green, compound foliage and, from late summer onwards, short, horizontal or hanging spikes of vivid rose-purple pea flowers. *Lespedeza bicolor* is more upright in habit, with slightly larger flowers. Best cut back hard each winter.

Soil preference: Any free-draining
Aspect: Sun
Season of interest: Summer
Height and spread: To 1.5m x 1.5m (5ft x 5ft)

Companion plants: Prettiest in a mixed border, in full sun, where the long stems can flop among lower shrubs such as Caryopteris or among late flowering perennials.

Chamaecytisus purpureus

Purple Broom, Purple False Broom   Hardy, deciduous shrub

A modest, spreading shrub with green winter twigs and, from spring, bright green three-lobed leaves. The pea-flowers, produced in profusion in late spring and early summer, are lilac mauve or pale purple, often with darker bases to the keels. In favourable conditions, the rootstock will creep.

Soil preference: Any free-draining
Aspect: Sun or part shade
Season of interest: Spring, early summer
Height and spread: 45cm (1ft 6in), spreading by 60cm (2ft)

Companion plants: Lovely for furnishing the ground below a wall, perhaps contrasting with such other pea relatives as *Genista lydia* or some of the paler hued brooms such as *Cytisus* x *kewensis*.

Salvia greggii

Autumn Sage   Marginally hardy shrub

A fast growing, shrub or sub-shrub with dark skinned stems and small, leathery, mildly aromatic leaves. The hooked flowers are borne on short spikes and have broad, showy lower lips, usually in shades of pink or red. Varieties include salmon pink 'Peach', cream-flowered 'Sungold' and 'Magenta'. Very similar to *S. microphylla* with which it readily crosses.

Soil preference: Any free-draining, not too dry
Aspect: Sun
Season of interest: Summer, autumn
Height and spread: 90cm x 1m plus (3ft x 3ft 3in)

Companion plants: Long-flowering and valuable for a bright summer border where it harmonises well with such other American plants as Rudbeckia, Penstemon, perennial asters or Anaphalis.

Salvia officinalis   Common or Culinary Sage   Hardy sub-shrub

The familiar aromatic culinary herb which originates from the Mediterranean and has simple, oval, pointed grey-green leaves which are slightly roughened but downy to the touch. In summer, spikes of rich royal blue, hooked flowers appear and are irresistible to bees. Varieties with decorative leaves included 'Purpurascens' (purple leaves), 'Icterina' (gold variegated) and 'Tricolor' (pictured), whose foliage is cream, pink, purple and green.

Soil preference: Any free-draining
Aspect: Sun
Season of interest: Year round
Height and spread: To 1m x 1m (3ft 3in x 3ft 3in)

Companion plants: Natural companions to such other culinary herbs as thymes, rosemary and marjoram. Beautiful with old shrub roses, in mixed cottage borders with lavender or as container plants.

Berberis x stenophylla

Hardy, evergreen shrub

A vigorous, sprawling shrub with small, spiny, leathery leaves which are held close to the prickly stems and each spring to early summer, a display of bright, golden yellow flowers. In late summer and autumn the black fruits are coated with a pale greyish-white bloom. Varieties include the pale flowered 'Lemon Cream', the yellow 'Corallina Compacta' (pictured) and the red-flowered 'Crawley Gem'.

Soil preference: Any, free-draining, not too dry
Aspect: Sun or part shade
Season of interest: Year round
Height and spread: 3m x 4m (10ft x 14ft)

Companion plants: Handy, windproof shrub for a shelter belt, perhaps with the more lusty viburnums such as *V. rhytidophyllum* or with hollies, laurels or *Cornus mas.*

Cistus x purpureus

Purple Rock Rose   Near hardy evergreen shrub

A tough, drought tolerant evergreen shrub with oval, dull green, leathery leaves on sparse stems and, from early summer, a succession large, saucer-shaped, dark centred pinkish purple flowers which last but a day. Other large flowered rock roses include *C. laurifolius* (white) and *C.* x *pulverulentus* (pink).

Soil preference: Any free-draining
Aspect: Sun
Season of interest: Summer
Height and spread: To 1.5m x 1.5m (5ft x 5ft)

Companion plants: Excellent with any lover of hot dry conditions. Phlomis and many of the salvias make good companions, as do such annuals as *Cerinthe major*, poppies and grasses such as *Lagurus ovatus* or *Briza maxima.*

Colutea x media

Bladder Senna   Hardy deciduous shrub

A big, ramshackle shrub with erect, then arching stems and grey-green, compound leaves. The pea flowers are produced throughout the growing season, in small clusters, and are rusty orange. The form 'Copper Beauty' is particularly good, with orange flowers followed by reddish seed pods.

Soil preference: Any free-draining
Aspect: Sun
Season of interest: Summer
Height and spread: 3m x 3m (10ft x 10ft)

Companion plants: Easy, tolerant plants whose bright flowers bring relief to the summer monotony of such shrubs as Ribes, Forsythia or Exochorda and which contrast with *Caryopteris* x *clandonensis* or late-blooming Ceanothus.

Cornus sericea   Winter Stem Dogwood   Hardy deciduous shrub

A fast growing shrub with creeping rootstock from which rises a thicket of stems which, when young, have decorative bark. The foliage is neutral green; the flowers insignificant. The form 'Flaviramea' (pictured) is one of the most sought-after, having yellow-green stems which, in winter sunlight are almost luminescent. Best pruned hard back each spring to stimulate the production of colourful new stems.

Soil preference: Moist, reasonably fertile
Aspect: Sun or part shade
Season of interest: Winter, year round
Height and spread: 2m x 3m (6ft x 10ft)

Companion plants: Superb winter garden plants, especially with pollarding willows such as *Salix irrorata*, *S. daphnoides* or *S. alba* var. *vitellina* 'Britzensis'.

Deutzia x elegantissima   Hardy deciduous shrub

Suckering shrubs, producing arching canes with simple, slightly downy, dull green leaves. Year-old stems branch to produce elegant sprays of small, many petalled white or pink flowers. Varieties of great value include 'Rosealind' – arching stems of white flowers, flushed pink – and the deeper pink 'Fasciculata'. Other excellent Deutzia varieties include 'Mont Rose' (pictured) and the pure white *Deutzia gracilis*.

Soil preference: Free-draining, reasonably fertile
Aspect: Sun or part shade
Season of interest: Spring, early summer
Height and spread: Variable to 2m x 2m (6ft x 6ft)

Companion plants: An attractive alternative to mock orange perhaps to follow such early spring shrubs as Ribes and forsythias. In a mixed border, the flowers make a pleasant background to pink or plum-coloured oriental poppies, or to blend with early shrub roses such as *Rosa* 'Fruhlingsmorgen' or 'Nevada'.

Olearia macrodonta

Daisy Bush, New Zealand Holly, Arorangi   Marginally hardy evergreen shrub

A robust species with large, oval, toothed, leathery leaves, dark green on top with pale grey undersides and, in early summer, generous clusters of white, daisy flowers. The foliage is attractive in mid-winter, as is the gnarled, greyish bark, but this Australasian plant will not tolerate prolonged, sustained frost.

Soil preference: Free-draining, reasonably fertile
Aspect: Sun or part shade
Season of interest: Summer, year round
Height and spread: To 3m x 2m (10ft x 6ft)

Companion plants: Valuable as a screen plant or background plant, making a superb dark foil for buddleias or *Cytisus aetnensis* but also dramatic to harmonize with laburnums or big shrub roses.

Cotoneaster frigidus

Himalayan Tree Cotoneaster   Hardy deciduous shrub

A very large shrub with oval, mid-sized leaves and a long run of small, white, five-petalled, bee-alluring flowers. In autumn, a heavy crop of glistening, bright red berries hangs in attractive clusters, providing food for winter birds as well as winter colour. The heavy-cropping 'Cornubia' has leaves which burnish in winter.

Soil preference: Any, free-draining
Aspect: Sun, part shade
Season of interest: Year round
Height and spread: 8m x 8m (26ft x 26ft)

Companion plants: Excellent, though very large, in a shrubbery or grown as a small tree alongside dogwoods, maples, Crataegus or mid-sized willows.

Salix   Shrubby Willow   Hardy deciduous shrubs

Medium or large shrubs, usually with rapid-growing wands which branch as they mature and bear, in late winter or spring, silky upright catkins which turn golden yellow as their stamens emerge. *Salix daphnoides* has grey stems and shiny grey catkins; *S. caprea* (pictured) has big silver catkins and is pollinated by earl bumble bees. Best pollarded, in a small garden. Some species have invasive roots.

Soil preference: Any, not too dry
Aspect: Sun, part shade, shade
Season of interest: Winter, spring, autumn
Height and spread: Variable to 3m x 3m (10ft x 10ft)

Companion plants: Perhaps best in a winter garden where the attractive winter stems can harmonize with dogwoods such as *Cornus alba* or with decorative maples. Lovely underplanted with aconites, snowdrops, hellebores and crocus.

Rosa   Roses (for hips)   Hardy deciduous shrubs

Most rose species have compound, slightly toothed leaves, five-petalled, frequently fragrant flowers with central tufts of stamens and brightly coloured fruits. For wildlife, *R. villosa* and *R. andersonii* have pink flowers and red hips. *R. moyesii* produces scarlet bottle-shaped hips in autumn and *R. rugosa* (pictured) follows its intensely fragrant blooms with fleshy, pink-orange hips. *R. spinossissima* has little black hips.

Soil preference: Any free-draining
Aspect: Sun, part shade
Season of interest: Summer, autumn
Height and spread: Variable to 3m x 3m (10ft 9in x 10ft 9in)

Companion plants: Plant tall growers to arch out from among taller trees or to make focal points in mixed shrub borders, with cotoneasters, sorbus species or hawthorns. Shorter, neater varieties of *R. rugosa* and *R. spinossissima* are suitable for mixed borders.

Gaultheria mucronata   Hardy evergreen shrub

Low growing, modest shrubs with small, rounded, dark green, semi-glossy leaves. During autumn and winter, females bear a rich crop of large, attractively coloured berries in white or shades of pink or purple. 'Mulberry Wine' has purple berries; 'Wintertime' has white fruits; 'Signaal' (pictured) has dark pink berries throughout winter and the berries of 'Parelmoer' are pale pink.

Soil preference: Lime-free, humus-rich, most but free-draining
Aspect: Shade or part shade
Season of interest: Winter
Height and spread: To 1m x 1m (3ft 3in x 3ft 3in)

Companion plants: A fine companion for such other lime-haters as dwarf rhododendrons and azaleas. Also pretty with low-growing daphnes such as *D. blagayana* or *D. laureola*, and with creeping *Persicaria vacciniifolia*. Plant a male to ensure berries.

Ruscus aculeatus

Butcher's Broom   Hardy evergreen shrub

A curious, spiky little evergreen with suckering habit growing as thickets of stiffly erect stems which are densely branched and bear small, triangular leaves, each ending in a sharp point. The flowers are insignificant but female plants carry large, bright red berries through winter.

Soil preference: Any, not too wet
Aspect: Shade, part shade
Season of interest: Year round
Height and spread: 75cm (2ft 6in), spreading

Companion plants: A plant for the woodland floor, best with such shade-lovers such as epimediums, Solomon's seals, hellebores and ferns.

Viburnum lantana

Wayfaring Tree   Hardy deciduous shrub

A stout, erect to slightly arching shrub with diamond-shaped, pale green leaves and, in spring, conspicuous umbels of creamy white, somewhat rank-smelling flowers. By late summer, the scarlet fruits are beginning to ripen and contrast well with the pale foliage which takes on golden hues shortly before falling.

Soil preference: Any free-draining. A lime-lover
Aspect: Sun or part shade
Season of interest: Spring, autumn
Height and spread: 2m x 2m (6ft x 6ft)

Companion plants: A beautiful companion to other viburnums, or for incorporating in a mixed wildlife-sustaining hedge along with hollies, beech, hawthorn and field maple.

Rhododendron Hardy evergreen shrubs

A huge group of familiar shrubs, usually with broad, oblong-pointed, glossy leaves and flowers produced in large clusters in spring or early summer. Examples include the Loderi group which grow up to 4m (13ft) and include 'Loderi King George' (pink buds, white flowers) and 'Loderi Venus' (mid-pink flowers). *R. maccabeanum* has large, long leaves and huge trusses of pale yellow fragrant blooms and *R. arboreum* (red, pink or white) grows into a substantial tree. *R.* 'Pink Pearl' (pictured) has conical trusses of deep lilac-pink.

Soil preference: Lime-free, moist and humus-rich
Aspect: Sun, shade or part shade
Season of interest: Spring
Height and spread: Variable to 10m (35ft)

Companion plants: Camellias make ideal companions for many rhododendrons, as do late winter and spring flowering Corylopsis, Kalmias and Pieris species.

Ilex x meserveae Blue Holly Hardy evergreen shrubs or trees

Beautiful hollies with small to medium-sized leaves with short prickles. Their dark green hue has a bluish tint and the leaves tend to burnish in hard weather. Small, blood red berries are produced in profusion by female clones. Top choices are 'Blue Angel' (pictured), 'Blue Princess' and the more spreading 'Blue Maid'. 'Blue Prince' is a male, similar in habit to 'Blue Maid'. Lime tolerant but not happy on very poor limestone or chalk soils.

Soil preference: Any, not too dry but free-draining
Aspect: Sun, shade or part shade
Season of interest: Winter, year round
Height and spread: Variable to 3m (10ft)

Companion plants: Perfect hollies for smaller gardens where they bring winter structure and are pretty when under-planted with winter bulbs and hellebores, or teamed with hazel for catkins, or medium willows such as *Salix acutifolia* for catkins.

Buddleja globosa

Orange Ball Tree Hardy, semi-evergreen or deciduous shrub

A coarse-growing, many branched shrub whose vivid green leaves have pale undersides and are roughened or wrinkled. In early summer, spherical clusters of bright orange flowers make a slightly understated display. Pruning regime is different from that of *Buddleja davidii* hybrids, since the flowers appear on previous season's growth. The hybrid *B. x weyeriana* is a worthy alternative, but flowers in late summer.

Soil preference: Any free-draining
Aspect: Sun or part shade
Season of interest: Early summer
Height and spread: 3m x 3m (10ft x 10ft)

Companion plants: Adds a sub-tropical flavour beneath Eucalyptus and in combination with the lilac-purpled *Abutilon vitifolium* or *Solanum crispum* 'Glasnevin'.

Viburnum rhytidophyllum   Hardy evergreen shrub

A big, erect, rather coarse shrub from China with leathery, wrinkled, oblong leaves which hang down rather lugubriously. In spring, dome-shaped umbels of cream to white flowers are borne in profusion followed by fruits which turn first red, and then black as they mature. Not a ravishing beauty but virtually indestructible out of the wind.

Soil preference: Any
Aspect: Sun or part shade and sheltered from the wind
Season of interest: Year round
Height and spread: 4m x 3m (13ft x 10ft)

Companion plants: Teams well with buddlejas, hazel, Cotinus and Philadelphus as part of a sheltering screen but also handy as a host plant through which to train herbaceous climbers such as *Clematis texensis* hybrids or such perennial peas as *Lathyrus rotundifolius* or *L. latifolius*.

Elaeagnus pungens

Hardy evergreen shrub

Well shaped, many-branched shrubs with mid-sized, oval, pointed leaves with grey undersides and shiny green or variegated upper surfaces. The flowers, though small and insignificant, are fragrant and are sometimes followed by small red berries. For ornamental use, *E. p.* 'Maculata' (pictured) has bold yellow leaves, margined with green; 'Dicksonii' has pale yellow edges to its green leaves; and 'Frederici' has pale primrose and green leaves.

Soil preference: Any free-draining, not too dry
Aspect: Sun or part shade
Season of interest: Year round
Height and spread: 3m x 3m (10ft x 10ft)

Companion plants: Robust plants for a windy spot, good with Cytisus, Escallonia and the tougher of the Ceanothus cultivars.

Escallonia   Hardy evergreen shrub

Handsome shrubs whose arching branches form a dome-shaped outline. The stems and leaves are slightly glutinous, when young, but are attractively glossy and dark green, making a pretty contrast with the brightly coloured flowers. Colours range from red, through pinks to white. 'Apple Blossom' and 'Donard Seedling' are pale pink; 'Red Elf' is a compact form with red flowers.

Soil preference: Any free-draining, not too dry
Aspect: Sun or part shade
Season of interest: Year round
Height and spread: 2.5m x 2.5m (8ft x 8ft)

Companion plants: Superb hedge plants, especially for mild maritime sites, but also handsome when planted with such fellow South Americans as Berberis, Desfontainea or hardy fuchsias. A beautiful backdrop for Achillea, Anchusa, Echinops or Geranium.

Cotoneaster x watereri 'John Waterer'

Hardy semi-evergreen shrub

A vigorous cotoneaster with small, oval, glossy, dark green leaves and clusters of small but showy white flowers in summer. The berries, which ripen from late summer, are small, rounded and exceptionally glossy. 'John Waterer' was the first named hybrid of many developed from three species: *C. frigidus*, *C. salicifolius* and *C. rugosus*.

Soil preference: Any reasonably fertile
Aspect: Sun, part shade
Season of interest: Summer, autumn
Height and spread: 4m x 4m (13ft x 13ft)

Companion plants: Excellent screen plant, capable of growing into a tree, or to form a loose, colourful hedge, perhaps blended with other cotoneasters, Escallonia or *Viburnum rhytidophyllum*.

Skimmia japonica   Hardy evergreen shrub

Despite the dimensions above, many garden forms are much smaller. A member of the orange family with simple, oval, evergreen leaves and in spring and early summer, clusters of sweetly fragrant blossoms followed, in female plants, by persistent red berries. 'Fragrans' grows to 1.5m (5ft) and is male; *S. j.* subsp. *reevesiana* is an hermaphrodite, with narrower leaves and deep red berries.

Soil preference: Any, well-drained, humus-rich and not too limy
Aspect: Part shade, shade or sun
Season of interest: Year round
Height and spread: Variable to 6m x 6m (20ft x 20ft)

Companion plants: The rounded shape of *S. japonica* is useful to raise the height of a low-level planting scheme, perhaps of such ground covers as *Geranium macrorrhizum*, periwinkles or heathers.

Clerodendrum trichotomum

Hardy deciduous shrub or small tree

A loose-limbed, vigorous shrub whose simple, broad leaves are slightly downy. The scented flowers appear in clusters, in late summer, followed by bright kingfisher blue fruits whose colour is set off by the conspicuous red calyces. The form *C. t.* var. *fargesii* has deep purplish bronze buds and young leaves.

Soil preference: Any free-draining
Aspect: Sun
Season of interest: Summer, autumn
Height and spread: 4m x 3m (13ft x 10ft)

Companion plants: A fine plant to grow on its own, as a specimen, or to site with such sun-loving shrubs as Buddleja, Indigofera, Colutea or Lavatera.

Decaisnea fargesii   Hardy deciduous shrub

A suckering shrub with thick, twiggy canes and large, highly decorative, pinnate leaves. The flowers, produced in late spring or early summer, are yellow-green and are followed by conspicuous, dumpy, sausage-like pods which are pale blue-grey.

Soil preference: Moist and fertile, but free-draining
Aspect: Sun or part shade
Season of interest: Summer, autumn
Height and spread: 5m x 6m (16ft x 20ft)

Companion plants: Best in a naturalistic planting scheme, perhaps among mid-sized maples, rhododendrons or camellias.

Vaccinium corymbosum

High Bush or Swamp Blueberry   Hardy deciduous shrub

A dense growing shrub with many thin, wiry branches furnished with narrow, simple green leaves which turn fiery red and russet before falling in autumn. The flowers, produced in late spring, hang on small racemes and are white or pale pink. These are followed by the familiar edible blueberries – rounded, blue-black with a soft grey bloom, and are sweet and delicious.

Soil preference: Moist, lime-free, humus-rich
Aspect: Sun or part shade
Season of interest: Spring, summer, autumn
Height and spread: 1.5m x 1.5m (5ft x 5ft)

Companion plants: A lovely species to provide an 'upper layer' among plantings of such heathers as Daboecia, Calluna and summer flowering species of Erica. Also suitable as a container plant for autumn colour and fruit.

Viburnum opulus

Guelder Rose   Hardy deciduous shrub

A vigorous, branching, sprawling shrub with three-lobed leaves and, in early summer, 'lace cap' umbels of creamy white flowers whose outer, sterile florets are large and showy. Soft, brilliant red berries follow and persist through much of winter. The leaves often colour purplish bronze in autumn. *V. o.* 'Compactum' stays small and is densely branched; 'Xanthocarpum' has yellow berries.

Soil preference: Any free-draining
Aspect: Sun, part shade
Season of interest: Spring, autumn
Height and spread: To 3m x 3m (10ft x 10ft)

Companion plants: A fine hedgerow species, perfect to blend with field maple, holly, beech and yew in a mixed hedge or to grow in a mixed shrubbery with other viburnums.

Sambucus nigra 'Variegata'

Variegated Elder, Elderberry   Hardy deciduous shrub

Vigorous shrub or small tree, whose leaves and stems have a tom-cat aroma. The leaves are compound and the tiny white or pinkish flowers are produced in huge, flat umbels, in early summer, followed by a heavy crop of small black fruits. 'Aureomarginata' has yellow and green leaves; 'Albovariegata' has paler cream leaf margins. Best when regularly pollarded.

Soil preference: Any
Aspect: Sun, part shade, shade
Season of interest: Spring, summer, autumn
Height and spread: To 6m x 5m (20ft x 16ft)

Companion plants: Fun to group with dark leaved elders, or with vigorous smoke bush varieties such as *Cotinus* 'Grace'.

Buxus sempervirens

Common Box, Boxwood   Hardy evergreen shrub

The familiar hedging plant, which is described in its non-variegated forms, on page 290. Variegated forms include *B. s.* 'Argenteo-variegata', whose small, oblong leaves are edged with pale cream; 'Latifolia Maculata' has leaves marked with yellow; 'Marginata' has gold leaf tips; and the margins of *B. s.* 'Elegantissima' (pictured) are creamy white.

Soil preference: Any free-draining
Aspect: Sun, shade or part shade
Season of interest: Year round
Height and spread: Any required to 2m (6ft)

Companion plants: Coloured forms are handy to use in conjunction with green, in formal low hedging – such as in knot gardens – but are also pretty to sculpt as structure plants among less formal groups of roses perhaps, or with mixed perennials or bedding.

Rhamnus alaternus

Italian Buckthorn   Hardy evergreen shrub

An upright shrub, but whose branches arch as they lengthen. The leathery leaves are small, oval and glossy and are joined in late spring by hundreds of small, insignificant yellowish green flowers followed, in autumn, by small red or black fruits. The form 'Argentovariegata' (pictured) has decorative, cream edged leaves.

Soil preference: Any
Aspect: Sun or part shade
Season of interest: Year round
Height and spread: 4m x 3m (13ft x 10ft)

Companion plants: A useful and colourful foliage accent shrub for mixed planting, especially with dark leaved shrubs such as rhododendrons or evergreen azaleas, or to contrast with large-leaved hostas.

Philadelphus coronarius 'Aureus'

Gold Leaf Mock Orange   Hardy deciduous shrub

A dome-shaped, suckering shrub with erect, then gently arching stems which carry paired leaves whose colour is a penetrating lime green. The short sprays of strongly fragrant creamy white flowers are almost lost among the intensity of the foliage. Protect the plant from harsh, direct sun which will cause leaf scorch.

Soil preference: Any free-draining, not too dry
Aspect: Part shade
Season of interest: Spring, summer, autumn
Height and spread: 2m x 1.5m (6ft x 4ft)

Companion plants: Superb shrub for lighting up a dull corner, especially when placed with dark-leaved herbage for contrast. Pollarded red hazel, *Corylus maxima* makes an even stronger contrast.

Cotinus coggygria 'Golden Spirit'

Smokebush   Hardy deciduous shrub

A vigorous shrub with curving branches bearing flattened, spoon-shaped leaves and, on mature specimens, large, loose panicles of tiny pinkish, feathery blooms which, with help from the imagination, give the impression of smoke. In 'Golden Spirit' (pictured) the leaves are an intense yellow-green.

Soil preference: Any free-draining
Aspect: Sun or part shade
Season of interest: Summer, autumn
Height and spread: 3m x 3m (10ft x 10ft)

Companion plants: Exciting to plant with the more commonly grown purple-leaved smoke bushes, or to go with blue summer flowers such Perovskia or Anchusa.

Physocarpus opulifolius 'Dart's Gold'

Ninebark   Hardy deciduous shrub

A shrub with erect stems whose bark in mature specimens turns soft tan and peels attractively. The leaves are toothed, simple or lobed and golden green. Small, pink-tinged white flowers are borne in corymbs in summer and in autumn the gold of the leaves intensifies. The form 'Luteus' has bright gold young growth which ages green and then turns bronze.

Soil preference: Any, free-draining, not too dry
Aspect: Part shade
Season of interest: Summer, winter
Height and spread: To 2m x 2m (6ft x 6ft)

Companion plants: The winter stems make a pretty foil for spring bulbs such as early daffodils or tulips, especially when the gold leaf buds are breaking. For autumn, rosy purple Colchicums look delightful with the deepening colour.

Corylus maxima 'Purpurea'

Red Filbert   Hardy deciduous shrub

Large, toothed, rounded leaves in a rich reddish purple, turning beetroot coloured just as they fall in autumn. In late winter, the pendulous male flowers (catkins) are pink tinged and the young nuts, as they form, are sheathed in red leafy tissue. Best when coppiced every second year, to encourage young stems which bear extra-large leaves.

Soil preference: Any free-draining
Aspect: Sun or part shade
Season of interest: Year round
Height and spread: To 5m x 3m (16ft x 10ft)

Companion plants: The rich red foliage makes a striking colour contrast with apricot or salmon flowers. With the rose 'Buff Beauty' or 'Albertine' or 'Climbing Lady Hillingdon' it is superb, especially when planted with drifts of apricot foxgloves.

Cotinus 'Grace'   Smoke Bush   Hardy deciduous shrub

A very vigorous shrub with long, arching branches and large, flattened, spoon-shaped leaves whose colour is a bewitching blend of purple, green and grey. Leaves colour more richly in full sun than those in shade and in summer, panicles of smoke-like flowers appear. Easy to keep to size by regular pruning.

Soil preference: Any, not too dry but free-draining
Aspect: Sun or part shade
Season of interest: Summer, autumn
Height and spread: To 6m x 5m (20ft x 16ft)

Companion plants: Not for a small garden, but superb among other grey-greens, such as with Eucalyptus, or with glaucous conifers. Where plants have the space to reach their full size, try growing a rambling rose such as 'Veilchenblau' or 'Paul Transon' among the branches.

Acer palmatum 'Bloodgood'

Japanese Maple   Hardy shrub or small tree

Slow growing, elegant plant with well spaced branches, forming an upright, then spreading outline. The five or seven-lobed, palmate leaves are a rich purple red in spring and summer, their hue intensifying just before they fall. The flowers are small and greenish yellow, followed by two-winged seeds. Winter twigs are dark purple to black.

Soil preference: Free-draining, humus rich, not too dry
Aspect: Part shade
Season of interest: Year round
Height and spread: 3m x 2m (10ft x 6ft)

Companion plants: An outstanding Japanese maple, suitable for growing as a shrub and lovely underplanted with such winter goodies as *Hepatica nobilis*, *Anemone nemorosa* or blue scillas and *Iris reticulata*.

Cytisus battandieri

Pineapple Broom, Moroccan Broom   Marginally hardy deciduous shrub

A fast growing shrub native to Morocco, whose three-lobed, silvery grey leaves are joined in summer by a mass of upright, densely packed racemes of vivid yellow pea flowers which smell strongly, not of fresh pineapple, but of a cooked pineapple confection. Will not tolerate exposure to cold winds.

Soil preference: Any free-draining
Aspect: Sun
Season of interest: Summer
Height and spread: 5m x 4m (16ft x 13ft)

Companion plants: In cold areas, this plant is best trained on a wall, perhaps sharing its space with morning glories or with a blue potato vine eg. *Solanum crispum* 'Glasnevin'.

Perovskia atriplicifolia   Russian Sage   Hardy sub-shrub

A grey-looking sub-shrub whose erect stems and deeply divided leaves are coated with a silvery white down. From late summer to mid-autumn, tall branched spikes of equally silvery flower buds open to reveal rich purple-blue lipped flowers. The variety 'Blue Spire' has flowers in a deeper, violet blue.

Soil preference: Any free-draining
Aspect: Sun
Season of interest: Summer
Height and spread: 1m x 1m (3ft 3in x 3ft 3in)

Companion plants: Equally happy with herbaceous perennials, in a dry border, or with other shrubs, the silvery effect works especially well with Anaphalis, artemisias or to contrast its colours with salvias such as *S. microphylla* or *S. greggii*.

Brachyglottis greyii

Hardy evergreen shrub

Neat, low-growing, mound-forming shrub with oval to rounded grey-green leaves with silvery undersides, and downy, white to grey stems and buds. From mid-summer, showy sprays of bright yellow, daisy flowers appear and bloom for a long period. One of the most useful, neat shrubs for a sunny spot.

Soil preference: Any free-draining
Aspect: Sun
Season of interest: Year round
Height and spread: 1m x 1.5m (3ft 3in x 5ft)

Companion plants: A good companion to almost any sun-lover, especially pretty with *Euphorbia characias* or with *Coronilla valentina* and charming when the yellow flowers can contrast with blue Anchusa or harmonize with orange Eschscholzia.

Calycanthus occidentalis Spicebush Hardy shrub

A quietly handsome shrub with open habit and oblong, oval, pointed leaves, which are aromatic when crushed. Through summer, a sporadic succession of curious, brownish red flowers are produced with clustered, thick-textured petals which smell of apple. When grown in sun, the leaves colour up to rich yellow in autumn.

Soil preference: Any
Aspect: Sun or part shade
Season of interest: Summer
Height and spread: 2.5m x 2m (8ft x 6ft)

Companion plants: Interesting for its summer blooms, and therefore worth blending with spring flowering shrubs to provide later colour. Also makes an attractive backdrop to hydrangeas or as a summer companion to the related winter-flowering *Chimonanthus praecox*.

Citrus species Citrus fruit Tender evergreen shrubs

All the citrus species and varieties are desirable as garden plants. The simple, glossy evergreen foliage is strongly – and pleasantly – aromatic and, in winter or early spring, the blossoms are intensely fragrant. The fruit – lemons (*right*), oranges, citron – is invariably decorative and highly durable. None is hardy and all need full protection from frost.

Soil preference: Preferably lime free, well-drained
Aspect: Sun
Season of interest: Year round
Height and spread: Variable to 6m (20ft)

Companion plants: Highly successful as container plants, most citrus make great companions to shrubs such as olive or pomegranate. They will not object to small bulbs or low-growing summer species such as Callibrachoa or Sutera being planted in their containers as companions.

Cydonia oblonga Quince Hardy shrub or small tree

A spreading, open-habit shrub whose mature branches develop muscle-like outlines. The simple leaves are pale green with paler undersides, and are joined, in mid-spring by solitary, five petalled blossoms which are pale pink in bud, opening white. The fruits, which mature in autumn, are pear-shaped and a distinctive shade of citron yellow. Though tart and hard, they are excellent for cooking, particularly for quince jelly.

Soil preference: Any rich, free draining
Aspect: Sun
Season of interest: Year round
Height and spread: 4.5m x 5m (15ft x 16ft)

Companion plants: One of the prettiest fruit trees, made even more attractive if underplanted with springtime pulmonarias and small bulbs such as Erythroniums or low-growing Narcissus.

Desfontainea spinosa   Marginally hardy shrub

A very densely growing evergreen from the Andes whose deep green, glossy, prickly leaves resemble those of holly. From late summer onwards, tubular, yellow-tipped orange-red flowers hang from the branches. Needs protection from sustained frost and is happiest sheltered from cold winds.

Soil preference: Lime-free, free draining but not too dry
Aspect: Sun or part shade
Season of interest: Year round
Height and spread: 2m x 2m (6ft x 6ft)

Companion plants: Lovely with its fellow South Americans, particularly *Fuchsia magellanica*, Escallonia species and *Crinodendron hookerianum*.

Ricinus communis   Castor Oil Plant   Tender shrub

A widespread species from Africa and Asia frequently used immature as an accent plant in bedding schemes. Thick, fast-growing stems carry large, showy, palmate leaves which are dark when young. As the plant matures, dense flower clusters develop and are then followed by rusty red, spiny fruits. 'Impala' has dark, bronze foliage. All parts of the plant are poisonous.

Soil preference: Any free draining
Aspect: Sun
Season of interest: Summer
Height and spread: 3m x 3m (10ft x 10ft)

Companion plants: Best treated as an annual, or short-term perennial, and grown in a tropical scheme, perhaps with cannas, bananas and other lush-leaved species.

Fatsia japonica   Hardy shrub

A rather sombre but imposing evergreen shrub with stiff, upright stems, very large, palmate leaves and, in autumn, big, showy umbels of greenish cream flowers. Though tolerant of dense shade, it will not take prolonged, sustained frost.

Soil preference: Any well-drained
Aspect: Shade, part shade
Season of interest: Year round
Height and spread: 2m x 2m (6ft x 6ft)

Companion plants: A fine choice for a dark corner, wonderful with such ferns as *Polystichum polyblepharum*, with the more shade tolerant flowering azaleas or with winter flowering hellebores.

Contrasting textures and colours from *Rubus cockburnianus* 'Goldenvale', red valerian and other perennials.

Spiky Siberian iris leaves associated with the bright golden foliage of *Cornus alba* 'Aurea'.

Rubus cockburnianus with Other Herbaceous Plants

A mixed planting with mostly herbaceous perennials whose seasonal focal point is the vivid golden foliage of *Rubus cockburnianus* 'Goldenvale'. This is a suckering shrub which can be troublesome with its invasive habit, but whose year-round interest makes it a strong candidate for a mixed planting scheme. In autumn, the golden hue of the leaves intensifies before they fall. Any flowers or fruits that may be produced are worthless but after leaf fall, the suckering stems are clothed with a pale greyish white bloom, which makes them stand out in winter gloom with a ghostly outline. In spring, the young, emerging foliage is intensely gold, but this hue subsides to yellow-green as summer advances.

The habit of spreading by stolons (arching stem tips which take root) can be prevented by pruning all canes away annually in spring, just as the new foliage is about to emerge. Other plants in this border include foxgloves and valerian, for early colour, with campanulas and lilies behind. There would have been columbine flowers, for the recently concluded spring – the seed capsules are still visible – and a cedar tree brings height and winter interest. The planting, overall, is quiet and unobtrusive, enabling the beautiful rural background to be enjoyed without too much distraction in front.

Different Effects for Different Seasons from the Same Plants

Certain shrubs, when pollarded or coppiced – in other words, cut hard back to a low stump each year – will change their growth habits and appearance. The golden leaved *Cornus alba* 'Aurea' was cut back a month or two before this picture was shot. The young stems and large golden leaves make a beautiful contrast with the Siberian iris behind. Earlier, the iris bore deep blue flowers, but for now, the seed capsules are forming and in time will turn bright tan.

In winter, when the foliage has fallen from the Cornus, its bare young stems will become bright red, making an interesting harmony with the tan seed stalks and capsules of the iris. Other winning winter combinations might include the stinking hellebore (*Helleborus foetidus*), planted with *Cornus alba* 'Sibirica' – red stems against pale green flowers. *Salix daphnoides* has blue-grey stems and looks lovely underplanted with snowdrops, followed by winter crocuses such as *C. chrysanthus* or *C. ancyrensis*.

Alchemilla mollis teams up with the candy-striped blooms of
Rosa gallica 'Versicolor', also known as Rosa Mundi.

The New Zealand native, *Brachyglottis* 'Sunshine', makes
a happy host to floriferous *Potentilla napalensis*.

Floral Friendships

Shrubs, particularly low-growing or mound-forming types, can look beautiful when herbaceous plants are persuaded to flower among them. The old fashioned bi-coloured rose, *Rosa gallica* 'Versicolor' – often called Rosa Mundi – is a natural companion to its close botanical relative, *Alchemilla mollis* (Lady's Mantle). The lime-green flowers and lacy sprays complement the showy rose blooms pleasingly, but the Lady's Mantle will continue to flower and to produce decorative, rounded foliage long after the rose's brief flowering period. (*R. gallica* does not repeat-flower.)

These are both seasonal plants which, despite their summer glory, tend to look nondescript in winter and spring. The lady's mantle would be cut back to ground level in autumn and the rose will need pruning, though not severely, immediately after flowering. Such treatment worsens winter bareness but this would be simple to remedy with an underplanting of tulips or other spring bulbs, perhaps backed up by primulas, wallflowers or forget-me-nots.

Floral Hot-spots

Evergreen shrubs for a hot dry spot have immense value and this *Brachyglottis* 'Sunshine' brings a summer bonus of brilliant golden-yellow daisy blooms. The flowery seasonal effect has been brought to a more exciting pitch, however, by allowing the charming perennial *Potentilla nepalensis* to come up through the shrub and scatter its pretty rose-shaped pink blooms among the grey foliage and yellow daisy flowers. The effect can be quite long-lasting, too, provided the spent stems are removed promptly to encourage the perennial to produce a second flush.

Since the Brachyglottis will be as valuable for its winter foliage as well as for the summer flowers, it is important to make sure that the accompanying herbaceous plants do not overcrowd the stems of the shrub. Plants such as the potentilla have an open, airy habit, and with semi-lax stems strike exactly the right balance, supporting and enhancing, rather than dominating.

trees

Betula pendula

European Silver Birch   Hardy deciduous tree

A fast-growing, broadly columnar tree with slender branches whose young stems are pendulous and whose bark, when aged, takes on a pale silvery hue. Small, toothed, diamond shaped leaves are emerald when young but turn custard yellow before falling. Thin, short hanging catkins appear in spring and in autumn, seed production is copious.

Soil preference: Any
Aspect: Sun, part shade
Season of interest: Year round
Height and spread: 24m x 8m
(8oft x 25ft)

Companion plants: Effective planted in small groups or grown multi-stemmed, where the pale winter trunks and limbs contrast with such darker evergreens such as hollies or laurels.

Carpinus betulus

Hornbeam   Hardy deciduous tree

Medium to fast-growing tree with spreading canopy, greyish, lined bark and oval, pointed, slightly toothed leaves, dull green in summer and parchment to tan when falling. Catkins form in spring, followed by attractive leafy 'fruits'. Shapely in outline, when naturally grown, but also excellent as a hedging plant. Alternative varieties include the upright *C. b.* 'Fastigiata'.

Soil preference: Any not too dry
Aspect: Sun or part shade
Season of interest: Year round
Height and spread: 24m x 18m
(8oft x 6oft)

Companion plants: Robust trees for providing shelter, happy on soils too heavy for the similar-looking beech. Lovely with such flowering trees as *Prunus avium* or *P. padus*, and under-planted with shade-lovers such as epimediums.

Fraxinus excelsior

European or Common Ash   Hardy deciduous tree

Common North European tree, broadly columnar or spreading in outline with grey bark and thick young twigs whose dormant buds are black. The leaves are pinnate, dark green with poor autumn colour; flowers are insignificant and followed by one-winged fruits (samaras). Traditionally valuable coppiced as a source of excellent firewood. *F. e.* 'Jaspidea' has golden twigs and trunk.

Soil preference: Any
Aspect: Sun, part shade, shade
Season of interest: Year round
Height and spread: 3om x 18m
(1ooft x 6oft)

Companion plants: Not suitable for small gardens but handy for large wind breaks or to establish speedy woodland. Woodland floor plants from anemones in spring to autumn colchicums would naturalize well.

Fagus sylvatica   European Beech   Hardy deciduous tree

A large, spreading tree with smooth, grey bark and well-spread, slender branches. The shiny, prominently veined leaves are fluorescent green when young, darkening with maturity and turning tan before falling. Small inconspicuous flowers are followed by pointed, bristling fruit (mast) which contain tiny, edible nuts. Numerous varieties are available.

Soil preference: Any, not too heavy. Tolerates chalk
Aspect: Sun, part shade, shade
Season of interest: Year round
Height and spread: 30m x 15m (100ft x 50ft)

Companion plants: Very large as a specimen tree, but superb in outline, perhaps among stately magnolias or on acid soil with camellias and rhododendrons. Also one of the best hedging plants in cultivation.

Quercus rubra

Red Oak, Northern Red Oak   Hardy deciduous tree

A large, spreading tree with fissured bark and lobed leaves, typical of oaks, but whose lobed margins are toothed, rather than rounded. Their summer colour is fresh green, colouring red, then bright tan before falling. Acorns are formed in small, shallow cups. There is a gold leaf form, 'Aurea' (see page 415).

Soil preference: Any, neutral to acid, not too dry
Aspect: Sun, part shade
Season of interest: Year round
Height and spread: 30m x 20m (100ft x 65ft)

Companion plants: A fine tree to provide leaf contrast, in a mixed planting, especially when strong autumn colour is sought. Superb alongside field maple, beech or *Liriodendron tulipifera*.

Taxus baccata

Common Yew, English Yew, Irish Yew   Hardy evergreen tree

A slow growing, exceptionally long-lived tree with upright, then spreading habit. The sombre green foliage resembles the flattened 'needles' of a conifer but is soft to the touch. Small fruits form with fleshy, rose-red arils which enfold highly poisonous seeds. The resilient timber, used in Mediaeval times for bow-making polishes magnificently. The Irish Yew, *T. b.* 'Fastigiata', is pictured.

Soil preference: Any
Aspect: Sun, shade, part shade
Season of interest: Year round
Height and spread: 15m x 8m (50ft x 25ft)

Companion plants: Sombre and dark, for a small garden, but clipped yew is one of the best plants for hedging or topiary. As a backdrop for roses or colourful herbaceous plants, it is ideal.

Acer pseudoplatanus

Sycamore   Hardy deciduous tree

Large tree with an open habit and spreading branches. The large leaves are five-lobed, dark green with paler undersides and the blossoms small, greenish yellow. In late summer, two-winged fruits are formed and distributed copiously. Selected forms include a dark leaved 'Atropurpureum' and 'Brilliantissimum' (pictured) whose young foliage is shrimp pink.

Soil preference: Any
Aspect: Sun, shade, part shade
Season of interest: Year round
Height and spread: 30m x 24m
(100ft x 70ft)

Companion plants: Often considered a 'weed' tree but capable of growing in poor conditions where it can make an effective shelter for such shrubs as lilac or mock orange.

Abies nordmanniana

Nordmann Fir   Hardy conifer

A tall, columnar, handsome fir from western Asia with soft, slightly curved, blunt-ended 'needles' which are emerald green above when young, with pale, silvery undersides. The colour darkens as they mature. The cones are cylindrical and greenish-brown. The form 'Golden Spreader' is very slow growing with lime-green to yellow foliage. A popular species for use as Christmas trees.

Soil preference: Any free-draining, not too dry
Aspect: Sun, shade, part shade
Season of interest: Year round
Height and spread: 40m x 6m
(130ft x 20ft)

Companion plants: The bright young foliage makes a pretty backdrop to light coloured shrub roses or to preside over a perennial border. Hard to team with deciduous trees, but effective with yew, Cupressus or Cryptomeria.

Catalpa bignonioides

Indian Bean Tree   Hardy deciduous tree

A distinctive species with broadly spreading habit, native to southern North America. Almost horizontal branches bear huge, heart-shaped leaves which are rank smelling if bruised. White, speckle-throated, trumpet-shaped flowers appear as showy, upright panicles in summer, followed by long thin, dangling pods. The golden leaf form 'Aurea' is a worthy alternative for smaller gardens.

Soil preference: Any free-draining
Aspect: Sun, part shade
Season of interest: Spring, summer, autumn
Height and spread: 15m x 12m
(50ft x 40ft)

Companion plants: A beautiful specimen tree to spread its branches over an informal lawn, perhaps underplanted with naturalized fritillaries, camassias or species tulips.

Davidia involucrata

Dove Tree, Pocket Handkerchief Tree   Hardy deciduous tree

A broadly columnar tree, sometimes irregular in its outline when young, with medium sized broad but pointed, serrated leaves. In early summer the small, tufted flowers are joined to large, pure white, oblong, hanging bracts which resemble handkerchiefs. Not easy to establish, and may need encouraging to grow straight when young.

Soil preference: Humus-rich, free-draining but not too dry
Aspect: Part shade, sheltered
Season of interest: Early summer
Height and spread: 18m x 9m (60ft x 30ft)

Companion plants: For a sheltered garden, this is a tree to stand on its own. In a larger, woodland situation, site it with earlier blooming magnolias, camellias or rhododendrons.

Gingko biloba

Maidenhair Tree   Hardy deciduous tree

A large, very long-lived tree whose curious leaves resemble large-size versions of the maidenhair fern. They are two-lobed and triangular, with veins that radiate in straight lines at equal angles from the base of the leaf and turn rich yellow in autumn. Female trees bear yellowish fruit in late summer, which is evil-smelling. Clones include Pendula Group and the erect-growing 'Fastigiata'.

Soil preference: Any
Aspect: Sun or part shade
Season of interest: Spring, summer, autumn
Height and spread: 30m x 8m (100ft x 25ft)

Companion plants: Beautiful grown in isolation, as a specimen, but lovely when its yellow autumn foliage can contrast with the oranges and red of maples or the purplish red of *Fraxinus* 'Raywood'.

Liriodendron tulipifera

American Tulip Tree   Hardy deciduous tree

A huge, stately tree with broadly spreading branches which become almost horizontal with age. The distinctive leaves are nearly square but with extended, pointed corners, mid-green in summer, turning custard yellow on falling. Mature trees carry a crop of understated, yellow-green, tulip-shaped flowers in late spring. The smaller, more compact *L. chinense* (Chinese tulip tree) is a worthy alternative.

Soil preference: Any, not too dry
Aspect: Sun or part shade
Season of interest: Year round
Height and spread: 30m x 12m (100ft x 40ft)

Companion plants: A beautiful tree to grow as a dominant specimen in a large design, perhaps with smaller shrubs at its feet. Also beautiful to team with fellow American species *Magnolia grandiflora*.

Abies procera

Noble Fir Hardy conifer

A tall, striking, conical fir, native to the forests of western North America. The blue-grey needles lie along the tops of the branches, giving a soft, smooth feel when stroked from the trunk outwards. The cones, produced on mature trees, are cylindrical, long and narrow. The foliage of *A. p.* Glauca Group has more distinctly blue-grey foliage.

Soil preference: Any free-draining but not too dry
Aspect: Sun, part shade, shade
Season of interest: Year round
Height and spread: 35m x 8m (115ft x 25ft)

Companion plants: An outstanding forest tree for high rainfall areas, suitable only for large gardens and then, best grown in groups rather than singly. Striking if mixed with the brighter green, deciduous larch.

Magnolia campbellii

Campbell's Magnolia Hardy deciduous tree

Huge, gently fragrant pink flowers are produced at the tree top in spring, followed by curious fruits which split to display red seed. A gigantic magnolia which, when grown from seed, may take more than 30 years to reach flowering size. When grafted onto the rootstock of smaller magnolias, typically *M.* x *soulangeana* flowering may occur in less than seven years.

Soil preference: Humus-rich, moist but free-draining, lime-free
Aspect: Sun or part shade
Season of interest: Spring
Height and spread: 30m x 9m (100ft x 30ft), often less if grafted

Companion plants: Best for a large garden, to include in a bold woodland planting where it can preside over rhododendrons, camellias and perhaps *Michelia doltsopa*.

Zelkova serrata Hardy deciduous tree

A bold, spreading relative of the elm, with simple, narrow, oval leaves which are toothed and pointed. The tiny flowers are insignificant but the tree's main attraction is its superb russet orange autumn colour. The bark is smooth but flaky, revealing a pattern of colours including tan, green and beige.

Soil preference: Any fertile but free-draining, preferably neutral or acid
Aspect: Sun, part shade or shade
Season of interest: Year round
Height and spread: 25m x 18m (80ft x 60ft)

Companion plants: For a large planting scheme, in shelter, this tree makes a fine centre point. It benefits from space to develop a stately spread, but looks beautiful underplanted with naturalized spring flowers such as wild narcissus, primroses, camassias or meadow grasses.

Tilia cordata   Small Leaved Lime, Linden   Hardy deciduous tree

A broadly columnar tree with grey bark and soft, mid-green, rounded or heart-shaped leaves. The greenish yellow blossoms hang in small corymbs, each with an elongated bract and, though inconspicuous, are richly fragrant and irresistible to bees. The leaves turn golden yellow in early autumn, and are among the first to fall. Suitable for pollarding or pleaching.

Soil preference: Any free-draining, especially limy
Aspect: Sun, part shade or shade
Season of interest: Summer, autumn
Height and spread: 25m x 15m (80ft x 50ft)

Companion plants: Handsome in formal avenue planting with its own kind, but also lovely as a specimen tree, especially on poor, limestone soil. In wild landscapes, *T. cordata* associates with ash, often with *Euphorbia amygdaloides*, *Paris quadrifolia* and bluebells as understorey.

Ailanthus altissima

Tree of Heaven   Hardy deciduous tree

A vigorous, suckering tree with erect, then hanging stems and large, pinnate leaves which may be 70cm (28in) in length. Mature trees produce panicles of greenish flowers followed by rusty red-brown fruits (samaras). Suckering can prove troublesome and, in some regions, this Chinese species has become invasive.

Soil preference: Any
Aspect: Sun, part shade or shade
Season of interest: Summer, autumn
Height and spread: 25m x 15m (80ft x 50ft)

Companion plants: Handy for quick shade and shelter, but needs thoughtful positioning. Useful to preside over spring and summer shrubs such as Spiraea, Exochorda or Deutzia.

Eucalyptus gunnii

Cider Gum   Hardy evergreen tree

A Tasmanian native and probably the hardiest of the eucalypts whose adult leaves are blue-green, long, narrow, pointed and richly aromatic. The bark is smooth, tan and white and the juvenile leaves (pictured) are rounded and pale glaucous blue-grey. Though likely to sustain damage by prolonged frost, the tree will often regenerate from mature limbs or from the roots.

Soil preference: Any
Aspect: Sun
Season of interest: Year round
Height and spread: 24m x 8m (80ft x 25ft)

Companion plants: A large, vigorous tree that needs thoughtful positioning, but attractive as part of a modern planting scheme perhaps with very large grasses, yuccas and cannas.

Large Trees

Large trees are not suitable for small spaces but may form part of the background scenery where a private garden is set in a broader landscape. Even in extensive gardens, it is important to plan long term when planting trees and to calculate what dimensions the plant may have in five, ten, 20 or more years.

1.   **Castanea sativa**
Sweet chestnut, Spanish Chestnut
A massive tree whose bark markings spiral with age. The simple leaves are long and serrated, and prickly fruits split to produce edible chestnuts. Castanets were made with chestnut wood.

2.   **Ostrya virginiana**
American Hop Hornbeam
A tall, tapering tree with toothed, pointed leaves, yellow spring catkins and in autumn, pale fruits which resemble hops.

3.   **Magnolia grandiflora**
An American species which, in favourable conditions, grows to a substantial tree with large, evergreen foliage and huge, fragrant, creamy white blossoms.

4.   **Nothofagus obliqua**
Roblé Beech
A South American beech with dark green, oblong leaves which colour to russet red or yellow in autumn. Most of the southern beeches are desirable for large areas.

5.   **Nyssa sylvatica**
Black Gum or Tupelo
An American native, grown mainly for its superb autumn colour. The simple leaves fire up to bright orange and red.

6.   **Pterocarya fraxinifolia**
Caucasian Wingnut
A vigorous, suckering, spreading tree with large, pinnate leaves and dramatically long, dangling strings of winged seeds. Deciduous.

1	2	3
4	5	6

Crataegus monogyna

Hawthorn, Quickthorn, May Blossom   Hardy deciduous tree

Beautiful European native with spreading, rounded habit and, in age, a characterful, gnarled outline. The bark is attractively crazed, the branches sparsely but fiercely thorned and the deeply lobed leaves turn russet in autumn. The white blossoms, presented in clusters, are followed by small blood red fruits (haws). The plant has immense wildlife value.

Soil preference: Any
Aspect: Sun or part shade
Season of interest: Year round
Height and spread: 8m x 8m
(25ft x 25ft)

Companion plants: Perfect as a small, free-standing tree for year round beauty. Alternatively, mix it in tapestry hedging with *Viburnum opulus*, *Acer campestre*, hollies, honeysuckle and sloe (*Prunus spinosa*).

Alnus glutinosa

Common Alder   Hardy deciduous tree

A fast-growing, broadly columnar tree with rounded, slightly toothed leaves and in aged specimens, thick, corky bark. Male flowers consist of golden catkins hanging in clusters with the females which resemble little fir cones. The seeds are popular in winter with small, seed-eating birds. Garden forms include the cut leaved 'Laciniata' and gold leaved 'Aurea'. Good in poorly drained or wet conditions.

Soil preference: Any not too dry
Aspect: Sun or part shade
Season of interest: Year round
Height and spread: 18m x 10m
(60ft x 35ft)

Companion plants: Fine wildlife trees and excellent to plant with willows to form a shelter belt.

Cupressus macrocarpa

Monterey Cypress   Marginally hardy conifer

A large columnar, then spreading conifer with soft, aromatic, deep green twigs bearing tiny scale-like leaves and, in mature specimens, rounded, brown cones approximately 3cm (1in) in diameter. The bark is tan, on mature trees. Garden forms include 'Goldcrest' and the spreading 'Horizontalis Aurea'. One parent of the Leyland Cypress, the other being *Chamaecyparis nootkatensis*.

Soil preference: Any
Aspect: Sun
Season of interest: Year round
Height and spread: 30m x 10m
(100ft x 30ft)

Companion plants: A fine hedging plant for maritime locations but also striking as a senior tree, especially when underplanted with big grasses or, in warmer regions, with succulents.

Gleditsia triacanthos   Honey Locust   Hardy deciduous tree

A North American native with rounded or spreading habit whose young trunk is armed with triple spines but whose foliage is soft and ferny. Insignificant, greenish flowers are followed by curved pods. *G. t.* 'Rubylace' is thornless and has purple foliage; 'Sunburst' has gold tinged leaves whose colour deepens in autumn.

Soil preference: Any free-draining
Aspect: Sun
Season of interest: Summer
Height and spread: 30m x 20m (100ft x 60ft) – usually smaller in cultivation)

Companion plants: Fine trees to bring height to a sunny shrubbery, blending nicely with the related *Acacia baileyana* or *A. dealbata* or to effect a foliage contrast with Catalpa or Paulownia.

Picea pungens

Colorado Spruce   Hardy conifer

A Rocky Mountain native with conical habit and branches growing in whorls from a single main stem. The short to medium length, curved needles are a striking blue-grey and in mature specimens, medium-sized, narrow, cylindrical cones form. Good garden selections include 'Hoopsii', which has pale blue-green foliage, and the rich silver-blue 'Koster'.

Soil preference: Any free-draining, not too dry
Aspect: Sun, part shade
Season of interest: Year round
Height and spread: 15m x 5m (50ft x 16ft)

Companion plants: Fine accent trees for conifer collections, but more attractive in groups rather than singly. With *Picea abies*, *P. breweriana* or *P. omorika*, they make a superb contrast.

Laburnum alpinum, L. anagyroides

Laburnum   Hardy deciduous trees

Ubiquitous, spreading trees, rather untidy and sprawling when young, with three-lobed leaves, light brown bark and, in spring, hanging racemes of bright yellow pea flowers. Both species are decorative but the hybrid *L.* x *watereri* is the most widely grown and its form 'Vossii' is sterile, producing no seed. (Laburnum seeds are toxic if swallowed.)

Soil preference: Any free-draining. Not too wet
Aspect: Sun, part shade
Season of interest: Spring
Height and spread: 8m x 8m (25ft x 25ft)

Companion plants: The 'laburnum tunnel' will appeal to some, underplanted with purple alliums. For the adventurous, a laburnum grove might be pretty, underplanted with drifts of late purple tulips, naturalized *Chelidonium majus* and *Meconopsis cambrica*.

Acer griseum

Paperbark Maple   Hardy deciduous tree

Rounded, spreading tree whose most delightful feature is the tan-coloured, peeling, papery bark. The leaves are palmate, divided into three leaflets and, though dull green all summer, fire up to orange before falling. Hanging clusters of small flowers precede two-winged fruits with large seeds. Beautiful grown as a multi-trunked specimen

Soil preference: Any free-draining, not too dry
Aspect: Sun or part shade, must be sheltered
Season of interest: Year round, autumn
Height and spread: 12m x 10m (40ft x 33ft)

Companion plants: A charmer among maples but to perform it needs shelter and sun to colour the autumn leaves. Effective as a mixed border feature, with such perennials as Echinops, Anchusa or oriental poppies which can be cut back in winter, the better to display the bark.

Amelanchier lamarckii

Snowy Mespilus, Lamarck Serviceberry   Hardy deciduous tree

Elegant small tree with rounded habit and spreading branches. The foliage is silvery when it first emerges, then bright pea green for summer and a brilliant fiery orange or scarlet before falling. Long-petalled, white blossoms appear, in generous clusters in early spring and are followed, in mid-summer, by bright red to purple black fruits.

Soil preference: Any, not too dry but free-draining
Aspect: Sun or part shade
Season of interest: Year round
Height and spread: 9m x 9m (28ft x 28ft)

Companion plants: Pretty grown either as a shrub or a single trunked tree, especially with spring displays of cherry blossom, under-planted with spring bulbs. Also beautiful when contrasting with dark foliaged conifers such as junipers or cypresses.

Cercis siliquastrum

Judas Tree, Red Bud   Hardy deciduous tree

Ancient species and a prominent feature of the Mediterranean landscape. Spreading branches are transformed, before the kidney-shaped leaves emerge, by masses of vivid purplish pink pea flowers which grow directly from the branches and even the trunk, on very short stems. Later massed pods develop – 'siliquastrum' means 'pod bearing' – and last throughout the rest of the year.

Soil preference: Any free-draining
Aspect: Sun
Season of inerest: Spring, year round
Height and spread: 10m x 10m (35ft x 35ft)

Companion plants: Superb as a street tree, or as part of a mixed garden planting scheme, perhaps with such fellow Mediterranean species as Styrax, oleanders, olives or *Teucrium fruticans*.

Koelreuteria paniculata

Golden Rain Tree   Hardy deciduous tree

A native of China and Korea, this spreading, rounded tree has bold, bipinnate leaves whose scalloped edge leaflets create a ferny effect. Big sprays of bright yellow flowers emerge in summer, followed by loose clusters of pinkish fruits. The young, emerging foliage is pinkish, turning green as it matures, but yellowing just before leaf fall.

Soil preference: Any free-draining, not too dry
Aspect: Sun
Season of interest: Year round
Height and spread: 9m x 9m (30ft x 30ft)

Companion plants: Pretty as a specimen tree, where the leaves can throw shadow patterns on a lawn or on paving. Also pretty when planted to contrast with the bold leaves of *Magnolia grandiflora*.

Magnolia x soulangeana

Hardy deciduous shrub

A spreading but open-habited tree which works best when grown with a short trunk and well-distributed main limbs. The large, oval leaves have pointed tips and turn yellow before falling. The flowers are large, tulip-shaped and held erect. Typically, they are white, flushed with pink, but 'Brozzonii' has white flowers with a trace of purple in the outer petal base; 'Rustica Rubra' has goblet-shaped, reddish purple flowers.

Soil preference: Any free-draining, not too dry
Aspect: Sun or part shade
Season of interest: Spring
Height and spread: 6m x 6m (20ft x 20ft)

Companion plants: The most popular of all magnolias, lovely with spring flowers such as wallflowers, forget-me-nots, hyacinths, tulips, white narcissus or primulas at its feet.

Robinia pseudoacacia

Black Locust, False Acacia   Hardy deciduous tree

A broadly columnar tree with brittle branches and deeply fissured bark when aged. Leaves emerge late in spring and are pinnate, delicate and ferny in appearance. Hanging racemes of white flowers emerge in mid-summer, followed by dark seed pods. The form 'Frisia' (pictured) has golden foliage whose colour deepens in autumn.

Soil preference: Any free-draining
Aspect: Sun, part shade
Season of interest: Summer, autumn
Height and spread: 25m x 15m (80ft x 50ft), garden forms often smaller

Companion plants: The late emerging foliage reduces the problems of shading, so this is an excellent choice for underplanting with all manner of spring flowers such as polyanthus, anemones, pulmonarias, *Lathyrus vernus* and epimediums.

Arbutus unedo   Strawberry Tree   Hardy evergreen tree

A handsome, though sometimes unevenly shaped shrub or tree, whose mature trunks have peeling tan bark. The leaves are oval, pointed, slightly toothed and a deep green, making a beautiful contrast, not only with the creamy white, Chinese lantern-shaped flowers, which hang in small clusters, but also for the conspicuous, rough-skinned, edible fruits which turn orange before ripening to red.

Soil preference: Any not too dry but free-draining
Aspect: Sun or part shade
Season of interest: Year round
Height and spread: 8m x 6m (25ft x 20ft)

Companion plants: Perfect for bringing evergreen structure to a mixed shrub planting scheme, perhaps associating with rhododendrons, or to add winter substance to groups of hydrangeas whose leafless stems will not hide the attractive trunks and mature limbs in winter.

Crinodendron hookerianum

Chilean Lantern Tree   Marginally hardy, evergreen tree

A stiff, upright shrub or small tree with narrow, dark green, slightly glossy leaves and, in spring and early summer, masses of hanging flowers whose rose red petals are thick and leathery. They are shaped exactly like Chinese paper lanterns. Will not survive sustained frost.

Soil preference: Any fertile, free-draining
Aspect: Sun or part shade
Season of interest: Year round
Height and spread: 6m x 2m (20ft x 6ft)

Companion plants: A distinctive plant which will bring both character and height to a sheltered mixed border, perhaps with such fellow South American plants as *Lobelia tufa*, *Drimys winteri* or escallonias.

Drimys winteri   Winter's Bark   Marginally hardy, evergreen tree

Attractively columnar trees, native to South America, with waxy, glossy, evergreen leaves dark on top but paler, bluish-green beneath. In late spring, a generous display of small, richly fragrant, star-shaped, creamy white flowers are held in generous umbels. Protection from frost is essential and shelter from wind recommended.

Soil preference: Fertile, free-draining but not too dry
Aspect: Sun or part shade, must be sheltered
Season of interest: Spring, early summer
Height and spread: 15m x 9m (50ft x 30ft)

Companion plants: Essentially a tree for a warm, sheltered garden, at home with Australian bottle brushes, *Grevillea rosmarinifolia* and perhaps even the red-flowered Waratah, *Telopea speciosissima*.

Pyrus nivalis   Snow Pear   Hardy deciduous tree

A small, attractively shaped tree with gently ascending branches and narrow, slightly downy leaves with silvery white undersides. In spring the tree flowers profusely with clusters of small, five-petalled, all white blossoms and in autumn, the tiny 'pears' are rounded and yellowish green.

Soil preference: Any free-draining, not too dry
Aspect: Sun or part shade
Season of interest: Year round
Height and spread: 9m x 6m (30ft x 20ft)

Companion plants: The texture and hue of this foliage looks beautiful as a background for pink or red roses, or as part of a white planting scheme with *Campanula alliariifolia*, *Leucanthemum* x *superbum* or *Achillea ptarmica*.

Fraxinus ornus

Manna Ash   Hardy, deciduous tree

A native of southern Europe with ascending, then spreading branches medium sized, pinnate leaves. In spring, showy clusters of white or creamy, fragrant blossoms appear and are followed, in autumn, by narrow, single-winged fruit (samaras). The name is derived from the nectar which the tree weeps when cut.

Soil preference: Any free-draining
Aspect: Sun, shade, part shade
Season of interest: Spring, summer
Height and spread: 15m x 12m (50ft x 40ft)

Companion plants: More elegant than common ash and effective as a sheltering tree, perhaps underplanted with *Cyclamen repandum* and the Helleborus species that often associate with it in wild habitats. Also a striking flower foil for blue or purple lilacs.

Corylus colurna

Turkish Hazel   Hardy, deciduous tree

A distinctive tree from Asia Minor whose leaves are bold and heart-shaped with serrated margins. They turn to an intense yellow in autumn. The bark is deeply fissured and corky, on aged specimens, and the golden catkins attractive in late winter. If nuts form, usually only after a hot summer, the sheaths are longer and more decorative than those of *C. maxima*.

Soil preference: Any fertile, free-draining
Aspect: Sun, part shade
Season of interest: Year round
Height and spread: 24m x 8m (80ft x 25ft)

Companion plants: A striking tree, best on its own as a single specimen or in a small group, perhaps with silvery stemmed birches or gold-leaved *Catalpa bignonioides*.

Medium Trees

Medium-sized trees, except in the largest of gardens, will tend to act as focal points or are likely to form the highest point of each planting scheme. As well as such temporary advantages as blossoms, autumn leaf colour or fruit crops, one must also consider outline, shape and habit when making a selection.

1. **Aesculus indica**
Indian Chestnut
A smaller, more refined version of the familiar conker tree (*A. hippocastanum*) with smooth, shiny, palmate leaves and, in mid-summer, 'candles' of white blooms.

2. **Eucryphia x intermedia 'Rostrevor'**
An upright, evergreen tree whose most valuable characteristic is the mass of waxy white blossoms produced in late summer, when few other trees bloom.

3. **Crataegus laevigata 'Rosa Flore Pleno'**
Double-flowered pink hawthorn
A garden selection of the familiar Midland Hawthorn, whose blossoms consist of tightly packed petals. No fruit is produced.

4. **Embothrium coccineum**
Chilean Firebush
An upright, columnar tree whose scarlet-orange spider-like flowers are borne in spring and summer. A member of the protea family.

5. **Acer negundo**
Box Elder
A maple, unrelated to the elders, but with compound leaves which are unlike those of most other acers. Coloured varieties include the pink, cream and green 'Flamingo'.

6. **Idesia polycarpa**
A spreading tree with attractively tiered branches and heart-shaped leaves. The flowers lack petals but are fragrant and, in female trees, are followed by red berries.

7. **Paulownia tomentosa**
Foxglove Tree
A fast-growing tree with large, simple, slightly hairy leaves and in spring, upright spikes of big, lilac mauve foxglove flowers. Late frosts can damage emerging blooms.

Cryptomeria japonica   Japanese Cedar   Hardy conifer

A distinctive conifer whose juvenile foliage is soft to
the touch, and consists of green, curled stems and tiny
scale leaves. The adult foliage grows along the stems with
soft needle tips pointing towards the end of the branch.
Selections for garden use include Elegans Group, which
retains juvenile foliage and colours bronze in frost; the
tiny, compact 'Nana'; and the scrunched-up dwarf
'Bandai-sugu'.

Soil preference: Any
Aspect: Sun or part shade
Season of interest: Year round
Height and spread: To 30m
(100ft), but garden forms smaller

Companion plants: The smaller varieties
are useful for winter structure, in small
gravel or courtyard plantings, perhaps with
Japanese cultivars of *Hepatica nobilis*, if
shaded, or *Euphorbia myrsinites* and a range
of succulents in sun.

Genista aetnensis

Mount Etna Broom   Hardy deciduous shrub or small tree

A spreading shrub which needs coaxing into tree form by
pruning away side stems until a reliable, straight trunk has
developed. The young stems which are pendulous, are
constantly grey-green to green and in summer, carry
sparse numbers of small, three-lobed leaves. The pea
blossoms, which appear from mid-summer, are bright
yellow, showy and sweetly scented.

Soil preference: Any free-
draining
Aspect: Sun
Season of interest: Summer
Height and spread: 8m x 8m
(25ft x 25ft)

Companion plants: Charming small tree
for a sunny spot, especially when its yellow
flowers can be cooled by under plantings of
blue Caryopteris, Perovskia or *Salvia patens*.

Juniperus communis

Common Juniper   Hardy conifer

A highly variable, widespread species whose leaves –
always juvenile – are tiny, triangular and thorny to the
touch. The tendency is for a narrow, upright outline, but all
manner of shapes and sizes occur including weeping and
prostrate forms. *J. c.* var. *depressa* is tiny and narrow, and
'Hibernica', larger and also upright.

Soil preference: Any free-
draining
Aspect: Sun or part shade
Season of interest: Year round
Height and spread: Variable to
6m x 1m (20ft x 3ft)

Companion plants: An essential genus for
conifer lovers, traditionally planted with
heathers but also handy as structure plants
in small landscapes for restricted spaces.
Associates with other junipers such as
J. conferta and with dwarf birch, *Betula nana*.

Pyrus salicifolia   Willow Leaved Pear   Hardy deciduous tree

Graceful tree with dense growth and thin, slightly pendulous branches which are mealy and pale grey when young. The longish, narrow leaves are covered with silky down, when young, and such a pale grey-green as to appear almost white. The white blossoms are inconspicuous among the leaves. Selected forms include 'Pendula' and 'Silver Cascade'.

Soil preference: Any free-draining
Aspect: Sun, part shade
Season of interest: Spring, summer, autumn
Height and spread: 8m x 4m (25ft x 12ft)

Companion plants: A superb tree to plant near water, for reflections, or to back up a white or pink planting theme. The foliage is striking among dark blue irises, or, on mature specimens, with a deep blue clematis twining among the branches.

Rhus typhina

Stag's Horn Sumach   Hardy deciduous tree or large shrub

A suckering plant with stiff, wide-branching stems, velvety in texture, especially when young, and furnished with large, long, pinnate leaves. In autumn, these turn from mid-green to bright gold, then rich orange red before falling. The flowers are uninteresting but are followed by mace-shaped clusters of ruddy fruits. The form 'Dissecta' (*syn.* 'Laciniata') has more finely divided leaves.

Soil preference: Any
Aspect: Sun or part shade
Season of interest: Year round
Height and spread: 5m x 5m (16ft x 16ft)

Companion plants: Traditionally used as a lawn tree, where its suckers are frequently problematic, but very beautiful for backing an autumn border, planted with asters, Helianthus and Rudbeckia.

Salix exigua   Coyote Willow   Hardy deciduous tree

A vigorous, suckering or thicket-forming plant with erect, flexible wands or branches and long, tapering, narrow, silvery-grey leaves. The greenish yellow catkins are produced among the leaves, in mid-spring. A plant of outstanding beauty, moving gracefully with the wind and happy on poor, sandy soils.

Soil preference: Any well-drained
Aspect: Sun, part shade
Season of interest: Summer, autumn
Height and spread: 4m x 5m (12ft x 16ft)

Companion plants: Immensely useful for difficult soils, where it can create a background for strongly coloured flowers – *Rosa rugosa*, perhaps – or for a softer scheme with *Verbena bonariensis*, and such medium and large grasses as *Stipa gigantea* or *Eragrostis curvula*.

Abies koreana   Korean Fir   Hardy conifer

A slow-growing, slim, elegantly formal tree whose outline is narrowly conical, and whose neatly whorled branches become more irregular and characterful with age. The short, blunt needles are deep green on their upper sides and silvery grey below. Dramatic purple cones are borne, even on relatively young specimens. More drought resistant than most firs.

Soil preference: Any, well-drained but not too dry
Aspect: Sun or part shade
Season of interest: Year round
Height and spread: To 15m x 1.5m (50ft x 5ft)

Companion plants: Charming specimen for bringing height and structure, perhaps with lower evergreen shrubs such as *Mahonia japonica* at its feet or in a small group, underplanted with epimediums, or with hellebores.

Acacia baileyana

Cootamundra Wattle   Marginally hardy, evergreen tree

A rare wildling discovered in Cootamundra, in the Riverina region of New South Wales, Australia. The soft pinnate leaves have the appearance and texture of grey-green feathers, on this much-branched, rounded tree, and are joined, in very early spring, by a riot of fluffy, fragrant, yellow flowers. The cultivar 'Purpurea' has leaves suffused with bronze to purple.

Soil preference: Any free-draining
Aspect: Sun
Season of interest: Year round
Height and spread: 6m x 6m (20ft x 20ft)

Companion plants: One of the finest small wattles available, lovely in a sheltered garden with *Chimonanthus praecox*, for fragrance, or to preside over white narcissus or blue scillas. The foliage is a perfect foil for summer perennials, too.

Aesculus parviflora

Bottlebrush Buckeye   Hardy deciduous shrub or small tree

An elegant shrub or small tree from south-eastern North America, with spreading branches and suckering habit. The big, palmate leaves are greenish brown when young, maturing dark green. In early summer, slender, upright spires of showy, pure white flowers develop. A woodland plant which does best in semi-shade, but needs a hot summer to mature its buds.

Soil preference: Moisture-retentive, humus-rich
Aspect: Sun or part shade
Season of interest: Spring, autumn
Height and spread: 3m x 3m (10ft x 10ft)

Companion plants: A happy companion to Japanese maples, perhaps with foxgloves or Asian Meconopsis to flower among the stems.

Oxydendrum arboreum   Sorrel Tree   Hardy deciduous tree

A columnar, slow growing tree, often multi-trunked, with rusty red, fissured bark and hanging, narrowly oval leaves. In late summer, elegant racemes of creamy flowers hang and in autumn, the foliage takes on remarkable hues of red, orange and purple. A lover of stream sides and moist places, not suitable for chalky soil or exposed sites.

Soil preference: Lime-free, moist
Aspect: Sun, part shade
Season of interest: Summer, autumn
Height and spread: 3m x 1.5m (10ft x 5ft)

Companion plants: A beautiful relative of the rhododendron happy with heathers, Fothergilla, or grown alone, in a sheltered spot, as a specimen tree.

Cornus kousa   Chinese Dogwood   Hardy deciduous tree

Tree with upright, then spreading or arching branches whose shining, paired leaves are oval, pointed and have undulating margins. In spring, tufts of small, green flowers are surrounded by large, cream to white bracts, edged in pink. Big, strawberry-like fruit follow to ripen among leaves which turn bronze or red before they fall. *C. k.* var. *chinensis* has paler leaves.

Soil preference: Fertile, humus-rich, not too dry
Aspect: Sun, part shade
Season of interest: Spring, summer, autumn
Height and spread: 8m x 4.5m (25ft x 15ft)

Companion plants: Superb tree to include in a mixed shrubbery, especially near camellias, magnolias or with rhododendrons. The autumn colour teams well with the turning leaves of maples and the startling red of *Euonymus alatus*.

Trachycarpus fortunei

Chusan Palm   Hardy palm

One of the world's hardiest palms, originating from China. The slender, erect trunk is thickly clothed with fibrous material which looks like woven sacking and the stumps of the old leaf stems. The fronds are fan shaped, dark green, glossy and somewhat irregularly shaped. Big clusters of greenish yellow flowers are followed by purplish black fruits.

Soil preference: Any free-draining
Aspect: Sun or part shade
Season of interest: Year round
Height and spread: 10m x 2.5m (33ft x 8ft)

Companion plants: Useful for providing a spurious sense of the tropics, in a cold garden, perhaps in the company of yuccas, cannas and the surprisingly hardy Japanese banana *Musa basjoo*.

Sciadopitys verticillata

Japanese Umbrella Pine   Hardy conifer

A slow-growing conifer, beautiful when young, with stiff, vertical main stem and horizontal branches, going right down to ground level, creating a conical shape. The needle-like leaves are stiff, dark green and attached in whorls to the stems and in mature specimens, small, rounded cones from. The bark peels with age, in long, vertical strips.

Soil preference: Fertile, humus-rich
Aspect: Sun or part shade
Season of interest: Year round
Height and spread: 21m x 6m (70ft x 20ft)

Companion plants: A distinctive conifer, suitable for bringing a strictly conical outline to an informal grouping of more rounded shrubs such as Cotinus, Enkianthus or for formal grouping.

Hoheria sexstylosa

Lacebark, Ribbonwood   Hardy deciduous tree

A pretty New Zealand native and member of the hollyhock family. Greyish green, toothed, simple leaves hang on longish pedicels on gracefully pendulous stems. In mid-summer, a generous crop of creamy white flowers, also on longish stems, give the tree a superficial resemblance to a wild cherry in full spring blossom.

Soil preference: Lime-free, well-drained but not too dry
Aspect: Sun, sheltered
Season of interest: Summer
Height and spread: 6m x 3m (20ft x 10ft)

Companion plants: Useful tree for a sheltered mixed border, perhaps with Correa, Iochroma and such large perennials as *Lobelia tupa*.

Styrax japonicus

Japanese Snow Bell   Hardy deciduous tree

A graceful tree whose canopy of spreading branches is as attractive naked, in winter, as when in full leaf. In early summer, the narrowly oval, dark green leaves are joined by masses of star-shaped blossoms which hang like garlands along the branches. The foliage colours to gold and orange for autumn. Fully hardy, but best in regions where winters are gentle and wet.

Soil preference: Humus-rich, well-drained, preferably lime-free
Aspect: Part shade
Season of interest: Year round
Height and spread: 6m x 4m (20ft x 13ft)

Companion plants: Lovely to include in a woodland planting, perhaps to share the ground with Fothergilla and such summer-flowering magnolias as *M. sieboldii*, underplanted with bluebells or trilliums.

Prunus incisa 'Kojo-no-mai' Hardy deciduous dwarf tree

Slow growing, twiggy, shrub-like tree whose branches turn slightly at each leaf joint, presenting a zigzag outline. The small, oval, serrated leaves are emerald green when young, darkening during summer and turning vivid russet in the autumn. Small, pale pink, semi-double blossoms adorn the branches before the new leaves emerge, occasionally followed by tiny, inconspicuous fruits.

Soil preference: Any free-draining, not too dry. Fully lime tolerant
Aspect: Sun, part shade
Season of interest: Year round
Height and spread: 2m x 1.5m (6ft 6in by 5ft)

Companion plants: A superb little tree for containers or small gardens, happy in a variety of conditions and pretty with spring bulbs such as scillas, muscari or dwarf narcissus, perhaps with the autumn flowering *Geranium wallichianum* to set off the turning foliage.

Ulmus x hollandica 'Dampieri Aurea'

Golden Dutch Elm   Hardy deciduous tree

A compact, conical form of the much larger Dutch elm, slow growing with erect branches which bear oval, toothed, rough-textured leaves. When young, they are golden green, the pale hue becoming more subtly suffused as they age. Autumn colour is custard yellow.

Soil preference: Any free-draining
Aspect: Sun, part shade
Season of interest: Year round
Height and spread: 8m x 3m (26ft x 10ft)

Companion plants: A useful specimen tree, making a strong focal point, perhaps with dark leaved evergreens such as *Olearia macrodonta* or with shrub roses such as 'Mrs Anthony Waterer' (wine red flowers) or the apricot-flowered 'Buff Beauty'.

Crataegus tanacetifolia

Tansy Leaved Hawthorn   Hardy deciduous tree

A spreading, rounded tree whose trunk and branches become attractively gnarled and fissured with age. Some shoots are modified to form long, very sharp spines. The leaves are deeply divided, greyish white as they emerge, subsiding to green for summer and turning golden before falling. Clusters of large, creamy blossoms appear in early summer, followed by amber to scarlet fruits.

Soil preference: Any free-draining
Aspect: Sun
Season of interest: Year round
Height and spread: 8m x 6m (25ft x 20ft)

Companion plants: Pretty as a lawn tree, thriving on thin chalky or limy soils, or planted with such silver-leaved perennials as artemisias, helichrysums or *Teucrium fruticans*.

Small Trees

A small tree is easy to keep within bounds and is often so slow-growing that it is unlikely to outgrow its space for a long time. Tree shape, particularly in small scale schemes, has a strong influence on the ultimate character of the landscape, so care must be taken when choosing between, for example, rounded, conical, columnar, spreading or compact varieties.

1. Acer pseudoplatanus 'Brilliantissimum'
A form of sycamore whose leaf colour begins pallid pink as the leaf buds open, later becoming streaked with cream and very pale green. Because of limited chlorophyll, this plant stays small (see pages 420–1 for more acers).

2. Halesia monticola var. vestita
A naturally occurring form of the snowdrop tree whose pink-tinged, white hanging blossoms are produced in late spring just after the leaves have emerged.

3. Morus alba 'Pendula' Weeping white mulberry
A highly decorative form of the silkworm's food plant. Fruits, when they are produced, are pale, ripening pink. This tree can be large, but is often grown as a short or medium standard.

4. Mespilus germanica 'Nottingham' (Medlar)
A pretty member of the rose family with simple leaves and single flowers which resemble apple blossoms and less attractive, edible fruits whose blossom ends crack characteristically.

5. Ptelea trifoliata 'Aurea' Hop Tree
An aromatic plant with three-part leaves and trusses of greenish white flowers, which are followed in autumn by pale green, winged fruits.

1	2	3
4	5	

Pinus nigra   Austrian Pine   Hardy conifer

A rugged pine with a narrow, conical outline when young, but becoming 'umbrella shaped' as it ages. The long, rigid, dark green needles, produced in pairs, are closely packed on the branches. The bark is dark brown to black and deeply fissured, in old trees. One of the best windbreak trees for a large space, resistant to salt-laden winds.

Soil preference: Any free-draining
Aspect: Sun, part shade, shade
Season of interest: Year round
Height and spread: 30m x 6m (100ft x 20ft)

Companion plants: Too large for small gardens, but mixed with hollies, oaks and Scots pines, it would contribute to a beautiful and effective shelter belt.

Pinus radiata   Monterey Pine   Marginally hardy conifer

A fast growing pine, widely used in commercial forestry and in some regions, an invasive plant. The outline is narrowly conical, at first, becoming wide-canopied in old age. The slender, flexible needles are produced in threes, and the long-lasting cones have open scales. Suitable as shelter trees in large gardens with mild climate. Will not tolerate sustained frost.

Soil preference: Any free-draining
Aspect: Sun or part shade
Season of interest: Year round
Height and spread: 30m x 8m (100ft x 25ft)

Companion plants: A tree that demands careful placing due to unwelcome self-sowing in some sensitive habitats, but stately and beautiful as a backdrop in a coastal garden. Striking with *Cupressus macrocarpa*, maybe with the bright flowers of Lampranthus or Arctotis in the foreground.

Pinus sylvestris

Scots Pine   Hardy conifer

A lovely pine, conical when young, becoming irregular shaped with age, whose mature bark takes on a rich tan hue. The needles, produced in pairs, are long, flexible and glaucous blue-green. Small, pointed cones appear on mature trees. Many garden forms include the upright Fastigiata Group, the yellow-leaved Aurea Group and dwarf 'Watereri'.

Soil preference: Any free-draining. Good in sand
Aspect: Sun, part shade
Season of interest: Year round
Height and spread: 25m x 6m (80ft x 20ft)

Companion plants: A handy companion to broad leaved evergreens such as hollies, laurels or *Olearia macrodonta*. Superb planted where the sun will shine on the tan trunks, perhaps with hip-bearing shrub roses such as *R. moyesii* as a foil.

Cedrus deodara   Deodar Cedar   Hardy conifer

An Asian native, huge when mature, but narrowly conical in shape, while young, with horizontal to slightly pendulous branches and longish, soft, pale green needles which grow in clusters along the stems. The canopy becomes wider spreading, with age; the cones are egg or barrel shaped. The variety 'Aurea' is slower-growing, with pale foliage.

Soil preference: Any free-draining, not too dry
Aspect: Sun, part shade
Season of interest: Year round
Height and spread: 60m x 9m (200ft x 30ft)

Companion plants: A fine structure tree, while young, good in a group growing in grass, or to create a wind-resistant back drop to mixed shrub planting.

Larix decidua

European Larch   Hardy deciduous conifer

A tall, narrow conifer with brown or tan bark and, tufts of needles which are a vivid emerald green when they emerge in spring and which turn straw yellow before falling in the autumn. The female flowers are purplish pink, making a pretty contrast with the young leaves, and ripen into small, cylindrical cones in autumn.

Soil preference: Any free-draining
Aspect: Sun, part shade, shade
Season of interest: Spring, summer, autumn
Height and spread: 30m x 10m (100ft x 33ft)

Companion plants: The fresh green foliage contrasts strikingly with white trunks of birches, or against darker evergreen screen plants such as camellias or hollies.

Populus tremula

Quaking Aspen   Hardy deciduous tree

A vigorous, suckering tree with invasive root system and grey bark. Mature trunks support a wide, spreading canopy but the plant's natural habit is to form dense thickets. The leaves are diamond shaped, pale grey-green and slightly toothed, displaying a unique shimmering or trembling effect – and sound like gently falling rain – when a breeze causes the slightest movement.

Soil preference: Any not too dry
Aspect: Sun, part shade
Season of interest: Summer
Height and spread: 15m x 10m (50ft x 33ft)

Companion plants: Handy trees for use where others will not grow, but unsuitable near walls or water courses due to invasive roots. Handsome with dark green conifers such as *Cupressus radiata* or *Pinus nigra*.

Juniperus communis 'Compressa'

Dwarf hardy conifer

A very slow growing conifer shaped like an exclamation point with tightly packed, vertical stems, each furnished with tiny needle-like scale leaves. The colour runs through subtle forms of blue-green to grey, through the season. The neat, formal shape is retained pretty well, even with aged specimens.

Soil preference: Any, free-draining
Aspect: Sun or part shade
Season of interest: Year round
Height and spread: 60cm x 20cm (2ft x 10in)

Companion plants: Perfect for a containerised miniature garden of such Alpines as Jovibarba, Sempervivum, Aubrieta, *Geranium farreri*, Gentians and little bulbs such as *Iris histrioides*, *Crocus sieberi* and *Leucojum autumnale*.

Aralia elata   Angelica Tree   Hardy deciduous tree

A distinctive, suckering plant, needing a large container. The thick, stumpy stems are armed with thorns when young and carry plump buds from which huge, compound leaves extend and are held almost horizontal. In late summer, mature stems produce big sprays of creamy white flowers. Remove suckers to encourage the single stem to flower.

Soil preference: Any humus-rich, free-draining but not too dry
Aspect: Sun or part shade, needs shelter
Season of interest: Spring, summer, autumn
Height and spread: To 10m x 2m (35ft x 6ft) – smaller in containers

Companion plants: A bold, brash plant, lovely to surround with containers planted with smaller, softer subjects such as fuchsias, heliotrope, pelargoniums and other summer flowers.

Luma apiculata

Chilean Myrtle, Temu   Near hardy evergreen tree

A strong-growing, though frost-sensitive myrtle from South America whose main feature is the beautiful bark which is dappled with deep cinnamon and contrasting pale grey. The dark green, glossy leaves are small and rounded and the flowers, produced in clusters, are creamy white. Small purple fruits follow.

Soil preference: Any humus-rich, free-draining
Aspect: Sun
Season of interest: Year round
Height and spread: 10m x 6m (30ft x 20ft)

Companion plants: In a large container, the bark and foliage make a striking feature, perhaps with such trailing plants as *Persicaria vacciniifolia* or Plectranthus to flow over the edge. Other containers of dwarf rhododendrons also associate attractively.

Chamaerops humilis

Mediterranean Fan Palm   Marginally hardy dwarf palm

A distinctive, suckering evergreen of the Mediterranean Garrigue and Maquis (scrubland) whose dark green, fan-palm leaves are attached to short, stiff trunks, often growing in dense clusters. The flowers are beige to yellow. A variable species which, in the wild, is usually short stemmed and spreading but which sometimes produces a single stem or group of stems exceeding the height stated below.

Soil preference: Any free-draining
Aspect: Sun
Season of interest: Year round
Height and spread: Variable
1.5m x 1m (5ft x 3ft)

Companion plants: A tough pot subject, suitable for a hot, dry spot and attractive with such succulents as Echeveria, Crassula and Agave.

Buxus balearica

Balearic Box   Hardy evergreen tree

A twiggy, dense-growing evergreen with small, shiny, oblong, deep green leaves and tiny, insignificant flowers. The habit is more upright than that of common box (see page 290) and the foliage colour a darker green with a hint of blue. Ideal for topiary or hedging – especially for upright shapes – but will not survive penetrating, sustained frost.

Soil preference: Any free-draining
Aspect: Sun or part shade
Season of interest: Year round
Height and spread: 5m x 2m
(15ft x 6ft)

Companion plants: A useful evergreen for living sculpture, whose leaf colour and shape will contrast with common box, hollies, rosemary or lavender.

Ilex crenata   Japanese Holly   Hardy, evergreen tree

A spreading, slow-growing, twiggy holly with stiff but semi-pendulous branches and tiny, oval, notched leaves. The small flowers are white and produce, on female trees, small black, or occasionally yellow, berries. Various garden forms of this slow but shapely plant include the gold leaved 'Golden Gem', upright 'Fastigiata' and silver variegated 'Shiro-fukurin'.

Soil preference: Any free-draining, not too dry
Aspect: Sun, part shade or shade
Season of interest: Year round
Height and spread: 5m x 3m
(15ft x 10ft)

Companion plants: Pretty as sole occupants of large containers, but also attractive in Alpine plantings with gentians, saxifrages and autumn or spring bulbs.

Fagus sylvatica 'Dawyck' Hardy deciduous trees

Candle flame shaped, or columnar trees whose branches are held at very acute angles to the main stem. The leaves are fresh green when very young, darkening with age and turning tan before falling. 'Dawyck Purple' has coppery red young foliage, darkening purple. 'Dawyck Gold' retains the golden green hue until mid-summer, but returns to gold before the leaves fall.

Soil preference: Any free-draining
Aspect: Sun, part shade
Season of interest: Year round
Height and spread: 18m x 5m (60ft x 16ft)

Companion plants: Fine specimen trees, but they do need space and will spread and splay with age. Gold and purple foliage is lovely when contrasted either by planting both colours or with golden elders *Sambucus nigra* 'Aurea', purple *Prunus cistena* or red hazel (*Corylus maxima* 'Purpurea').

Ilex aquifolium 'Green Pillar' Holly

Hardy evergreen tree

A superbly self-disciplined holly which retains its narrowly conical or columnar shape, producing short branches at very acute angles to the main stem. The lustrous, dark green foliage is classic holly-shaped, with deep scalloping and long prickles. A moderate to heavy crop of berries is produced, provided a male holly grows within bee range.

Soil preference: Any, free-draining, not too dry
Aspect: Sun, part shade
Season of interest: Year round
Height and spread: 2m x 10m (6ft x 30ft)

Companion plants: One of the most striking specimen trees, never boring and lovely if it can preside over Christmas roses (*Helleborus niger*) for winter, perhaps with *Cyclamen coum* and snowdrops among them. Also superb for planting in bold groups, possibly with *Betula utilis* for contrast.

Carpinus betulus 'Fastigiata' Hardy deciduous tree

A broadly candle flame-shaped tree the bottom of whose canopy broadens and spreads with age, but which retains the pointed, cone-shaped crown. The foliage is oval, pointed, toothed and a fresh green, turning beige to brown before falling. Flowers are in the form of attractive, leafy catkins, produced in late spring, followed by leafy 'fruits.' *Carpinus betulus* 'Columnaris' is more compact.

Soil preference: Any not too dry, but free-draining
Aspect: Sun, part shade
Season of interest: Year round
Height and spread: 15m x 10m (50ft x 30ft)

Companion plants: Good 'lawn trees' creating some shade, but not greedy for space until they age. Lovely underplanted with meadow subjects such as *Fritillaria meleagris*, wild narcissus, cowslips and, for autumn, colchicums.

Prunus 'Amanogawa'   Hardy deciduous tree

A multi-trunked tree with upright stems and branches and large, oval to oblong, toothed leaves which are coppery as they emerge, soon turning dull green and firing up again in the autumn. In spring, a large crop of mid- to pale pink, semi double, faintly fragrant flowers is produced. Trees are inclined to splay, with age, unless held in with wire hoops.

Soil preference: Any free-draining, not too dry
Aspect: Sun, part shade
Season of interest: Spring; Year round
Height and spread: 8m x 3m (25ft x 10ft)

Companion plants: A pretty tree for a focal point, perhaps among other shrubs such as low-growing cotoneasters, shrub roses for summer colour and autumn fruit, or with late-flowering herbaceous plants such as asters, phloxes, sidalceas or achilleas.

Juniperus scopulorum 'Skyrocket'

Upright Rocky Mountain Juniper   Hardy conifer

A medium paced juniper with a tall, slim outline. The adult foliage consists of small scale leaves covering loosely packed, upright twigs. The tree retains its formal shape for about 15 years, but with age the branches are inclined to splay outwards, especially after snow, unless held in place with wires.

Soil preference: Any free-draining
Aspect: Sun
Season of interest: Year round
Height and spread: Up to 6m x 75cm (20ft x 3ft)

Companion plants: A superb medium term landscape plant, striking in a group but also useful individually as a focal point for mixed perennial planting, or in gravel with grasses, sedges and rocks.

Quercus robur 'Fastigiata'   Hardy deciduous tree

A slow-growing, ramrod-straight tree which bulges only very slightly at the middle in age and whose branches are held at very acute angles to the main stem. The typical oak leaves are lobed and dark green, turning yellow, then brown before falling in late autumn. Acorns are produced on mature trees which may also bear several different kinds of gall.

Soil preference: Any free-draining
Aspect: Sun, part shade, shade
Season of interest: Year round
Height and spread: 15m x 3m (50ft x 10ft)

Companion plants: A beautiful and wildlife friendly tree, fine as a central statement singly, or to stand in a group with its own kind. Also beautiful with large-flowered Cornus species nearby or perhaps eucryphias for late summer blossoms.

Fraxinus excelsior 'Pendula'

Weeping Ash   Hardy, deciduous tree

A weeping form of the ash described on page 366. The tree benefits from training, while young, to achieve height before the branches are allowed to hang down, forming a huge, spreading dome of summer foliage and naked, rib-like branches in winter. There is also a golden form, *F. e.* 'Aurea Pendula', which grows smaller than the green.

Soil preference: Any
Aspect: Sun, shade or part shade
Season of interest: Year round
Height and spread: 15m x 15m
(50ft x 33ft)

Companion plants: This is really a solo plant, and needs plenty of space, but winter bulbs such as snowdrops, aconites and small bulbous iris usually have time to complete much of their life cycle before the leaves obscure them.

Betula pendula 'Youngii'

Young's Weeping Birch   Hardy deciduous tree

A slender, weeping form of the common silver birch described on page 366. The trunks and main limbs are the same pale silver-grey as those of common *B. pendula* but the branches are much more pendulous. Young trees need support to develop a good trunk before the branches can be allowed to weep.

Soil preference: Any free-draining
Aspect: Sun, part shade or shade
Season of interest: Year round
Height and spread: 8m x 4m
(26ft x 13ft)

Companion plants: A pretty tree to spread its branches over spring underplanting, particularly of daffodils or narcissus. Also excellent in a group.

Ilex aquifolium 'Argentea Marginata Pendula'

Silver Weeping Holly, Weeping Holly   Hardy evergreen tree

A graceful holly with reasonably upright main stem but pendulous branches whose sparsely prickled, glossy green leaves are subtly margined with silver variegations. Small white flowers are followed by a crop of blood red berries, provided there is a male tree in the vicinity for pollinating. *I. a.* 'Pendula' is a weeping holly with green leaves.

Soil preference: Any, free-draining, not too dry
Aspect: Sun, part shade, shade
Season of interest: Year round
Height and spread: 5m x 3m
(15ft x 10ft)

Companion plants: Charming as a poolside tree, or where it can weep over an informal planting scheme. The subtle foliage markings go well in a white garden, perhaps with *Anemone* 'Honorine Jobert' or with any white-flowered roses and lilies.

Laburnum alpinum 'Pendulum' Hardy deciduous tree

A slow growing, weeping form of the familiar laburnum (page 375) whose main trunk needs support to the desired height and whose branches are profoundly pendulous. Three-lobed leaves, emerald green in colour, set off the long racemes of bright yellow flowers in mid- to late spring. The seeds are poisonous.

Soil preference: Any free-draining
Aspect: Sun or part shade
Season of interest: Spring
Height and spread: 5m x 5m (16ft x 16ft)

Companion plants: A fine specimen tree, lovely if purple drumstick alliums are set to contrast or with drifts of intense yellow *Meconopsis cambrica* to harmonize.

Larix kaempferi 'Pendula'

Weeping Japanese Larch   Hardy deciduous conifer

The Japanese larch is very similar in habit to *Larix decidua*, described on page 391. The form 'Pendula' has gracefully hanging branches and a more spreading habit whereas *L. k.* 'Stiff Weeping' has more markedly down-turned limbs. Hybrid weeping larches include 'Varied Directions' whose horizontal limbs are hung with limp lateral branches.

Soil preference: Any free-draining
Aspect: Sun or shade. Pollution tolerant
Season of interest: Year round
Height and spread: 8m x 5m (25ft x 15ft)

Companion plants: Valuable feature trees for creating an interesting outline, perhaps over water, or as single focal points, under-planted with yellow winter aconites, perhaps, Welsh poppies or naturalized columbines.

Prunus 'Kiku-Shidare-Zakura'

Cheal's Weeping Cherry   Hardy deciduous tree

A spreading, weeping tree whose toothed, oval and pointed leaves are coppery when newly emerged, soon turning dull green, and whose heavy crop of pendant, fully double flowers are bright, shell pink. The leaves take on a gentle russet hue, in favourable autumn weather.

Soil preference: Any free-draining, not too dry
Aspect: Sun or part shade
Season of interest: Spring
Height and spread: 3m x 3m (10ft x 10ft)

Companion plants: A popular lawn tree, lovely underplanted with pulmonarias, hellebores, small daffodils or *Anemone blanda*.

Aesculus hippocastanum

Horse Chestnut, Conker   Hardy deciduous tree

Popular, fast growing tree with a broadly columnar or spreading habit. Thick twigs have tips in winter bearing large, glutinous ('sticky') buds which open to produce bold, palmate leaves. Late spring blossoms are held in erect spikes, but each flower has a small red pollen guide and prominent stamens. Fruits in autumn are sparsely armed with soft thorns and split to reveal highly polished seeds or 'conkers'.

Soil preference: Any
Aspect: Sun or part shade
Season of interest: Year round
Height and spread: 30m x 18m (100ft x 6oft)

Companion plants: A street tree, but cursed by having soft, brittle wood which can cause large limbs to fall. Valuable as a landscape tree for avenues or parkland or to use as a single specimen, best underplanted with spring bulbs.

Alnus incana   Grey Alder   Hardy deciduous tree

A variable species, very widespread in the wild, with grey bark, grey downy young shoots and simple, dull green leaves. The clusters of male catkins hang among more rounded female flowers which mature into cone-like fruits. Good forms include 'Aurea', whose gold-tinged leaves contrast with reddish young stems and 'Laciniata' which has narrowly lobed or cut leaves.

Soil preference: Any not too dry but free-draining
Aspect: Sun, part shade, shade
Season of interest: Year round
Height and spread: 20m x 9m (65ft x 3oft)

Companion plants: Equally handy as a specimen tree or as wind-proofing background. Large companions could include conifers, hollies, hawthorns. Underplanting could be with early spring perennials such as *Lathyrus vernus*, Thermopsis and *Brunnera macrophylla*.

Malus x scheideckeri   Crab Apple   Hardy deciduous tree

Compact, small trees with simple, dull green, toothed or serrated leaves which turn gold in autumn, before falling, and which are coppery when they emerge in spring. The spring blossoms appear just ahead of the leaves and are red or pink in bud, opening pale pink with white interiors. Fine garden forms include 'Hillieri' (scarlet buds opening pale pink) and 'Red Jade', whose pink blossoms are followed by red fruit.

Soil preference: Any fertile, free-draining
Aspect: Sun or part shade
Season of interest: Spring
Height and spread: 4.5m x 2m (15ft x 6ft)

Companion plants: Perfect for bringing drama to small gardens, these make excellent companions to spring shrubs such as Exochorda or lilacs; or use as solo trees, underplanted with primroses or cowslips.

Morus nigra   Black Mulberry   Hardy deciduous tree

A broadly spreading tree with attractively fissured, bright brown bark and large, rough-textured leaves whose edges are serrated and which turn yellow in autumn before falling. The luscious but tart fruits are pink when immature, turning black as they ripen. As they age, mulberry trees acquire great character.

Soil preference: Any
Aspect: Sun or part shade
Season of interest: Year round
Height and spread: 10m x 12m
(40ft x 50ft)

Companion plants: Superb specimens, to use on their own, simply underplanted with such naturalised bulbs as *Crocus tommasinianus*, *Fritillaria meleagris*, *Anemone blanda* and autumn colchicums planted in rough grass.

Platanus x hispanica

London Plane   Hardy deciduous tree

Familiar street tree with bark which sloughs off in patches, creating attractive patterns as well as helping the tree to resist air pollution. The leaves are three or five lobed, large, and very slow to rot down after falling. In late spring, small clusters of inconspicuous flowers develop and are followed by rounded, fibrous fruits.

Soil preference: Any
Aspect: Sun, part shade or shade
Season of interest: Year round
Height and spread: 30m x 20m
(100ft x 65ft)

Companion plants: A fine tree for pleaching or pollarding, and therefore useful for planting in avenues or groves. Lovely underplanted with bulbs.

Pyrus calleryana

Callery Pear   Hardy deciduous tre

Variable species with glossy, simple leaves and, in spring, a profuse and dramatic display of white blossoms. Small brownish fruits develop, in autumn, when the foliage fires up to a vivid russet or orange. The form 'Chanticleer' (pictured) has a semi-erect habit and flowers profusely.

Soil preference: Any, fertile, free-draining but not too dry
Aspect: Sun or part shade
Season of interest: Year round
Height and spread: 12m x 10m
(40ft x 33ft)

Companion plants: Valued as a street tree and excellent as a structure plant, either as a lone specimen, or associated with such other species as *Acer japonicum* or *A. palmatum*, whose foliage will help extend the autumn colour display.

Pyrus communis

Domestic pears (see also page 401)   Hardy deciduous tree

Most fruiting pear varieties are charming when grown as ornamentals. The foliage is glossy and pretty in spring; the blossoms make a pleasant display and the fruit look beautiful as well as tasting good. 'Conference' is a dependable self-pollinator with long, green fruit but 'Doyenne du Comice' produces beautiful plump pears which are suffused in copper red as they ripen.

Soil preference: Any free-draining
Aspect: Sun
Season of interest: Year round
Height and spread: Variable, depending on grafting rootstock

Companion plants: For formal effects, they can be trained as a cordon or espalier specimens, but are also beautiful when free-standing, perhaps near others in an orchard, or in a border with sun-loving shrubs such as Ceanothus or Buddleja.

Arbutus menziesii

Madron   Hardy evergreen tree

A shapely, spreading tree whose main distinguishing feature is the peeling cinnamon tan bark. The leaves are medium sized, oval, slightly serrated, leathery and dark green. The clusters of small, creamy white, lantern-shaped flowers are produced copiously during the first half of summer, followed by orange fruits.

Soil preference: Preferably lime-free, not too dry
Aspect: Sun or part shade
Season of interest: Year round
Height and spread: 15m x 15m (50ft x 50ft)

Companion plants: A superb tree for a moist climate, best grown in isolation so that its trunk may be admired. Companion plantings of such shrubs as *Pieris forestii*, dwarf rhododendrons, Fothergilla and perhaps *Cercis canadensis* 'Forest Pansy' help to complete the picture.

Cotoneaster serotinus

Hardy, evergreen shrub or tree

Large shrub, easy to train single trunked as a small, spreading tree with oblong, dark green leaves whose undersides are paler, and whose young stems slightly downy. Clusters of small white flowers are produced in summer and followed by a heavy crop of rounded, bright red berries which persist through autumn.

Soil preference: Any reasonably fertile, free-draining
Aspect: Sun or part shade
Season of interest: Year round
Height and spread: 8m x 3m (25ft x 15ft)

Companion plants: A fine berry tree to group with spring flowering lilacs or mock orange, or to set in a border with late flowering perennials such as asters or yellow daisies.

Tilia x euchlora   Hardy deciduous tree

A large, stately tree with large, heart-shaped, toothed, vivid green leaves and slightly pendulous branches. In mid- to late summer, small, loose clusters of greenish fragrant flowers appear, followed by hard green fruits. Unlike many limes, this one resists aphids and does not therefore drip honeydew.

Soil preference: Any free-draining
Aspect: Sun or part shade
Season of interest: Year round
Height and spread: 20m x 15m (70ft x 50ft)

Companion plants: A superb avenue tree, adaptable for pleaching or growing naturally. In formal plantings, pleached limes will associate well with clipped lavenders, box or bay.

Pyrus communis

Wild Pear (see also page 400)   Hardy deciduous tree

Original wild form from which domestic pears have been bred. The leaves are narrowly oval, glossy when mature and coppery as they emerge. The copious blossoms are pure white and produced in early to mid-spring. Small, hard, inedible pears follow. The form 'Beech Hill' is more narrowly columnar in shape.

Soil preference: Any free-draining
Aspect: Sun
Season of interest: Spring
Height and spread: 15m x 8m (50ft x 30ft)

Companion plants: A useful tree for natural growth as part of a screen, perhaps with crab apples and hawthorns, or set as a specimen grown in turf, with such climbers as honeysuckle or non-invasive clematis to grow through the branches.

Tilia cordata   Small Leaved Lime   Hardy deciduous tree

A European species common on calcareous soils, broadly columnar in shape and having heart-shaped serrated leaves accompanied, in mid-summer, by small clusters of pale green, intensely fragrant flowers which hang just below a long, narrow bract. The leaves turn yellow before falling, relatively early in autumn, and are late to emerge in spring.

Soil preference: Any free-draining, alkaline
Aspect: Sun, part shade, shade
Season of interest: Year round
Height and spread: 25m x 15m (82ft x 50ft)

Companion plants: One of the best species for pleaching or training and beautiful if underplanted with such woodland plants as *Iris foetidissima*, *Euphorbia amygdaloides*, *Anemone nemorosa*, snowdrops and violets.

Sorbus aucuparia

Rowan, Mountain Ash   Hardy deciduous tree

A slender-trunked, upright, then spreading tree with smooth, tan bark and pinnate leaves which are slightly toothed. In spring, umbels of creamy white, malodorous blossoms develop among the fresh foliage and are followed, in mid- to late summer by big clusters of fruits which turn orange, then red, contrasting with the yellowing leaves.

Soil preference: Any
Aspect: Sun or part shade
Season of interest: Year round
Height and spread: 10m x 8m
(30ft x 25ft)

Companion plants: Beautiful as part of a screen or for woodland planting with hazel, holly or hawthorn, or as a specimen tree underplanted with such late flowering species as *Cyclamen hederifolium* and autumn colchicums.

Crataegus orientalis (syn. C. laciniata)

Oriental hawthorn   Hardy deciduous tree

A much branched, sturdy tree with spreading branches and rounded habit. The deeply divided leaves are dark green, in summer, but turn yellow before falling. Corymbs of showy, creamy white blossoms appear in early to mid-summer, followed by large orange-red haws. A native of southern Europe and Asia Minor.

Soil preference: Any
Aspect: Sun or part shade
Season of interest: Year round
Height and spread: 6m x 6m
(20ft x 20ft)

Companion plants: A superb wildlife tree, hosting many invertebrates and providing nutritious fruits for winter birds. Suitable for under-planting with such wildlife-friendly plants as *Mahonia japonica* and *Iris foetidissima*. Honeysuckle could be woven through mature specimens.

Ilex aquifolium 'J. C. van Tol'

Holly   Hardy evergreen tree

A vigorous, handsome holly whose deep green, lustrous leaves are sparsely prickled and barely scalloped, and whose young stems have a purplish cast. Probably the most dependable berry producer, being partially self fertile. Berrying is heavier, however, if there is a male tree nearby. 'Golden van Tol' has yellow margined leaves.

Soil preference: Any free-draining, not too dry
Aspect: Sun, part shade, shade
Season of interest: Year round
Height and spread: 20m x 6m
(65ft x 20ft)

Companion plants: One of the best hollies for hedging or for making screens, especially if grown with a male such as *Ilex* x *altaclerensis* 'Hodginsii'. Also superb as a solo lawn tree.

Malus 'Golden Hornet'   Crab Apple   Hardy deciduous tree

A compact crab apple with neat habit and attractive winter outline. Simple, slightly serrated leaves are held on fairly upright branches which spread as the tree ages. The white blossoms open from pink buds and, in autumn, oblong yellow fruits develop and turn to old gold as they mature. The fruit, popular with wild birds, is also suitable for making jelly.

Soil preference: Any reasonably fertile, free-draining
Aspect: Sun or part shade
Season of interest: Spring, autumn
Height and spread: 7m x 5m (23ft x 16ft)

Companion plants: A useful tree for a wildlife-friendly garden, pretty alongside hawthorn and holly or to blend with such smaller shrubs as *Kerria japonica* and flowering currants.

Salix caprea

Goat Willow, Pussy Willow, Sallow   Hardy deciduous tree or large shrub

A variable, suckering tree with broadly oval, grey-green leaves and, from late winter, silvery catkins which, on male plants bear conspicuous golden anthers. Pollination is by bumble bees and by wind. Responds well to pollarding or hard pruning, but has an invasive root system. The weeping form 'Kilmarnock' (pictured) is often used, grafted to an upright stock.

Soil preference: Any not too dry
Aspect: Sun or part shade
Season of interest: Winter, spring
Height and spread: Variable, 5m x 5m (16ft x 16ft)

Companion plants: Food plant of several interesting moths; loved by early bumble bees, this willow teams well with other hedging materials such as field maple, hawthorn, blackthorn or holly.

Tilia 'Petiolaris'

Weeping Lime   Hardy deciduous tree

A graceful lime with upright stature, but gently pendulous branches. The heart-shaped, serrated leaves are pale silvery green on their undersides, darker on top, and in mid- to late summer, corymbs of sweet smelling, greenish yellow petalled flowers are produced in profusion, followed by hard fruits. The form 'Chelsea Sentinel' is more columnar in habit.

Soil preference: Any fertile but free-draining
Aspect: Sun or part shade
Season of interest: Year round
Height and spread: 30m x 20m (100ft x 6oft)

Companion plants: Though suitable for pollarding, this lime is superb as a free standing specimen or for a large avenue.

Conifers

Conifers were widely over-used during the 20th century but became somewhat passé by the 1990s. If selected prudently, however, such genera as Pinus, Picea, Abies, Cupressus, Tsuga and Juniperus can make a rich contribution to contemporary creative planting. Furthermore, since most are evergreen, their value for winter structure cannot be over emphasised.

1. **Araucaria araucana**
Monkey Puzzle
A southern hemisphere conifer from Chile whose pointed, scale-like leaves and symmetrical growth habit make it unmistakeable. On female trees, large, spiny fruits appear and contain edible nuts.

2. **Cupressus sempervirens**
'Stricta'
A narrow, columnar form of the Mediterranean or Italian cypress, much used in European landscape design and frequently seen in Mediaeval and Renaissance art.

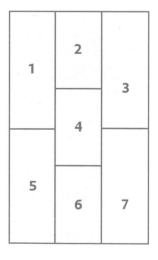

3. **Ginkgo biloba**
Maidenhair tree
The broad, two-lobed leaves on this ancient Chinese species differ from those of all other conifers.

4. **Picea abies**
Norway Spruce, Christmas Tree
Familiar European spruce with conical outline, sharp-ended needle leaves and long, pendulous cones.

5. **Pseudotsuga menziesii**
Douglas Fir
Named after the 19th Century Scottish plant hunter, David Douglas, this western North American native has short, soft 'needles,' narrow, pointed cones and reddish brown, corky bark on the mature trunk.

6. **Taxodium distichum**
Swamp Cypress
A deciduous conifer, familiar in the swamps and wetlands of Louisiana and the American South. Feathery leaflets are bright green, turning russet before falling.

7. **Tsuga heterophylla**
Western Hemlock
Stately and beautiful American species bearing short, flat, deep green needles with silvery undersides, and tiny cones. Shade tolerant and tough.

Amelanchier canadensis

Snowy mespilus   Hardy deciduous tree

An open habited tree whose young foliage is coppery tinted, soon turning bright green, and then colouring red or orange in autumn. The frail white blossoms are spectacular in spring, when they appear in large masses, followed by rose red berries in mid-summer.

Soil preference: Any, not too dry
Aspect: Sun or part shade
Season of interest: Year round
Height and spread: 8m x 5m (30ft x 16ft)

Companion plants: A fine accent tree for a mixed border. The autumn foliage is attractive with the blues or mauves of perennial asters to contrast, but the berries make an interesting foil for late summer roses.

Eriobotrya japonica

Loquat   Near hardy, evergreen tree

A stiff-branched tree with very large, pleated, oblong leaves which are remarkably durable and, even when they fall, are slow to rot. The off-white blossoms, produced in late winter or early spring, form at the stem tips, followed by clusters of edible, pear-shaped fruits which ripen to a warm, egg yolk yellow. Though frost-hardy, loquats will not tolerate sustained cold.

Soil preference: Any free-draining
Aspect: Sun
Season of interest: Year round
Height and spread: To 5m x 3m (15ft x 10ft)

Companion plants: A fine tree for a small space, even when grown in a container, where its dramatic foliage makes a backdrop for smaller, colourful plants such as pelargoniums, *Bidens ferulifolia*, *Solanum rantonnetii* or heliotropes.

Cotoneaster salicifolius 'Rothschildianus'

Hardy, evergreen or semi-evergreen shrub or tree

A spreading shrub, capable of being grown as a standard tree. The dark green leaves are narrow and long, with pale undersides and, in spring or early summer, large, showy cymes of white flowers are formed. Later a heavy crop of berries ripens to a brilliant golden yellow and persists long into the autumn.

Soil preference: Any fertile, free-draining
Aspect: Sun or part shade
Season of interest: Autumn
Height and spread: 5m x 5m (16ft x 16ft)

Companion plants: Superb to team with such red-berried shrubs as *Cotoneaster lacteus* or with hollies, skimmias or hawthorns.

Sorbus hupehensis Hubei Rowan Hardy deciduous tree

A graceful, upright tree with grey bark and large, pinnate leaves which colour to purplish bronze autumn. In spring, bold clusters of pale pink blossoms emerge soon after the new foliage and in late summer, a heavy crop of rose pink berries follows. The form *S. h.* var. *obtusa* has a blue-grey tinge to the foliage and dark, marbled pink berries.

Soil preference: Any free-draining, not too dry
Aspect: Sun or part shade
Season of interest: Year round
Height and spread: 8m x 6m (26ft x 20ft)

Companion plants: A charming specimen tree, also effective grouped with other rowans such as *S. aucuparia, S. cashmeriana* or *S.* 'Joseph Rock'.

Euonymus europaeus

Spindle Tree   Hardy deciduous tree or large shrub

The stems are dark green, even through winter and the simple, oval, pointed leaves are green through summer, colouring up to brilliant scarlet in autumn. Insignificant greenish blossoms appear in spring, but in late summer through autumn, the vivid foliage is joined by the amazing fruits whose outer husks are startling pink, contrasting with orange seeds. 'Red Cascade' has the best colour.

Soil preference: Any free-draining, a lime lover
Aspect: Sun or part shade
Season of interest: Summer, autumn
Height and spread: 3m x 2m (10ft x 6ft)

Companion plants: Grown either as a multi-stemmed shrub, or single trunked tree, this plant, like no other, brings vivid autumn colour. Team it with *Rosa moyesii* or with Japanese maples for a colourful fall.

Sambucus racemosa

Red Berried Elder   Hardy deciduous shrub

Fast growing, arching shrub with bold, compound leaves. White blossoms, in early summer, are followed in autumn by big, showy racemes of bright red berries. Best garden forms include 'Plumosa Aurea', whose golden leaves are more finely divided than the wild type and the similar 'Sutherland Gold', which is less likely to scorch in sun. *S. r.* 'Tenuifolia' lacks vigour but has filigree foliage.

Soil preference: Any
Aspect: Sun, part shade or shade
Season of interest: Summer, autumn
Height and spread: 3m x 3m (10ft x 10ft)

Companion plants: Gold forms are useful to place among other large shrubs, such as Syringa, Philadelphus or Weigela to introduce more interesting foliage. Also pretty with dark leaved evergreens such as holly or laurels.

Acer davidii   Snake Bark Maple   Hardy deciduous tree

A highly variable species from China, named after the Jesuit missionary and naturalist, Père David. The bark is often marked in reddish, green and grey streaks. The leaves are simple or slightly lobed, bright green, turning russet or gold in autumn. Small, yellow-green blossoms develop into two-winged fruits. Best forms include 'Ernest Wilson' for orange autumn foliage and 'Serpentine', whose young shoots are purplish.

Soil preference: Any moist but free-draining, preferably neutral or slightly acid
Aspect: Sun, part shade or shade
Season of interest: Year round
Height and spread: Variable, 8m x 6m (26ft x 20ft)

Companion plants: Fine as a specimen tree, especially at the edge of a dense planting screen, or to preside over a mixed border. Also beautiful with *A. japonicum*, *A. griseum* and the larger forms of *A. palmatum*.

Prunus serrula   Hardy deciduous tree

A Chinese native, distinctive for its shiny tan bark which retains its lustre by sloughing off a thin skin each year. The leaves are unremarkable, oval and pointed, and the flowers are small, white and insignificant. Most effective when grown as a multi-trunked three, or when the canopy is regularly thinned, to ensure a clear view of the gleaming limbs.

Soil preference: Any free-draining, not too dry
Aspect: Sun or part shade
Season of interest: Year round
Height and spread: 10m x 6m (33ft x 20ft)

Companion plants: Wonderful to underplant with vivid blue *Pulmonaria angustifolia* and the orange tan tulip 'Prinses Irene'.

Betula ermanii

Erman's Birch   Hardy deciduous tree

A handsome, broadly columnar birch from Siberia and Japan with creamy bark, sometimes pinkish or cinnamon tinged, and fresh, then dull green leaves which are mid-sized, slightly toothed and which turn ochre yellow before falling. Catkins hang in spring, among emerging leaves.

Soil preference: Any free-draining, not too dry
Aspect: Sun, part shade or shade
Season of interest: Year round
Height and spread: 20m x 12m (70ft x 40ft)

Companion plants: Grown largely for its conspicuous mature bark and perfect for a winter garden also featuring *Daphne bholua* witch hazels, *Cornus alba* or groups of *Helleborus foetidus*. Most effective in tight groups of three or five, or trained as multi-trunked trees.

Eucalyptus pauciflora subsp. niphophila

Snow Gum   Hardy evergreen tree

An upright, then spreading tree whose main feature, in maturity, is the brilliant white and grey bark which sloughs off in large pieces to reveal a new, pristine surface beneath. The young shoots are also white to pale grey and the aromatic, blue-grey to green leaves are oblong, pointed and have a smooth but leathery texture. The tufty cream flowers are held on small umbels.

Soil preference: Any free-draining
Aspect: Sun
Season of interest: Year round
Height and spread: 6m x 3m (20ft x 10ft)

Companion plants: Planted away from water pipes or foundations, to which it can cause damage, this makes a handsome specimen tree, best on its own or perhaps as focal point plant for a gravel scheme with grasses, phormiums or yuccas.

Salix alba var. vitellina 'Britzensis'

Hardy deciduous tree

A fast-growing, vigorous willow with invasive roots and, in mature specimens, craggy, fissured bark. The leaves are narrow, pointed and soft green with paler undersides and the male catkins are pale yellow-gold and mildly fragrant. The tree's most attractive feature, however, are the young stems and twigs which, in late winter, are vivid copper-orange.

Soil preference: Any moist
Aspect: Sun or part shade
Season of interest: Year round
Height and spread: 20m x 8m (65ft x 30ft) – less when pollarded

Companion plants: A superb tree for pollarding, in a garden, preferably atop a stem left tall enough to allow the ageing trunk to feature, surrounded by such wetland plants as ligularias, irises or hostas.

Parrotia persica   Persian Ironwood   Hardy deciduous tree

A vigorous tree with spreading, branches which become nearly horizontal with age. The oblong to oval leaves are dark green and slightly glossy on their upper surfaces, but turn to rich shades of russet, gold, tawny and tan as autumn advances. The flowers of this member of the witch hazel family are small and insignificant.

Soil preference: Any reasonably fertile, free-draining
Aspect: Sun or part shade
Season of interest: Summer, autumn
Height and spread: 8m x 10m (26ft x 33ft)

Companion plants: A fine tree for bringing crowning autumn glory to a planting of shrubs which might lack autumn interest. Contrast it with lilacs, forsythias and dark evergreens, or harmonise with *Fothergilla major*, Cercidiphyllum and *Euonymus europaeus*.

Prunus 'Taihaku'

The Great White Cherry   Hardy deciduous tree

A large ornamental cherry whose mature branches spread out to create a shapely canopy. The leaves are oblong, toothed and pointed, green in summer, colouring up to golden russet in autumn. The large, single or semi-double, pure white flowers hang in clusters, on longish stems and are fully developed before the leaves unfold.

Soil preference: Deep, humus-rich, fertile
Aspect: Sun or part shade
Season of interest: Spring, autumn
Height and spread: 8m x 6m (25ft x 20ft)

Companion plants: Perhaps the showiest of the big Japanese cherries, magnificent when grown in grass underplanted with white 'Pheasant Eye' narcissus or with bedded white and pink tulips nearby.

Prunus dulcis

Almond   Hardy deciduous tree

An upright, then spreading tree with relatively thick twigs on which, in late winter, the downy buds begin to swell and open, producing large, single pink or white flowers. The narrow, tapered leaves appear later and in late summer, velvety skinned fruits appear whose stones contain the edible almond nuts. Needs a hot summer to ripen the kernels.

Soil preference: Any
Aspect: Sun
Season of interest: Spring
Height and spread: 8m x 6m (25ft x 20ft)

Companion plants: A useful tree for early blossom, interesting when grown in association with forsythia, or Chaenomeles and also lovely when the blossoms can contrast with dark evergreen foliage of yew or holly.

Sorbus cashmiriana   Hardy deciduous tree

A fairly thick-stemmed rowan, with attractive winter buds and large, pinnate leaves whose leaflets are serrated. In spring, the showy umbels of small, densely packed, five-petalled blooms are pale pink, with a somewhat rank odour. Berries the size of children's glass marbles begin pale pink but ripen snow white and persist through winter.

Soil preference: Any free-draining but not too dry
Aspect: Sun or part shade
Season of interest: Year round
Height and spread: 8m x 6m (25ft x 20ft)

Companion plants: Whether multi-trunked or as a standard tree, this plant is a fitting companion to dark evergreen rhododendrons or to such foliage shrubs as *Physocarpus opulifolius* 'Diablo' or 'Dart's Gold'. Delightful when underplanted with winter flowers such as snowdrops.

Cornus nuttallii   Canadian Dogwood   Hardy deciduous tree

A sprawling tree with rounded or spreading habit and oval, dark green leaves which turn brilliant shades of russet, yellow and red in autumn. The small, greenish, late spring flowers are surrounded by conspicuous white bracts which flush pinkish as they mature. In autumn, salmon-orange, strawberry-like fruits are produced. The neater growing, smaller *C.* 'Eddie's White Wonder' has bigger, whiter flowers and is a hybrid of *C. nutallii* and *C. florida.*

Soil preference: Fertile, humus-rich, not too dry but well-drained
Aspect: Sun, part shade
Season of interest: Spring, summer, autumn
Height and spread: 15m x 12m (50ft x 40ft)

Companion plants: Makes an excellent tree for a large planting, perhaps with other American species such as *Catalpa bignonioides* or Arbutus. *C.* 'Eddie's White Wonder' is a better choice for a small garden and teams sweetly with camellias.

Cydonia oblonga

Quince   Hardy deciduous tree

A spreading tree, whose mature limbs become almost horizontal and which undulate with muscle-like contours. The simple, soft green leaves are silvery and felty, when young, and turn yellow in autumn. Solitary pink and white blossoms are borne in spring, followed by voluptuously pear-shaped, culinary fruits which turn rich chrome yellow when fully ripe.

Soil preference: Any fertile, free-draining
Aspect: Sun
Season of interest: Year round
Height and spread: 5m x 5m (16ft x 16ft)

Companion plants: A lovely and distinctive 'orchard' tree, worthy as an ornamental, particularly when underplanted with such colourful cottage plants as pulmonarias, *Brunnera macrophylla*, forget-me-nots or *Omphalodes cappadocica.*

Embothrium coccineum

Chilean Fire Bush   Borderline hardy, evergreen tree

A columnar South American tree belonging to the protea family. The simple leaves are narrowly oblong, dark green and make excellent foils for the orange-scarlet, spider-like flowers which are produced in late spring and the first part of summer. Yellow-flowered forms also exist. The tree has a suckering habit.

Soil preference: Fertile, free-draining, not too dry and lime-free
Aspect: Sun or part shade
Season of interest: Year round
Height and spread: 10m x 5m (33ft x 16ft)

Companion plants: High rainfall and a climate which lacks extremes seems to suit this natural companion to Desfontainea or escallonias. Rhododendrons, azaleas and most magnolias also thrive with embothriums.

Acer rubrum

Red Maple, Scarlet Maple   Hardy deciduous tree

A sturdy North American maple with broadly columnar habit and medium sized palmate leaves which, in some varieties, colour superbly to scarlet and crimson in autumn. Yellow blossoms flower as the leaves emerge and two-winged fruits follow. Best varieties include the upright 'Scanlon' and the glossy-leaved, more spreading 'October Glory'.

Soil preference: Fertile, humus-rich, free-draining
Aspect: Sun or part shade
Season of interest: Year round; autumn
Height and spread: 20m x 10m (70ft x 33ft), often less

Companion plants: A fine species for isolated planting, or to contrast with the yellow autumn leaves of *Liriodendron tulipifera*, perhaps, or with *Prunus* 'Umineko'.

Betula medwedewii

Transcaucasian Birch   Hardy deciduous tree or large shrub

A big shrub or tree which grows naturally with several trunks. These begin upright, but gradually splay outwards creating an attractive, spreading effect. The shiny winter buds open to reveal slightly toothed, dark green leaves which, in autumn, turn ochre to russet and then brownish tan. The showy spring catkins are 10cm (4in) long.

Soil preference: Any free-draining, not too dry
Aspect: Sun, part shade or shade
Season of interest: Year round
Height and spread: 5m x 5m (16ft x 16ft)

Companion plants: A small but handsome birch, lovely on its own, with ground cover, or with its branches spread above shade-loving perennials such as Heuchera, Tiarella or Tolmeia. Bergenias, epimediums, Uvularia and *Lysimachia nummularia* would also go well at its feet.

Cercidiphyllum japonicum

Katsura   Hardy, deciduous tree

A broadly columnar tree whose rounded or heart-shaped leaves resemble those of a Judas tree, Cercis. The tiny red flowers are insignificant, but the tree's most striking feature is the rich, rusty gold autumn colour accompanied, in mature specimens, by a distinctive and strong aroma of cooking caramel or toffee.

Soil preference: Any, fertile, humus-rich
Aspect: Sun, part shade, shade
Season of interest: Year round
Height and spread: 20m x 12m (70ft x 40ft)

Companion plants: A charming tree to grow in a woodland clearing, or to use as a free-standing specimen at the edge of a lawn or shrubbery.

Fraxinus angustifolia   Narrow Leaved Ash   Hardy deciduous tree

A rather variable, broadly columnar to spreading tree with
dark grey, fissured bark and pinnate leaves whose oval,
pointed leaflets are narrower than those of common ash.
The flowers are insignificant and are followed by winged
seeds. Best known form is 'Raywood', the 'claret ash',
whose autumn foliage in sun turns rich beetroot red.

Soil preference: Any free-
draining, not too dry
Aspect: Sun
Season of interest: Year round,
autumn
Height and spread: 20m x 12m
(65ft x 40ft)

Companion plants: Fine tree for dark,
brooding autumn colour, but not suitable
for a small garden. Associates well with
species of Sorbus, for their berries, or
Crataegus persimilis 'Prunifolia' for even
more autumn colour.

Prunus sargentii

Sargent's Cherry   Hardy deciduous tree

An upright, then spreading tree with attractively smooth
bark, when mature, and leaves which are coppery when
young, pale green during summer, and then rich maroon,
scarlet and orange in the autumn. The small but showy,
bright pink blossoms appear in spring before the first
leaves emerge.

Soil preference: Any humus-rich,
fertile, free-draining
Aspect: Sun
Season of interest: Spring;
autumn
Height and spread: 18m x 12m
(60ft x 40ft)

Companion plants: A superb specimen
tree for a lawn, or to grow with shrubs such
as *Rosa moyesii* for its autumn and spring
harmonizing or set above groups of
hydrangeas for an interesting late summer
show.

Liquidambar styraciflua   Sweet Gum   Hardy deciduous tree

A broadly columnar, elegant tree with well spaced
branches and maple-like, lobed leaves which grow
alternately on the stems. Flowers and fruits are
insignificant, but the tree's main feature is its rich, warm
autumn colour. Garden varieties include 'Worplesdon',
whose leaves turn purple in autumn, and the variegated
'Golden Treasure'. 'Burgundy' has striking autumn colour.

Soil preference: Fertile, free-
draining, but not too dry
Aspect: Sun or part shade
Season of interest: Year round
Height and spread: 25m x 12m
(80ft x 40ft)

Companion plants: The distinctive shape,
bold foliage and changing colour make this a
superb choice as a specimen tree, to stand
alone or in a bold group of its own kind.
Companions plants could include eucalyptus
or *Quercus rubra*.

Chamaecyparis lawsoniana (golden forms)

Hardy evergreen conifers

Among the easiest and most adaptable of the soft or scale-leaved conifers and available in a number of fine gold-leaf forms. The best known are probably 'Elwoods Gold', which has custard yellow fronds and grows tall, 'Lutea', whose leaves are paler gold, and 'Aurea Densa', a form with dense, compact growth.

Soil preference: Any
Aspect: Sun, part shade
Season of interest: Year round
Height and spread: Variable to 30m x 3m (100ft to 10ft)

Companion plants: Once the mainstay of suburban gardens, conifers are used more judiciously nowadays but make charming background plants for bright-coloured perennials, for formal beds or clipped as hedging.

Thuja occidentalis   Arborvitae, White cedar   Hardy conifer

Common and variable species from Eastern North America which grows as a broadly or narrowly conical tree with a neat, symmetrical shape. Small scale leaves cover the twigs, making a soft, green effect. Golden forms include the popular 'Rheingold', whose foliage becomes bronze tinted in hard weather and 'Golden Globe' is a rounded, compact dwarf form.

Soil preference: Free-draining, humus-rich
Aspect: Sun, shade or part shade
Season of interest: Year round
Height and spread: 20m x 4m (65ft x 13ft) – many forms much smaller

Companion plants: Thuja is one of many choice evergreens for background use, in mixed borders or to make up part of a general conifer scheme. 'Rheingold' is a compact plant, ideal to contrast with the purple foliage of *Prunus cistena* or *Fagus sylvatica* 'Dawyck Purple'.

Populus alba 'Richardii'

Golden white poplar   Hardy deciduous tree

A suckering, fast growing tree with invasive roots whose young stems and buds are covered with felty white hairs. The leaves are golden green on their upper sides but pale and downy beneath. Mature trees produce short-lived catkins, and in autumn, the golden colour of the foliage is amplified just before the leaves fall.

Soil preference: Any not too dry
Aspect: Sun or part shade
Season of interest: Spring, summer, autumn
Height and spread: 12m x 3m (40ft x 10ft)

Companion plants: A beautiful tree to set with other plants in a golden green theme, especially in moist conditions. Try it with *Euphorbia palustris*, *E. griffithii*, *Crocosmia* 'Lucifer' and for earlier in summer, dark blue *Iris sibirica* cultivars.

Taxus baccata **Fastigiata Aurea Group**

Golden Irish Yew   Hardy evergreen tree

A slow-growing, upright yew (see page 367) whose short, flattened needle-like leaves are golden green to yellow. Other forms of golden yew included the prostrate 'Repens Aurea' and dwarf, very golden 'Standishii'.

Soil preference: Any
Aspect: Sun, shade or part shade
Season of interest: Year round
Height and spread: 5m x 2m (16ft x 6ft)

Companion plants: Excellent plants for hedging and for formal use, but also striking as stand-alone features. Imagine an old Iris Yew with an antique seat beneath it, and perhaps a pink moss rose or a *Daphne bholua* nearby for fragrance.

Quercus rubra **'Aurea'**

Golden Red Oak   Hardy deciduous tree

Spreading tree with rounded canopy described on page 367 The golden form is slightly smaller and more compact with foliage that is vivid golden green, when young, subsiding to pale green during summer but turning to a rich, golden orange in autumn.

Soil preference: Any, preferably neutral, not too dry
Aspect: Sun
Season of interest: Year round
Height and spread: 15m x 10m (47ft x 33ft)

Companion plants: A large tree, but lovely as a specimen, especially where the foliage can be viewed against a bright blue sky. Attractive underplanted with fellow American natives such as *Smilacina racemosa*, violets, trilliums and *Aquilegia formosa*.

Acer cappadocicum

Cappadocian Maple, Caucasian Maple   Hardy deciduous tree

A stately tree with broadly columnar habit and mid-sized to large, lobed or almost palmate leaves. The blossoms are pale yellow, unremarkable and are followed familiar, winged maple fruits. The gold leaved form 'Aureum' grows less tall and has yellow foliage, when young, turning green for summer, and then going bright gold before falling.

Soil preference: Any
Aspect: Sun, shade or part shade
Season of interest: Spring, autumn
Height and spread: 20m x 15m (65ft x 47ft)

Companion plants: Best for a sizeable garden, where the spread can be enjoyed without restriction. Fine as a specimen tree, or in groups, underplanted with woodland plants.

Acer platanoides

Norway Maple   Hardy deciduous tree

A vigorous, rather coarse-growing maple, with spreading habit and large, glossy, oval leaves whose lobes are tipped with fine points. Selected cultivars, ideal for garden use, include 'Crimson King' (pictured), whose foliage is dark purple, and 'Crimson Sentry', a purple leaved fastigiate form. Other fine cultivars include subtly variegated 'Drummondii' and the round-headed 'Globosum'.

Soil preference: Any
Aspect: Sun, part shade, shade
Season of interest: Spring, summer, autumn
Height and spread: 12m x 5m (40ft x 17ft)

Companion plants: Fine trees to create shade and give screens. 'Crimson King' looks inspiring when its newly emerged foliage backs mauve, purple or blue lilacs, or when planted alongside *Robinia x margaretta* 'Pink Cascade'.

Cercis canadensis   Eastern Redbud   Hardy deciduous tree

A rounded or spreading tree, usually much branched with a short trunk and large, rounded leaves. In late winter or early spring, small, reddish or pink pea flowers bloom on the naked branches but are joined by emerging foliage before they fall. The variety 'Forest Pansy' (illustrated) has pink blossoms and deep purple-red leaves which are very dark when newly emerged.

Soil preference: Any humus-rich, free-draining
Aspect: Sun or part shade
Season of interest: Spring, summer, autumn
Height and spread: 9m x 9m (30ft x 30ft)

Companion plants: *C. c.* 'Forest Pansy' is an outstanding tree for a mixed border, setting off flowers in the purple, mauve or pink range to perfection. Delightful with *Dicentra spectabilis* in spring, followed by dark astrantias or pale foxgloves in early summer and purple asters later.

Betula pendula 'Purpurea'

Hardy deciduous tree

A striking form of silver birch whose bark and young stems are purple tinged, and whose foliage is suffused with dark pigment, producing a purple or near-black effect. The leaves tend to lose their striking colour in summer, but in autumn, they turn an interesting range of colours from dirty grey to dull bronze.

Soil preference: Any free-draining
Aspect: Sun or part shade
Season of interest: Spring, autumn, summer
Height and spread: 10m x 7m (33ft x 23ft)

Companion plants: A fine tree to contrast with the fresh foliage of, say, larch, golden forms of *Catalpa bignonioides* or to blend with big shrub roses, buddleias and lilacs.

Olea europaea   Olive   Tender or marginally hardy evergreen tree

The classical, biblical, Mediterranean tree with small, simple, silvery grey-green leaves and dark, flaky bark. The blossoms are small, green and unexciting, but are followed by plum-shaped, bitter-tasting, oil-rich fruits which turn black when ripe. Some forms are said to be hardier than others.

Soil preference: Any free-draining
Aspect: Sun
Season of interest: Year round
Height and spread: 6m x 6m (20ft x 20ft)

Companion plants: The perfect 'crowning' tree for a Mediterranean style garden, beautiful with such native companions as rosemary, lavender, Phlomis, rock roses, pomegranate and the little palm *Chamaerops humilis*. Also an outstanding tree for a large container.

Abies concolor   Silver Fir, Colorado White Fir   Hardy conifer

A tall, stately fir, native to western North America where mature specimens are remarkable for their erect trunks and narrowly tapering shape. Foliage is dark, dull green, consisting of short, blunt needles which in some forms, have a bluish grey cast. Cones are long and cylindrical, green at first, eventually turning brown. Garden forms include the very dwarf 'Compacta', Violacea Group (bluish foliage) and 'Argentea' (silver needles).

Soil preference: Free-draining, but not too dry
Aspect: Sun or part shade
Season of interest: Year round
Height and spread: 36m x 8m (120ft x 25ft)

Companion plants: *A. c.* 'Compacta' seldom exceeds 3m and is ideal for planting with heathers or other dwarf conifers. The more normal sized varieties need space but are beautiful while young, planted in groups, perhaps with *Abies amabilis*.

Cedrus atlantica   Atlas Cedar   Hardy conifer

Dramatic conifers from the Atlas Mountains, tall and tapered while young, but eventually developing a broad, flattened canopy, often with a series of wide, horizontal limbs. The bark is attractively fissured and grey, the needles arranged in tuft-like rosettes and the cones, on mature specimens, are rounded or egg shaped. Good varieties include Glauca Group – blue-green needles – and the weeping 'Glauca Pendula'.

Soil preference: Any, free-draining
Aspect: Sun, part shade
Season of interest: Year round
Height and spread: 24m x 9m (8oft x 30ft)

Companion plants: Best as specimen plants which, though pretty while young, are seen at their finest in mature gardens or arboreta. The young look striking alongside spring flowering magnolias.

Idesia polycarpa

Hardy deciduous tree

A deciduous tree with broadly spreading habit and, when mature, a stately appearance. The deep green, glossy leaves are heart-shaped with pointed tips. Male specimens bear tiny but fragrant greenish flowers and females, in time, bear clusters of red berries.

Soil preference: Well drained, fertile and lime-free
Aspect: Sun, shade
Season of interest: Summer
Height and spread: 12m x 12m (40ft x 40ft)

Companion plants: A fine plant for a large, woodland garden, perhaps with fellow Japanese natives such as Cercidiphyllum, Asian maples and the conifer, *Cryptomeria japonica*.

Magnolia campbellii   Deciduous tree

A large tree with upright habit during its first 30 years or so of life, but ultimately spreading with a wide canopy. The flowers, produced in spring, are enormous, fragrant and have loose petals, the inner ones forming a cup shape and the outer making a 'saucer'. Colours vary from pure white, through shades of pink.

Soil preference: Well-drained but fertile and preferably neutral or acid
Aspect: Sun or part shade
Season of interest: Spring
Height and spread: 15m x 10m (50ft x 30ft)

Companion plants: Suitable only for large spaces, preferably with other magnificent trees. In a medium-sized or small garden, it will need space, but is superb for underplanting with spring bulbs such as *Fritillaria meleagris*, crocuses, camassias and, for later summer, naturalized lilies.

Metasequoia glyptostroboides

Dawn redwood   Deciduous conifer

A tall, columnar or narrowly conical tree with attractive, flaky, tan trunk and branches whose feathery foliage is vivid green in spring when it emerges, and which turns burnished gold before falling in autumn.

Soil preference: Any, but not too dry
Aspect: Sun, part shade
Season of interest: Year round
Height and spread: 30m x 5m (100ft x 16ft)

Companion plants: A beautiful specimen tree to set as the high point of a general planting scheme, especially among evergreens such as rhododendrons, or as a waterside tree among such marginals as *Iris laevigata*, *Carex elata* 'Aurea' or to preside over a collection of hostas.

Nothofagus obliqua   Deciduous tree

A southern hemisphere beech with considerable vigour, columnar at first, but spreading more as it ages. The leaves are oblong, medium size and attractively pleated, with deep veining. They colour up to a tawny red or golden yellow in the autumn.

Soil preference: Any free draining
Aspect: Sun, part shade
Season of interest: Year round
Height and spread: 20m x 10m (65ft x 30ft)

Companion plants: Southern beeches grow into impressive trees and all have attractive foliage, making them superb backdrops for flowering shrubs such as roses, buddlejas or spring shrubs.

Paulownia tomentosa

Foxglove Tree, Princess Tree   Hardy deciduous tree

A fast-growing tree with wide, well-spaced branches, a spreading habit and large, simple heart-shaped or rounded leaves which may be dark when immature. On mature trees in late spring, the branches are laden with spikes bearing tubular flowers which resemble foxgloves, but which are soft purple-mauve, in hue. A spectacular sight, when in full bloom, but the flowers are vulnerable to late spring frost.

Soil preference: Any free-draining
Aspect: Sun
Season of interest: Spring, summer
Height and spread: 10m x 8m (35ft x 30ft)

Companion plants: Best as a solo specimen and a fine choice as a lawn tree. You could sacrifice the flowers and pollard annually. The dramatic result is that the tree produces huge leaves which make a perfect foil for summer perennials of every kind.

Phoenix canariensis

Canary Palm   Tender palm

A tender palm species from the Canary islands, which, with climate change, is surviving winters now where previously it perished. The trunk is stout and straight; the leaves very large and long, set off in male specimens by creamy gold flowers and in females by clusters of light tan or golden fruits. Suitable when young for a large container, but must be protected from frost.

Soil preference: Any
Aspect: Sun
Season of interest: Year round
Height and spread: up to 18m x 15m (60ft x 50ft)

Companion plants: Effective on a sheltered terrace or as a centrepiece for a tropical border surrounded, perhaps, by Brugmansia, Hedychium, *Melianthus major* and Yuccas.

Acers

Most acers, or maples, produce wonderful autumn colours when foliage can become bright red, maroon, orange or yellow. In spring, the new leaves are fresh and vibrant and one or two species have spectacular bark which may be patterned and marked, or may become papery, flaking with age. Asia, particularly Japan, is the source of some of the finest garden maples.

1.   Acer palmatum 'Bloodgood'
A variety of Japanese maple with dark, almost black stems and palmate, deep purple foliage which turns red in autumn.

2.   Acer palmatum var. dissectum Dissectum Atropurpureum Group
A small maple with divided, dark purple leaves which turn fiery crimson in autumn, just before falling.

3.   Acer palmatum var. dissectum 'Garnet'
A very small, dome-forming maple whose leaves are deeply divided and

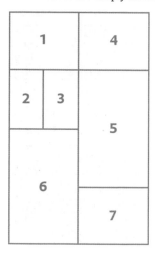

dissected to create a feathery appearance. Green summer colour gives way to russet orange in autumn.

4.   Acer japonicum 'Aconitifolium'
One of the handsomest maples for a small garden. The leaves are elegantly divided, bronze-edged when young and turning beetroot red in autumn.

5.   Acer griseum
The paper bark maple whose distinguishing characteristic is the bark which sloughs off in thin layers, like paper.

6.   Acer cappadocicum 'Aureum'
The leaves of this western Asian native are bright gold in spring, green in summer and mellow to old gold before falling in autumn.

7.   Acer negundo 'Kelly's Gold'
A gold-leaf form of the box elder. Regular pruning can result in production of larger, more highly coloured leaves in decorative varieties of this fast-growing species.

water plants

Aponogeton distachyos

Water Hawthorn, Cape Pondweed   Aquatic perennial

A distinctive aquatic with long, oval leaves which lie flat on the surface. The strange looking white flowers open in a vee-shaped spike during summer and are sweetly scented. In their native South Africa, the fleshy flower spikes are eaten as a vegetable.

Soil preference: Silt, mud or gravel, must be under water
Aspect: Sun, part shade. Not fully hardy
Season of interest: Spring, summer, autumn
Height and spread: Minimum depth 30cm (1ft); maximum 1m (3ft 3in)

Companion plants: Attractive placed near the sides of a pond, growing out from the bases of marginal plants, rather than among water lilies which might swamp them. The floating leaves make contrasting shapes to sedges, rushes, irises and other plants with sword-shaped leaves.

Hydrocharis morsus-ranae

Frogbit   Aquatic perennial

An aquatic which spreads by forming stolons or runners of rounded, floating leaves that resemble those of a miniature water lily. During summer, white, three-petalled flowers open in a steady succession. Can be invasive.

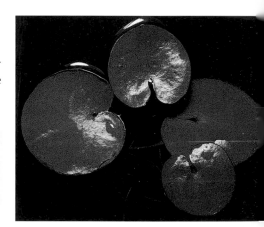

Soil preference: Floating, so not applicable
Aspect: Sun
Season of interest: Summer
Height and spread: Spreading, can be invasive

Companion plants: A pretty wild plant of ponds and slow-moving streams, lovely when accompanying grasses, sedges and reed mace (bull rushes).

Hottonia palustris   Water Violet   Aquatic perennial

A good oxygenating weed for neutral or lime-free waters, with feathery submerged foliage. In early summer, flower spikes appear, bearing whorls of primrose-like blossoms in a delicate lilac mauve. Beneficial to submerged invertebrates and one of Britain's loveliest aquatic wildflowers.

Soil preference: Mud, silt or gravel, must be under water; acid or neutral
Aspect: Sun or part shade
Season of interest: Early summer
Height and spread: Submerged. Flower stems 30cm (1ft) above water surface

Companion plants: This is not easy to establish, but makes a perfect centre point to a wildlife pond margined with kingcup, water forget-me-not, yellow flag iris and wild sedges. Good fellow submerged plants include Potamogeton and river crowfoot, *Ranunculus fluitans*.

Eichhornia crassipes

Water Hyacinth   Tender aquatic perennial

An invasive water species from tropical South America which floats on the surface by means of inflated bladders in the leaf stems. Mature plants which grow in loosely bonded colonies produce short, well-packed spikes of mauve to blue flowers, each with a yellow centre. Frost protection is essential.

Soil preference: Floating, so not applicable
Aspect: Sun or part shade
Season of interest: Summer
Height and spread: 45cm (18in), spreading

Companion plants: A plant that must be kept in check, but beautiful to team with tropical water lilies. Can be introduced to outdoor ponds as a summer plant in colder regions.

Persicaria amphibia

Amphibious bistort   Aquatic or marginal perennial

Only suitable for a large pond or watercourse, this member of the dock family has narrow, oblong leaves which float on the water surface. In summer, it produces short, erect flower spikes which carry densely packed, pinkish blooms.

Soil preference: Mud or pond bed
Aspect: Sun
Season of interest: Summer
Height and spread: Spreading

Companion plants: A good one to blend, in large ponds, with *Ranunculus lingua* or with vigorous varieties of water lily, including the yellow *Nuphar lutea*.

Trapa natans

Water Chestnut   Tender aquatic annual

An Asian or African native with nettle-like, floating leaves, which are bright green with bronze markings. White flowers appear at the leaf joints and are followed by four sided, spiny, hard fruits. Protection from frost is essential.

Soil preference: Water
Aspect: Sun or part shade
Season of interest: Summer
Height and spread: Floating – no height; indefinite spread

Companion plants: Best treated as a summer plant in cold regions where it can be over-wintered under glass, but set out in a summer pond along with hardier aquatics such as Stratiotes.

Water lilies

Water lilies are not only among the most beautiful of aquatic plants for an ornamental pond, but are also the most useful. Their floating leaves provide essential shade, keeping water temperatures down and thereby raising oxygen levels and supporting more aquatic life. As summer advances, the leaves multiply, increasing that vital shade as needed. Flower colours are rich and varied, from deep pink, through blush tones to white or to yellow. Among the different cultivars, there is also considerable variation in size. It is important to select dwarf varieties for small ponds.

1. Nymphaea 'Chromatella'
Large leaves, suffused with bronze streaking, and large, double flowers which open to a soft, primrose yellow make this one of the best choices for a medium or large pond. A minimum of 45cm (18in) water depth is needed for this plant to thrive.

2. Nuphar lutea
Wild Yellow Waterlily, Brandy Bottles
Familiar wild plant of European waterways and suitable only for large ponds and slow-moving streams. The buttercup yellow, single flowers appear through summer and are followed by bottle-shaped seed capsules. Prefers a minimum of 1m (3ft 3in) depth.

3. Nymphaea 'Gladstoneana'
A large, vigorous water lily whose deep green leaves may exceed 30cm (1ft) in diameter. The big, double white flowers are similar in size and shape to the wild European white lily, *Nymphaea alba*.

4. Nymphaea 'Perry's Pink'
Deep green leaves accompany tidy flowers with well-packed petals in clear, mid-pink. Less abundant than many cultivars, but a beautiful variety nonetheless.

5. Nymphaea 'Albatross'
A compact variety, suitable for small ponds, with rounded, green foliage and well-shaped, pure white flowers. The pointed petals create a somewhat starry effect.

6. Nymphaea 'Carnea'
Despite its name, the large flowers carry just a hint of blush pink on this large, vigorous variety, and contrast well with the large, dark green leaves. The stamens are rich, egg-yolk yellow.

7. Nymphaea 'Odorata Sulphurea'
Bronze streaks and stipples mark the foliage of this excellent, compact variety whose broad-petalled flowers are bright yellow with deeper, golden stamens.

Myosotis scorpioides   Water Forget-me-not   Perennial

Oblong, narrow leaves on somewhat lax stems rise above a slowly creeping rootstock bearing sprigs of tightly curled buds, which gradually open and straighten to release sky blue or white flowers (as for the Albino form pictured), each with a tiny primrose yellow centre. Tolerant of a surprising range of conditions.

Soil preference: Any wetland soil, in or out of the water
Aspect: Sun or part shade
Season of interest: Spring and summer
Height and spread: Up to 30cm (1ft); indefinite spread

Companion plants: Beautiful in spring, with marsh marigolds (*Caltha palustris*) and in summer with great spearwort (*Ranunculus lingua*). The plants also love to scramble among iris rhizomes, water mint *Mentha aquatica* and between the stems of rushes, reeds and sedges.

Pontederia cordata

Pickerel Weed, Pickerel Rush   Aquatic or marginal perennial

A vigorous, invasive bog or aquatic perennial from the Americas and Caribbean with bold, paddle-shaped leaves and tall, springy stems bearing tight spikes of dark blue or white flowers. Excellent for large ponds, where the stems and leaves make good wildlife cover, but best confined to a container in a small pond.

Soil preference: In water or very wet soil
Aspect: Sun
Season of interest: Summer
Height and spread: 120cm x 75cm (4ft x 2ft 6in)

Companion plants: Beautiful with the golden yellow-flowered European native, *Ranunculus lingua*, and with aquatic iris species such as *I. pseudacorus* or *I. sanguinea*.

Iris pseudacorus   Yellow Flag   Marginal or aquatic perennial

Huge clumps of sword-like leaves emerge from a network of knobbly rhizomes. The branched flower stems appear in early summer, carrying typical iris blossoms in clear, bright yellow (pale lemon in the form 'Bastardii'), each with brownish veins at its centre. Chunky, prism-shaped seed capsules follow. Favoured as launching vegetation for emerging dragonfly and damsel fly nymphs.

Soil preference: Damp or in shallow water
Aspect: Sun
Season of interest: Late spring, summer
Height and spread: 1.2m x 1.5m (4ft x 5ft)

Companion plants: Beautiful with other water irises such as *I. laevigata* and with pickerel weed. In bog gardens, the leaves make a textural contrast with rounded foliage of Rodgersia or *Ligularia clivorum*.

Butomus umbellatus   Flowering Rush   Aquatic perennial

Narrow, erect, rush-like foliage, dark coloured when young, but fading green as it ages. The flower stems emerge in summer and carry terminal umbels of clear mid-pink flowers. There are white forms, as well as a deeper pink, 'Rosenrot'. Valuable for growing in shallow water.

Soil preference: Any soil, mud or gravel, preferably under water
Aspect: Sun or part shade
Season of interest: Summer
Height and spread: 60-120cm x 75cm (2-4ft x 2ft 6in)

Companion plants: Handsome on its own, but better when grown among the floating flat leaves of water lilies and Aponogeton. A good 'link plant' connecting the margin with the open water.

Caltha palustris   King Cup, Marsh Marigold   Hardy perennial

Bold, rounded leaves develop on fleshy stems in early spring and are soon accompanied by rounded buds which open to large, single flowers whose intense golden yellow make them the highlight of a springtime water garden. The leaves continue to expand after flowering and are accompanied by crown-like seed heads. A free seeder, but not likely to become invasive. Constant damp or wet soil is essential.

Soil preference: Wetland or at the water margin
Aspect: Sun or part shade
Season of interest: Spring
Height and spread: To 60cm x 60cm (2ft x 2ft)

Companion plants: A beautiful companion for the first of the water forget-me-nots, with which it can contrast, but an earlier plant than most other aquatics. Useful for developing a textural contrast with the fresh, young leaves of grasses and sedges.

Mimulus ringens

Alleghany Monkey Flower   Aquatic or marginal perennial

Vigorous perennial with pointed, willow-like foliage and purple-blue, narrow, tubular flowers, which flare to a trumpet shape at their tips. White and pink versions are sometimes available. Happy growing in water, at a pond margin or in very moist soil in a bog or damp garden.

Soil preference: Any damp or wet soil
Aspect: Sun or part shade
Season of interest: Summer
Height and spread: 1m x 1.2m (3ft 3in x 4ft)

Companion plants: Different from other mimulus species which tend to come in hotter, brighter colours. The soft mauve co-ordinates gently with golden or variegated grass-like plants or contrasts with the flat, floating water lily leaves. Beautiful when nestling among reeds or rushes.

Ranunculus fluitans   River Crowfoot   Aquatic perennial

From small beginnings, large, submerged beds of long, tangled stems develop, bearing feathery leaves and small white roots along the stems. In spring and early summer small, white, five-petalled buttercup flowers are held just clear of the water. There are several other species of aquatic crowfoot, all of which have value for wildlife ponds.

Soil preference: Any, must be under water. Loves limy (hard) water
Aspect: Sun
Season of interest: Spring and summer
Height and spread: Indefinite, spreads under the water

Companion plants: Grow this with Aponogeton or with starwort (Callitriche) as submerged plants, and allow it to run at the feet of marginals such as Lysimachia, Lythrum, Caltha or Butomus to aid biodiversity. A key plant for natural trout streams.

Utricularia vulgaris

Common Bladderwort   Aquatic perennial

Bronze to green, feathery leaves, always submerged and bearing small bladders at whose necks spring-loaded trap doors catch waterborne creatures which are then digested. In summer, the bright yellow, snapdragon flowers are held clear of the water on thin stems.

Soil preference: Silt or mud, must be submerged and lime free
Aspect: Sun or part shade
Season of interest: Summer
Height and spread: Flower spikes 10–15cm (4–6in) above water; indefinite spread

Companion plants: Attractive to grow with water violet – *Hottonia palustris* – but quite difficult to establish. Will associate with potamogeton and with marginal plants such as *Iris ensata*.

Myriophyllum aquaticum

Parrot Feather   Near-hardy aquatic perennial

A fast growing waterweed from the tropics with feathery submerged foliage and ferny, vivid green stems which emerge and are held erect above the water surface. Greenish flowers grow from the submerged stems. In frost-free areas, this species can become invasive.

Soil preference: Water
Aspect: Sun or part shade
Season of interest: Summer
Height and spread: 15cm (6in), above water. Indefinite spread.

Companion plants: The bright green feathers look pretty contrasted with darker, more solid marginal plants such as *Iris pseudacorus* and with floating aquatics such as water lilies.

Stratiotes aloides   Water Soldier   Aquatic perennial

A remarkable plant which floats, forming rosettes of spiky leaves. From the centres of these, in summer, appear showy, three-petalled white flowers which flush pink as they age. In winter, the leaf rosettes sink and stay out of sight until the weather warms up again.

Soil preference: Floating, so not applicable
Aspect: Sun
Season of interest: Summer
Height and spread: Spreading

Companion plants: Interesting to add to the general pond flora, making a good contrast with the flat surfaces of floating water lily leaves or with the oblong water-surface foliage of Aponogeton.

Ranunculus lingua

Great Spearwort   Hardy aquatic perennial

A handsome but invasive buttercup which is happy in bog or in water. Thick, fleshy stems carry strap-shaped leaves and, in summer, large, golden yellow flowers. The plant creeps by means of a vigorous rhizome network.

Soil preference: Any, wet
Aspect: Sun
Season of interest: Summer
Height and spread: 1.5m (5ft) spreading

Companion plants: Not suitable for small ponds, but where there is space, it is superb with *Lythrum salicaria* or with water-loving irises. (Note: Lythrum is a troublesome weed in parts of North America.)

Callitriche hermaphroditica

Water Starwort   Aquatic perennial

A part submerged water weed of considerable benefit to ponds, especially if they have a natural mud bottom. A mass of thin stems develops, during summer, with submerged, narrow leaves. Where the plant approaches the surface, the top leaves of each stem are slightly taller and float on the surface.

Soil preference: Mud or pond bed
Aspect: Sun, part shade
Season of interest: Spring, summer
Height and spread: Spreading

Companion plants: To help keep water clear, and to provide refuge for water-dwelling invertebrates, this plant will colonize areas beneath water lilies or along a pond margin at the feet of *Iris pseudacorus*, *Caltha palustris* or among water forget-me-not.

index

picture credits

The majority of the photographs in this book were taken by Tim Sandall.

A number of additional pictures were taken by the author, and the Publishers would also like to thank the following individuals and organisations for supplying the images listed below:

(Key: T = Top; C = Centre; B = Bottom; TL = Top Left; TC = Top Centre; TR = Top Right; ML = Middle Left; MC = Middle Centre; MR = Middle Right; BL = Bottom Left; BC = Bottom Centre; BR = Bottom Right)

Garden Picture Library: 356(T)

Garden World Images: 21(T) J. Swithinbank, 26(T), 28(B) R. Coates, 36(T&B), 37(C), 40(T), 41(T), 51(C), 55 (T) R. Ditchfield, 86(T) T. Cooper, 92(B), 116(T), 118(T) S. Keeble, 119(C), 122(T), 123(T), 149(C) T. Sims, 160(C&B), 166(C), 168(C), 173(T), 185(C), 187(T), 188(T), 194(T), 197(B), 198(C), 200(T), 202(C), 203(C), 216(B) C. Hawes, 226(B), 246(C), 247(T) B. Gadsby, 251(BC), 253(TL), 253(BL), 254(C) R. Ditchfield, 255(C), 256(C) R. Coates, 256(B) R. Shiell, 259(T), 262(MC&MR), 279(B), 281(T), 287(B) R. Cox, 292(T) G. Kidd, 338(C), 394(C), 395(T), 396(T,C,B), 397(B), 401(T), 402(C), 406(B), 414(T), 414(B), 415(C), 416(B).

Heather Angel: 38(T), 51(T), 55(B), 56(T), 98(B), 120(C), 121(T), 125(B), 141(BC), 144(C), 145(B), 149(T), 164(T), 165(B), 166(B), 167(B), 179(B), 187(B), 194(T&B), 198(B), 223(B), 232(T), 253(CR), 255(B), 266(C), 277(C), 390(T), 391(B), 392(T), 403(T), 408(C), 410(C), 412(T), 413(C).

Oliver Matthews: 381(BL), 418(T).